Regulation and Performance of Communication and Information Networks

Regulation and Performance of Communication and Information Networks

Edited by

Gerald R. Faulhaber

Professor Emeritus of Business and Public Policy, University of Pennsylvania, USA

Gary Madden

Professor of Economics and Director, Communication Economics and Electronic Markets Research Centre, Curtin University, Australia

Jeffrey Petchey

Professor of Economics and Head of Research, School of Economics and Finance, Curtin University, Australia

Edward Elgar
Cheltenham, UK • Northampton, MA, USA

Published by
Edward Elgar Publishing Limited
The Lypiatts
15 Lansdown Road
Cheltenham
Glos GL50 2JA
UK

Edward Elgar Publishing, Inc.
William Pratt House
9 Dewey Court
Northampton
Massachusetts 01060
USA

A catalogue record for this book
is available from the British Library

Library of Congress Control Number: 2011939347

ISBN 978 0 85793 098 9

Printed and bound by MPG Books Group, UK

Contents

Contributors

Rob Albon, Principal Economist at the Australian Competition and Consumer Commission (ACCC), has over thirty years' professional experience in universities, government agencies and consulting. He was based at The Australian National University (where, *inter alia*, he attained his PhD and directed the Centre for Applied Economics) for 25 years, before joining the ACCC in 2000. He has over 100 professional publications including in applied welfare economics, taxation, housing market analysis and the economics of utilities and regulation. Professional experience in telecommunications covers the analysis of fixed-line, wireless and convergent networks. *Inter alia*, he was lead adviser on telecommunications economics at the ACCC from 2000 to 2006; an international expert to the Indian telecommunications regulator; and conducted a course in telecommunications economics at the New Zealand Commerce Commission. He has made numerous conference and seminar presentations including in Australia, China, Germany, Japan, New Zealand, Spain, the UK, and the US. Publications on telecommunications economics include two policy monographs, journal articles (including three in *Telecommunications Policy*), contributions to conference volumes and other collections, and co-authoring *Telecommunications Economics and Policy Issues* at the Industry Commission (1997).

Edmond Baranes obtained a PhD in Industrial Organisation from the University of Paris I Panthéon-Sorbonne, France. He is Professor of Economics at the University of Montpellier. His main fields of work are industrial organisation, competition policy, regulation, telecommunications and energy economics. Edmond Baranes is also on the International Editorial Board of the journal *Communications & Strategies*.

Johannes M. Bauer is a professor in the Department of Telecommunication, Information Studies, and Media at Michigan State University where he is also the Director for Special Programs of the Quello Centre for Telecommunication Management and Law. He holds MA and PhD degrees in Economics from the Vienna University of Economics and Business Administration, Vienna, Austria and joined Michigan State University in 1990. Prof. Bauer was affiliated as a visiting professor with the Delft University of Technology, the Netherlands (2000-2001), the University of International Business and Economics in Beijing, China (2002), and the University of Constance, Germany (summer 2010). He is currently the Chairman of TPRC, Inc., the Research Conference for Communications, Information and Internet Policy; serves on the Board of the International Telecommunications Society (ITS); and is a member of the International Scientific Advisory Board of LIRNEasia (Colombo, Sri Lanka).

Erik Bohlin is Professor and Head of the Division of Technology & Society, Department of Technology Management & Economics at Chalmers University of Technology, Gothenburg. He has published in a number of areas relating to the information society - policy, strategy and management. He is Chief Editor of *Telecommunications Policy*; Chair of the International Telecommunications Society; Member of the Scientific Committee of the Florence School of Regulation (Communications & Media); and Member of the Royal Academy of Engineering Sciences. Erik Bohlin obtained his graduate degree in Business Administration and Economics at the Stockholm School of Economics (1987) and his PhD at Chalmers University of Technology (1995).

Martin Cave is BP Centennial Professor at the London School of Economics for 2010/11 and a visiting professor at Imperial College Management School. From 2002 to 2010, he was a professor at Warwick Business School. He is a regulatory economist specialising in the communications sector. He has written a number of academic articles in this area. He is co-author of *Essentials of Modern Spectrum Management* (2007) and of *Understanding Regulation* (2011), and co-editor of *The Handbook of Telecommunications Economics* (2002, 2005) and of the *Oxford Handbook of Regulation* (2010). He has consulted widely for regulators in several countries and for the European Commission, and conducted a number of regulatory reviews for the UK and other governments.

Barbara A. Cherry is Professor of Telecommunications at Indiana University in Bloomington, Indiana. Her research is primarily focused on evaluation of deregulatory policies, governance structures, comparative analysis of infrastructure industries both domestically and internationally, and framing of analyses from a complexity theory perspective. Dr. Cherry's research reflects an interdisciplinary academic background integrated with policymaking experience in the telecommunications industry and government. She has held positions of Senior Counsel in the Office of

Strategic Planning and Policy Analysis at the Federal Communications Commission; Associate Professor and Associate Director of the James H. and Mary B. Quello Centre for Telecommunication Management and Law at Michigan State University; and Director of Public Policy Studies at Ameritech; and Regional Attorney for State Government Affairs at AT&T.

Dr. Cherry holds a PhD in Communication Studies from Northwestern University, a J.D. from Harvard Law School, and an MA in Economics and Law from Harvard University. Dr. Cherry has published articles in scholarly social science journals and law reviews, including *Telecommunications Policy*, *Information Economics and Policy*, *The Information Society*, *International Journal of Communications*, *Federal Communications Law Journal*, and *CommLaw Conspectus*. Her books include *The Crisis of Telecommunications Carrier Liability*, and *Making Universal Service Policy: Enhancing the Process through Multidisciplinary Evaluation* (coedited with S. Wildman and A. Hammond). Dr. Cherry is a Board Member of the International Telecommunications Society.

Kurt DeMaagd is an assistant professor at Michigan State University in the Department of Telecommunication, Information Studies, and Media. His primary research area is on the value of information networks for economic growth, with a particular emphasis on using complex adaptive systems and agent-based models to study the mechanisms and impacts of ICT investments. He teaches courses on programming and network infrastructure. His PhD is from the Ross School of Business at the University of Michigan. He is currently leading the ICT for Development initiative, which is a joint program between the Department of Telecommunication and the Department of Electrical and Computer Engineering (ECE). In addition to various ICTD classes, the program includes semi-annual trips with Telecom and ECE students to Tanzania to deploy broadband Internet connections in rural regions. Back in Michigan, he works with the Michigan Department of Information Technology on the state broadband initiative.

Nicholas Economides is Professor of Economics at the Stern School of Business of New York University and Executive Director of the NET Institute. He is an internationally recognised academic authority on network economics, e-commerce and public policy. His fields of specialisation include the economics of networks (including the Internet, information, computers and telecommunications), the economics of technical compatibility and standardisation, industrial organisation, the structure and organisation of financial markets and payment systems, antitrust, application of public policy to network industries, strategic analysis of markets, and law and economics. He has published over one hundred articles in top academic journals. He holds a PhD and an MA in Economics from the University of California at Berkeley, as well as a BSc (First Class Honours) in Mathematical Economics from the London School of Economics. He previously taught at Columbia University and Stanford University. He is Editor of the *Journal of Economics and Management, Netnomics*, *Quarterly Journal of Electronic Commerce*, *The Journal of Financial Transformation*, *The Journal of Network Industries*, *Economics of Networks Abstracts* by SSRN, and is on the Advisory Board of the Social Science Research Network. His website on the 'Economics of Networks' (www.stern.nyu.edu/networks/) has been ranked as one of the top four economics sites worldwide by *The Economist*. He is advisor to the US Federal Trade Commission, the governments of Greece, Ireland, New Zealand and Portugal, major telecommunications corporations, a number of the Federal Reserve Banks, the Bank of Greece and major financial exchanges. Dr Economides also serves on the Advisory Board of the Economist Intelligence Unit and Quadrisev.

Gerald R. Faulhaber is Professor Emeritus of Business, Public Policy and Management at the Wharton School, University of Pennsylvania, and Penn Law School, US. He has previously served as Chief Economist at the Federal Communications Commission, US. His current research includes spectrum policy, network neutrality, the wireless industry and the open Internet. Dr Faulhaber has been a Visiting Scholar at INSEAD, Fontainebleau, France, the Institut Analisi Economica in Barcelona, Spain, and at Tsinghua University School of Economics and Management, Beijing, China. Prior to his academic career, Dr Faulhaber was Director of Strategic Planning and Financial Management at AT&T, after holding the position of Head, Economics Research at Bell Laboratories.

Benoît P. Freyens is Senior Lecturer at University of Canberra, in the Australian Capital Territory. He concurrently holds a Senior Research position at the Centre of Law and Economics, at the Australian National University, and is Honorary Fellow of the Centre for Human and Social Capital Research at the University of Wollongong. Dr Freyens has long been associated with research projects conducted by the Australian Communications and Media Authority, a collaboration which resulted in the release of several industry reports and the publication of academic papers on spectrum policy, spectrum licensing and radio transmission technologies. Aspects of this research have been published in *Information Economics and Policy*, *Telecommunications Policy, Info, Telematics and Informatics, Telecommunications Journal of Australia,* several book chapters and in the proceedings of various refereed *IEEE* conferences. A committed interdisciplinary scholar, his research interests also include the economics of employment protection (the theme of his PhD dissertation), optimal contracting for human services, inequality and poverty measurement, and some aspects of human capital policy, such as workforce planning and knowledge transfer. In his earlier working life, he was a statistical expert at Eurostat, Luxembourg, and taught economics at Deakin University, at the University College of University of New South Wales and at University of Wollongong.

Rob Frieden serves as Pioneers Chair and Professor of Telecommunications and Law at Penn State University, US. He writes extensively and recently completed *Winning the Silicon Sweepstakes: Can the United States Compete in Global Telecommunications?* published by Yale University Press. Before accepting an academic appointment, Professor Frieden provided business development and regulatory functions for the IRIDIUM mobile satellite venture, held senior government policy making positions in international telecommunications and practised law in Washington, DC. Professor Frieden holds a BA, with distinction, from the University of Pennsylvania and a JD from the University of Virginia.

Shane Greenstein is the Elinor and Wendell Hobbs Professor of Management and Strategy at the Kellogg School of Management, Northwestern University. He is a leading researcher in the business economics of computing, communications and Internet infrastructure. Many of these essays and other commentary are on his blog called virulent word of mouse. He is presently writing a history of the development of the commercial Internet in the United States. Greenstein is co-director of the program on the economics of digitization at the National Bureau of Economic Research, and business/economics section of the Communications of the ACM. He was administrative head of the Management and Strategy Department from 2002 to 2005. Greenstein received his BA from University of California at Berkeley in 1983, and his PhD from Stanford University in 1989, both in economics. He also continues to receive a daily education in life from his wife and children.

Harald Gruber is Head of the Digital Economy and Education division at the Projects Directorate of the European Investment Bank based in Luxembourg. He oversees project appraisal and has contributed to the Bank's strategy papers on the telecommunications sector and the knowledge economy in general. He has recently published *The Economics of Mobile Telecommunications* at Cambridge University Press. He has co-authored articles in particular on the mobile telecommunications sector in scholarly journals such as *Economic Policy, European Economic Review, Telecommunications Policy, Information Economics and Policy* and

International Journal of Industrial Organization. He has been professor at Bocconi University (Milan) for telecommunications economics. Previously he has researched the semiconductor industry, publishing several articles and a book titled *Learning and Strategic Product Innovation - Theory and Evidence for the Semiconductor Industry* (North Holland). He is on the editorial board of *Telecommunications Policy* and *Information Economics and Policy*. Harald Gruber holds a PhD in Economics from the London School of Economics.

Jerry A. Hausman is the John and Jennie S. MacDonald Professor of Economics at MIT in Cambridge, Massachusetts, USA. He is Director of the MIT Telecommunications Economics Research Program. Professor Hausman received the John Bates Clark Award from the American Economics Association in 1985 for the most outstanding contributions to economics by an economist under 40 years of age. He also received the Frisch Medal from the Econometric Society. Professor Hausman has done research and been a consultant in telecommunications since 1974. He has served as a consultant for major US telecommunications firms as well as companies in Canada, the UK, France, Germany, New Zealand, Australia, India, the Netherlands, Finland, and Hong Kong. He has also advised regulatory agencies in the US, the UK, Sweden, Spain, Australia, Mexico, Sri Lanka, and Hong Kong. Professor Hausman has published a number of academic papers in telecommunications. He has authored two books and published numerous articles on mobile telecommunications in academic journals. He first estimated the consumer surplus from cellular telephone in the US in 1996 and determined the loss to the US economy from regulatory delay. He also authored the chapter on mobile telecommunication in the *Handbook of Telecommunications Economics*.

Christiaan Hogendorn is an associate professor of economics at Wesleyan University and co-editor of *Information Economics and Policy*. His research focuses on market structure and competition in deregulated infrastructure industries. He is currently working on projects studying network neutrality, ownership structure in two-sided markets, and the prospects for wired versus wireless competition in broadband. He was formerly a Member of Technical Staff at Bell Laboratories, and he has been a visiting scholar at the Columbia Institute for Tele-Information (CITI) and the Research Institute in Industrial Economics (IFN) in Stockholm.

Gary Madden is Professor of Economics at Curtin University, Perth, Western Australia, and Director of the Communication Economics and Electronic Markets Research Centre (CEEM). His research is primarily focused on examining empirical aspects of communication economics, electronic markets, productivity measurement, cost of living indexes, real options, network economics and digital divide issues. As Director of CEEM, Gary organises workshops and conferences on various topics in telecommunications policy. Gary has published articles in the fields of industrial organisation and aspects of the economics of networks, particularly on telecommunications and the Internet, in scholarly journals including *Review of Industrial Organization*, *Review of Economics and Statistics*, *Industrial and Corporate Change*, *Journal of Forecasting*, *International Journal of Forecasting*, *Economics of Innovation and New Technology*, *Information Economics and Policy*, *Applied Economics*, *Journal of Media Economics* and *Telecommunications Policy*. Dr Madden is an Associate Editor of Telecommunications Policy and a member of the Editorial Board of several International Journals. He is a Board Member of the International Telecommunications Society and Chairman of its Publications Committee. Gary has served as an economic advisor to the Australian Government and international agencies.

Aaron Morey is a research assistant at the Communication Economics and Electronic Markets Research Centre (CEEM). His research interests are in the areas of network economics, regulatory analysis and information economics.

Jeffrey Petchey is a professor of economics and is Head of Research of the School of Economics and Finance at Curtin University, Australia. He is also Director of the Fiscal Federalism Research Unit and has published on issues in fiscal federalism and public economics, both in Australia and internationally. Recent publications include papers in prestigious international journals including the *Journal of Development Studies*, *Regional Studies*, and *Regional Science and Urban Economics*. His main areas of research include international capital and labour mobility, tax competitions between jurisdictions and equilibrium concepts in fiscal competition games, national systems of fiscal equalisation and public infrastructure issues. Jeff has worked as an advisor to AusAid, the Financial and Fiscal Commission (South Africa), the Commonwealth Grants Commission (Canberra) and the Western Australian Treasury.

Brian Viard is Assistant Professor of Strategy and Economics at Cheung Kong Graduate School of Business (CKGSB) in Beijing, China. Prior to joining CKGSB, he was a professor at Stanford Graduate School of Business. His research primarily examines pricing, product, and entry decisions with a focus on information, technology, and communications industries. In these industries, he has studied the effect that competition has on pricing, product variety, and the adoption of new technologies by firms and consumers. He has also studied the role of switching costs in market competitiveness and frequency reward programs. His research has implications for government regulation and policies toward telecommunications and broadband Internet adoption. Brian has published articles in the field of industrial organization in scholarly journals including *The RAND Journal of Economics, Quantitative Marketing and Economics,* and *American Economic Journal.*

Ingo Vogelsang is a professor of economics at Boston University. He received his doctorate in Economics from the University of Heidelberg in 1969. From 1968 to 1975, he was a managing limited partner of Vogelsang & Schönfeld, an international fuel-trading firm in Hamburg, Germany. He subsequently taught economics at the University of Bonn until 1980. From 1981 on, he has been at Boston University. He is an Associate Editor of *Information Economics and Policy* and on the editorial board of several other journals, including the *Journal of Regulatory Economics*. His major consultancies include the RAND Corporation, the World Bank, the European Commission, the German Ministry of Economics (BMWi), the German Monopoly Commission, the German regulatory agency (BNetzA), and regulatory agencies in a number of countries.

He has published sixteen books and monographs and many articles on public utility regulation, public enterprises, privatisation and institutional problems in network industries. Among others, he has developed regulatory mechanisms that formed the basis for price caps. He also helped design a major cost-benefit framework for the World Bank for evaluating the privatisation of public enterprises. In recent years, his research and consulting interest outside telecommunications has focused on methods for regulating electricity transmission networks. In telecommunications he has taken up interconnection regulation and its relationship with the development of competition.

Cuong Huong Vuong was a PhD student in economics at ERMES, Université Pathéon-Assas, France. His research interests lie in the field of regulation and competition in telecommunications, especially in mobile industry. Prior to carrying out PhD research, he studied economics at University of Toulouse 1, France and University of Essex, U.

Foreword

Glenn Woroch

It has become routine to marvel at the extraordinary dynamism of the modern communications marketplace. This sector – whether in developed or developing nation – does not cease to amaze observers with its feats. A few of those feats deserve repeating: In just the last two decades the number of mobile users worldwide went from less than 1 to over 70 per hundred people, and starting from zero the internet is now used by 30 per cent of the world's population. Twenty years ago people watched video programming at home on their TV sets received over the air or off a coaxial cable. Today video is also delivered by satellite networks, by cell phones, and by broadband connections to an expanding array of screens and devices, and some viewers are now the source of videos and images shared with the world. This connectivity is not just enabling high-tech social interaction, but is providing the means to generate wealth through market information at the micro level as well as to shape broad national trends and regional politics.

While progress in communications services has been relentless, the path has not been linear by any means. The quick twists and turns without much warning make it difficult to get a firm grip on the underlying forces driving the industry. Academic research is handicapped in an undertaking of this sort because it is based on historical evidence – as it should be – and so destined to always be out of date. The urge to forecast the future, however, is nearly irresistible. Who would not want to identify the next big development before it dislodges established incumbents and sweeps in new technologies and business models? Of course, this is a fool's errand. Time and again, history has confirmed the futility of these exercises.

This volume, edited by Gerald R. Faulhaber, Gary Madden and Jeffrey Petchey, is able to straddle the turbulent past of the telecoms sector and yet contributes to its exciting, though unpredictable, future. It does so by conducting positive analysis of communications policies adopted in the past and using that analysis to deduce lessons that can guide policy makers in the future. On occasion, the volume also takes the tack of calibrating structural models using historical data and then using those models to numerically simulate counterfactual regulatory policies or corporate strategies. It is these kinds of research strategies that preserve the scientific method while providing relevant policy analysis for this fast-changing sector.

One advantage of the backward looking nature of academic research that is too often overlooked is the lessons offered by past failures. It is important to keep in mind this sector has filled a large cemetery of failed technologies, companies and their business models and practices, and regulatory policies. The invention of the telephone in 1876 is held up as the birth of the telecommunications industry only to ignore that it was the beginning of the end for the telegraph. Nevertheless, it took 130 years, until 2006, before Western Union ceased sending telegrams. Its demise may have begun with the telephone but it was sealed by email and text messaging. Yet some new popular technologies never displace the established ones. Despite fears to the contrary, television has not made radio obsolete – though digital transmission of sound and picture clearly is displacing the earlier analogue equivalent. Mobile phones may be making payphones and pagers extinct but fixed line penetration remains high in the developed world.

Make no mistake: communications services and technology have much left to do. Despite several digital initiatives, most medical records remain on paper. Few workers telecommute, even those in advanced economies, but rather spend countless hours and tremendous amounts of fossil fuel traveling back and forth to work. Education, with few exceptions, is consumed by students seated in buildings in front of teachers, and not at home or work in front of a computer screen. The challenge to imagine and build a digital economy that efficiently and effectively meets these goals is what makes communications research so intriguing. This volume provides the reader with a good blueprint of how best to pursue this project.

Acknowledgements

Our primary obligation is to the authors of the chapters that comprise *Regulation and Performance of Communication and Information Networks*. We appreciate the authority, talent and imagination with which they prepared their drafts, the willingness to accept comment and efforts to meet deadlines.

We also want to thank Matthew Pitman, Editor at Edward Elgar who was enthusiastic about signing on to publish this book. Edward Elgar provided all the support we could have hoped for.

Thien Tran and Warren Kimble provided superb support from the conference proposal to final publication, support which is critical to the book's timely completion. Their exceptional copyediting, desktop publishing and indexing skills are gratefully acknowledged.

Dedicated administrative support from Robyn Pease is greatly appreciated as well.

Gerald R. Faulhaber, Gary Madden and Jeffrey Petchey
July 2011

Introduction

Gerald R. Faulhaber, Gary Madden and Jeffrey Petchey

Digital markets worldwide are in rapid flux. The Internet and World Wide Web have traditionally evolved in a largely deregulated environment, but recently governments have shown great interest in this rapidly developing sector and have been imposing regulations for a variety of reasons that are changing the shape of these industries. For good or ill, the industrial organizations of broadband ISPs, Internet backbone providers and content/application providers are in turmoil; even the immediate future is highly uncertain. Broadband ISPs no longer simply provide a conduit for service delivery, they are involved in producing content and transaction services themselves, in competition with content and delivery providers. Further, the traditional lines between and among all three of these sectors is blurring, as each enters into the others' markets. We are seeing the emergence of powerful, competing platforms, linked in complex ways that challenge traditional economic analyses.

In this context, debate focuses on vertical relations between downstream Internet service providers and upstream Internet backbone providers regarding transit arrangements and pricing for interconnection. Particular issues relate to appropriate service quality discrimination and interoperability standards. In particular, mobile operators must now compete with virtual mobile network (sometimes branded) resellers. These circumstances, along with convergence driven telecommunications operator and information technology provider rivalry, leaves a complex chain of substitutions in end-users' markets to be analysed. For instance, the wireless-only household market segment has recently emerged. This phenomenon has implications for the delivery of triple-play service and the optimal ownership of rural telecommunications utilities. This volume examines the microeconomics of platform structure and firm competition within and between digital markets, modern theoretical treatments of regulatory intervention in digital markets and the consideration of forward-looking experimental analysis of demand for yet to be provided services.

The volume is divided into four parts: governance issues; regulation and investment; next-generation service markets; and wireless communication. Final remarks are provided by Shane Greenstein. The structure of the volume is guided by the basic themes considered at the International Telecommunications Society's Africa-Asia-Australasia Regional Conference 'Mobile Technology and Broadband Application Developments', which was held in Perth, Western Australia on 16–18 August 2009. The volume contains a selection of parallel session papers presented at the conference as well as seven invited papers commissioned to augment the volume. The invited papers are authored by Rob Frieden (Chapter 3), Ingo Vogelsang (Chapter 4), Harald Gruber (Chapter 6), Nicholas Economides and Brian Viard (Chapter 7), Christiaan Hogendorn (Chapter 8), Jerry A. Hausman (Chapter 13), and Edmond Baranes and Cuong Huong Vuong (Chapter 14).

The Conference was sponsored by: Arnold & Porter LLP, the Australian Competition & Consumer Commission, Axiata, BT, Concept Economics, Curtin Business School, DotEcon, Edward Elgar Publishers, Electronic and Telecommunications Research Institute, France Telecom, Global Competition Review, IBBT, IDATE, Inderscience Publishers, InfoCom Research, Inc., National Telecommunications Commission of Thailand, NERA Economic Consulting, NTT DoCoMo, Pacific Telecommunications Council, Sheppard Mullin, Telecom Italia, Telenor and Telus. The conference was attended by 150 researchers, practitioners and regulators involved in telecommunications market analysis.

I: GOVERNANCE ISSUES

The volume begins with three chapters concerned with aspects of national and transnational governance of information network infrastructures. These analyses are important as network platforms act as a conduit for service delivery and as a means to conduct market transactions. A unifying theme of the analyses is regulators' desire to stimulate the development of next-generation broadband networks, whilst not imposing a technological winner. In particular, in Chapter 1, 'Challenges of institutional governance for network infrastructures: Reinstitution and expansion of legal innovations', Barbara Cherry examines how recent US deregulatory telecommunications policy, particularly that related to broadband and the Internet, may create conditions for future instability. Cherry argues that the elimination of common carriage for broadband as a means 'to push *laissez-faire* policy, advocated by the large incumbent telecommunications carriers and many economists, to decrease the role of government rather than a response to a crisis.' Instead, the divergent path may trigger its own crises, creating a demand for re-imposition of the dismantled rules associated with the common carriage framework. Adding to this complexity is the accelerated pace of technological and societal activities and change which are undermining the temporal presuppositions that underlie the division of powers among the branches of government. Scheuerman (2004) asserts that the conflation among the temporal roles of the various branches of government poses difficulties for the maintenance of the rule of law within a liberal democracy.

Rob Albon (Chapter 2 'Beyond traditional regulatory models: Emerging governance for new networks') traces the evolution of ICT regulation and governance across the OECD since the 1980s liberalisation. Albon's principal finding is that telecommunications has a relatively advanced regulatory design. These designs are relatively transparent and consultative compared to other infrastructure areas. EU directives also appear to be catalysts for the liberalisation and formation of economic regulation. Additionally, a move away from telecommunications-only regulation is identified, with governments combining telecommunications with spectrum management, broadcasting and posts as part of a communications-sector-wide regulator. Finally, many countries encounter difficulty in dealing with government desires to further develop broadband on a national scale with greater data rates, including the need to address structural and competition issues beyond the traditional regulatory ambit. The leading countries in broadband penetration and data speed have a diversity of provision by technology, and below average DSL. No country in this position is embarking on a large-scale NBN initiative.

In Chapter 3 ('Government oversight of next generation wireless networks'), Rob Frieden examines the regulatory status of wireless carrier-delivered video content to determine the 'necessary' scope and nature of government oversight. Past practices of the US FCC in regulating the cable industry are reviewed to highlight the disparate treatment of wireless-delivered video content. Frieden concludes that the FCC, and other NRAs, must balance the carriers' interests in finding new revenue centres to pay for next generation network upgrades with subscribers' interests in maximizing their options for wireless handset use. NRAs should also aid wireless carriers to exploit technological innovations that enable the provision of telecommunications, information and video programming service combinations. However, regulators need to guard against carriers' anti-competitive strategies that favour their services by handicapping access to alternative sources. Frieden concludes that as most NRAs seek to promote video programming competition and access for wired cable TV ventures, these NRAs should undertake similar efforts to promote wireless access, because wireless carriers have equivalent incentives and abilities to blunt competition.

II: REGULATION AND INVESTMENT

The next three chapters analyse traditional areas of concern to firms and regulators in telecommunications markets, that is, investment and the appropriate role for regulation. Ingo Vogelsang (Chapter 4, 'Incentive regulation, investments and technological change') provides a review of the academic literature about the relationship between price regulation and investment. Vogelsang then develops policy proposals on pricing assuming that regulators can commit to incentive regulation. Because prices are set after investment, the wish for lower prices creates an ex-post conflict with the ex-ante desire for high investment (Brito et al., 2008). Lack of commitment leads to ex-post policy that inhibits investment. Anticipating such policy, the regulated firms refrain from investing. The introduction of the regulatory commitment issue shows the potential tension between the inability of regulators to commit over the long time horizon of infrastructure investments and the provision of cost-reducing incentives. This leads to policy proposals balancing the investment and incentive aspects. Next, the difference between ordinary and innovative investments are examined as reasons to abandon regulation altogether.

In Chapter 5, 'Policy and regulation for next generation networks', Martin Cave focuses on the policy and regulatory challenges posed by the introduction of NGAs. In developed countries with ubiquitous networks, for the first time in decades governments and regulators are not facing operators with fully sunk costs in the most monopolised part of the network, the local loop. Thus, their problems have increasing similarity with those faced by regulators of other infrastructures seeking to elicit efficient investment decisions, except that telecommunications have the extra complication, or benefit, of operating in an environment where no element of the value chain is conclusively a natural monopoly. However, a faster pace of technological change entails a greater risk of obsolescence than is present in the case of many infrastructures. Accordingly, the regulatory approaches to NGAs being adopted in various jurisdictions are reviewed. Then the role of central government in promoting high-speed broadband, as part either of a long-term policy or of a recovery plan is critically assessed.

Chapter 6 by Harald Gruber ('Sector regulation and investment incentives: The European experience') argues European telecommunications regulatory reform is inspired by open access regulation to bottleneck elements in the customer access infrastructure. Competitive access is seen as the means for eliminating the deadweight loss from monopoly and for establishing efficient service provision in fixed-line telecommunications. Cost-based access pricing regimes are introduced to favour competitive entry. In this sense the ladder of investment concept worked to illustrate the entry mode with increasing own facilities over time. However, it failed to deliver significant investment for inter-platform competition. This issue is now compounded by the fact that FTTH becomes in many contexts the only option for high-speed broadband access. This therefore requires a stepping up of regulation towards a utility style regulation with warranted rates of return for providers of open access fibre networks. The implicit rate of return should provide for sufficient incentives to invest, but there remains the problem that competitive pressure may not be as high as desired by policy makers. This therefore requires substantial public support for the roll out of NGA networks. A further issue for regulatory policy is to create incentives for dynamic efficiency in terms of the sector pursuing innovation in technology and services.

III: NEXT-GENERATION SERVICE MARKETS

The next four chapters focus on modelling issues related to virtual goods markets, spillovers and network neutrality. In particular, Nicholas Economides and Brian Viard (Chapter 7, 'Pricing of complements and network effects') examine a monopolist of a base good that benefits from a complementary good provided either by it or another firm. Use of the complementary good requires the base good, but not the reverse. The model assesses and calibrates the extent of the positive influence on the base good profits that are created by the existence of the two sources (internal or external) of the complementary good. An equivalence between a model of a base and complementary good, and a reduced-form model of the base good where network effects are assumed in the utility function as a surrogate for the presence of direct network effects (i.e., a consumer's utility directly increases in the number of users) or indirect network effects (i.e., arising from increased variety of complementary goods produced by other firms) is established. This allows examination of the pricing of the complementary good under different market structures and in the context of the effect of other complementary goods via the network effects. Additionally, the study assesses and calibrates the influence of the intensity of network effects and quality improvements in the complementary good on profits from the base good. Also evaluated is the incentive that a monopolist has to improve the quality of the base good rather than that of a complementary good that it produces.

Christiaan Hogendorn (Chapter 8, 'Spillovers and network neutrality') considers that the practices addressed by network neutrality include an ISP:

offering content providers an ability to prioritize their traffic; preferring one service or one set of applications over others; or choosing to block or slow a service or set of services. Clearly any of these would be a large change from current practice, but the question is why that should be a public policy concern? The reason is that the ISP would choose preferred services or differential prices based on private valuations of those services. That is, the ISP will base its preferred services and fees on what it can privately appropriate from content provider's revenue. Hogendorn suggests three main reasons for divergence. First, the Internet is a GPT, which means that the applications of content providers often have public values in excess of their private value. Second, the Internet is a network of networks, and so network effects are rampant throughout all Internet-associated products. These take time to grow and they accrue to users beyond the content provider, so the dynamic, public value is likely to be higher than the static, private value. Finally, the Internet is an innovation-spawning technology, so that most of its content is rapidly changing and developing, adding new value. This means that the static value of content may be much less than the dynamic value, since successful development causes future increases in value.

Kurt DeMaagd and Johannes Bauer (Chapter 9, 'Network neutrality and sector performance: Exploring policy options with simulation methods') argue that the main concern of the network neutrality debate is a clarification of the principles that ought to govern the relations between network operators and providers of applications and content. A broad range of economic and non-economic goals is advanced by stakeholders. For example, not only is the need for mandated network neutrality rules contested in the political realm, where broader political objectives also are deliberated; it is far from being settled theoretically and empirically within the community of economic researchers. Considerable progress has been made in a short period of time, but theoretical explorations have yielded a broad range of possible outcomes, contingent on specific model assumptions and theoretical frames. This chapter explores whether progress in addressing these questions by means of simulation methods, capable of coevolving populations of heterogeneous agents, can be used to study policy interventions in communications systems.

IV: WIRELESS COMMUNICATIONS

The final five complementary chapters deal with wireless communications markets. In Chapter 10 ('Mobile communications: Economic and social impact'), Gerald R. Faulhaber examines US voice subscriptions and usage growth in comparison to wireline telephony. The extensions of voice mobile into forms of data services are also discussed. World trends are reviewed, particularly in the developing world. Specifically compared are the deployment and growth of mobile to PCs, broadband, wireline and Internet users. In the penultimate section, both empirical results and anecdotal evidence regarding the substantial impact of mobile telephony on the economies of developing countries, and the pivotal role of mobile telephony as an engine of economic development are reviewed. Faulhaber concludes that to ensure that mobile fulfils its promise there must be a release of large amounts of spectrum for use by mobile service operators; more technological innovation be encouraged by reducing the cost of low-end devices and systems; maintenance of light touch regulation; and for poor rural areas, encourage the deployment of power delivery systems so customers can charge their mobiles.

Gary Madden, Aaron Morey and Erik Bohlin (Chapter 11, 'Regulator incentives and third generation national mobile telecommunications market entry') argue the potential for increased competition arising from entry into national mobile markets is recognised by the EC. Recently, research on the assignment of spectrum licences is concerned with the design and success of auction assignments. However, the determinants of market entry have received little attention. The analysis herein suggests that ex-post payment modes encourage entry, and that incumbents win licences with less onerous deployment obligations. Further, entrants that win licences with direct assistance from NRAs appear to receive more favourable licence conditions. These findings suggest that incumbents have advantages in 3G spectrum assignments, that result in them winning licences in more attractive markets. However, the analysis also suggests NRAs can, and do, design spectrum packages that increase the likelihood of entry. Thus, it would seem that EC directives on mobile entry are consistent with NRA decision-making across the world, and that mobile markets are evolving accordingly.

Benoît P. Freyens (Chapter 12, 'Licensing options for digital dividend spectrum: An Australian perspective') reports that by end-2013, the switchover of analogue television for DTV services will release a sizeable portion of 700 MHz UHF spectrum for use by non-broadcasting services. The main digital dividend allocation policy issues concern: consistency with the objectives of the Act; and resolving legal conflicts over the high-value of the spectrum and incumbents' rights. A bespoke approach can contribute to clarifying both issues. First, the more tailored are licences to meet the needs of certain users in particular bands, the better the fit with market aspirations and legislated objectives. Second, resolving legal conflict concerning UHF band reallocation may require compromise. Given the deeply rooted nature of incumbent spectrum rights under the Broadcasting Act 1997, it is doubtful other approaches will be effective. Whereas wholesale replacement of the apparatus-licenced digital dividend by spectrum licences will polarise positions, a bespoke licensing approach may conciliate incumbent and future user views. Finally, a bespoke approach would better address the needs of providers of wireless access services that face different market structures, while addressing long-term objectives of the Act.

In Chapter 13, ‘Two-sided markets with substitution: Mobile termination revisited’, Jerry A. Hausman argues that regulators consider that fixed-to-mobile prices are set too high. This inference follows typically as mobile termination is seen as a monopoly problem, where mobile carriers do not face competition to terminate calls to their customers. This view misses two important economic factors. First, some or all of the excess of price over cost for mobile termination is used to lower prices for mobile subscription, as would be expected in a two-sided market. The second economic factor is that consumers who want to reach someone on-the-go can substitute mobile-to-mobile calls for fixed-to-mobile calls, and do so given relative prices. When allowed for substitution to mobile-to-mobile calls, which are assumed to be prices at cost, the monopoly termination implication no longer holds true. In terms of a policy recommendation it is concluded that regulating termination charges on the basis of costs is unjustified. When prices in the mobile markets are set competitively, such market intervention seems misguided. While the calibrated results suggest welfare may be enhanced by lowering termination charges below the market-determined rate, they also suggest it is well beyond usual regulatory calculations to determine the optimal prices.

Edmond Baranes and Cuong Huong Vuong (Chapter 14, ‘Policy implications of asymmetric termination rate regulation in Europe’) argue that the setting of asymmetric termination rate regulation between fixed and mobile operators, and different sized MNOs, should be replaced by symmetric regulation. In principle, asymmetric regulation is only appropriate when there is a demonstrated need. Furthermore, the regulator should reduce asymmetry via a glide path with MNOs well established in the market. This approach avoids the ‘cash cow’ problem and allows the incumbent to invest, especially in further deploying the FTTH network. Another consideration is distortion in the MTR. In this case implementing asymmetric MTR regulation is necessary when MTRs are above cost or there are tariff-mediated effects. It may be that both types of asymmetric regulation can be replaced by symmetric regulation simultaneously. This situation is relevant in an environment in which fixed and mobile services offered by an MNO and the incumbent become closer substitutes; and in the context when important investments are required to deploy further network infrastructure by all players.

V: FINAL REMARKS

The final chapter in this volume (Chapter 15, ‘The absence of data for measuring the economic impact of IT in the US’) by Shane Greenstein illustrates the state of US data collection for the Internet economy. Greenstein indicates that the available data is inadequate, and that this is pervasive throughout many of the key questions in Internet economic policy. Moreover, US policy formulation across a range of issues is poorer as a result. Importantly, this knowledge gap is not restricted to the US.

1. Challenges of institutional governance for network infrastructures: Reinstitution and expansion of legal innovations

Barbara A. Cherry

INTRODUCTION

Recent experience under deregulatory policies reveals an acute challenge for institutional governance to support sustainable policies.[1] More specifically, government must develop greater regulatory resilience, i.e., create regulatory structures and policy that are more adaptive to the complexity and increasing pace of technological innovation and ensuing economic and social changes – that must also be constrained by sustainability of the rule of law.[2] The financial crisis in the US and its global diffusion are illustrative of the unpredictability and rapidity with which market instabilities can appear and cascade to potentially catastrophic levels, and for which the difficulties of institutional governance are already apparent.[3]

This chapter examines how recent deregulatory telecommunications policies, particularly those related to broadband and the Internet adopted in the US, may be creating conditions for similar future instability. In so doing, it stresses important legal innovations – encompassing both bodies of law and governance structures – that evolved in the 19th and early-20th centuries to address certain societal and economic problems arising from technological innovations in network infrastructures. Unfortunately, many of these legal innovations have been dismantled under US deregulatory policies during the latter portion of the 20th century, reintroducing historical problems and associated instabilities. Societal demand for broadband infrastructure that is widely available, affordable and reliable will create pressure for reinstitution of important aspects of common carriage principles that successfully provided the legal foundation for the development of previous network infrastructures with such properties.

ACHIEVING SUSTAINABILITY THROUGH REGULATORY RESILIENCE AND THE RULE OF LAW

This chapter expands on a prior lineage of research, examining the challenges in institutional governance for designing sustainable telecommunications policies during the recent phase of deregulatory policies in the co-evolution of technology, economy, and the law. Some research examined sustainability of specific policies, such as universal service,[4] rate rebalancing,[5] and liability rules under detariffing.[6] Others broadened inquiry to look at sustainability problems arising from fundamental attributes of the US governance structure and bodies of law, including enforcement of basic US constitutional principles,[7] attempts to retrench from public utility regulation,[8] and effects of eliminating common carriage obligations to broadband access services.[9]

More recently, research applied a complexity theory perspective to examine policy sustainability problems, both stressing the need for a new paradigm of policy analysis and pressing new inquiries for understanding fundamental challenges of institutional governance.[10] Such a new paradigm 'explicitly recognizes the evolutionary dynamic inherent in policymaking systems and the systems they endeavour to influence',[11] and rejects the traditional paradigm whereby 'policy recommendations are developed based on optimization of some measure of . . . efficiency . . . using models that are essentially mechanic and deterministic'.[12]

As more fully described in Resilience within the Rule of Law, insights for institutional governance from this later stage of research using a complexity theory perspective include:

> (1) the general strength of federalism as a policymaking algorithm, given its mechanisms for both order and experimentation; (2) the need for specific legal rules to enable the evolution of certain emergent properties, such as the desired emergent properties of widespread availability, affordability, and reliability of critical communications infrastructures; (3) the criticality of conducting policy analysis in a historically accurate context, such as when evaluating the evolving interrelationship among general business and industry-specific legal regimes; and (4) the importance of liability rules for complex adaptive systems with the potential for catastrophic failures.[13]

Moreover, '[n]otwithstanding the need for regulatory resilience, the adaptability of a policymaking process and its policies must not undermine the rule of law'.[14] Yet, sustainability of the rule of law – an emergent property of legal and policymaking institutions[15] – is arguably being undermined by a historical process of accelerated technological and social change referred to by Prof. William Scheuerman as 'the social acceleration of time'.[16]

This chapter expands on these insights to further probe the historical evolution of the US governance structure for several purposes. First is to understand how the adoption of the US Constitution – a legal innovation in establishing shared sovereignty under federalism – and its subsequent implementation enabled the emergence of the rule of law for a sustainable republic.

Second is to examine the legal innovations that evolved under the US governance structure to address inadequacies of certain common law principles, their English origins predating the creation of the US as a nation, to changing technological and economic circumstances during the Industrial Revolution. The relevant common law principles embodied a pre-existing distinction between industry-specific legal obligations under common carriage and treatment of commercial transactions among general businesses that constitute restraints of trade.

Third is to explain how crises triggered the development of these legal innovations, which in turn were emergent solutions to address perceived system instabilities. Similar forces underlay the various crises: fear of abuse of power, and the needs of interstate commerce. Furthermore, the emergent solutions had a common characteristic: providing a framework for on-going negotiation to apply legal rules or principles to changing circumstances over time. In so doing, these innovations provided resilience within the rule of law.

Fourth is to explore how recent US deregulatory telecommunications policies related to broadband and the Internet, through dismantling of common carriage regulation, are recreating conditions for instabilities and future crises that the prior legal innovations evolved to address. Importantly, the statutory framework of common carriage, from which deregulatory policies are evolving, was the result of successive layers of policy evolution and legal innovation. Each layer evolved, in turn, to address problems of abuse of power and the needs of interstate commerce. The network neutrality debate is a response to the need to impose a legal framework to replace the resultant legal gap arising from the elimination of common carriage to broadband. Viewed through a deeper historical understanding of governance, that provided sustainability through resilience and the rule of law, such a 'new' framework will likely result in reinstitution of important aspects of the previous industry-specific common carriage regime and associated legal innovations to broadband. Moreover, as discussed in Resilience within the Rule of Law, further legal innovations will also likely be required to meet the changing temporal conditions in which human activities are being conducted under the social acceleration of time.

ESTABLISHING A SUSTAINABLE REPUBLIC

Having won independence from England, the greatest institutional challenge after the American Revolution was to establish a sustainable republic among the States. The initial framework provided in the Articles of Confederation that was ratified in 1781 created a weak federal government that 'accurately reflected both the ideology that justified the American Revolution as well as the mentality and experience of most American citizens'.[17] However, after only a few short years, 'anarchy seemed to threaten, for the Revolution had unleashed new expectations and a new rhetoric of equality and political participation. These new ideas threatened a social revolution that would destroy not only their own fortunes but also the rule of law'.[18]

The Threat of Anarchy to the Republic and Interstate Commerce

Fundamentally, the threat of anarchy to the republic arose from divisive relationships among the sovereign States, creating what James Madison[19] referred to as political vices. Such vices included the States' failure to honour their tax obligations during the war and to fund veterans' pensions after the war; encroachment on federal authority by the States signing their own separate peace treaties with Indian tribes; and a wide variety of state laws, lacking any uniform system of justice.[20]

Moreover, the nation's founders discovered a dark side of independence, including the loss of advantages of membership in the British Empire. The American merchant marine no longer enjoyed the protection of the British navy.[21] Furthermore; there was lingering post-war depression in the South and New England, with the British military campaigns leaving the Carolinas' economies in shambles and the Northern States' economies suffering from peacetime.[22]

The economic problems intensified State rivalry with devastating consequences for interstate commerce.[23] States 'refused to cooperate on internal improvements like roads and canals and . . . blocked efforts to facilitate interstate trade'.[24] 'With duties to pay at every state border, even the most intrepid merchant or shipper found interstate commerce a nightmare. States with natural advantages made every effort to abuse those without them'.[25] 'Other sovereign rights [e.g., each state using its own currency] claimed by the states hurt domestic trade'.[26] 'By 1785 the conflict and chaos created by thirteen independent mercantile systems was obvious, yet calls for commercial cooperation that year and the following year were met with suspicion, resistance – and a decided lack of interest'.[27] 'Despairing of this localism sooner than most, . . . Alexander Hamilton, bemoaned the fact that so few Americans "thought continentally"'.[28]

The Innovation of Federalism

Seeing the republic 'at the edge of anarchy', key Revolutionary leaders feared inaction to address the inadequacies of the confederation.[29]

> The word that Madison, along with most critics of the current confederation, used to describe the consequences of inaction was 'anarchy', a term suggesting utter chaos, widespread violence, possible civil war between or among the states, and the likely intervention of several European powers eager to exploit the political disarray for their own imperial purposes.[30]

Madison argued that – based on appraisal of historical Greek, Italian, German, and Dutch confederations – confederations were an inherently transitory political configuration.

> Confederations were an inherently transitory political configuration headed either toward dissolution, which was the usual outcome, or toward unity, the rare but obviously preferred destination. The political lessons that history provided, then, were unambiguous. Either the confederated republic of the United States came together as one nation or it suffered the sad fate of its European predecessors, which was some combination of civil war, anarchy, and political oblivion.[31]

Madison and Washington concluded 'that the full promise of the American Revolution could be secured only by a stable and wholly consolidated nation-state',[32] even though 'such a national government contradicted the most cherished political values the American Revolution claimed to stand for'.[33]

It is this fear of anarchy that created the sense of crisis that led to the Constitutional Convention held in Philadelphia in May 1787 to address the inherent weaknesses of the Articles of Confederation.[34] At the Convention '[t]here was consensus on only one thing: A new and more effective government was essential. But there was no consensus on what powers that government should have, the form that government should take, or how representation in that government should be determined'.[35] Fearing the concentration of power in a new government, Madison developed the Virginia Plan, which provided for the diffusion of power among three branches of government – legislative, executive, and judicial.[36] During the Convention, the delegates' 'blueprint was the Virginia Plan, which they had accepted in principle but not in its specifics'.[37]

The delegates at the Convention encountered major obstacles in developing and agreeing on the specifics of organizational design for a proposed government. First, a major stumbling block facing the Convention was the States' resistance to shared sovereignty.[38] There was an inevitable 'tug-of-war between the states and the central government, [as] any power granted to one must, of necessity, diminish the autonomy of the other'.[39] Second, there was fear of excess power in any hands.[40] The Convention had a collective fear of abuse of power, anxiety about conspiracies, and a 'near obsession with setting trip wires and booby traps to ensnare the abusers and the conspirators'.[41] '[T]heir lawyerly obsession with anticipating every pitfall, protecting against every contingency, making airtight every clause seemed to them a great asset in assuring . . . protection'.[42] Yet, some believed that any design of government, at best, might only forestall decline into tyranny.[43]

Throughout the Convention these two themes – States' resistance to shared sovereignty and the fear of abuse of power in any hands – 'bled into each other . . . no matter how the discussion began'.[44] Given the unprecedented form of government the delegates were attempting to design, 'it often proved difficult to decide what constituted a radical notion and what constituted a conservative one'.[45] Characteristic of innovative processes, the process at the Convention itself often appeared chaotic,[46] with the delegates moving back and forth from one issue to another.[47] Yet, 'there was in fact a logic to the endless to-and-fro. Because the government the delegates envisioned was made up of interconnected parts, the smallest tinkering or adjustment to one required changes in another. The branches had to be able to cooperate, but they also had to be able to restrain one another'.[48]

As debate progressed at the Convention, the delegates 'essentially declared the theoretical question of state versus federal sovereignty politically irresolvable . . . The only workable solution was to leave the sovereignty question unclear'.[49] The resulting complex design 'of sovereignty that was at once shared and divided raised the [political] compromises reached at the Constitutional Convention to the level of a novel political discovery: to wit, the notion that government was not about providing answers, but rather about providing a framework in which the salient questions could continue to be debated'.[50] More specifically, the organizational design in the US Constitution ultimately ratified by the States in 1788 'was a new and wholly unprecedented version of federalism, [that] emerged from the messy political process itself rather than from the mind of any single thinker'.[51] '[T]he Constitution . . . created a political framework in which state versus federal sovereignty was an on-going negotiation to be resolved on a case-by-case basis . . . Instead of a fatal weakness, the deliberate blurring of sovereignty was an abiding strength'.[52]

The governance structure created in the US Constitution was a legal innovation, 'simultaneously a conservative and radical act'.[53] '[T]he Framers . . . introduced an entirely new concept to the [political] discourse, that of federalism, and in the doing, created a *novus ordo seclorum:* a new order of the ages'.[54] Furthermore, federalism was an emergent solution, 'emerg[ing] from the messy political process itself rather than from the mind of any single thinker',[55] to address the anarchy of an unsustainable republic.

The Sustainability Properties of Federalism

The US Constitution thus far provided a sustainable framework of republican governance for the United States. Other nations and groups of nations have since created federalism structures as well, including Canada and the European Union. As discussed in greater depth in Implications for Federalism, the sustainability properties of federalism are analytically better understood when viewed from a complexity theory perspective.

> [F]ederalism is a patching algorithm that confers system advantages for adaptability through diversity and coupling of policymaking jurisdictions. Such diversity and coupling is important for adaptability of the policymaking process itself by providing mechanisms for both experimentation and stability that are essential for development of sustainable policies.[56]

Federalism also continued to evolve under the US Constitution, in large part from the federal and state governments operating in distinctly separate spheres (dual federalism) toward sharing of federal and state authority (cooperative federalism).[57] Some aspects of such evolution have been legal innovations in their own right, including those that arose during the 19th century to address growing problems of interstate commerce. The development of further legal innovations within federalism relevant to the development of essential network infrastructures, such as transportation and communications, are discussed in the following section.

INNOVATING TO ADDRESS THE NEEDS OF INTERSTATE COMMERCE

The English common law was the foundation of the law in the American colonies and of the common law of the US after the colonies became an independent nation. The common law is case law, by which policy change occurs incrementally through decisions rendered by the judicial branch of government. With its basis on English common law, common law in the US derives from centuries of development in legal doctrine predating creation of the US Constitution. Thus, further development of American law has and continues to evolve from the foundation of the US Constitution and English common law heritage.

The Rise of Statutorification and Corporate Power

Evolution of the common law continued to be the primary source of legal change in the US until the 19th century. However, changes in technology driving the Industrial Revolution exposed certain inadequacies of the common law system that led to statutorification as the primary source of law.[58] Fundamentally, the writ system of common law pleading strictly limited the scope of legal causes of action; and the recognition of new causes of action evolved very slowly. Changes in economic relationships driven by changes in technology gave rise to disputes not recognized by the writ system and thereby to growing societal frustration at the lack of remedies. The only option for more immediate policy change was the enactment of legislation to override the common law.

The rise of statutorification – law-making by legislatures – led to further legal innovations to address commerce. As increased commercial activity initially expanded on an intrastate basis, legislative activity dramatically increased first in the States. The increased burden on state legislatures led to some legal innovations. One – of ultimately great, but largely unforeseen consequences – was the change in method for creating corporations. 'The first method by which charters of incorporation were obtained in the United States was the special incorporation statute. Each charter was generally a separate bill . . . Each such private bill would generally require separate enactment by a state legislature'.[59] Each charter described the intentions of the corporation, its organization features, and any specific privileges or restrictions placed on the corporation.[60] Early business organizations that were granted charters included banks, insurance companies, canals, turnpikes, and later railroads.[61] As the demand for corporate charters increased, another method developed, starting in the early-19th century and more widespread after 1820, known as general incorporation.[62] General incorporation permitted pro forma incorporation without action of the legislature, making corporations more standard and easily available.[63]

By the late-19th century the ease with which corporations could be established, combined with the development of new transportation and communications technologies, provided an opportunity for business corporations to accumulate vast levels of capital and to conduct interstate business on an unprecedented scale.[64] As discussed below, common law remedies did not adequately address the economic abuses of large corporations, and the corporations' interstate activities were beyond the jurisdictional reach of the States. The only viable solutions were statutory responses by Congress to create federal regulation of interstate commerce. Congress' responses led to further legal innovations with passage of the Interstate Commerce Act (ICA) of 1887 to regulate railroads[65] and the Sherman Act of 1890 to prohibit certain anti-competitive and monopolistic practices by all general businesses.[66]

The Common Law Origins of Industry-Specific and General Business Regimes

Under the English common law the concept of 'public callings' developed during the Middle Ages. Under feudalism, service performed within the feudal relationship of lord to man was considered a private employment; however, any service performed for the public outside this relationship was considered a public employment, or public calling. Examples of public callings were common carriers, innkeepers, blacksmiths, and surgeons.

Public callings were simply undertakings to serve the public, and bore various legal duties or obligations under tort law merely by virtue of their status as public employments. 'These obligations evolved . . . to address numerous situations of economic coercion, exploitation and the illegal wielding of bargaining power'.[67] Public callings were required to serve upon reasonable request without discrimination, to charge just and reasonable prices, and to exercise their calling with adequate care, skill and honesty.[68] Importantly, 'public callings bore these obligations merely by engaging in the activity, not because the parties to the transaction agreed to such obligations in the context of negotiating an agreement'.[69]

With the decline of feudalism and rise of *laissez-faire* ideals, the meaning of public callings waned. By the early-19th century, most businesses in the US came to be governed by the evolving common law of contracts. For general businesses, increased reliance was placed on the freedom to contract, and the scope of court intervention to protect parties from unequal bargaining power eroded. However, the tort obligations of public callings remained for a few classes of businesses, including common carriers, and were also imposed on a new class of businesses – public utilities – that evolved during the 19th century.[70] As for the interrelationship between tort and contract law, the common law also continued to impose restrictions on common carriers' attempts to exempt or limit their tort liability in contracts with customers.[71]

The businesses for which the tort obligations remained were referred to collectively as 'businesses affected with a public interest'.[72] During the 19th century, the scope of permissible government regulation under the US Constitution was deemed to be greater for businesses 'affected with a public interest' than for other general businesses.[73] Therefore, the validity of government regulation often hinged on the governments' ability to convince the courts that the business subject to regulation fell into one of the classes of business affected with a public interest. Businesses affected with a public interest fell into three categories, one of which included common carriers and public utilities.[74]

In 1934, in the case of Nebbia v. New York,[75] the US Supreme Court effectively broadened the scope of permissible regulation under government's police power for any business. Yet the Court still maintained that permissible regulation as to a given business depends on the specific circumstances in each case.

> It is clear that there is no closed class or category of businesses affected with a public interest, and the function of courts in the application of the Fifth and Fourteenth Amendments is to determine in each case whether circumstances vindicate the challenged regulation as a reasonable exertion of governmental authority or condemn it as arbitrary or discriminatory.[76]

Thus, given that the Court found government's police power to be coextensive with regulation in the public interest, the need for government to prove that a business did or did not fall into the historical classes of business affected with a public interest fell into disuse.[77] Based on the holding and analysis by the Court in Nebbia v. New York, a wider range of businesses can now be subject to some government regulation; but what constitutes reasonable exertion of government authority would still likely be greater for a business in which circumstances are similar to those underlying the traditional justifications for regulating 'businesses affected with a public interest'.[78]

The Statutory Evolution of Common Carriage

By the 19th century, the common law of common carriage was derivative of the common law for public callings that had emerged from the Middle Ages. The tort obligations of common carriers were applied to specific factual situations on a case-by-case basis. In so doing, the meaning of key concepts – such as 'upon reasonable request', 'just and reasonable price', and 'without discrimination' – evolved over time and in varying contexts. A vestige of the status of public callings was also retained in the concept of 'businesses affected with a public interest'.

Late in the 19th century, common law remedies did not adequately address the economic abuses of large corporations, and corporations' interstate activities were beyond the jurisdiction of the States' police powers. In 1885, Congress created a special Senate Select Committee on Interstate Commerce, popularly known as the Cullom Committee (named after Sen. Cullom), to review the economic abuses associated with large corporations, particularly with regard to the railroad industry.[79]

In early 1886, the Cullom Committee issued its report, known as the Cullom Report.[80] The Cullom Report provides a comprehensive record of the Committee's investigation and recommendation for federal legislation. At this juncture the recommendation for legislation was limited to the railroad industry. Later that same year, a definitive ruling by the US Supreme Court in Wabash, St. Louis & Pacific Railway Co. v. Illinois[81] – that the States lacked jurisdiction to regulate railroad transportation in interstate commerce –

further precipitated a crisis for Congress to act. The following year Congress passed the Interstate Commerce Act of 1887 based on the recommendation of the Committee.

Recognizing the need for policy change

In the Cullom Report, the Committee emphasized that the general question of policy before them was how to control the growth and influence of corporate power and to regulate its relations to the public. Corporations engaged in transportation naturally received the most consideration, given their public visibility and importance to commerce.

> The interest everywhere manifested in its investigation has convinced the committee that no general question of governmental policy occupies at this time so prominent a place in the thoughts of the people as that of controlling the steady growth and extending influence of corporate power and of regulating its relations to the public; and as no corporations are more conspicuously before the public eye, and as there are none whose operations so directly affect every citizen in the daily pursuit of his business or avocation as the corporations engaged in transportation, they naturally receive the most consideration in this connection.[82]

The Committee then stated that the industry and commercial welfare of the country is materially affected by the wisdom or unwisdom of policy affecting the respective rights and obligations of citizens and railroads.[83] Therefore, the Committee's investigation focused on railroad corporations.

The Committee proceeded to describe how, within the past fifty years, the development of improved means of communication and transportation had revolutionized commercial, social, and political relations of nations.[84] Moreover, the Committee asserted, '[r]ailroads are the arteries through which flows the life-blood of the world's commerce; and to promote the interests of commerce is their manifest destiny and the purpose they are especially fitted to serve'.[85]

The Committee then discussed why government policy for the past fifty years had left development of railroads to the private sector.

> The question then was how to get railroads, not how to control them . . . It was a matter of necessity in a new country with undeveloped resources and struggling with other burdens which fully taxed its capacity that the work of railroad construction was left to private enterprise . . . A method of uniform regulation adopted at the outset might have prevented a needless waste of capital and might have obviated or mitigated existing evils, but it would assuredly have retarded the building up of the country in comparison with the progress attained under freedom from legislative restrictions.[86]

However, the Committee stated that such policy may no longer be appropriate and regulation may now be needed.[87]

After reviewing the results of railroad building during the past half century, the Committee asserted that '[t]he policy which has been pursued has given us the most efficient railway service and the lowest rates known in the world; but its recognized benefits have been attained at the cost of the most unwarranted discriminations'.[88] The effect of this policy has been to build up the strong at the expense of the weak, to give the large dealer an advantage over the small trader, to make capital count for more than individual credit or enterprise, to concentrate business at great commercial centres; to necessitate combinations and aggregations of capital that foster monopoly, to encourage the growth and extend the influence of corporate power, and to throw control of commerce into the hands of the few.[89]

As a result of these 'acknowledged evils' incident to the business of railroad transportation, the Committee recognized that public sentiment was nearly unanimous that Congress should undertake in some way to regulate interstate commerce.[90] The Committee then turned its attention to why federal regulation of interstate commerce was necessary and in what manner the public interest could be best served by legislation.[91]

Identifying the reasons for federal regulation of interstate commerce

The Committee found that Congressional action was necessary and expedient for several reasons. First, the Committee concluded that, in the absence of regulation, 'the carrier is practically and actually the sole and final arbiter upon all disputed questions that arise between shipper and carrier as to whether rates are reasonable or unjust discrimination has been practiced'.[92] Throughout the investigation the railroads had argued that: arbitrary or oppressive rates cannot be maintained as they are sufficiently regulated by competition; that such discriminations as exist are unavoidable; that owners and managers of railroads are the best judges of the conditions and circumstances that affect the cost of transportation and what compensation should be received; and that the common law affords the shipper an adequate remedy and protection against abuse or infringement of his rights.[93] But the Committee stated that the railroads' argument fails to recognize the public nature and obligations of the carrier, and the right of the people to have a voice in the management of a corporation which performs a public function; that competition is not sufficient to secure the shipper from abuse and unjust discrimination; and that the common law does not afford the shipper effective remedy for grievances.[94]

As for the inadequacy of legal remedies, the Committee first recognized that the States had found common law remedies to be insufficient in intrastate commerce. Consequently, nearly every State had passed legislation, and many also established commissions, to provide shippers prompt and effective remedies.[95] The Committee stated that the reasons for the failure of recourse to the common law 'apply with even greater force to the more complicated transactions of interstate commerce than to State traffic, because the former involve more perplexing questions and are affected by a greater diversity of varying conditions'.[96] The Committee then elaborated on the hardships borne by a shipper that did seek redress for grievances under the common law. The shipper bears the burden of proof yet the railroad possesses nearly all the evidence; the railroad has ample resources and legal talent to wear out the shipper; the railroad has the power to determine the success or failure of the shipper in business; and, finally, the expense involved and uncertainty faced in litigation have made common law remedies obsolete and useless.[97]

Second, the Committee concluded it is the duty of Congress to regulate because of the railroads' admitted abuses of management and acknowledged discrimination between persons and places that only Congress has the power to remedy under the US Constitution. In this regard, the Committee asserted that competition constitutes effective regulation only under certain conditions, such as for larger shippers and in commercial centres or localities where competition is most active,[98] but that such conditions do not exist for shippers and areas where the protection afforded by competitive forces are inadequate or non-existent, and additional safeguards are needed.[99]

Third, the Committee recognized that federal legislation is necessary because the operations of the transportation system are, for the most part, beyond the jurisdiction of the States. Under the US Constitution, the States have no power to regulate interstate commerce; furthermore, 'even [State] control of their own domestic traffic is restricted and frequently made inoperative by reason of its intimate intermingling with interstate commerce and by the present freedom of the latter from any legislative restrictions'.[100] The Committee asserted that federal regulation would supplement, and render effective, State regulation.[101]

Fourth, the Committee concluded that federal legislation was necessary 'because the business of transportation is essentially of a nature which requires that uniform system and method of regulation which the national authority can alone prescribe'.[102] In this context, the Committee stressed the need for uniformity of regulation in commerce with foreign nations, which only Congress could provide.

Fifth, and finally, the Committee stated that the failure of Congress to act enables the railroads to regulate commerce in their own way and in their own interests.[103] Notwithstanding the achievements of the railroads, there are still inequalities and discriminations that characterize the operations of the system in its entirety. To equalize through and local rates, and to give them uniformity and stability, must involve a complete readjustment and reconstruction of the commercial relations and business methods of the whole country.[104] 'How this is to be accomplished is the secret which underlies the satisfactory solution of the railroad problem'.[105] Judging from past experience, the Committee concluded it was highly improbable that the railroads would eventually work out its solution.[106] The Committee did not believe that a satisfactory solution could ever be secured without the aid of wise legislation.[107]

Developing a solution to the railroad problem

The Committee then took on the task of designing legislation to address the railroad problem. In so doing, it started with an examination of the causes of complaint against the railroad system. The Committee concluded that the essence of the complaints is 'based upon the practice of discrimination in one form or another'.[108] The Committee stated that:

> [t]he first question to be determined . . . is whether the inequalities complained of and admitted to exist are inevitable, or whether they are entirely the result of arbitrary and unnecessary discrimination on the part of the common carriers of the country; and the consideration of this question suggests an inquiry as to the proper basis upon which rates of transportation should be established.[109]

The Committee then engaged in a lengthy analysis of the principles upon which railroad rates should be established, and the limitations within which discrimination may be justifiable.[110] Its analysis examined the following issues: charging 'what the traffic will bear'; the classification of freights; uniformity of classification; discrimination between persons; concessions to large shippers; discriminations between places; the impracticability of fixing rates by legislation; and rates on long and short hauls.

The Committee ultimately made two fundamental recommendations, upon which specific proposed legislative language was based. First, 'one of the chief purposes of . . . legislation . . . should be to secure the fullest publicity, both as to the charges made by common carriers and as to the manner in which their business is conducted'.[111] For 'the maintenance of stable and reasonably uniform rates, [publicity] is the surest and most effective preventive of unjust discrimination'.[112] Furthermore, for publicity to serve this preventive role, 'any deviation from [the posted rates] should be declared unlawful, except when the schedule [of rates] is changed in such manner as may be provided'.[113] However, to provide some flexibility for railroad rates to vary with circumstances, including to meet price cuts by competitors,[114] the proposed legislation suggests time frames for advance notice of rate changes that the Committee believes 'would be reasonable and sufficient notice and not unduly oppressive'.[115] The Committee concluded, '[w]hile it is impossible to foresee the exact effect of legislation requiring the operation of the transportation lines of the country upon a system of fixed rates, . . . the committee believes that the experiment should be tried'.[116]

Second, a federal commission should be established for the enforcement of the proposed legislation.[117] Upon review of the evidence before it, the Committee found that nearly all those expressing an opinion on the matter favoured the creation of a federal commission or other special tribunal to enforce legislation enacted to regulate interstate commerce.[118] Furthermore, in light of the evidence before it, the Committee concluded 'no statutory regulations which may be enacted can be made fully effective without providing adequate and suitable machinery for carrying them into execution . . . Such enactments cannot possibly be self-enforcing'.[119] Therefore, the Committee was convinced that a federal commission is essential to carry out remedial legislation.[120]

Such a commission should 'be authorized to prescribe the manner in which and the extent to which rates should be published'.[121] A commission should also be given ample authority to acquire information, to prescribe the manner in which railroad corporations shall keep their accounts, and to require uniform reports as it may designate.[122] However, citizens 'shall be free to pursue his remedy at common law or under the statute herein recommended, at his own discretion'.[123]

The Committee acknowledged that, '[i]n undertaking regulation of inter-State commerce Congress is entering into a new and untried field'.[124] For this reason, '[i]ts legislation must be based on theory instead of experience'.[125] However, the Committee believed that work intelligently performed by a federal commission 'would year by year remove "the railroad problem" farther from the realm of conjecture and speculation, and would make it possible to gradually build up a system of regulation upon the safe and enduring foundation of certain knowledge'.[126]

The following year Congress passed the Interstate Commerce Act (ICA) of 1887 based on the Committee's recommendation. The ICA was the first federal statute to regulate interstate commerce, and created the first federal regulatory agency, the Interstate Commerce Commission (ICC), to oversee its enforcement.

The Statutory Evolution of Federal Antitrust Law

The Cullom Report identified 'how to control the growth and influence of corporate power and to regulate its relations to the public' as the critical general question of policy.[127] However, the Interstate Commerce Act of 1887, subsequently passed based upon the Report's recommendation, provided a federal regulatory framework only for the railroad industry in interstate commerce. Addressing the policy question of how to regulate corporate power in general had been deferred. Only three years after passage of the ICA, Congress responded with passage of the first federal statute to regulate interstate commerce for general businesses, the Sherman Act of 1890.

Recognizing the need for policy change

From the legislative history of the Sherman Act, it is clear that Congress was motivated to act in response to rising concentration of commercial power on the general public. For example, during a session of the US Senate, Senator George asked:

> We find everywhere over our land the wrecks of small, independent enterprises thrown in our pathway. So now the American Congress and the American people are brought face to face with this sad, this great problem: Is production, is trade, to be taken away from the great mass of the people and concentrated in the hands of a few men who, I am obliged to add, by the policies pursued by our Government, have been enabled to aggregate to themselves large, enormous fortunes?[128]

Senator Sherman, after whom the eventual legislation was named, acknowledged the benefits of large corporations:

> Experience has shown that [corporations] are the most useful agencies of modern civilization. They have enabled individuals to unite to undertake enterprises only attempted in former times by powerful governments. The good results of corporate power are shown in the vast development of our railroads and the enormous increase of business and production of all kinds.[129]

But he also stressed the negative consequences arising from the decline of competition.

> The sole object of [trusts] is to make competition impossible. It can control the market, raise or lower prices, as will best promote to selfish interest . . . Its governing motive is to increase the profits of the parties composing it. The law of selfishness, uncontrolled by competition, compels it to disregard the interest of the consumer.[130]

Identifying the reasons for federal regulation of interstate commerce

Congress identified problems similar to those encountered in addressing the railroad problem. Congressional response was necessary due to the inadequacy of common law remedies and the lack of State jurisdiction over interstate commerce.

Legal remedies were inadequate under both federal and state law. First, there was no relevant federal common law.[131] Second, the States' common law was not designed to preserve competition. 'The historical concern of the common law of contracts in restraint of trade was coercion, or the elimination of noncontracting parties' freedom to contract'.[132] But '[t]he classical doctrine of contracts in restraint of trade had little or nothing to do with the emerging neoclassical economic theory of competition'.[133] That the doctrine was not designed to preserve competition is clear from the way in which the courts employed the doctrine.[134] '[C]ompletely voluntary agreements to eliminate competition, such as by price-fixing, were not generally enforceable in court, [but] neither were they indictable offenses or even challengeable by third parties in civil actions'.[135] Thus, the law intervened only when parties to the contract combined to force a recalcitrant contract party to adhere to the contract terms.[136]

As for the jurisdictional problem,

> [f]ederal jurisdiction seemed necessary because multistate firms were then largely beyond the reach of any single state. State courts could not easily attach property located in other states, and corporations often evaded judicial penalties by reincorporating elsewhere or moving their principle place of business. By 1890, it was widely believed that only the federal government could deal effectively with trade restraints.[137]

Developing a solution to the rising concentration of commercial power

The Sherman Act was enacted to prevent restraints on competition arising from the conduct of large businesses, often organized as 'trusts'.

> [The Sherman Act] was enacted in the era of 'trusts' and of 'combinations' of businesses and of capital organized and directed to control of the market by suppression of competition in the marketing of goods and services, the monopolistic tendency of which had become a matter of public concern. The end sought was the prevention of restraints to free competition in business and commercial transactions which tended to restrict production, raise prices or otherwise control the market to the detriment of purchasers or consumers of goods and services, all of which had come to be regarded as a special form of public injury.[138]

However, Congress faced the challenge of designing a statutory framework to achieve the intended purposes.

Given the lack of relevant pre-existing federal common law, the '[c]reation of a new federal jurisdiction inevitably required the courts to receive, apply, and develop "the common law" in the same way that a new jurisdiction customarily does'.[139] For this reason, Areeda and Hovenkamp assert:

> [T]he Sherman Act may be seen not as a prohibition of any specific conduct but as a general authority to do what common law courts usually do: to use certain customary techniques of technical reasoning, to consider the reasoning and results of other common law courts, and to develop, refine, and innovate in the dynamic common law tradition.[140]

The brevity of the legislation – to prohibit every contract, combination or conspiracy in restraint of trade and to prohibit monopolization of any part of trade in interstate commerce – and its subsequent enforcement by the courts for over a century support this characterization. The Sherman Act provided the statutory foundation for a new body of law that provided flexibility to evolve in the courts consistent with the common law tradition.

PROVIDING AN INSTITUTIONAL INFRASTRUCTURE TO SUSTAIN A MARKET ECONOMY AND ESSENTIAL NETWORK INFRASTRUCTURES

A complexity theory perspective provides powerful insights for understanding how governance structures and legal rules affect the sustainability of commercial activities. This section incorporates and expands upon the results of prior research examining institutional infrastructure necessary for the sustainability of a market economy and essential network infrastructures. As will be discussed, market capitalism requires an institutional infrastructure, including the rule of law, to create and sustain it. Furthermore, specific legal rules are required for the sustainability of critical network infrastructures, such as communications, with the desired properties of widespread availability, affordability and reliability. Historically, the institutional infrastructure in the US – through federalism and evolution of the key common law principles of common carriage and public utility – has provided both the rule of law and specific legal rules for such network infrastructures. However, as further discussed below, sustainability problems have been created by deregulatory policies for broadband in particular, and, as discussed in Resilience within the Rule of Law*,* by the forces underlying the social acceleration of time in general.

The Importance of the Rule of Law to Support a Market Economy

An important concept from complexity theory is emergence.[141] Emergence refers to 'order that spontaneously develops as collective properties from interacting system components'.[142] The spontaneous order that emerges from free markets 'as if by an invisible hand' is an emergent property of a market economy (under certain conditions).[143]

It is now well recognized that government plays a critical role in providing an institutional infrastructure to support a market economy, and thereby deriving the benefits, under appropriate conditions, of the invisible hand.[144] Such an infrastructure includes bodies of law, such as property rights and contract principles, as well as a governance structure for their enforcement.[145] Moreover, sustainability of market capitalism also requires limits on government power through the rule of law.[146] Constraints on government power are necessary to protect investors from vulnerability to expropriation of their investments by arbitrary exercise of administrative power.[147]

The core concept of the rule of law is 'a government of laws and not of men'.[148] It describes a system of governance in which the sovereign is limited by the law.[149] Importantly, however, 'the rule of law is not itself a legal rule, but a political ideal'.[150] In other words, the rule of law itself is an emergent property of some legal and policymaking institutions.

The rule of law is deemed to have first emerged as a tradition in the West during the Middle Ages,[151] and has since become 'the preeminent legitimating political ideal in the world today'.[152] The emergence of federalism in the US Constitution as a solution to the problem of anarchy among the States enabled the extension of the rule of law on a much broader geographic scale than had previously existed.[153] At the time of the Constitutional Convention in 1787, '[t]he conventional assumption, most famously articulated by Montesquieu, held that republics worked best in small geographic areas, where elected representatives remained close to the interests of the citizens who elected them'.[154] But, 'Madison took [a] theoretical step, generally regarded by most historians and constitutional scholars as his most brilliant contribution to modern political science'.[155] Madison asserted that an extensive republic was an asset rather than a liability.

> Small republics, like the states, were actually more vulnerable to factional squabbling and sectarian divisions than large republics, because the larger scale of the enterprise vastly increased the number of competing factions, thereby producing 'a greater variety of interests, of pursuits, of passions, which check each other . . . So an extensive republic meliorates the administration of a small Republic.'[156]

'[T]he very novelty of the idea, which essentially turned a core assumption of revolutionary ideology on its head, . . . was an idea so far ahead of its time that no one could fully appreciate its originality'.[157] Thus, a novel theoretical idea was an important contribution to the eventual emergent solution of a governance structure based on federalism to extend the rule of law to republics of broader geographic scope.

The Importance of Legal Infrastructure for Sustainability of Network Infrastructures

The legal infrastructure necessary to sustain a market economy must also support the development of critical network infrastructures for transportation and communications. Today, most nations seek the development of critical network infrastructures that are widely available, affordable, and reliable. From a complexity theory perspective, these desired attributes of network infrastructures are emergent properties. This section incorporates and expands on the results of prior research that examines 'the fundamental question as to what legal rules are necessary for the sustainability of critical communications infrastructures that generate the desired properties of widespread availability, affordability and reliability'.[158] Common law principles of common carriage and public utility have historically provided key components of the legal infrastructure in the US for the establishment of critical network infrastructures of transportation and communications with the desired emergent properties of widespread availability, affordability and reliability.

Establishment of the federal postal system

In the US the federal government's role in establishing a critical network infrastructure began with the federal postal system. Under the US Constitution, Congress was granted the exclusive power to establish post offices and postal roads.[159] Congress passed the Post Office Act of 1792, which not only established the US Postal Service (USPS), but, unlike Europe or Canada, subsidized newspaper delivery and exchange through reduced postal rates.[160] Furthermore, Congress abandoned the requirement that each post office be financially self-sustaining, allowing revenues of more profitable post offices to subsidize new post offices as the nation expanded westward.[161] The result of these policy choices was the creation of the news network, which Paul Starr refers to as 'America's First Information Revolution'.[162]

Importantly, the federal postal system was considered a common carrier, as it provided to the public the distribution of information through physical means of transportation. In this respect, the postal system represented the convergence of transportation and communications networks. Furthermore, under a policy of subsidizing new post offices from existing profitable ones in order to expand its geographic accessibility, the postal system operated much like a public utility. However, the postal system was unlike a public utility in that, under its meaning in the US, the latter is a private corporation.[163] Thus, the postal system operated under an industry-specific legal framework.

Diffusion of common carriage regulation based on successive layers of policy innovation

As technologies evolve and commercialize, societal response tends to follow subsequent phases that Spar refers to as 'creative anarchy' and the 'demand for rules'.[164] Creative anarchy refers to the chaos that arises from problems – whether for innovators, pioneers in commercializing the innovations, or society at large – from the prior phases of innovation and commercialization. These problems often relate to issues of property rights, coordination, and competition.[165] Demand for rules refers to those responses that seek to end the creative anarchy through the quest for rules.[166] Rules may come from various sources, such as monopoly power, industry standards, or government.[167]

During the 18th century, technological innovations revolutionized society and commerce through new forms of transportation and communications networks. These new technologies include railroads, telegraphy, and telephony. In the US, the demand for rules response has historically followed, in many respects, a similar trajectory for these three technologies.[168]

Although each of these technologies was utilized by the postal system, they remained under private ownership and control. However, similar to the postal system, all three technologies were considered common carriers under the common law.[169]

The creative anarchy phase creating a demand for federal statutory rules developed first for railroads. As previously discussed, both competition and common law remedies were deemed insufficient to constrain the abuse of economic power in the railroad industry, and the States lacked jurisdiction over interstate commerce. The solution that emerged from Congress' deliberations, superbly described in the Cullom Report, was the ICA of 1887. The statutory framework of the ICA: (1) started by codifying the common law principles of common carriage as its foundation; (2) established a new regulatory framework for the interrelationship of interstate and intrastate commerce based on shared sovereignty with the States under federalism; and (3) created a new type of federal government entity, an independent federal regulatory agency, to oversee implementation of the statute in interstate commerce.

Articulated in this way, we see that the ICA was the result of successive layers of policy evolution and legal innovation. Each layer, in turn, was the response to prior demands for rules from prior phases of creative anarchies; and each of the earlier phases of creative anarchy arose from the consequences of abuse of power and the needs of commerce. The first layer, or foundation, was composed of the principles of common carriage, which were the result of centuries of legal innovation by the courts with deep roots in the Middle Ages, consisting of fundamental obligations originally borne by all public employments to address forms of economic coercion and retained for certain classes of 'businesses affected with a public interest' notwithstanding the rise of capitalism and the common law of contracts. The second layer was the US Constitution, its framework of federalism constituting an innovative solution by the Constitutional Convention of 1787 to the anarchy of the early republic. The third layer was an innovation of Congress through the process of statutorification that was more frequently invoked starting in the 19th century, creating a new federal government entity to oversee the complexities of implementation of the legislation. In this regard, Congress emulated the innovation of the States, many of which had already created state commissions to regulate the activities of railroads in intrastate commerce.

Congress later applied the same statutory framework, or template, to address issues arising from the growing role and influence of telegraphy and telephony. In 1910, Congress amended the ICA to extend the jurisdiction of the Interstate Commerce Commission (ICC) to the interstate activities of telegraphy and telephony. In this way, Congress diffused its experimental framework of regulation from railroads to electronic communications technologies. The States did likewise through creation of state commissions, often lineal descendants of those established to regulate railroads, to regulate telephony.[170] In 1934, the same framework – copying much of the language verbatim from the ICA – was established in the Communications Act of 1934 (FCA), which created the Federal Communications Commission (FCC) with jurisdiction over telephony, telegraphy, and radio. By the time the Telecommunications Act of 1996 (TA96) was enacted, Congress' experiment had lasted and diffused for over 100 years.

Diffusion of public utility law

In the US, the common law of common carriage was the bedrock of the legal infrastructure supporting the development of network infrastructures with the emergent properties of widespread availability, affordability, and reliability. However, its critical role was augmented by the evolution of public utility law. With the imposition of additional public utility obligations, railroad and telecommunications network infrastructures became even more widely available and more affordable to more people, businesses, and geographic areas.

The common law of public utilities evolved in the US during the 19th century. A public utility is a private corporation that provides service of public importance or necessity under a government grant of privilege; and this grant of privilege imposes an affirmative duty to render service demanded by any member of the public.[171] For network services, the government grant of privilege was access to public rights-of-way and, often for railroads and telecommunications carriers, the right of eminent domain.

In essence, a public utility had an affirmative duty to extend facilities to provide service with a corresponding barrier to exit; in exchange for which it was in some way protected from competitive entry.[172] It is the set of mutual obligations between the private entity and government contractual obligations that is distinctive of a public utility relationship, including the scope of government power within it.

> For public utilities, the nexus for greater government regulatory power was the existence of the contractual relationship between government and the private service provider. This contractual relationship arose from the government's grant of some privilege to a private entity to be exercised for the benefit of the public; in exchange for which, whether express or implied, the private entity agreed to be bound by certain obligations (Wolfe Packing Co. v. Court of Industrial Relations of Kansas, 1923).[173]

A public utility arrangement is the legal mechanism by which access to the network infrastructures of railroads and telephony was further extended. Over time, the ICA was amended to include provisions that both restricted entry and exit as well as imposed obligations to extend facilities. Similar provisions were retained in the Communications Act of 1934. With regard to intrastate commerce for telephony, the public utility framework evolved first in municipal franchises and was later codified in state public utility statutes.

It is the principles underlying public utility law that gave rise to what has come to be referred to as universal service policy in the US. With regard to telephony, universal service has generally come to mean access to basic service at affordable rates.[174] Through a complex array of government interventions implemented over decades, such as implicit subsidies within the price structure of services and explicit funding mechanisms, by the early-1980s household penetration rates for wireline telephony service exceeded 90 per cent for the nation overall.

For transportation carriers and in varying ways, public utility obligations also took the form of implicit subsidies in the price structure and explicit funding mechanisms.[175] Such government interventions also contributed to the more widespread availability and affordability of railroad and airline services throughout the US.

Therefore, by the time the US responded to technological changes in the late 20th century, the existent regulatory framework also included a public utility law heritage. For this reason, as analysis progresses it is important to modify the previous description of the successive layers of policy evolution and innovation to better reflect the layers of the prevailing statutory, regulatory framework from which deregulatory policies were being developed. These layers, stated more briefly and modified, are: (1) codification of common law principles of common carriage and public utility; (2) a regulatory framework based on federalism; and (3) oversight by a federal independent administrative agency and in some cases also by state administrative agencies.

UNDERSTANDING THE SUSTAINABILITY PROBLEMS OF DEREGULATORY POLICIES FOR BROADBAND

US deregulatory policies for both transportation and communications carriers have introduced numerous problems for the sustainability of critical network infrastructures with the emergent properties of widespread availability, affordability and reliability. This section incorporates and expands upon the results of prior research examining these sustainability problems. Recent US deregulatory telecommunications policies related to broadband and the Internet, through dismantling of common carriage regulation are recreating conditions for instabilities and future crises that the prior legal innovations evolved to address. The network neutrality debate is a response to the need to impose a legal framework to replace the resultant legal gap arising from the elimination of common carriage to broadband. This section probes more deeply into the sustainability properties of common carriage principles that provided the legal foundation for the sustainability of critical network infrastructures. From this perspective, societal demand for broadband infrastructure that is widely available, affordable and reliable will likely create pressure for reinstitution of important aspects of common carriage principles that successfully provided the legal foundation for the development of previous network infrastructures with such properties.

Sustainability Problems Created by Deregulatory Policies

In the US deregulatory policies in transportation preceded those for telecommunications. Given their common legal heritage, experience with deregulatory transportation policies provides valuable insights for both evaluating recent deregulatory telecommunications policies and informing prospective policy change in telecommunications under intermodal competition. The analysis in Back to the Future[176] is dedicated to this task, and some important findings are summarized here.

Correctly identifying the original regulatory regimes

The analysis in Back to the Future starts with correctly identifying the original regulatory regimes from which deregulatory policies are evolving and thus serve as the appropriate basis for comparative evaluation. In this regard, the original legal regime for both transportation and telecommunications carriers is that of the common law upon which the statutory regimes later evolved. Unfortunately, the analyses of numerous scholars either explicitly or implicitly characterize the statutory, and not the common law, regimes as the original paradigm from which deregulatory changes have evolved.

Serious analytical problems arise in analyses based on such a misidentification of the original paradigm. '[T]here is a preoccupation with changes in the statutory obligations but inadequate evaluation of changes relative to the common law obligations'.[177] The analytical problems have been manifested in various ways.

First, given that deregulatory policies have changed various statutory requirements, some scholars' analyses incorrectly claim – either explicitly or implicitly – that deregulatory transportation regimes have eliminated common carriage. Such assertions as to the non-existence or irrelevance of common carriage under the deregulatory regimes mischaracterize the current state of transportation law. Furthermore, such assertions fail to appreciate the policy reasons underlying the development of the original common law obligations as status-based rules, imposed simply by virtue of one's status of engaging in the business and not as the result of the existence of monopoly power.[178]

Second, as a result of this tendency to dismiss the relevance of common carriage under the deregulatory regimes, such analyses are preoccupied with evaluating regulation governing the wholesale market but devote inadequate attention to regulation governing the retail market.[179] Consequently, when considering deregulatory communications policies, they fail to discuss the common law origins of common carrier and public utility regulation or problems in the retail market that the original common law principles of common carriage evolved to address. Furthermore, such analyses stop short of asking whether their own policy recommendations will enable sustainability of critical communications infrastructure in the long term.[180]

By correcting mischaracterizations of common carriage under transportation deregulation, the previously discussed analytical problems become clear. The current transportation regimes still retain many attributes of the original common law regime albeit with significant modifications to the initial statutory regimes; retain a significant degree of industry-specific regulation with agency oversight; and impose common carriage obligations in varying ways among carriers both across and within transportation modes. Furthermore, considerable energies have and continue to be devoted to addressing issues related to the retail market.

Identifying sustainability and transition problems

By commencing analysis from the appropriate temporal point in legal history under the common law, experience under deregulatory transportation policies foreshadows evolution of communications policies. In this regard, both policy sustainability and transition problems that have arisen under deregulatory transportation policies are already appearing under deregulatory telecommunications policies.

First, mechanisms established to fulfil public utility functions under the transportation deregulatory regimes are having recurring sustainability problems.[181] By eliminating entry barriers in order to embrace competition, the mechanisms for extending access to targeted customers or geographic areas that would not otherwise be served had to be modified by increasing reliance on explicit funding programs. Programs funded through appropriations by Congress – such as Amtrak for intercity passenger rail service and the Essential Air Service program for airline service to small, isolated communities – are considered unsustainable at historical funding levels, but do not reliably receive adequate funding from Congress.[182]

Likewise, by eliminating entry barriers for the telecommunications industry, mechanisms for achieving universal service objectives had to be modified by shifting reliance from implicit subsidies within the price structure to explicit funding programs. The current funding mechanism for support of federal universal programs established under the Telecommunications Act of 1996 is already considered to be unsustainable.[183]

Second, there have been transition problems in implementing the transportation deregulatory regimes that relate to litigation of claims in the retail market.[184] Some problems have arisen from judicial interpretation of the effects of detariffing, which were ultimately resolved by the US Supreme Court.[185] Others have arisen from ambiguity as to the applicability of other federal or state causes of action – based on legal grounds outside of the industry-specific legal regimes – that may be brought by or on behalf of customers against transportation carriers. Unfortunately, many of these – such as the interpretation of savings clauses or pre-emption clauses – still remain unresolved.

Similar transition problems related to detariffing and the scope of federal pre-emption of state claims have already arisen under deregulatory telecommunications policies.[186] There is a conflict among the Federal Court of Appeals as to the legal implications and effects of detariffing, but thus far it has been unaddressed by the US Supreme Court.[187] In addition, the US Supreme Court has not eliminated uncertainties regarding the viability of state causes of action given the coexistence of various federal pre-emption and savings clauses.[188]

The Legal Gap Created for Broadband

There is, however, a major divergence in the evolutionary trajectories of the legal regimes for the transportation and telecommunications sectors. Recent FCC policy decisions affecting broadband access services have eliminated common carriage in both the wholesale and retail markets, also rendering public utility obligations inapplicable.[189] From the perspective of deregulatory transportation policies, this broadband policy is of a radical nature. For this very reason, deregulatory transportation policies are not instructive of the unique policy trajectory for broadband. This section incorporates and expands upon the results of recent research related to network neutrality,[190] consumer sovereignty,[191] and the search for critical legal rules to enable sustainable communications infrastructures[192] to reveal an even deeper layer of sustainability problems.

Relevance of the differential evolution of the common carriage and antitrust regimes

As discussed, both the statutory industry-specific regime of common carriage and the statutory general business regime of antitrust evolved to address a crisis of corporate power in interstate commerce, but with different solutions in the different contexts. These coexisting industry-specific and general business regimes have since coevolved, creating complex interrelationships between them.

The federal antitrust law post-dates the initial federal statutory framework of common carriage established for railroads and later applied to telecommunications. From differential starting points, the respective regimes further coevolved. Recognizing this temporal sequencing is critical, as the antitrust evolved as an adjunct to the common carriage framework. As a result, in numerous cases and circumstances the antitrust law has been pre-empted or superseded by the common carriage statute, and, for such situations, further evolution of the antitrust law thereby addressed issues not covered by the traditional common carriage framework.

As the common carriage framework changes under deregulatory policies, the resulting interrelationships between the common carriage and antitrust laws necessarily shift. The complexity of redrawing the boundaries between the common carriage and antitrust laws is already apparent from recent US Supreme Court cases.[193]

A legal framework for broadband access services is still evolving. Because the FCC classified broadband access services as information services, they are not subject to common carriage regulation under Title II of the Communications Act of 1934. As a result, the FCC's regulatory authority over broadband access is limited to its ancillary jurisdiction under Title I, which is ill-defined. Therefore, a new and different interface with antitrust law must be built. Meanwhile, bifurcation in the development of common carriage and antitrust law – particularly with the former predating the latter – means that elimination of the common carriage layer for broadband access services creates a legal gap that the antitrust law does not automatically fill.

The network neutrality debate

The network neutrality debate in the US is a response to the phase of creative anarchy triggered by the legal gap for broadband. The network neutrality debate is complex because the issues raised under that rubric embody a diversity of alleged goals, problems, and remedies.[194] Yet, the issues arise from the same root cause: the inapplicability of the statutory common carriage framework for broadband access services, at both the wholesale and retail levels. However, because many analyses intentionally or unintentionally ignore the common law origins of common carriage, the previously discussed analytical problems reappear in the network neutrality debate.[195]

The analytical problems include a preoccupation with evaluating regulation governing the wholesale market and inadequate attention to regulation governing the retail market.[196] This led to assumptions or assertions that reliance on antitrust law for wholesale market problems will, as if by an invisible hand, trickle down to adequately address problems in the retail market. However, the statutory framework of common carriage evolved because competition was insufficient even under the common law framework of common carriage to adequately address problems in the retail market. The elimination of the centuries-old common law principles of common carriage constitutes a new experiment with which the US had no prior experience.

The overall effect of misidentifying or ignoring the original regulatory paradigm under the common law has been to mislead the discourse of network neutrality away from critical questions related to problems in the retail market.[197] One set of questions relates to whether a broadband network infrastructure will evolve with the desired emergent properties of widespread availability, affordability and reliability. Another set of questions relates to the sustainability of policy goals that had been achieved under the traditional telecommunications, common carriage regime. In this regard, subjecting broadband and narrowband telecommunications services to asymmetric regulatory frameworks may undermine the sustainability of policy goals associated with the latter.[198] Due to competition between asymmetrically regulated narrowband and broadband networks, ultimately no common carriage-provided service may be available to some classes of customers in some geographic areas.[199]

Yet, another set of sustainability problems may be created due to inter-infrastructure effects. Notably, deregulatory broadband policies may adversely affect the financial sustainability and ubiquitous deployment of the postal system (USPS).[200] Electronic substitution over the Internet of first class mail has undermined the financial viability of the USPS. To address the financial unsustainability of the USPS's current business model, in 2003 the President's Commission on the US Postal System recommended that the USPS become more Internet-dependent, both for coordinating internal operations and for providing value-added services.[201] How the postal system will be affected by the elimination of common carrier obligations for the provision of broadband access services to the Internet is unclear. Adverse consequences could arise, such as de facto erosion of common carriage postal services and deterioration in the geographic availability of postal service. The cascading implications for the postal system have thus far not penetrated policymakers' attention in the context of network neutrality.

Sustainability Properties of Common Carriage

Successive layers of policy evolution and innovation of the statutory regulatory framework from which deregulatory policies are developing were modified as follows: (1) codification of common law principles of common carriage and public utility; (2) a regulatory framework based on federalism; and (3) oversight by a federal independent administrative agency and in some cases also by state administrative agencies. These layers are restated here as a reminder of the temporal sequencing of the respective legal innovations, which deepens appreciation of the previously discussed sustainability problems arising from the FCC's elimination of the bedrock layer of common carriage for broadband access services. Attributes of the first layer are now probed more deeply in order to better appreciate sustainability properties inherent in the common law principles of common carriage.

Federalism is a form of patching algorithm that confers advantages for system adaptability by providing mechanisms for both experimentation and stability. Federalism also provided a solution to the anarchy of a weak confederation of sovereign states. The solution to this form of sustainability problem is a political framework in which the salient questions could continue to be debated, that is, a political framework in which state versus federal sovereignty was an on-going negotiation to be resolved on a case-by-case basis. The framework of on-going negotiation, in which the theoretical question of state versus federal sovereignty is politically irresolvable, is federalism that has inherent sustainability properties.

The framework established by common law principles of common carriage is similar to that of federalism. Common carriage principles provide a framework in which the salient questions continue to be debated, that is, a framework for on-going negotiation on a case-by-case basis as to what is unjust or unreasonable discrimination, a just and reasonable price, and an adequate level of service. As with federalism, common carriage principles provide mechanisms for both experimentation and stability that confer advantages for adaptability over time and changing circumstances. Given the longevity of the common carriage principles and the success of US experimentation under statutorily modified frameworks, the empirical realities support the theoretical expectations.

What changed from the Middle Ages to the 20th century was not the core set of common law principles of common carriage but the governance structure by which the principles were enforced. For transportation common carriers, deregulatory policies further altered the governance structure for enforcement of common carriage policies but preserved the foundational layer of common carriage. However, for broadband access services the entire foundational layer of common carriage has been removed. As a result, the inherent sustainability properties of common carriage provided through on-going negotiation on a case-by-case basis have been eliminated for broadband. For this reason, the depth of sustainability problems for broadband appears far more acute.

The elimination of common carriage principles has reintroduced forces for instability that the common carriage regime had evolved to address. It is unclear whether a legal framework can be developed that will enable broadband infrastructure to be widely available, affordable and reliable without re-imposition of requirements similar to those of common carriage, as many of the network neutrality recommendations propose.

CONCLUDING REMARKS

The elimination of the common carriage framework for broadband access services to the Internet in the US is a radical departure from deregulatory policies for other transportation and telecommunications network infrastructures. It removed a critical layer of the legal institutional infrastructure that had successfully supported the development of previous network infrastructures with the desired emergent properties of widespread availability, affordability and reliability. In so doing, the US has embarked on a new, experimental policy trajectory.

However, unlike the crises that triggered prior paths of legal innovation – creation of federalism, federal regulation of interstate commerce, and administrative agencies – the reasons for deviating onto this new path are less compelling. The elimination of common carriage for broadband appears to have been the exploitation of a window of opportunity to push *laissez-faire* policy, advocated by the large incumbent telecommunications carriers and many economists, to decrease the role of government rather than a response to a crisis.[202] Instead, the divergent path may likely trigger its own crises, creating a demand for re-imposition of the dismantled rules associated with the common carriage framework. The recent financial crisis in the US arising from deregulatory policies and reliance on the neoclassical economics paradigm are instructive of the system instabilities and sustainability problems that can ensue.[203]

Adding to the complexity of these problems is a recent historical process that is generating an even deeper set of core sustainability problems for institutional governance. This historical process – which Scheuerman refers to as the social acceleration of time[204] – is arguably threatening the sustainability of the rule of law itself. In this regard, Scheuerman asserts that the accelerated pace of technological and societal activities and change are undermining the temporal presuppositions that underlie the division of powers among the branches of government: that the legislature is deliberate and future-oriented, the executive is expeditious and present-oriented, and the judiciary is retrospective and past-oriented.[205] Each branch of government is under pressure to respond outside of its intended temporal role – for the legislature to change laws with greater rapidity and less deliberation, for the executive to augment its power to address exigencies, and the judiciary to take on forward-looking legislative tasks.[206] Scheuerman asserts that the conflation among the temporal roles of the various branches of government poses difficulties for the maintenance of the rule of law within a liberal democracy.

Given the premise of Scheuerman's argument, '[a]n unresolved issue is what further innovations to policymaking systems can be made to address the temporal challenges of the social acceleration of time'.[207] Any such further innovations would need to be incorporated into the evolution of broadband policy, further complicating the trajectory of the latter. The implications of the social acceleration of time represent another area of research that needs to be incorporated into analyses of future broadband policies.

NOTES

1. '[S]ustainable policies are defined as rules that are politically adoptable and for which the desired policy goals are reasonably likely to be achievable', Cherry (2007a, p. 374) (emphasis omitted) (hereinafter Implications for Federalism), quoting Cherry and Bauer (2004) (hereinafter Adaptive Regulation).
2. See Cherry (2008a) (hereinafter Resilience within the Rule of Law).
3. See Cherry (2008a, p. 27–30).
4. See Cherry and Wildman (1999, p. 45).
5. See Cherry (2000) (hereinafter Deregulation Role Reversal) and Cherry and Bauer (2002).
6. See Cherry (2003a) (hereinafter Improving Network Reliability).
7. See Cherry and Wildman (2000).
8. See Cherry (2003b, p. 758–60) (hereinafter Political Realities).
9. See Cherry (2003c) (hereinafter Essentiality of Access) and Cherry (2006, p. 484) (hereinafter Misusing Network Neutrality).
10. See Cherry (2007a, 2008a), Cherry and Bauer (2004), Cherry (2008b, p. 947) (hereinafter Maintaining Critical Rules).
11. See Cherry (2007a, p. 374).
12. See Cherry (2007a, p. 374).
13. See Cherry (2008a, p. 7).
14. See Cherry (2008a, p. 7).
15. See Emergent Properties (describing emergence as properties or substances that '"rise" out of more fundamental entities and yet are "novel" or "irreducible" with respect to them').
16. See Cherry (2008a, p. 19–23) and Scheuerman (2004). Scheuerman (2004) defines the social acceleration of time as:

    [A] long-term yet relatively recent historical process consisting of three central elements: technological acceleration (e.g. the heightening of the rate of technological innovation), the acceleration of social change (referring to accelerated patterns of basic change in the workplace, e.g.), and the acceleration of everyday life (e.g., via new means of high-speed communication or transportation).
17. See Ellis (2007, p. 92).
18. See Berkin (2002, p. 5).
19. Key revolutionary leaders – often referred to as founding fathers, some of whom are mentioned in this section – include George Washington, James Madison, Thomas Jefferson, Benjamin Franklin, and Alexander Hamilton.
20. See Ellis (2007, p. 104).
21. See Berkin (2002, p. 13).
22. See Berkin (2002, p. 13–4).
23. See Berkin (2002, p. 14–6).
24. See Ellis (2007, p. 104).
25. See Berkin (2002, p.15) (emphasis added).
26. See Berkin (2002, p.15).
27. See Berkin (2002, p.16) (emphasis added).
28. See Berkin (2002, p.17) (emphasis added).
29. See Ellis (2007, p. 91–2).
30. See Ellis (2007, p. 93) (emphasis added; footnote omitted).
31. See Ellis (2007, p. 103) (footnote omitted).
32. See Ellis (2007, p. 94).
33. See Ellis (2007, p. 89).
34. See Ellis (2007, p. 6–7).
35. See Berkin (2002, p. 71).
36. See Berkin (2002, p. 73).
37. See Berkin (2002, p. 77).
38. See Berkin (2002, p. 44).

39. See Berkin (2002, p. 45).
40. See Berkin (2002, p. 91).
41. See Berkin (2002, p. 78).
42. See Berkin (2002, p. 78–9).
43. See Berkin (2002, p. 79).
44. See Berkin (2002, p. 91).
45. See Berkin (2002, p. 77).
46. See Berkin (2002, p. 78).
47. See Berkin (2002, p. 94).
48. See Berkin (2002, p. 95).
49. See Ellis (2007, p. 110).
50. See Ellis (2007, p. 123) (emphasis added).
51. See Ellis (2007, p. 90) (emphasis added). Federalism is '[a] federal system of governance arises when a group of equally-sovereign states combine to form a union in which they cede some sovereignty to a central government and retain some sovereignty.', see Ulen (1998) (citation omitted).
52. See Ellis (2007, p. 124) (emphasis added).
53. See McDonald (1985, p. 261).
54. See McDonald (1985, p. 262).
55. See Ellis (2007, p. 90).
56. See Cherry (2007a, p. 372).
57. See Cherry (2007a, p. 386–388).
58. See Calabresi (1982, p. 1–7).
59. See Creighton (1990, p. 51).
60. See Creighton (1990, p. 51).
61. See Creighton (1990, p. 38).
62. See Creighton (1990, p. 52).
63. See Creighton (1990, p. 52).
64. See Hurst (1977).
65. See Schwartz (1973).
66. See Areeda and Hovenkamp (2000).
67. See Cherry (2003c, p. 257).
68. For a discussion of the history of public callings, see Cherry (2003c, p. 256–7), Cherry (2003b, p. 763-4), and Cherry (2008b, p. 962).
69. See Cherry (2003b, p. 763).
70. See Cherry (2003c, p. 257, n. 31). 'A public utility is a private corporation that provides a service of public importance, or necessity, under a government grant of privilege. This grant of privilege imposes an affirmative duty to render service demanded by any member of the public. Public utilities were initially created by local government grants of franchises, which were subsequently pre-empted by the codification of public utility law in state statutes.', Cherry (2003c, p. 257). Thus, unlike a common carrier under the common law, a public utility had the affirmative duty to extend facilities to serve an entire community, Cherry (2003c, p. 257). A few businesses, such as railroads and telecommunications companies, are both common carriers and public utilities, Cherry (2003c, p. 257, n. 37).
71. See Cherry (1999, p. 12–6) (hereinafter Crisis in Telecommunications).
72. For a discussion of the history of 'businesses affected with a public interest', see Cherry (2003c, p. 259–60) and Cherry (2003b, p. 763–7).
73. Here the legal issue concerned constitutional limitations on the ability of government to exercise its police power. See Cherry (2003b, c).
74. Wolff Packing Co. v. Court of Industrial Relations of Kansas (1923), 262 US 522, 535.
75. Nebbia v. New York (1934), 291 US 502.
76. Nebbia v. New York (1934), 291 US 502, 536.
77. See Cherry (2003b, p. 765–7).
78. See Cherry (2003b, p. 765–7).

79. See Schwartz (1973, p. 31).
80. Report of the Senate Select Committee on Interstate Commerce (1886) (hereinafter Cullom Report).
81. Wabash, St. Louis & Pacific Railway Co. v. Illinois (1886), 118 US 557.
82. Cullom Report (1886, p. 2–3) (emphasis in original).
83. Cullom Report (1886, p. 3).
84. Cullom Report (1886, p. 3–4).
85. Cullom Report (1886, p. 4).
86. Cullom Report (1886, p. 5).
87. Cullom Report (1886, p. 6).
88. Cullom Report (1886, p. 7) (emphasis added).
89. Cullom Report (1886, p. 2–3) (emphasis added).
90. Cullom Report (1886, p. 175).
91. Cullom Report (1886, p. 175).
92. Cullom Report (1886, p. 176).
93. Cullom Report (1886, p. 176).
94. Cullom Report (1886, p. 176–7).
95. Cullom Report (1886, p. 176–7)
96. Cullom Report (1886, p. 177).
97. Cullom Report (1886, p. 177).
98. Cullom Report (1886, p. 178).
99. Cullom Report (1886, p. 178).
100. Cullom Report (1886, p. 178).
101. Cullom Report (1886, p. 178).
102. Cullom Report (1886, p. 179).
103. Cullom Report (1886, p. 179)
104. Cullom Report (1886, p. 180).
105. Cullom Report (1886, p. 180).
106. Cullom Report (1886, p. 180).
107. Cullom Report (1886, p. 180).
108. Cullom Report (1886, p. 180) (emphasis added).
109. Cullom Report (1886, p. 180) (emphasis added).
110. Cullom Report (1886, p. 182–98).
111. Cullom Report (1886, p. 198).
112. Cullom Report (1886, p. 198).
113. Cullom Report (1886, p. 200).
114. Cullom Report (1886, p. 206).
115. Cullom Report (1886, p. 202).
116. Cullom Report (1886, p. 208) (emphasis added).
117. Cullom Report (1886, p. 213).
118. Cullom Report (1886, p. 208).
119. Cullom Report (1886, p. 213).
120. Cullom Report (1886, p. 213).
121. Cullom Report (1886, p. 207).
122. Cullom Report (1886, p. 215).
123. Cullom Report (1886, p. 214).
124. Cullom Report (1886, p. 214).
125. Cullom Report (1886, p. 214).
126. Cullom Report (1886, p. 215).
127. See Cullom Report (1886, p. 2–3), and accompanying text.
128. 21 Cong. Rec. 2598 (1890) (emphasis added).
129. 21 Cong. Rec. 2457 (1890).
130. 21 Cong. Rec. 2457 (1890).
131. See Areeda and Hovenkamp (1978, §302, p. 3)
132. See Areeda and Hovenkamp (2000, §104a, p. 63).

133. See Areeda and Hovenkamp (2000, §104a, p. 68).
134. See Areeda and Hovenkamp (2000, §104a, p. 69).
135. See Areeda and Hovenkamp (2000, §104a, p. 63).
136. See Areeda and Hovenkamp (2000, §104a, p. 63).
137. See Areeda and Hovenkamp (1978, §302, p. 4).
138. Apex Hosiery Co. v. Leader (1940), 310 US 469, 492–3 (footnote omitted).
139. See Areeda and Hovenkamp (1978, §302, p. 4).
140. See Areeda and Hovenkamp (1978, §302, p. 4).
141. See Areeda and Hovenkamp (1978, §380) and Cherry (2008a, p.7).
142. See Cherry (2007a, p. 380).
143. See Cherry (2008b, p. 953–4).
144. See North (2005, p. 133) and Fligstein (2001, p. 3).
145. See De Soto (2000, p. 153–72), and Kovacic (2001, p. 269–72).
146. See North (2005, p. 83–5,133–6), Tamanaha (2004, p. 97), and Zakaria (2003, p. 77).
147. See Levy and Spiller (1996).
148. See Cass (2001, p. 2) (quoting Mass. CONST. art. XXX).
149. See Tamanaha (2004, p. 144).
150. See Tamanaha (2004, p. 58).
151. See Tamanaha (2004, p. 15).
152. See Tamanaha (2004, p. 4).
153. See Ellis (2007, p. 104–7).
154. See Ellis (2007, p. 105).
155. See Ellis (2007, p. 105).
156. See Ellis (2007, p. 105–6) (emphasis added).
157. See Ellis (2007, p. 107).
158. Cherry (2008b, p. 949).
159. Art. I, Sec. 8, Clause 7, US Constitution.
160. See Starr (2004, p. 88–92).
161. See Starr (2004, p. 88–92). In this respect, US policy was different from that in Europe, contributing to greater density of post offices in the US For example, just before the American Revolution the colonial Post Office had 67 offices, or about 4.5 per 100,000 inhabitants. As of 1828, the number of post offices per 100 thousand inhabitants was 74 in the US compared to 17 in Great Britain and 4 in France (Starr, 2004, p. 87–98).
162. See Starr (2004, p. 83–111).
163. See note 70.
164. See Spar (2001, p. 11–22). Spar discusses four distinct phases of societal response along the technological frontier: innovation, commercialization, creative anarchy, and rules. She provides a vivid recounting of these phases of societal response along the technological frontier through a series of technological revolutions, beginning with the development of the compass in the early Middle Ages, following with the development of telegraph and radio during the 19th century, and turning to satellite television and the Internet in the 20th century. These phases should be understood as describing a general pattern, and may not necessarily follow a rigid path of progression as some phases may interact with each other or even with those of other technologies.
165. See Spar (2001, p. 15–8)
166. See Spar (2001, p. 18–22).
167. See Spar (2001, p. 18–22).
168. For a comparison of the historical legal regimes of railroads and telecommunications, see Cherry (2008c, p. 273) (hereinafter Back to the Future).
169. See Cherry (1999, p. 14–28). However, comparing the evolution of the liability rules of common carriage among the respective technologies is considerably more complex, Cherry (1999). See Cherry (2003a).
170. See Stone (1991).
171. See note 70.

172. For a more detailed discussed of the evolution of public utility law, see Cherry (1999, p. 50–7).
173. See Cherry (1999, p. 55) (emphasis in original).
174. The evolution of the meaning of 'universal service' has its own complex history. Milton Mueller traces its origins to problems of interconnection between the Bell system and independent telephone companies during the early 19th century. However, certainly by the second half of the 20th century, the term has come to have the general meaning stated here. See Mueller (1993).
175. See, for example, Cherry (2008c, p. 275–83).
176. See Cherry (2008c, p. 273).
177. See Cherry (2008c, p. 277).
178. See Cherry (2008c, p. 277).
179. See Cherry (2008c, p. 277).
180. See Cherry (2008c, p. 277–8).
181. See Cherry (2008c, p. 283).
182. See Cherry (2008c, p. 277).
183. See Cherry (2008c, p. 286).
184. See Cherry (2008c, p. 284).
185. See Cherry (2008c, p. 284).
186. See Cherry (2008c, p. 286–7).
187. See Cherry (2008c, p. 286–7).
188. See Cherry (2008c, p. 277). For a discussion of uncertainty related to judicial interpretation of several savings clauses under federal law applicable to telecommunications services, see Cherry (2007b) (hereafter Consumer Sovereignty).
189. In the matter of inquiry concerning high-speed access to the Internet over cable and other facilities, Declaratory Ruling and Notice of Proposed Rulemaking, 17 FCC Rcd 4798 (2002) (cable modem access to the Internet is an information service not subject to common carriage regulation); In the matter of appropriate framework for broadband access to the Internet over wireline facilities, universal service obligations of broadband providers, Report and Order, 20 F.C.C.R. 14,853 (2005) (DSL access to the Internet is an information service not subject to common carriage regulation).
190. See Cherry (2006).
191. See Cherry (2007b, 2008b).
192. See Cherry (2008b).
193. Verizon Communications Inc. v. Trinko, 540 US 398 (2004) (interpreting the antitrust-specific savings clause in the Telecommunications Act of 1996; neither recognizing nor repudiating the essential facilities doctrine); Bell Atlantic Corp. v. Twombly, 127 S. Ct. 19955 (2007) (changing the standard for pleading an agreement in restraint of trade). For a discussion of the uncertainties created by these cases, see Cherry (2007b, p. 15–9).
194. See Cherry (2006, p. 485–90).
195. See Cherry (2006, p. 500–5).
196. See Cherry (2006, p. 484).
197. See Cherry (2006, p. 500–5).
198. See Cherry (2006, p. 497–500).
199. See Cherry (2006, p. 498).
200. See Cherry (2006, p. 507–10).
201. See 'Embracing the Future: Making the Tough Choices to Preserve Universal Mail Services' (2003, p. 143–57).
202. This interpretation is supported by the analysis of agenda denial strategies in Barbara A. Cherry (2007c).
203. See Cherry (2008a, p. 27–30).
204. See note 16.
205. See Scheuerman (2004, p. 26–7).
206. See Scheuerman (2004, p. xvi–xvii, 44–6).
207. See Cherry (2008a, p. 23).

REFERENCES

Areeda, P. and Hovenkamp, H. (1978), *Antitrust Law: An Analysis of Antitrust Principles and their Application,* Vol. II, Boston: Little, Brown and Company.

Areeda, P. and Hovenkamp, H. (2000), *Antitrust Law: An Analysis of Antitrust Principles and their Application,* Vol. I, New York: Aspen Law & Business.

Berkin, C. (2002), *A Brilliant Solution*, New York: Harcourt, Inc.

Calabresi, G. (1982), *A Common Law for the Age of Statutes*, Cambridge: Harvard University Press.

Cass, R. (2001), *The Rule of Law in America*, Baltimore: Johns Hopkins University Press.

Cherry, B. (1999), *The Crisis in Telecommunications Carrier Liability: Historical Regulatory Flaws and Recommended Reform*, Norwell, MA: Kluwer Academic Publishers.

Cherry, B. (2000), 'The Irony of Telecommunications Deregulation: Assessing the Role Reversal in US and EU Policy', in I. Vogelsang and B. Compaine (eds), *The Internet Upheaval: Raising Questions, Seeking Answers In Communications Policy*, Cambridge: The MIT Press, 355–86.

Cherry, B. (2003a), 'Improving Network Reliability – Liability Rules Must Recognize Investor Risk/Reward Strategies', in L. Cranor and S. Wildman (eds), *Rethinking Rights and Regulations: Institutional Responses to New Communications Technologies*, Cambridge: The MIT Press, 309–34.

Cherry, B. (2003b), 'The Political Realities of Telecommunications Policies in the US: How the Legacy of Public Utility Regulation Constrains Adoption of New Regulatory Models', *Michigan State University Law Review*, **3**, 757–90.

Cherry, B. (2003c), 'Utilizing "Essentiality of Access" Analyses to Mitigate Risky, Costly, and Untimely Government Interventions in Converging Telecommunications Technologies and Markets', *Commlaw Conspectus,* **11**, 251–75.

Cherry, B. (2006), 'Misusing Network Neutrality to Eliminate Common Carriage Threatens Free Speech and the Postal System', *Northern Kentucky Law Review*, **33**, 483–512.

Cherry, B. (2007a), 'The Telecommunications Economy and Regulation as Coevolving Complex Adaptive Systems: Implications for Federalism', *Federal Communications Law Journal*, **59**, 369–402.

Cherry, B. (2007b), 'Consumer Sovereignty: Redrawing the Boundaries between Industry-Specific and General Business Legal Regimes for Telecommunications and Broadband Access Services', presented at the Telecommunications Policy Research Conference 2007, Arlington.

Cherry, B. (2007c), 'Analysing the Network Neutrality Debate through Awareness of Agenda Denial', *International Journal of Communication*, **1**, 580–94.

Cherry, B. (2008a), 'Institutional Governance for Essential Industries under Complexity: Providing Resilience within the Rule of Law', *CommLaw Conspectus*, **17**, 1–31.

Cherry, B. (2008b), 'Maintaining Critical Rules to Enable Sustainable Communications Infrastructures', *Georgia State University Law Review*, **24**, 947–75.

Cherry, B. (2008c), 'Back to the Future: How Transportation Deregulatory Policies Foreshadow Evolution of Communications Policies', *The Information Society*, **24**, 273–91.

Cherry, B. and Bauer, J. (2002), 'Institutional Arrangements and Price Rebalancing: Empirical Evidence from the United States and Europe', *Information Economics and Policy*, **14**, 495–517.

Cherry, B. and Bauer, J. (2004), 'Adaptive Regulation: Contours of a Policy Model for the Internet Economy', presented at the ITS 15th Biennial Conference, September 22. Retrieved from: http://userpage.fu-berlin.de/~jmueller/its/conf/berlin04/Papers/Cherry_paper.pdf.

Cherry, B. and Wildman, S. (1999), 'Unilateral and Bilateral Rules: A Framework for Increasing Competition while Meeting Universal Service Goals in Telecommunications', in B. Cherry, S. Wildman, S. Hammond IV and A. Hammond (eds), *Making Universal Service Policy: Enhancing the Process through Multidisciplinary Evaluation*, Mahwah: Lawrence Erlbaum Associates.

Cherry, B. and Wildman, S. (2000), 'Preventing Flawed Communication Policies by Addressing Constitutional Principles', *Michigan State University Law Review*, 2000, 55–105.

Creighton, A. (1990), *The Emergence of Incorporation as a Legal Form for Organizations*, Unpublished PhD dissertation, Stanford University.

De Soto, H. (2000), *The Mystery Of Capital: Why Capitalism Triumphs in the West and Fails Everywhere Else*, New York: Basic Books.

'Embracing the Future: Making the Tough Choices to Preserve Universal Mail Services' (2003), Report of the President's Commission on the United States Postal System. Retrieved from: http://www.ustreas.gov/offices/domesticfinance/usps/ pdf/report.pdf.

'Emergent Properties' (2006, Oct 23), Stanford Encyclopaedia of Philosophy. Retrieved from: http://plato.stanford.edu/entries/ properties-emergent/.

Ellis, J. (2007), *American Creation*, London: Vintage Books.

Fligstein, N. (2001), *The Architecture of Markets: An Economic Sociology of Twenty-First-Century Capitalist Societies*, Princeton: Princeton University Press.

Hurst, J. (1977), *Law and Social Order in the United States*, Ithaca: Cornell University Press.

Kovacic, W. (2001), 'Institutional Foundations for Economic Legal Reform in Transition Economies: The Case of Competition Policy and Antitrust Enforcement', *Chicago-Kent Law Review*, **77**, 265–315.

Levy, B. and Spiller, P. (1996), *Regulations, Institutions, and Commitments: Comparative Studies of Telecommunications*, Cambridge: Cambridge University Press.

McDonald, F. (1985), *Novus Ordo Seclorum: The Intellectual Origins of the Constitution*, Lawrence: University Press of Kansas.

Mueller, M. (1993), *Universal Service: Competition, Interconnection, and Monopoly in the Making of the American Telephone System*, Cambridge: The MIT Press.

North, D. (2005), *Understanding the Process of Economic Change*, Princeton: Princeton University Press.

Report of the Senate Select Committee on Interstate Commerce (1886), 49th Congress, 1st session.

Scheuerman, W. (2004), *Liberal Democracy and the Social Acceleration of Time*, Baltimore: Johns Hopkins University Press.

Schwartz, B. (1973) (ed.), *The Economic Regulation of Business and Industry,* Vol. I, New York: Chelsea House Publications.
Spar, D. (2001), *Ruling the Waves: Discovery, Chaos, and Wealth from the Compass to the Internet*, New York: Harcourt Trade Publishers.
Starr, P. (2004), *The Creation of the Media: Political Origins of Modern Communication*, New York: Basic Books.
Stone, A. (1991), *Public Service Liberalism*, Princeton: Princeton University Press.
Tamanaha, B. (2004), *On the Rule of Law: History, Politics, Theory*, Cambridge: Cambridge University Press.
Ulen, T. (1998), 'Economic and Public-Choice Forces in Federalism', *George Mason Law Review*, **6**, 921–51.
Zakaria, F. (2003), *The Future of Freedom: Illiberal Democracy at Home and Abroad*, New York: W. W. Norton & Company.

2. Beyond traditional regulatory models: Emerging governance for new networks

Rob Albon

INTRODUCTION

This chapter considers the evolution of regulatory and governance arrangements for information and communications technology (ICT) across major Organisation for Economic Co-operation and Development (OECD) Member Countries.[1] Three phases of reform are recognized. In the first phase (during the 1980s), independent regulatory institutions are established (or modified) and commercial operations (other than in the United States and Canada where operation are private) are corporatized. Prior to this, outside North America, telecommunications are operated as politicized government-owned statutory monopolies where governance is typically internalized in government departments that both operate and regulate telecommunications. The second phase occurred as mobile networks emerged during the 1990s, digital subscriber line (DSL) technology breathed new life into traditional copper, and an element of convergence occurred between information technology (IT), broadcasting and telecommunications. Driven by technological imperatives, regulatory and governance arrangements more generally are typically reviewed, with a tendency toward formation of communications-sector-wide regulatory institutions, often with clearer links to competition and antitrust institutions. The third round of institutional and design change is currently taking place, and relates particularly to government desires in a number of countries to establish high-speed broadband networks with substantial ubiquitous geographic coverage. Existing regulatory and governance institutions established to cope with more competitive circumstances are not always ideally equipped to address all the necessary issues associated with government broadband objectives.

LIBERALISATION AND INDEPENDENT REGULATION OF TELECOMMUNICATIONS IN THE 1980s AND EARLY-1990s

Telecommunications reform began in the 1980s and early-1990s when major OECD Member Countries moved from statutory monopoly to competitive telecommunications markets; and those countries not previously exhibiting private ownership moved to privatise (in part or full) government-owned incumbent telecommunications operations. Whereas telecommunications operations and governance had been within government departments, the first round of reforms separated operation from governance, and separated both from departmental operation.

Removal of Statutory Monopoly

In the surveyed countries, until the 1980s or 1990s, telecommunications are supplied by operators with comprehensive statutory monopoly power. Other than in Canada and the United States (US), nationwide telecommunications services are supplied by government-owned statutory monopolies operating nationally. In Canada, telecommunications services are supplied by six regional statutory monopolists, while telecommunications in the US are traditionally supplied by privately owned regional monopoly Bell system local-operating companies, controlled by AT&T. Beginning in either the 1980s or 1990s, statutory monopoly is abolished across the OECD, and some competition subsequently emerged. In most cases, telecommunications are the first major infrastructure industry subject to this form of liberalisation and associated regulation. Newly formed regulators assumed powers to regulate access to the incumbent's network. The emphasis is initially on access to predominant fixed-line networks; particularly to the public switched telephone network (PSTN). Mobile networks are either in their infancy or non-existent at the time.

Ownership and Privatisation

The incidence of private ownership also increased markedly, beginning in the 1980s. While North American incumbents are traditionally privately or locally owned, those in other OECD countries typically are fully government-owned. Complete privatisations of incumbent telecommunications carriers in the United Kingdom (UK) and New Zealand in the 1980s are amongst the first in the OECD. Since then, previously government-owned incumbents, including those in Australia, Germany, Ireland, Korea (1994-2002) and the Netherlands are fully privatised, while those in Japan, France, and Sweden are partially privatised. New entrants into telecommunications markets are almost always privately owned, leading to the further dilution of government ownership.

Structural Change

Structural issues are addressed in the early reform stage in a number of the countries considered, e.g., the US, Japan and Australia.

Following an antitrust case, in 1982, AT&T reached a settlement with the US Department of Justice whereby AT&T would divest its local operating companies. These companies are subsequently split into seven independent Regional Bell Operating Companies (RBOCs). Each RBOC provided telecommunications services within a designated local access transport area, with AT&T restricted to providing long-distance service. The RBOCs have subsequently merged to form the current three major regional companies in the US, viz., AT&T, Verizon and Qwest.

In Japan, the incumbent, Nippon Telephone and Telegraph (NTT), is split into the regional companies NTT East and NTT West in 1999. Both companies are owned by the partially-privatised NTT Holdings.

In Australia, there are important structural changes when the domestic statutory monopolist, Telecom, is amalgamated with the statutory monopolist for international services, Overseas Telecommunications Corporation (OTC), to become Telstra in 1991. In the same year, the government-owned satellite operator, AUSSAT, was sold to Optus, and became the second licence holder entitled to operate all kinds of telecommunications services. A third mobile operator (Vodafone) is licenced in 1993.

Retail Price Regulation and Changes to USO Arrangements

Across the surveyed countries, governments required monopoly carriers to look after the special interests of particular users, sometimes defined by the type of service (e.g., local calls); the attributes of the users (e.g., the low income and disabled; 'vulnerable' consumers in the UK) or the geographic location of users (Universal service obligation or USOs). Funding these arrangements is usually through cross subsidy (charging other users above-cost prices to generate funds for subsidies); and sometimes through explicit government subsidies from consolidated revenue. As, outside North America, telecommunications operations are traditionally part of a government department, pricing decisions are made by government under advice from the responsible department, and perhaps other departments. Cross subsidies are embedded in these pricing decisions, including uniform national pricing for key services.

As operations are separated from government, retail prices came to be regulated by an independent body. For example, in Germany the regulator assumed a role in approving retail tariffs for carriers with significant market power. Several countries including Australia adopted a 'RPI minus X' form of regulation, where the weighted average price of a basket of services can increase at no greater than the percentage change in the retail price index minus a percentage X. Independent price regulation previously existed in the US and Canada because of the separation of private operation from government. The prices of the main intra-state telephony services are subject to controls by state regulators.

Anti-competitive Conduct

In all countries considered, incumbent statutory monopolies did not – by definition – operate in competitive markets, so anti-competitive conduct is not an issue. However, following liberalisation and the weakening (and ultimate removal) of statutory monopoly, competitive conduct and antitrust became relevant. All standard antitrust and trade practices issues became applicable in relation to practices like predatory pricing and failure to supply. However, in nearly all countries considered, these competition functions are in bodies other than the regulator, e.g., the Competition Commission in Canada.

Independent Economic Regulation

The substantial changes to the institutional and market arrangements in telecommunications led governments to introduce explicit economic regulation, independent of operation, and, in most cases, independent of the government department in which it is previously embedded.

While the US and Canada had regulators in place, in each case the changes to market structure and competition led to a broadening of the powers and functions of the regulatory body; especially rivals' access to incumbent networks. The unique industry structure in the US required a unique regulatory solution to introduce national competition to regional monopolies that are subject to State rather than Federal jurisdictions. The Federal Communications Commission (FCC) had no direct authority to enforce the Telecommunications Act locally, and thus could not compel local exchanges to open to competition. To facilitate market opening, the Telecommunications Act provided incentives to the local exchange carriers to liberalise their markets. The FCC did not authorise entry of the local exchange carriers into the long-distance market unless the local incumbent opened its own market for regional services to competition. To determine whether a local exchange carrier had opened its market to competition, the FCC developed a checklist that had to be verified by the state regulator. State regulators arbitrate disputes. To facilitate a consistent approach to pricing by state regulators, the FCC established national pricing principles.

In the UK, the Office of Telecommunications (Oftel) is established as the telecommunications-specific economic regulator in 1984. Its responsibilities increased through time, (now the Ofcom) with broad responsibilities across telecommunications, spectrum, broadcasting and postal services. Elsewhere in Europe, the tendency is initially to retain ministerial decision-making, and then to move to independent regulators under the influence of the European Union (EU). In France, e.g., the Telecommunications Regulatory Authority was established in 1996; and in Germany, the Regulatory Authority for Telecommunications and Posts (part of the FNA since 2004) is formed in January 1998.

In Australia, regulatory responsibilities were initially vested in the AUSTEL, but economic regulation is later transferred to the Australian Competition and Consumer Commission (ACCC; access and anti-competitive conduct) and the Australian Communications and Media Authority (ACMA) (USO and spectrum). Regulation of telecommunications in New Zealand became the responsibility of the Commerce Commission (NZCC), with access being initially based on the general anti-monopoly provisions of the *Commerce Act*.

In both Japan and Korea, specific independent regulators are not established initially, with ministerial decision-making retained.

MOBILE TELEPHONES, DSL AND CONVERGENCE FROM THE LATE-1990s: BROADER REGULATORY ARRANGEMENTS

The 1990s are a time of rapid change in the telecommunications industry. There are four major strands to the changes. First, mobile technology began to be deployed (sometimes with different standards), and mobile penetration increased at an accelerated rate through the 1990s. Second, broadband became commercially available, through both HFC cable (often deployed for cable TV) and DSL technology, using existing ubiquitous copper wires. Third, there is the beginning of the convergence of telecommunications with IT and broadcasting, manifested in, *inter alia*, the rapid spread of email, the advent of Voice over Internet Protocol (VoIP) and use of telecommunications for content-as-well-as-calling. Fourth, the move from statutory monopoly had given rise to many new entrants. This created opportunities for incumbents to engage in anti-competitive behaviour and also gave rise to opportunities for mergers and takeovers. These changes placed pressure on existing regulatory arrangements and other aspects of governance.

Further Market Opening

In the original round of market opening focus is on the fixed-line PSTN and the interconnection of downstream competitors using the PSTN as an 'essential facility' in providing rival services. As new networks emerged for which there was a demand for access, the importance of determining what should be opened became more important amongst the functions of regulators. The interrelationship between fixed and mobile networks became important, as mobile carriers used their bottleneck power in termination of calls from fixed-line networks on their mobile networks (Albon and York, 2006).

While all countries reviewed opened networks to third-party access, they achieved this in different ways – in some regulatory regimes, regulation is applied asymmetrically, while in others, regulatory regimes applied to all providers of certain services.

Under the EU Access Directive, access obligations in Member States are only imposed on operators that are found to have significant power in a market (SMP) following market analysis. Where a competition problem is identified in relation to third-party access, available remedies include obligations related to cost-recovery, price controls and accounting separation, as well as obligations of transparency, non-discrimination and good faith in negotiating access. Under the Authorisation Directive it is necessary to establish a general authorisation for all types of electronic communication services and networks (including fixed and mobile networks and services; data and voice services; and broadcasting transmission networks and services) rather than a system whereby individual licences are issued by Member States to network and service providers. The Directive limits the type of conditions, which may be included in general authorisations, to ensure service providers are treated in a non-discriminatory, objective, transparent and proportionate fashion. Member States also must encourage the use of standards to ensure interoperability of service. The EU benchmark countries generally transposed these Directives into national laws.

In the Netherlands, the regulator publishes a 'market analysis decision' in which it sets out its broad approach to pricing and non-price access issues for a range of regulated services. This approach specifically addresses the perceived problem of a high number of individual access disputes appearing before the regulator.

In Japan's access regime, only a dominant carrier of specified services is subject to regulation. The Telecommunications Business Dispute Settlement Commission (TBDSC) is established within the Ministry of Internal Affairs and Communication (MIC) specifically to deal with dispute resolution in telecommunications, offering an alternative channel to the ministerial ordinances for consultation or award for dispute settlement.

The Australian regime provided for the ACCC to determine pricing principles at the time a service is declared and to issue model terms and conditions for certain 'core services'. Industry-specific access regimes apply to 'declared services' based on a 'long-term interests of end-user' test conducted by the ACCC. In New Zealand, the NZCC is able to make a 'standard terms' determination on which a designated access or specified service must be supplied.

Structural Change

In most of the countries reviewed, telecommunications incumbents remain vertically integrated, but some form of 'operational separation' occurred in several countries. Operational separation of vertically-integrated operators is prescribed in, *inter alia*, the UK and New Zealand. British Telecom (BT), in the UK, is subject to an undertaking setting out commitments in respect of operational separation of its wholesale and retail functions and offering a wholesale line-rental product to third-parties on a non-discriminatory basis. Telecom in New Zealand is subject to a separation undertaking setting out obligations to operate access network, wholesale and retail business units at an arm's length. In Australia, the incumbent, Telstra, remained both horizontally and vertically integrated, but became subject to a relatively weak form of operational separation in conducting wholesale, retail and network businesses; implemented as a statutory condition of Telstra's carrier licence.

Social Objectives and Universal Service Obligations

These matters are often dealt with in the first phase of telecommunications reform as part of the corporatisation of commercial operations. Obligations and funding needed to be more clearly defined. In the second phase, the advent of new services placed pressure on governments to broaden the reach of USOs to include these emerging services. The Canadian legislation placed particular emphasis on USO and affordability given its large land mass and low population density. In Europe, the EU Directives established a minimum level of availability and affordability of basic communications services. The USO administered by the Ofcom includes giving special tariffs to persons on low incomes, reasonable access to public phone boxes, and basic tailored telephony services for disabled people. In Australia, USOs and customer service guarantees are the responsibility of the ACMA.

Implications for Governance

In the first phase of reform, regulatory institutions sometimes emerged as part of a process based on a set of principles applied across all main infrastructure areas, and in other cases the process is less coordinated. Nonetheless, across the countries reviewed, telecommunications regulatory regimes are sophisticated relative to most other infrastructure areas. They universally have features of advanced regulatory design and transparent and consultative decision-making processes. Possible explanations of this include the importance of telecommunications to the economy as a whole, particularly in the context of greater internationalisation of OECD economies. Because all carriers are globally interconnected, telecommunications is always subject to some international influence.

A common feature of telecommunications regulation in the second phase is the convergence of regulatory responsibility into a communications-wide regulatory body, covering telecommunications and at least two of spectrum allocation, broadcasting and postal services. There appear to be at least three advantages of this grouping of regulatory functions:

First, the bunching of communications-wide responsibilities allows for the sharing of expertise. The economic expertise that is required to analyse telecommunications, broadcasting and postal services are sufficiently similar that people with similar skills can easily move between the different parts of the portfolio, allowing economies of scope and knowledge diffusion to be realized. Similarly, the legal and engineering skills required to operate successfully in 'communications' have strong similarities across different components.

Second, this arrangement facilitates the general-equilibrium efficiency analysis of pricing and other proposals. The convergence associated with technological change is particularly important in driving institutional change. The existence of substitutability and complementarity in demand and supply between different communications media means that a general-equilibrium approach rather than a partial-equilibrium approach is necessary to identify bottlenecks and to assess pricing impacts. This is similar to the circumstances in both energy and transport, where sector-based regulation is also becoming increasingly common.

Third, the convergence of regulatory functions may help avoid regulatory capture. The early literature on the economics of regulation is concerned about the possibility of 'capture' by the regulated industry. As exposited particularly by Stigler (1971), an industry-based regulator could be unduly influenced by the regulated industry. For example, commissioners tend to be appointed from the industry itself, and may have too great an affinity with the industry. In response, regulatory designers could cause a diffusion of power of incumbents in each ICT area by including them all in a single sector regulator.

Telecommunications is now regulated by sector-wide institutions in nearly all countries considered, e.g., the US (FCC), Canada (CRTC), the UK (Ofcom), France (ARCEP), Ireland (ComReg), the Netherlands (OPTA), Sweden (Swedish Post and Telecom Agency, PTS) and Korea (Korea Communications Commission). Japan's new government in the lead up to the 2009 election promised that a sectorial regulatory body along the lines of the FCC in the US would be formed (Japan Ponders, 2009), however this did not eventuate.

In Germany, the FNA covers nearly all utility areas, but decision making for telecommunications, spectrum and posts is spread across autonomous 'ruling chambers'. In broadcasting, the FNA's role is limited to spectrum management, assigning frequencies for broadcasting within the federal states' jurisdiction and the use of free-traffic ways. Some broadcasting regulation is the responsibility of state governments. In Australia, spectrum, USO and broadcasting functions lie with the ACMA; and in New Zealand, posts (which is effectively not regulated) and broadcasting lie outside the NZCC.

Integration with Competition Policy and Antitrust

In most cases the functions of enforcing anti-competitive conduct rules are conducted by the general competition (or antitrust) body such as the Competition Commission in Canada, the Federal Cartel Agency in Germany and the Japan Fair Trade Commission (JFTC) in Japan. Institutional arrangements are more complex in the US and the UK where, in each case, there are two bodies responsible for these functions, with some apparent overlap. In Australia and New Zealand the regulatory and competition functions are in the same body.

Australia appears to be unique in also having a telecommunications-specific competition law set out in Part XIB of the *Trade Practices Act*. Among other things, Part XIB provides the ACCC with additional enforcement powers enabling a rapid response to anti-competitive conduct in the telecommunications industry, under the 'competition rule'. The ACCC is able to issue a competition notice in response to a breach of the competition rule. A competition notice calls on the recipient to cease the allegedly anti-competitive conduct or else face the prospect of proceedings for pecuniary penalties and/or damages. Part XIB also allows the ACCC to issue tariff filing directions to certain carriers and carriage service providers and to make rules requiring carriers and carriage service providers to keep and retain records. The ACCC is also required to report each year on competitive safeguards within the telecommunications industry and monitor charges for declared carriage services.

EMERGING GOVERNANCE – FACILITATING TECHNOLOGICAL ADVANCE AND NATIONAL BROADBAND

The institutional convergence of regulatory functions, and attention to the relationship between competition and regulatory bodies in the second phase, is not completely successful in dealing with all emerging ICT issues. Continuing technological change and market demands present carriers and customers with difficult decisions, and the regulatory and governance stance is likely to bear on those choices. The dynamics between fixed and mobile telecommunications are not completely played out. The UK communications regulator, the Ofcom, is continually undertaking 'strategic reviews'; e.g., the 2008 review of mobile telecommunications is in response to significant changes in the industry in recent years. Spectrum issues also re-emerged with regard to the 'digital dividend', i.e., the increase in efficiency with which the spectrum is used for digital broadcasting, including the clearance of a large amount of spectrum for new services (Ofcom, 2005). Specifically with respect to broadband, its penetration, geographic availability and speed are important issues in all major OECD countries. Because of these pressures, there are on-going national reviews of the need for, and appropriate form of, regulation and governance more generally in the ICT sector. In the US, the recent focus is 'net-neutrality' (e.g., Faulhaber, 2009a), although this now appears overshadowed by national broadband initiatives (reviewed below).

Broadband Penetration and Technology

Broadband penetration appears to be something of a status symbol amongst advanced economies, with the broadband penetration (on a per population basis)[2] differing substantially across countries according to latest (June 2010) OECD figures (OECD, 2011). Ireland, Australia and New Zealand have relatively low penetration; the Netherlands, Sweden, France and Korea are leaders amongst the countries considered. Across all thirty OECD countries the majority of fixed broadband provision is via DSL (around 58 per cent), however DSL is much higher than this in most of Europe and in Australasia (typically 80-90 per cent); and much lower in North America, Japan and Korea (20-40 per cent). Cable (29.3 per cent overall) is relatively important in the US, Canada, the Netherlands and Korea; but below-OECD average elsewhere. Fibre (11.6 per cent) is most advanced in Japan, Korea, and Sweden, but is very low or negligible in the other countries surveyed. Wireless broadband was largely excluded from OECD data until June 2010, when wireless broadband was included for most OECD countries, albeit separately from fixed-line broadband. The limited data available show that wireless penetration is substantial and growing rapidly in many countries.

While Korea, Sweden and Japan are high in both fixed and wireless broadband rankings; the Netherlands, Germany and France have a lower ranking in wireless than in fixed. In contrast, Australia and Ireland are considerably higher in wireless broadband ranking than they are in fixed. The United States is higher in wireless broadband than it is in fixed, and this is reflected in its current policy focus (see below).

Broadband Policy and Governance

According to Atkinson (2007), proactive broadband policy should focus on stimulating both the supply of, and the demand for, high-speed broadband. Most countries reviewed pursue policy aimed at expanding broadband availability (geographical and socioeconomic penetration) and increasing data rates. Approaches range from the government building an (National Broadband Network (NBN) (Australia); a combined government and private NBN solution (New Zealand); extension of USO-type arrangements to cover broadband (e.g., UK)[3], use of stimulus funding in 2009 to subsidize broadband extension (e.g., Canada and the US) and the use of targeted demand-side subsidies (e.g., Korea). The Netherlands, with the highest fixed-line broadband penetration, has a more *laissez-faire* approach based on competition between copper and cable, which is argued to 'put it way ahead of those countries in which government is actively encouraging the establishment of broadband markets' (OPTA, 2010, p. 7). Sweden also emphasizes competition as the underlying principle guiding broadband policy. Interesting themes emerge from an examination of these approaches.

First, the higher is fixed penetration and the greater the diversity of fixed broadband technologies, the less likely an interventionist approach is adopted. Countries previously adopting fixed-line broadband technologies other than DSL, such as Japan, Korea and Sweden (cable and fibre); Canada, the Netherlands and the US (cable), are not contemplating NBN-type broadband deployments. All six countries are in the top half of the OECD table for fixed broadband. In contrast, countries where overall fixed penetration is lower and where DSL penetration is much higher than average, such as Australia and New Zealand, exhibit a strong intention to build a nationwide broadband network deploying mainly fibre technology. France and Germany, that both have high proportions of DSL-based broadband, also have high fixed penetrations and also are restricted by EU Law in the extent that broadband deployment can be subsidized by the state.

Second, where the path involves the development of an NBN at least partially independent of existing networks, current governance arrangements are challenged. For example, building an NBN may be perceived to require intervention in relation to the structure of fixed-line incumbents (requiring powers beyond the regulator's ambit) and direct government intervention. For instance, in Australia, an announcement by the Minister for Broadband,

Communications and the Digital Economy (Conroy, 2009) mapped a plan for the structural separation of Telstra and divestiture of operational segments. A new government-owned enterprise, known as NBN Co, is established to deploy the NBN. While the arrangements do allow private sector involvement, at this stage NBN Co is entirely government owned. The New Zealand model (Funston, 2010) involves private and government involvement in building an NBN, but the details are still being decided. There may also be a requirement by the builder of the NBN that it be protected from competition from alternative means of providing broadband, sometimes called 'preventing over-build'. This normally requires legislative change, and thus is outside the jurisdiction of the regulator. Greater penetration of wireless broadband with faster data rates is creating an interesting dynamic in several countries, including the United States with its explicit emphasis on '4G' wireless, and Australia and Ireland, with high rankings in wireless broadband combined with lower-middle rankings in fixed.

Third, a number of countries (including France, Germany, Ireland, and the UK) opted for more limited intervention involving the extension of geographic penetration and high data rates into rural areas. Such initiatives require subsidisation, and there needs to be a source of funding to achieve this. Explicit subsidies from consolidated revenue may be required, and/or adjustments to USO arrangements made. EU Member States are restricted by EU Law with respect to the extent and purpose of subsidising carriers. The plan in *Digital Britain* (2009) is based on three technologies (viz., DSL, Fibre-to-the-Cabinet (FTTC) and wireless), and are to be partly funded by a tax of £0.50 per month on all copper lines. Similarly, the New Zealand government announced the replacement of the TSO (New Zealand for USO) with a Telecommunications Development Levy (TDL) where funds are applied to subsidize rural broadband.

Finally, the US experience is complicated because of the link with economic stimulus measures. The *Recovery and Reinvestment Act of 2009* (the 'stimulus package') mandated that the FCC develop a national broadband plan to address broadband deployment, adoption, affordability, and the advanced use in areas of priority (FCC, 2009). Broadband Initiatives funded by the package are intended to accelerate broadband deployment throughout the US, to create jobs or provide other public benefits (Broadband USA, 2009).[4] The FCC is now implementing the *21st Century Communications and Video Accessibility Act of 2010*. While details of the US approach are still being developed, there is strong emphasis on three things – transforming universal service, removing barriers to broadband build-out and unleashing mobile broadband (Genachowski, 2011).

CONCLUDING REMARKS

This study considers the way the economic regulation of telecommunications is designed across the OECD and, in the broader research underlying this chapter, in comparison with other infrastructure areas like energy and transport. In particular, the study traces the evolution of regulation and governance of ICT since the 1980s liberalisation, concentrating on how regulatory design changed alongside the metamorphosis from telephony to ICT.

The main conclusions arising from the analysis are:

First, there is a tendency for telecommunications to have relatively advanced regulatory design and to be relatively transparent and consultative compared with other infrastructure areas. Telecommunications regulation began at least twenty years ago in most OECD countries (related to the early liberalisation of telecommunications) and typically has relatively more frequent reviews from within and without the regulator (related to the pressure of continuing technological advance (Noam, 2010); seemingly more rapid than in other important infrastructure areas). Regulatory arrangements are also impacted by the rapid internationalization of telecommunications.

Second, as emphasized in the broader research underlying this chapter, ICT is a sector where the EU appears to have substantial influence in shaping regulation across Member States. In some cases, EU directives appear to be a catalyst of liberalisation and played a major role in the form of economic regulation of telecommunications adopted. Further, EU Law has acted as a brake on the subsidisation of telecommunications carriers in Member States.

Third, there is a trend to move away from telecommunications-only regulation with governments combining telecommunications with spectrum management, broadcasting and posts as part of a communications-sector-wide regulator. This institutional convergence reflects technological and market convergence across the ICT industries. Much of the regulatory debate in the US revolved around the issue of 'net neutrality'.

Fourth, many countries share a common difficulty in dealing with government desire to further develop broadband on a national scale with greater data rates, including the need to address structural and competition issues beyond the traditional regulatory ambit. The leading countries in broadband penetration and data speed (including Korea, the Netherlands, and Sweden) all have a diversity of provision by technology, and below average DSL. No country in this position is embarking on a large-scale NBN initiative.

ACKNOWLEDGEMENTS

The author acknowledges the many helpful comments of his colleague, Su Wu and the assistance of Gary Madden in the development of the paper. Both are absolved of any responsibility for errors, and any views in this paper are the author's own, and may not coincide with the views of the Australian Competition and Consumer Commission.

NOTES

1. See the Appendix for a description of the regulatory benchmarking project. It covers eleven OECD countries, but other OECD countries (including Korea) are considered herein.
2. Countries with low average household size could be interpreted to be understated by use of the per population measure.
3. The UK Department of Culture, Media and Sport's *Digital Britain Report* targets the 10 per cent of households that do not have at least 2 Mbps data rate.
4. See Adamski (2009) and Faulhaber (2009b).

REFERENCES

Adamski, D. (2009), 'Broadband Stimulus Policy in Europe and the US: A Comparative Review', *Media Law and Policy*, **18**, 45–63.

Albon, R. (2006), 'Fixed-to-Mobile Substitution, Complementarity and Convergence', *Agenda*, **13**, 307–20.

Albon, R. and R. York (2006), 'Mobile Termination: Market Power, Externalities and their Policy Implications', *Telecommunications Policy*, **30**, 368–84.

Atkinson, R. (2007), *The Case for a National Broadband Policy*. Retrieved from: http://www.itif.org/files/CaseForNationalBroadbandPolicy.pdf.

Broadband USA (2009), *Broadband USA*. Retrieved from: http://www.broadbandusa.gov/.

Conroy, S. (2009), 'Regulatory Reform for 21st Century Broadband', *Joint Media Release: Prime Minister, Treasurer, Minister for Finance and Minister for Broadband*. Retrieved from: http://www.minister.dbcde.gov.au/media/media_releases/2009/021.

Department of Culture, Media and Sport (UK) (2009), *Digital Britain Report*. Retrieved from: http://www.culture.gov.uk/what_we_do/broadcasting/5631.aspx.

Faulhaber, G. (2009a), 'Network Neutrality: Theory and Practice', in Russel Cooper and Gary Madden (eds), *The Economics of Digital Markets*, Cheltenham, UK and Northampton, MA, USA: Edward Elgar Publishing, pp. 325–49.

Faulhaber, G. (2009b), 'A National Broadband Plan for Our Future: A Customer Centric Framework', *International Journal of Communication*, **3**, 742–79.

Federal Communications Commission (2009), *Recovery Act Broadband Initiatives*. Retrieved from: http://www.fcc.gov/recovery/broadband/.

Federal Networks Association (BNetzA, Germany) (2009a), *Key Elements for Progressing Modern Telecommunications Networks and Creating Powerful Broadband Infrastructures*. Retrieved from: http://www.bundesnetzagentur.de/enid/f92f33a605b29681c703fb835a21d603,0/Regulierung_Telekommunikation/Next_Generation_Access__NGA__5n6.html.

Federal Networks Association (BNetzA, Germany) (2009b), 'Notes on the Consistent Regulation of Rates as Required under Section 27(2) of the Telecommunications Act(TKG)'. Retrieved from: http://www.bundesnetzagentur.de/enid/f92f33a605b29681c703fb835a21d603,0/Konsistenzgebot/Hinweise_konsistente_Entgeltregulierung_5n5.html.

Funston, K. (2010), 'National Broadband Deployment Approach: New Zealand', WIK International Conference on National Strategies for Ultrabroadband Infrastructure Deployment: Experiences and Challenges, Radisson Blu Hotel, Berlin, 26-27 April.

Genachowski, J. (2011), '"The Clock is Ticking" Remarks on Broadband', 16 March, Washington DC.

Japan Ponders Broadcasting Watchdog (2009, September 20), *The Yomiuri Shimbun*. Retrieved from: http://www.tmcnet.com/usubmit/2009/09/20/4380137.htm.

Minister for Broadband, Communications and the Digital Economy (2009), *Historic Reforms to Telecommunications Regulation*. Retrieved from: http://www.minister.dbcde.gov.au/media/media_releases/2009/088.

Noam, E. (2010), 'Regulation 3.0 for Telecom 3.0', *Telecommunications Policy*, **34**, 4–10.

OECD (2011), *OECD Broadband Portal*. 13 April. Retrieved from: http://www.oecd.org/sti/ict/ broadband.

Ofcom (2005), *The Ofcom Digital Dividend Review (DDR)*. Retrieved from: http://www.ofcom.org.uk/media/news/2005/11/nr_20051117.

Ofcom (2008), *Mobile Citizens, Mobile Consumers*. Retrieved from: http://www.ofcom. org.uk/consult/condocs/msa08/.

OPTA (2010), *Market Monitor 2009*. Retrieved from: http://www.nfia.nl/files/publications/20100601_OPTA_marketmonitor_2009_EN.pdf.

Post and Telecom Agency (Sweden) (2009), *Broadband Survey 2008*. Retrieved from: http://www.pts.se/upload/Rapporter/Internet/2009/broadband-survey-2008-pts-er-2009-8.pdf.

Stigler, G. (1971), 'The Economic Theory of Regulation', *Bell Journal of Economics and Management Science*, **2**, 3–21.

APPENDIX

Project on Benchmarking International Regulatory Design, Processes and Practice

ACCC staff conducted research on the economic regulation of infrastructure across a number of major OECD countries. The research was carried out for the ACCC's Infrastructure Consultative Committee (ICC), comprised of infrastructure providers, industry bodies and user groups from all main infrastructure areas regulated or monitored by the ACCC or AER. The eleven OECD countries surveyed are (in order in the report) Japan, Australia, New Zealand, France, Germany, Ireland, the Netherlands, Sweden, the UK, Canada and the US. The European Union was also surveyed because of its influence on the Member States, six of which were included in the survey. There is also a chapter on state regulation in the US. The seven infrastructure areas covered are energy (electricity and gas); telecommunications; posts; water and wastewater; rail; airports and ports.

The information on economic regulation of the seven infrastructure areas in the eleven countries is set out in the country-based review. There are chapters on each country and on the EU and state regulation in the US. The country chapters contain background information on the economy, geography, polity and legal structure of each country and then describe the market situation, regulatory institutions and regulatory processes (consultation, timeliness, information management, decision-making and appeals) in each infrastructure area.

The second part of the report is more interpretative, drawing out insights for the best practice of the economic regulation of infrastructure. It considers institutional and design features, and a range of process issues from when matters get before the regulator, ranging through consultation, information management and decision-making, to the availability and nature of appeals.

Information about the ICC and the report itself (in two parts) can be found at: http://www.accc.gov.au/content/index.phtml/itemId/875207.

3. Government oversight of next generation wireless networks

Rob Frieden

INTRODUCTION

Wireless handsets increasingly deliver a combination of telephone, computer and television (TV) functions. These devices provide users a 'third screen' alternative for accessing multimedia content[1] that currently are available from TV and computer monitors. However, for these devices to exploit fully what converging technology can offer, wireless manufacturers, carriers and content providers must agree on business models that generate sufficient revenue from advertising and consumers to pay for content creation and delivery. Additionally, legislatures and regulators have to confront the fact that a single wireless medium offering convergent services will trigger different legacy regulatory models, i.e., print, broadcast, cable television and telephony. Both business and regulatory models will have to adapt to convergent technology and markets as third screens will combine services that trigger divergent views on the proper scope and reach of government oversight.

In the United States (US), the Communications Act of 1934, as amended, establishes mutual exclusivity[2] between telecommunications,[3] information[4] and cable TV[5] services notwithstanding the convergence of these services. Wireless carriers mostly provide service bundles that include conventional (regulated) telephone services, Internet access (treated as a largely unregulated information service), and audio and video services that trigger different regulations than telephone services. The Federal Communications Commission (FCC or Commission) is disinclined to apply two different regulatory regimes to the same venture when it offers services that fit into more than one regulatory classification. Accordingly, the FCC treats wireless carriers as qualifying for largely unregulated status, despite these carriers continuing to provide regulated telecommunications services and that their video programming could readily fit within the cable classification.

This chapter examines the regulatory status of wireless carrier-delivered video content with an eye toward determining the necessary scope and nature of government oversight. Past practices of the FCC in regulating the cable industry are examined to highlight the disparate treatment of wireless-delivered video content, despite the fact that ventures from both categories soon will distribute identical or similar content. The chapter concludes that the FCC, and other national regulatory authorities (NRAs), must balance the carriers' interests in finding new revenue centres to pay for next generation network upgrades with subscribers' interests in maximizing their options for wireless handset use. NRAs should aid wireless carriers exploit technological innovations that make it possible to provide a combination of telecommunications, information and video programming services. However, regulators also must guard against carriers' anti-competitive strategies designed to favour their services by handicapping access to alternative sources. The chapter concludes that because most NRAs seek to promote video programming competition and access for wired cable TV ventures, these regulatory authorities should undertake similar efforts to promote wireless access, because wireless carriers have equivalent incentives and abilities to blunt competition.

THE REGULATORY QUANDARY PRESENTED BY THIRD SCREEN CONVERGENCE

The versatility of modern wireless handsets presents a regulatory quandary for NRAs. Innovations in wireless handsets make it possible for devices to provide access to information, communications and entertainment (ICE) services including telephone calling, information services, e-commerce applications, position location functions, as well as access to the Internet and video programming. Wireless handsets have become an electronic Swiss Army knife capable of exploiting ICE convergence and easily toggling between first-, second- and third-generation wireless functions. In the first generation of wireless handsets, users made mobile telephone calls almost exclusively. With digitization in the second generation, subscribers engaged in text messaging, photography, music downloading, and functions that rely on memory storage, keypads, and video screens. In the evolving third generation,[6] wireless handsets switch between legacy and new functions that can convert the handset into a platform for accessing much multimedia content available from personal computers and TV sets.[7]

The FCC and other NRAs appear ill equipped to apply different regulatory regimes to third-generation wireless carriers offering subscribers opportunities to switch from telephone, to video, to Internet access. Prior to the onset of robust technological and market convergence, NRAs could erect different and mutually exclusive regulations based on the single function any one company offered. Acting on a legislative mandate, the FCC established different regulatory requirements for broadcasters, cable TV operators, telephone companies, and Internet service providers (ISPs) based on the characteristics of operator types. The FCC is yet to address the impact of convergence that allows wireless carriers to offer a combination of services and functions that run the gamut of regulatory classifications.

To make matters even more complicated in the wireless marketplace, vertically integrated carriers blend content and conduit making it all but impossible to establish 'bright line' regulatory demarcations between the provision of telecommunications transmission services and the content these links transmit. In previous regulatory regimes, the FCC could separate the content provider from the content carrier subjecting the former to little, if any, government oversight while subjecting the latter to extensive common carrier price, quality of service and non-discrimination regulation.

Using service definitions created by the national legislature,[8] the FCC applies the largely unregulated information services category, to as many convergence services as plausible with an eye toward promoting marketplace driven competition and innovation largely free of government oversight.[9] The FCC opted to ignore or subordinate the conduit function provided by carriers, which if separately identified would trigger the obligation for the Commission to enforce the more extensive regulations applied to telecommunications service providers. When wireless carriers offer a convergent blend of telecommunications access to telephony, video content and information services, the FCC emphasizes the multimedia service delivered to subscribers' wireless handsets and deemphasizes the fact that the wireless carriers use a telecommunications network to deliver such content.[10] Reviewing courts endorsed the FCC's determination that the least burdensome regulatory classification should apply.[11]

The FCC has not applied a similarly deregulatory model for treatment of other convergent services, such as VoIP[12] that blends telecommunications transmission links with information services. The FCC appears inclined to treat convergent services as unregulated information services, but because these services compete directly with pre-existing (legacy) common carrier telephone companies, TV broadcasters and cable TV operators, the Commission has determined the need to reapply some traditional regulations. Rather than treat VoIP carriers with the same sort of regulatory forbearance it applies to wireless telephone service and increasingly to wireline service, the FCC has 'saddled' VoIP service with regulatory burdens that make VoIP service more like conventional telephone service, at the expense of reducing VoIP's competitive cost advantage.[13] VoIP service providers, which offer subscribers telephone calling access to the conventional wireline public switched telephone network (PSTN), must contribute to universal service funding,[14] reconfigure their service to provide wiretapping capabilities to law enforcement authorities,[15] provide caller location identification and emergency 911 access[16] and offer service to disabled users.[17] Despite extensive rhetoric about refraining from imposing regulation on both emerging technologies and competitive services,[18] the FCC chose not to allow the marketplace to determine whether considerable service discounts available from VoIP service providers outweigh the greater risk in an emergency and greater inconvenience for some users. Even though the FCC generally wants to allow wireless carriers' need to qualify for a deregulated 'safe harbor,'[19] the Commission will make exceptions when it sees the need to protect incumbent technologies from new technologies that generally qualify for less burdensome government oversight.

WIRELESS CARRIERS' INCENTIVE AND ABILITY TO LOCK DOWN ACCESS

By qualifying for the information service provider exemption from most regulation,[20] wireless carriers receive operational flexibility, including the ability to offer subscribers easy access to a packaged 'walled-garden'[21] of content. In the absence of traditional common carrier non-discrimination requirements, wireless carriers have an incentive and ability to steer subscribers into a walled garden and to make it costly, inconvenient and more difficult for them to seek and receive other content. The FCC appears willing to allow wireless carriers to deprive subscribers of freedom and flexibility mandated for access via wireline carriers based on the perception that wireless carriers need to create and serve new markets if they are to afford the costs incurred in competitively bidding for radio spectrum[22] and in building next generation network infrastructure. In light of such risk taking, these carriers predictably seek to evade, or at least limit, any government regulatory oversight that might constrain their ability to recoup investment, particularly by diversifying services and increasing the monthly average revenue per user (ARPU).

However, a requirement that carriers operate in a non-discriminatory manner constitutes a fundamental component of conventional common carrier telecommunications service regulation and is still applicable to wireless carriers when they provide voice services.[23] Title II of the Communications Act of 1934, as amended, requires telecommunications service providers, *inter alia*, to charge just and reasonable rates, to operate in a non-discriminatory manner and to submit to scrutiny by the FCC that bears a legislative mandate to resolve consumer complaints. In their capacity as information and video programming providers, wireless carriers do not trigger conventional telephone service regulation. These carriers want the FCC and the public to conclude that even though these carriers must comply with most Title II common carrier telecommunications service regulations,[24] the FCC nevertheless should refrain from enforcing these rules in light of the fact that the carriers offer other services that qualify for little regulatory oversight.

Wireless carriers should not evade regulation[25] simply because a portion of what they offer qualifies for comparatively less regulatory oversight than what offering telecommunications service triggers. Nevertheless, a prominent *Wall Street Journal* industry analyst concluded that the wireless carriers have succeeded in creating the inference that they are not able to be regulated:

> A short-sighted and often just plain stupid federal government has allowed itself to be bullied and fooled by a handful of big wireless phone operators for decades now. And the result has been a mobile phone system that is the direct opposite of the PC model. It severely limits consumer choice, stifles innovation, crushes entrepreneurship, and has made the US the laughingstock of the mobile-technology world, just as the cell phone is morphing into a powerful hand-held computer. . . . That's why I refer to the big cell phone carriers as the 'Soviet ministries.' Like the old bureaucracies of communism, they sit athwart the market, breaking the link between the producers of goods and services and the people who use them.[26]

The FCC needs to remedy carriers' tactics that are detrimental to market competition, but instead the Commission strongly prefers to 'shoehorn' any and all converged services into the lightly regulated information services 'safe harbor,' including wireless broadband Internet access.[27] With rare exception, the FCC appears reluctant to hold wireless operators to the applicable Title II requirements, despite having not untaken the administrative process necessary to forbear officially from regulating based on changed circumstances favouring competition and self-regulation.[28] Regardless of the regulatory posture undertaken by the FCC, or what regulatory classification the Commission applies to particular wireless services, fundamental public interest and consumer protection concerns require the Commission to assess whether wireless carriers have an incentive and ability to discriminate unlawfully. Wireless carriers' efforts[29] to frame the debate in terms of whether their broadband and video programming services qualify for deregulation as information services largely shifts attention from the need to determine whether government oversight remains legislatively mandated.

CURBING CABLE TV MARKET POWER IN VIDEO PROGRAMMING ACCESS

The FCC's aggressive and expanding regulation of cable companies stands in sharp contrast to the Commission's reluctance to enforce valid regulations of wireless carriers, despite the similarity of content consumers' access via either option. The FCC expressed longstanding concerns that cable TV ventures have an incentive and ability to harm consumers by establishing vertically integrated firms[30] that create and distribute 'must see' content while restricting or denying access to multi-channel video programming distributor (MVPD) competitors. The major cable TV companies own ventures that create video programming as well as the companies that distribute such content to consumers. The FCC regulated cable TV companies so that the same enterprise cannot limit the customer's choice to make it more likely that the customer will watch the video programming created by an affiliate of the cable company.

In 2007, the FCC specifically found that cable companies tied programming and distribution, and where this happened the programming available to MVPD competitors is reduced:

> [W]e conclude that there are no good substitutes for some satellite-delivered vertically integrated programming and that such programming therefore remains necessary for viable competition in the video distribution market. Based on this finding, we conclude that vertically integrated programmers continue to have the ability to favour their affiliated cable operators over competitive MVPDs such that competition and diversity in the distribution of video programming would not be preserved and protected absent the rule. . . . [W]e also find some trends that increase their incentive to withhold programming, such as the increase in horizontal consolidation of the cable industry, the increase in cable clustering, and the recent emergence of new competitors. We also find specific factual evidence that, where the exclusive contract prohibition does not apply, such as in the case of terrestrially delivered programming, vertically integrated programmers have withheld and continue to withhold programming from competitive MVPDs.[31]

Because cable TV companies generate most popular video content and control the major medium for distributing it, the FCC expressed concern[32] that the cable companies can stifle competition, extract rates above competitive levels from subscribers, favour affiliated content providers and stifle the development of new content sources. This concern for consumer protection and the determination of market failure contrasts with the Commission's lack of concern with vertically-integrated providers of wireless video services.

Ban on Exclusive Contracts between Programmers and Cable Operators

In light of grave concerns about the incentive and ability of cable TV ventures to stifle consumer access to content, the FCC decided to extend for five more years a ban on exclusive contracts between vertically integrated programmers and cable operators to October 5, 2012.[33] The Commission determined that vertically integrated programmers still have an ability[34] and the incentive[35] to favour the operators with whom they are affiliated over other competitive providers.[36] The FCC reaffirmed its conclusion that vertically integrated ventures still control, content, for which no viable substitute exits.[37] The Commission retained the prohibition against exclusive content distribution contracts from ventures that vertically integrate content production and distribution to consumers.

The FCC declined to narrow its ban on exclusive contracts based on programmer suggestions that restrictions should vary with the popularity of the programming network and the competitive climate in specific regions served by a cable operator.[38] Additionally the Commission refused to limit the restriction to conventional cable TV operators, which would exclude other MVPDs, or to limit the restriction to cable operators that have been in the MVPD market for more than five years, have extensive resources, and have entered into exclusive contracts for programming.[39] This shows the FCC's strong resistance to vertically integrated carriers' control of content provided to users.

In contrast, the FCC declined to expand the exclusive contract prohibition to apply to non-cable-affiliated programming, for example, content created by vertically integrated direct broadcast satellite (DBS) operators and new MVPDs such as AT&T and Verizon. The FCC has evidenced great concern about consumer access to content controlled by cable operators, but the Commission has no such concern that vertically integrated telephone companies would secure exclusive content distribution agreements.

Prohibition on Content Tier-Buy through Requirements

The FCC also limits the ability of cable operators to force subscribers to pay for content they do not want, so that they can 'qualify' for accessing desired content. Section 3 of the 1992 Cable Act[40] prohibits cable TV operators, operating in a market without effective competition, from requiring subscribers to 'buy through'[41] intermediate tiers of programming to access desired content in a higher service tier. This means that consumers do not have to subscribe to enhanced basic service tiers, which bundle cable TV programming, before they can view content offered on a per view or per channel basis, such as individual premium channels like Home Box Office. Former FCC Chairman Kevin Martin promoted the prospect of allowing consumers to select content on an *à la carte*, network-by-network basis in lieu of service tiers that contain many channels of content, some of which individual consumers consider offensive.[42] In contrast the FCC imposes no regulations on how wireless carriers package and price video content access.

Forced Alternatives to Mandatory Set Top Box Leases

The FCC also established rules designed to enable cable TV subscribers to access content via 'cable ready' TV sets[43] without the expense of having to lease a device (set top converter) to descramble signals. The FCC prohibits cable TV companies from offering set top converters that combine security functions, e.g., descrambling, and features such as channel selection and navigation, electronic program guides, and pay per view, on-demand access to content. The prohibition prevents cable companies from requiring all subscribers to lease set top boxes.[44] With the integration ban, cable TV companies have to provide subscribers with a cheaper alternative to leased set top boxes (CableCard) that subscribers insert into most recent vintage TV sets.[45]

Despite the duty to support CableCard access, cable TV operators largely thwarted the Congressional mandate that consumers have the option of using alternatives to the operator leased set top boxes. However, while a competitive market for such devices has not evolved and few consumers even know about the CableCard option, recent innovations in digital video recorders may incorporate many of the features provided by the cable operators. From recent decisions by the FCC, it appears that cable operators will no longer succeed in stalling compliance with Section 629 of the Communications Act[46] that promotes set top box alternatives.

REASONS WHY WIRELESS CARRIERS SHOULD BEAR CONTENT NON-DISCRIMINATION REQUIREMENTS LIKE THOSE BORNE BY CABLE OPERATORS

In light of wireless carriers' practice of marketing handsets bundled with service, the concentrated nature of the industry, and the rewards accruing from walled gardens, the FCC should subject wireless carriers to the same sort of non-discrimination rules applied to cable operators. In light of the likelihood that wireless handsets increasingly will become a competitive alternative to TV and computer terminals, regulatory parity requires that vertically integrated wireless ventures bear similar burdens as cable operators if both type of ventures have similar incentives and ability to exploit market power.

Public Benefit and Harm from Bundling Wireless Service with Handsets

US wireless carriers can restrict the versatility and utility of handsets primarily because most subscribers acquire subsidized handsets in exchange for a two-year service commitment[47] and acceptance of carrier-imposed limitations on handset use. By taking the subsidy of the handset, subscribers also accept restrictions on use. Wireless subscribers have become accustomed to acquiring 'free' or inexpensive handsets, and perhaps this benefit offers ample compensation notwithstanding the fact that wireless service rates factor in the cost of the subsidy and subscribers incur substantial financial penalties for changing carriers before completion of the two-year service commitment.[48]

However, wireless carriers can reduce the versatility of the handset and the utility consumers derive from the handset by locking access to content and locking out content providers' access to handset users. Set out below is a list of existing lockout strategies:

- Locking handsets so that they cannot access competitor networks (by frequency, transmission format, firmware or software); in the US;
- carriers even lock handsets designed to allow multiple carrier access by changing an easily inserted Subscriber Identity Module (SIM);
- Using firmware 'upgrades' to 'brick,' i.e., render inoperative, the handset or alternatively disable third-party firmware and software;
- Disabling handset functions, i.e., bluetooth, Wi-Fi access, Internet browsers, GPS services, and email clients;
- Specifying formats for accessing memory, i.e., music, ringtones and photos;
- Creating walled garden access to favoured video content of affiliates and partners; and
- Using proprietary, non-standard interfaces making it difficult for third-parties to develop compatible applications and content.

The FCC needs to impose safeguards that prevent wireless carriers from imposing limitations on handsets that have nothing to do with legitimate network management and everything to do with favouring affiliated content providers and erecting barriers to subscriber access to third-party service providers. These safeguards should specify that subscribers have the right to use any technically compatible handset to access any available source of content, software, or computer application whether or not affiliated with the wireless carrier providing the link.[49]

Long ago the FCC rejected any attempt by wireline carriers to limit, block, or disable access by handsets bought from unaffiliated suppliers.[50] Consumers take for granted the right to buy and operate their own telephones for accessing wireline networks and the same principle should apply for access to wireless networks.[51] The FCC specifically mandated this consumer right in the Carterfone policy, established by the Commission in 1968 that requires all wireline telephone companies to allow subscribers to attach any technically compatible device.[52]

Already many purchasers of Apple iPhones and other cell phones have resorted to self-help[53] tactics to eliminate manufacturer or carrier-imposed limitations on the handset's versatility, features, and access to third-party applications and content. Rather than all but criminalize such tactics, the FCC should establish a handset technical certification process to allow any handset, operating in the proper format and frequency, to access any carrier's network. At the very least, the FCC should forbid wireless operators from imposing handset restrictions unrelated to legitimate network management requirements.

Wireless Carrier Market is as Concentrated and Anti-competitive as Cable TV

The FCC recognizes that vertical integration in video content creation and distribution requires regulatory intervention. CMRS operators, the term used by the FCC to identify cellular radiotelephone carriers, benefit from having a similarly concentrated and vertically integrated industry. The top two CMRS carriers, AT&T and Verizon, control at least 53.4 per cent of the wireless market,[54] and are owned by the ventures that have substantial market share in broadband wireline access, e.g., digital subscriber line (DSL),[55] fibre-optic cable links and wireline telephone service. In addition to the possible market power accruing from a commanding share of the wireless industry, AT&T and Verizon vertically integrate by securing exclusive content distribution rights for carriage via their wireless networks. They horizontally integrate by bundling triple-play[56] and quadruple-play service packages[57] combining wireless service with wireline telephony, Internet access and wireline video program access. With such a broad wingspan of packaged services, these ventures can become a 'one stop shop' that can result in further industry consolidation, less competition and greater market share held by a few firms.

Incentives and Rewards from Wireless Walled Gardens

Walled gardens can help wireless carriers generate higher revenues by improving the odds that subscribers either will pay for carrier-supplied content, or view advertising supported content that appears in the carrier's walled garden. When subscribers must make an effort to access content outside the walled garden, many may make do with what the carrier provides. For subscribers using a subsidized handset, a wireless carrier can block subscribers from using the handset to access competing carriers' networks and limit or burden subscribers' access to unaffiliated content sources. The carrier typically reserves the right to impose such access restrictions in the non-negotiable subscription agreement few customers read and understand. The imposition of restrictions and financial penalties for early termination of service converts the delivery of a 'free' wireless handset into an instalment-sales contract containing lawful restrictions on subscriber use. Yet, even for subscribers who own their handset, whether by completing the initial two years of 'rent to own' period, or acquiring an unsubsidized unit, the FCC does not outlaw restrictions that could provide wireless subscribers with more freedom to access preferred content and software applications.

INFORMATION SERVICE SAFE HARBOR LIMITS THE FCC'S ABILITY TO REGULATE WIRELESS CARRIERS

Despite several successful attempts to re-regulate aspects of VoIP telephone service, the FCC likely will face an incredulous appellate court review if the Commission were to impose mandatory, quasi-common carrier regulatory safeguards for wireless Internet access, even if the FCC framed the issue in terms of subscriber handset access freedom guaranteed by the Commission's 1968 Carterfone policy. In 2005 the Commission articulated four essential 'Internet Freedoms' emphasizing non-discrimination in the manner by which ISPs provide Internet access to end users and the delivery of content.[58] The FCC expects all ISPs, regardless of corporate affiliation and technology, to provide subscribers with the freedom to: (a) access the lawful content of their choice; (b) run applications and services of their choice, subject to the needs of law enforcement; (c) connect their choice of legal devices that do not harm the network; and (d) benefit from competition among network providers, application and service providers, and content providers.[59] However, an appellate court reversed the FCC's decision to sanction an ISP, Comcast, for violating transparency and non-discrimination articulated by the Internet Freedoms policy.[60]

Even though the FCC did not formalize rules, it considers its 2005 articulation of Internet Freedoms an enforceable policy and attempted to enforce it. The Commission decided that Comcast violated this policy when the company used network management techniques to choke peer-to-peer (P2P)[61] transfers even when the company experienced no congestion and could have handled the traffic without imposing delays. By a 3-2 vote, the FCC concluded that Comcast violated the Commission's 2005 Internet Policy Statement in using software applications to block or delay subscriber P2P file transfers.[62] The Commission chided Comcast for unduly interfering with Internet users' right to access the lawful Internet content and to use the applications of their choice:

> Although Comcast asserts that its conduct is necessary to ease network congestion, we conclude that the company's discriminatory and arbitrary practice unduly squelches the dynamic benefits of an open and accessible Internet and does not constitute reasonable network management. Moreover, Comcast's failure to disclose the company's practice to its customers has compounded the harm.[63]

Specifically, the Commission found that Comcast had deployed deep packet inspection[64] equipment throughout its network to monitor the content of its customers' Internet connections and to block specific types of P2P connections such as the use of BitTorrent software.[65] Comcast used software to enable the company to masquerade as the recipient of a P2P file transfer session and issued a command to reset, that is, to stop sending traffic and start again. Comcast forged so-called TCP reset packets[66] even though the company could have handled the actually occurring traffic volume without having to degrade anyone's traffic.[67] While Comcast initially disclaimed any responsibility for its customers' problems, tests conducted by the Associated Press and Electronic Frontier Foundation[68] suggested that the company selectively interfered with subscribers' file sharing sessions using P2P applications, a user practice that did not violate FCC rules, or Comcast's service terms and conditions.[69] Comcast later acknowledged [70] that it did target its subscribers' P2P traffic for interference, but claimed that such interference was limited to times of network congestion.[71]

The FCC concluded that Comcast's practices did not constitute legitimate network management, because Comcast discriminated against specific applications without regard to whether the specific use actually caused congestion by depleting the Comcast network of sufficient bandwidth:

> On its face, Comcast's interference with peer-to-peer protocols appears to contravene the federal policy of 'promot[ing] the continued development of the Internet' because that interference impedes consumers from 'run[ning] applications . . . of their choice,' rather than those favored by Comcast, and that interference limits consumers' ability 'to access the lawful Internet content of their choice,' including the video programming made available by vendors like Vuze. Comcast's selective interference also appears to discourage the 'development of technologies' – such as peer-to-peer technologies – that 'maximize user control over what information is received by individuals . . . who use the Internet' because that interference (again) impedes consumers from 'run[ning] applications . . . of their choice,' rather than those favored by Comcast. [72]

The Commission noted that Comcast had an anti-competitive motive to interfere with customers' use of P2P applications, because such software provides Internet users with a high-quality video access alternative to cable television services.[73] Such video distribution might compete with Comcast's video-on-demand (VOD) service.[74] The Commission thus concluded that Comcast's practices were not minimally intrusive, as the company claimed, but rather invasive in substantially impeding subscribers' ability to access preferred content and applications.[75]

The Commission also concluded that Comcast exacerbated the situation by failing to disclose its practices to consumers. Because Comcast hid from its customers the fact that it interfered with customers' use of P2P applications, customers had no way of knowing when Comcast would interfere with their connections.[76] As a result, the Commission found that many consumers experiencing difficulty using only certain applications would blame not Comcast, as deservedly, but rather on the applications themselves, to the further disadvantage of the companies offering such applications in a competitive marketplace.[77] A majority of the FCC Commissioners concluded that Comcast's discriminatory practices so harmed consumers and competitors alike that the Commission had to curb such behaviour, despite having concluded that Internet access constitutes a lightly regulated information service. The Commission's pro-consumer zeal and uncustomary readiness to regulate juxtaposes with its *laissez-faire* attitude toward perhaps even more egregious instances of wireless carrier imposed limitations on subscribers' access to content and software applications.

Attempting to Establish FCC Jurisdiction over Internet-based Practices

In establishing its 2005 Internet Policy Statement, the FCC made clear its intention to incorporate the Policy Statement's principles 'into its ongoing policymaking activities.'[78] Along with the 2005 Internet Policy Statement, the Commission released its Wireline Broadband Order that largely eschewed regulation, but warned that '[s]hould we see evidence that providers of telecommunications for Internet access or IP-enabled services are violating these principles, we will not hesitate to take action to address that conduct.'[79]

Anticipating that Comcast would appeal its Order, the Commission extensively outlined its statutory authority for having substantive jurisdiction over Comcast's Internet-based practices and for reaching an administrative decision without a formal rulemaking before adjudication. The Commission claimed to have jurisdiction to resolve disputes regarding discriminatory network management practices based primarily on two statutory mandates: (a) Section 230(b) of the Communications Act of 1934, as amended, where Congress stated that it is the policy of the US 'to preserve the vibrant and competitive free market that presently exists for the Internet' as well as 'to promote the continued development of the Internet;' and (b) Section 706(a) of the Act, where Congress directs the Commission to 'encourage the deployment on a reasonable and timely basis of advanced telecommunications capability to all Americans.'[80] Comcast and other parties considered these broad statutory mandates insufficiently specific in light of the requirements the FCC decided to impose on Comcast.[81]

In particular, the FCC opted to exercise jurisdiction over P2P Internet connections based on the fact that such connections use 'communication by wire.'[82] With that direct link to the general jurisdiction conferred under Title I of the Communications Act, the Commission exercised its ancillary jurisdiction on the premise that Comcast's practices undercut national Internet policy.

The Commission rejected Comcast's argument that any regulation of network access and management violates the Commission's 27-year old policy of leaving information services unregulated:

> [T]he Commission previously indicated that it would not hesitate to take action in the event that providers violated the principles set forth in the Internet Policy Statement. Moreover, the Commission repeatedly has stated its willingness to exercise the full range of its statutory authority to ensure that providers of cable modem service meet the public interest in a vibrant, competitive market for Internet-related services. For instance, in the Wireline Broadband Order, the Commission found that it had jurisdiction over providers of broadband Internet access services and stated that 'we will not hesitate to adopt any non-economic regulatory obligations that are necessary to ensure consumer protection and network security and reliability in this dynamically changing broadband era.' Specifically with regard to cable modem service, in the 2002 Cable Modem Declaratory Ruling sustained by the Supreme Court in Brand X, the Commission sought comment on a wide range of statutory bases for exercising ancillary jurisdiction over cable modem service, including section 230(b) of the Act. The Commission also explicitly mentioned the blocking or impairing of subscriber access by a cable modem service provider as possible triggers for Commission 'intervention.'[83]

While deciding that it should act on a case-by-case basis, the Commission held that it did not have to conduct a rulemaking or hearing to investigate and remedy Comcast's practices:

> And to the extent that Comcast implies that our ancillary authority does not extend to adjudications but rather must first be exercised in a rulemaking proceeding, it is simply wrong. The question of whether the Commission has jurisdiction to decide an issue is entirely separate from the question of how the Commission chooses to address that issue. Perhaps more to the point, the D.C. Circuit has affirmed the Commission's exercise of ancillary authority in an adjudicatory proceeding and in the absence of regulations before.[84]

D.C. Circuit Court of Appeals Rejects the FCC's Jurisdictional Claims

The FCC's attempt to sanction Comcast for interfering with subscribers' peer-to-peer traffic absent legitimate network management requirements failed to pass muster with the D.C. Circuit Court of Appeals.[85] This decision severely side-tracks the Commission's attempt to establish binding network neutrality policies, rules and regulations absent an explicit legislative mandate.

Noting that the Commission invoked no express statutory authority, the court considered whether 'barring Comcast from interfering with its customers' use of peer-to-peer networking applications is 'reasonably ancillary to the . . . effective performance of its statutorily mandated responsibilities.'[86] Notwithstanding the Supreme Court's broad deference to the FCC's assertion of ancillary jurisdiction in the Brand X case,[87] here the Court affirmed the FCC's determination that cable modem provided Internet access constitutes a lightly regulated information service, the D.C. Circuit required evidence that the FCC's regulatory action had a direct link to its statutorily mandated responsibilities.[88] The court vacated the FCC's sanctioning order of Comcast based on the view that the FCC could only refer to congressional statements of policy which do not provide a precedent for creating such responsibilities and to various sections of the Communications Act that the court deemed inapplicable for substantive and procedural reasons.

The D.C. Circuit vacated the Commission's reprimand of Comcast based on the court's refusal to accept the Commission's claim of ancillary jurisdiction. The court referred to the three major cable TV cases[89] where the Supreme Court had affirmed the FCC's ancillary jurisdictional claim 'at a time when, as with the Internet today, the Communications Act gave the Commission no express authority to regulate such systems.'[90] As it had done in the case rejecting the FCC's attempt to require television set manufacturers to build units capable of processing digital right management, 'broadcast flags,' the court distilled the precedent for ancillary jurisdiction established by these cases into a two part test whether: '(a) the Commission's general jurisdictional grant under Title I [of the Communications Act] covers the regulated subject and (b) the regulations are reasonably ancillary to the Commission's effective performance of its statutorily mandated responsibilities.'[91] The court determined that the FCC had not satisfied the second part of the test.[92]

The court flatly rejected the FCC's attempt to infer congressional intent for the Commission to extend its regulatory wingspan to include Internet access. In a series of references to provisions of the Communications Act,[93] the Commission expansively read congressional policy as sufficient ground for undertaking regulatory policy:

> Instead, the Commission maintains that congressional policy by itself creates 'statutorily mandated responsibilities' sufficient to support the exercise of section 4(i) ancillary authority. Not only is this argument flatly inconsistent with Southwestern Cable, Midwest Video I, Midwest Video II, and NARUC II, but if accepted it would virtually free the Commission from its congressional tether.[94]

The court concluded that the FCC would unlawfully invoke ancillary jurisdiction to apply any number of regulatory requirements to cable modem provided Internet access without explicit congressional authority to do so.[95]

ACHIEVING A LEVEL PLAYING FIELD AND SERVING THE PUBLIC INTEREST

Industry observers and interested parties disagree over whether wireless carriers robustly compete, or whether four national carriers share an oligopoly with a market share exceeding ninety per cent. The FCC believes in the former.[96] Even given such characterization, competitiveness by itself still did not dissuade the Commission from attempting to remedy anti-competitive and anti-consumer restrictions on Internet access imposed by Comcast, a largely unregulated information service provider.[97]

The FCC's unwillingness to apply legislatively mandated consumer safeguards, i.e., conventional telecommunications service regulation, subject to streamlining based on current wireless marketplace conditions, results in both the lack of regulatory parity with competing technologies and the reduction in consumer benefits accruing from greater handset use freedoms. The FCC has refrained from stating explicitly what regulatory requirements wireless carriers incur when they provide both content and conduit for next-generation ICE services. Having a predisposition to support marketplace competition and deregulation, the FCC has given wireless carriers *carte blanche* to assume that they can avoid conventional telecommunications regulatory burdens. In the US wireless carriers have actively and aggressively limited subscribers' handset flexibility and freedom without punishment.

Rather than wait for a consumer revolt, the FCC should state explicitly that:

1. Wireless subscribers have the right to attach any handset that complies with standards designed to protect networks from technical harm; Wireless operators should bear the burden of proving that a particular handset would cause technical harm and therefore should not receive FCC certification;
2. Wireless subscribers have the right to use their handsets to access any service, software, application and content available by subscriber imputed commands or instructions. The FCC should expressly state that wireless operators should have an affirmative duty to receive, switch, route and transmit such subscriber keyed commands or instructions; and
3. Suppliers of software, applications, services and content accessible via wireless networks have the right to offer them to subscribers subject to

> a reasonable determination by carriers that such access will not cause technical harm to the carriers' networks. The FCC should reserve the right to mediate and resolve disputes over technical compatibility of any software, applications, services and content accessible via a wireless carrier network.

Additionally, the FCC needs to exercise vigilance to identify instances of excessive market consolidation. When wireless carriers acquire market share by buying out competitors consumers have fewer opportunities to 'vote with their feet' when dissatisfied with service provided by their existing carrier. Already wireless carriers can engage in 'consciously parallel' conduct where they offer roughly the same terms and conditions for service. For example, in the US no carrier offers a discounted rate for existing or prospective customers who already have a handset available and who do not trigger a subsidy by seeking a new phone. Indeed most cellular carrier advertisements emphasize how well their networks operate, without much discussion about price and service versatility.

Lastly, the FCC needs to force wireless carriers to operate in a more transparent and forthright manner so that subscribers understand the total cost of service and the limitations imposed on their handset freedom. Many wireless carriers have managed to insert into consumers' bills surcharges that appear as a tax or other type of compulsory fee. Without the duty to file tariffs and standard service terms and conditions, some wireless carriers can impose unanticipated charges. When handsets can access a much larger array of ICE services it becomes more essential that wireless carriers fully disclose instances where they offer subscribers superior access to content and preferential access to subscribers for specific content providers. Not all quality-of-service and price differentials violate a reasonable conceptualization of fairness and neutrality. Conversely, the failure to disclose instances of price and quality of service discrimination creates the appearance of impropriety and anti-competitive conduct.

Requiring transparency and fair dealing by carriers providing the underlying transmission capacity for ICE services serves the national interest. Unfortunately, the issue of imposing such straightforward requirements has become submerged in a larger debate about how much flexibility ISPs should have to diversify services and what regulator-created incentives are necessary to encourage investment in next-generation networks. The network neutrality debate[98] addresses what constitutes lawful price and service discrimination by ISPs, but opponents have managed to frame the debate as an unlawful attempt to impose common carrier responsibilities. While ISPs do not operate as telecommunications common carriers, wireless radiotelephone companies do, in addition to their information and video programming, delivery services. The FCC and other NRAs have lawful authority to impose network neutrality obligations on wireless carriers in the carriers' capacity as telecommunications service providers.

NRAs face a regulatory quandary when wireless carriers augment telecommunications with new ICE services. The carriers want to claim that by offering new information and video services the NRA no longer has any legal basis for regulating any wireless service, particularly in light of the apparent inability of the FCC and other NRAs to subject a single enterprise to more than one regulatory regime. However, the onset of new services, which may qualify for classification as something other than a common carriage telecommunications service, does not by itself vitiate or justify elimination of the initial regulatory requirements. NRAs and wireless carriers will need to learn how to operate in an environment where two or more regulatory regimes apply when handsets offer an amalgam of telecommunications, information and video services.

NOTES

1. See, e.g., Wingfield (2008); International Telecommunication Union, ITU New Initiatives Programme: The Regulatory Environment for Future Mobile Multimedia Services, World Wide Web Site. See http://www.itu.int/osg/spu/ni/multimobile/index.html.
2. '[T]he language and legislative history of [the Communications Act of 1996] indicate that the drafters . . . regarded telecommunications services and information services as mutually exclusive categories.' ('Federal-State Joint Board on Universal Service, Report to Congress', 13 FCC Rcd. 11501, 11522 (1998)); see also Vonage Holdings Corp., 290 F. Supp.2d at 994, 1000 (applying the FCC's dichotomy).
3. Telecommunications is defined as 'the transmission, between or among points specified by the user, of information of the user's choosing, without change in the form or content of the information as sent and received.' (47 U.S.C. § 153(43)). Telecommunications service means 'the offering of telecommunications for a fee directly to the public, or to such classes of users as to be effectively available directly to the public, regardless of the facilities used.' (47 U.S.C. § 153(46)). The Communications Act defines telecommunications carrier as 'any provider of telecommunications services, except that such term does not include aggregators of telecommunications services (as defined in section 226). A telecommunications carrier shall be treated as a common carrier under this Act only to the extent that it is engaged in providing telecommunications services, except that the Commission shall determine whether the provision of fixed and mobile satellite service shall be treated as common carriage.' (47 U.S.C. § 153(44)). While information service providers use telecommunications to transmit bitstreams, the FCC has chosen not to separate this functionality from the information processing that also occurs. In other words the FCC considers telecommunications to be subordinate to and fully integrated with the predominant information service.
4. Information service is defined as 'the offering of a capability for generating, acquiring, storing, transforming, processing, retrieving, utilizing, or making available information via telecommunications, and includes electronic publishing, but does not include any use of any such capability for the management, control, or operation of a telecommunications system or the management of a telecommunications service.' (47 U.S.C. § 153(20)).
5. Cable service is defined as '(A) the one-way transmission to subscribers of (i) video programming, or (ii) other programming service, and (B) subscriber interaction, if any, which is required for the selection or use of such video programming or other programming

service.' (47 U.S.C. § 522(6)). The term 'cable system' refers to 'a facility, consisting of a set of closed transmission paths and associated signal generation, reception, and control equipment that is designed to provide cable service which includes video programming and which is provided to multiple subscribers within a community, but such term does not include (A) a facility that serves only to retransmit the television signals of 1 or more television broadcast stations; (B) a facility that serves subscribers without using any public right-of-way; (C) a facility of a common carrier which is subject, in whole or in part, to the provisions of title II of this Act, except that such facility shall be considered a cable system (other than for purposes of section 621(c)) to the extent such facility is used in the transmission of video programming directly to subscribers, unless the extent of such use is solely to provide interactive on-demand services; (D) an open video system that complies with section 653 of this title; or (E) any facilities of any electric utility used solely for operating its electric utility systems.' (47 U.S.C. § 522(7)). 'Video programming' means 'programming provided by, or generally considered comparable to programming provided by, a television broadcast station.' (47 U.S.C. § 522(20)).

6. 'AWS is the collective term the Commission uses for new and advanced wireless applications, such as voice, data and broadband services provided over a variety of high-speed fixed and mobile networks, and which are popularly referred to as International Mobile Telecommunications-2000 (IMT-2000) or "third generation" (3G) systems. The 3G nomenclature is based on the popular view that analogue cellular systems represent the first generation of advanced wireless devices, that digital cellular and broadband Personal Communications Service systems represent the second, and that the next deployment of wireless technologies (which are included in the collective term AWS) represents the third generation.' ('Service Rules for Advanced Wireless Services in the 1.7 GHz and 2.1 GHz Bands, WT Docket No. 02-353, Report and Order', 18 FCC Rcd. 25162, 25163 (2003)).
7. 'Convergence in telecommunications gives many consumers access to multiple technologies or platforms that can be used to send and receive voice communications. Consumers are no longer limited to wireline platforms: they can choose from a range of platforms, including wireless and broadband. As wireless and broadband technologies have become more widely available to and used by consumers, they have increasingly become part of the competitive continuum. As more consumers view and use wireless and broadband services as substitutes for wireline services, the extent to which wireline and broadband services are competitive with wireline services will increase.' (Rosenberg, 2007).
8. See note 5 and 6.
9. See, e.g., 'Appropriate Regulatory Treatment for Broadband Access to the Internet over Wireless Networks, Declaratory Ruling' (22 FCC Rcd. 5901 (2007)).
10. 'Inquiry Concerning High-Speed Access to the Internet Over Cable and Other Facilities, Declaratory Ruling and Notice of Proposed Rulemaking' (17 FCC Rcd. 4798 (2002)), *aff'd sub nom.*, Nat'l Cable & Telecomms. Ass'n v. Brand X Internet Servs., 545 U.S. 967 (2005).
11. Nat'l Cable & Telecomms. Ass'n v. Brand X Internet Servs., 545 U.S. 967 (2005) (upholding the FCC's determination that cable modem provided Internet access constitutes an information service). See also Frieden (2006).
12. VoIP offers voice communications capabilities, much like ordinary telephone service, using the packet switched Internet, for all or part of the link between call originator and call recipient. VoIP calls originating or terminating over the standard, dial up telephone network require conversion from or to the standard telephone network's architecture that creates a dedicated circuit-switched link, as opposed to the ad hoc, best efforts packet switching used in the Internet.
13. See Frieden (2008a).
14. 'Universal Service Contribution Methodology, Report and Order and Notice of Proposed Rulemaking', (21 FCC Rcd. 7518 (2006)) (extending section 254(d) permissive authority to require interconnected VoIP providers to contribute to the USF), *petition for review*

denied, and vacated in part on other grounds, Vonage Holding Corp. v. FCC, 489 F.3d 1232 (D.C. Cir. 2007).

15. 'Communications Assistance for Law Enforcement Act and Broadband Access And Services, ET Docket No. 04-295, RM-10865, First Report and Order and Further Notice of Proposed Rulemaking' (20 FCC Rcd. 14989, 15001 (2005)) (citations omitted), *aff'd*, American Council on Education v. FCC, 451 F.3d 226 (D.C. Cir. 2006).
16. 'IP-Enabled Services; E911 Requirements for IP-Enabled Service Providers, WC Docket Nos. 04-36, 05-196, First Report and Order and Notice of Proposed Rulemaking' (20 FCC Rcd 10245 (2005)), *aff'd*, Nuvio Corp. v. FCC, 473 F.3d 302 (D.C. Cir. 2006).
17. 'IP-Enabled Services, WC Docket No. 04-36, Implementation of Sections 255 and 251(A)(2) of the Communications Act Of 1934, as Enacted by the Telecommunications Act of 1996: Access to Telecommunications Service, Telecommunications Equipment and Customer Premises Equipment by Persons With Disabilities' (Docket No. WT 96-198, 22 FCC Rcd. 11275 (2007), *on partial recon*., 22 FCC Rcd. 18319 (2007)).
18. For example, the FCC classified wireless broadband Internet access as a lightly regulated information service: '[W]e find that classifying wireless broadband Internet access service as an information service furthers the goals of sections 7 and 230(b)(2) of the Communications Act, and section 706 of the Telecommunications Act of 1996. As noted above, wireless broadband Internet access technologies continue to evolve at a rapid pace. Through this classification, we provide the regulatory certainty needed to help spur growth and deployment of these services. Particularly, the regulatory certainty we provide through this classification will encourage broadband deployment in rural and underserved areas, where wireless broadband may be the most efficient broadband option. Additionally, we believe that wireless broadband Internet access service can provide an important homeland security function by creating redundancy in our nation's communications infrastructure.' ('Appropriate Regulatory Treatment for Broadband Access to the Internet Over Wireless Networks', 22 FCC Rcd. 5901, 5911 (2007)). Section 706 of the Telecommunications Act of 1976, Pub. L. 104-104, Title VII, § 706, Feb. 8, 1996, 110 Stat. 153, as amended Pub. L. 107-110, § 1076, Jan. 8, 2002, 115 Stat. 2093, requires '[t]he Commission and each State commission with regulatory jurisdiction over telecommunications services . . . [to] encourage the deployment on a reasonable and timely basis of advanced telecommunications capability to all Americans (including, in particular, elementary and secondary schools and classrooms) by utilizing in a manner consistent with the public interest, convenience, and necessity, price cap regulation, regulatory forbearance, measures that promote competition in the local telecommunications market, or other regulating methods that remove barriers to infrastructure investment.' Section 706(c)(1) defines advanced telecommunications capability 'without regard to any transmission media or technology, as high-speed, switched, broadband telecommunications capability that enables users to originate and receive high-quality voice, data, graphics, and video telecommunications using any technology'. See also 47 U.S.C. § 157; 47 U.S.C. § 230(b)(2) (stating that it is the policy of the US 'to preserve the vibrant and competitive free market that presently exists for the Internet').
19. A safe harbour constitutes '[a]n area or means of protection [or a] provision (as in a statute or regulation) that affords protection from liability or penalty.' (*Black's Law Dictionary*, 2004).
20. A federal appellate court in the US determined that the FCC lacked jurisdiction to sanction an ISP for non-transparent and discriminatory traffic management practices that did address legitimate network management and congestion problems. See Comcast Corp. v. F.C.C., __F.3d __, slip op. (D.C. Cir. April 6, 2010) (No. 08-1291); available at: http://pacer.cadc.uscourts.gov/common/opinions/201004/08-1291-1238302.pdf.
21. 'Although US mobile service providers tend to keep tight control on what applications are available and what services consumers can access on mobile handsets by selling content through their own branded portals (the 'walled garden' approach), operators have begun selectively to allow third-party content providers to market multimedia content directly to their subscribers, in exchange for a share of the revenue generated by the sale of these

services.' ('Implementation of Section 6002(B) of the Omnibus Budget Reconciliation Act of 1993, Annual Report and Analysis of Competitive Market Conditions with Respect to Commercial Mobile Services, WT 07-71, Twelfth Report', 23 FCC Rcd. 2241, 2315 (2008)).

22. See FCC, Auctions Summary, http://wireless.fcc.gov/auctions/default.htm?job=auctions_all.
23. The FCC uses the term Commercial Mobile Radio Service (CMRS) to identify the basic telephone services provided by wireless carriers. See Omnibus Budget Reconciliation Act of 1993, Pub. L. No. 103-66, 107 Stat. 312, amending Section 332 of the Communications Act of 1934, to create the CMRS carrier category. The law defines CMRS as 'any mobile service . . . that is provided for profit and makes interconnected service available (A) to the public or (B) to such classes of eligible users as to be effectively available to a substantial portion of the public.' (47 U.S.C. § 332(d)(1) (2006)). CMRS operators do receive regulatory forbearance of some specified regulations, e.g., the need to file tariffs that establish the terms and conditions for service. However, for regulation not explicitly removed, CMRS carriers must comply with Title II common carrier, telecommunications service regulatory requirements and the FCC can forbear from applying any of the remaining regulations, only upon determining that consumers will remain protected against unreasonable and discriminatory service and that the public interest supports forbearance. 'A person engaged in the provision of a service that is a commercial mobile service shall, insofar as such person is so engaged, be treated as a common carrier for purposes of this chapter, except for such provisions of subchapter II of this chapter as the Commission may specify by regulation as inapplicable to that service or person. In prescribing or amending any such regulation, the Commission may not specify any provision of section 201, 202, or 208 of this title, and may specify any other provision only if the Commission determines that— (i) enforcement of such provision is not necessary in order to ensure that the charges, practices, classifications, or regulations for or in connection with that service are just and reasonable and are not unjustly or unreasonably discriminatory; (ii) enforcement of such provision is not necessary for the protection of consumers; and (iii) specifying such provision is consistent with the public interest.' (47 U.S.C. § 332(c)(1)(A)i-iii (2006)). See also 47 U.S.C. § 160(a) (2006) (establishing similar forbearance criteria for other telecommunications service providers). Put another way, CMRS operators do not avoid most basic common carrier responsibilities simply because they provide wireless services, subject to partial regulatory forbearance.
24. 47 U.S.C. § 201 *et seq.* (2008).
25. The FCC reminded cellular telephone companies of this regulatory 'fact of life': [W]e clarify that automatic roaming is a common carrier obligation for commercial mobile radio service (CMRS) carriers, requiring them to provide roaming services to other carriers upon reasonable request and on a just, reasonable, and non-discriminatory basis pursuant to Sections 201 and 202 of the Communications Act. We reiterate the Commission's earlier determination that roaming is a common carrier service because roaming capability gives end users access to a foreign network in order to communicate messages of their own choosing. Thus, the provision of roaming is subject to the requirements of Section 201, 202, and 208 of the Communications Act. ('Reexamination of Roaming Obligations of Commercial Mobile Radio Service Providers, WT 05-265, Report and Order and Further Notice of Proposed Rulemaking', 22 FCC Rcd. 15817 (2007)) (specifying that cellular operators must provide their subscribers automatic access to other carriers for making and receiving telephone calls when travelling outside subscribers' home service regions).
26. See Mossberg (2007).
27. See 'Appropriate Regulatory Treatment for Broadband Access to the Internet Over Wireless Networks, Declaratory Ruling' (WT Docket No. 07-53, FCC 07-30 (rel. March 23, 2007), available at: http://fjallfoss.fcc.gov/edocs_public/attachmatch/FCC-07-30A1.pdf).
28. Section 10 of the Telecommunications Act, *codified at* 47 U.S.C. §160(a)(1)-(3) (2006) authorises the FCC to forbear from applying specific aspects of Title II regulation if

enforcement of such regulation is no longer necessary to ensure just and reasonable charges, is not necessary for protecting consumers and forbearance would serve the public interest. See also, Telecommunications Corp. v. American Telephone & Telegraph Co., 512 U.S. 218 (1994) (absent explicit legislative authorisation the FCC could not exempt designated non-dominant carriers from the Communications Act's Title II requirement that all carriers file a public contract, known as a tariff, specifying the terms and conditions of service).

29. 'Cingular Wireless [AT&T's cellular telephone company name prior to the acquisition of BellSouth] also argued that there is a statutory basis for not applying generic broadband regulation to CMRS operators. Section 332, it argued, differentiates CMRS from other delivery technologies by limiting state authority and requiring the Commission to forbear from unnecessary common carrier regulation. A CMRS operator's broadband Internet access service, it asserted, is part of a CMRS service offering and cannot be subjected to levels of regulation that the Commission finds appropriate for other providers.' ('Appropriate Regulatory Treatment for Broadband Access to the Internet Over Wireless Networks', WT 07-53, 22 FCC Rcd. 5901, 5905-6 (2007)). 'Cingular Wireless & BellSouth and Cisco contended that wireless broadband Internet access service should be classified as an information service, asserting that the deregulatory features of CMRS allowed under section 332 were not sufficient'. (22 FCC Rcd. 5901, 5905 (2007)).
30. Vertical integration refers to the combination of separate market activities by a single enterprise. 'Vertical relationships may have beneficial effects, or they may deter competitive entry in the video marketplace and/or limit the diversity of programming.' ('Annual Assessment of the Status of Competition in the Market for the Delivery of Video Programming, Twelfth Annual Report', 21 FCC Rcd. 2503, 2575 (2006)). 'Beneficial effects can include efficiencies in the production, distribution, and marketing of video programming, and providing incentives to expand channel capacity and create new programming by lowering the risks associated with program production ventures.' (21 FCC Rcd. 2503, n. 565 (2006)). 'Possible detrimental effects can include unfair methods of competition, discriminatory conduct, and exclusive contracts that are the result of coercive activity.' (21 FCC Rcd. 2503, n. 566 (2006)).
31. 'Implementation of the Cable Television Consumer Protection and Competition Act of 1992, Development of Competition and Diversity in Video Programming Distribution: Section 628(c)(5) of the Communications Act: Sunset of Exclusive Contract Prohibition Review of the Commission's Program Access Rules and Examination of Programming Tying Arrangements' (22 FCC Rcd. 17791, 17810 (2007)).
32. 'Despite the increase in available programming over the past five years, we find that cable operators still own popular programming for which there are no close substitutes. The availability of new, non-integrated networks does not mitigate the adverse impact on competition of a competitive MVPD's inability to access popular vertically integrated programming. The record reflects that numerous national programming networks, RSNs, premium programming networks, and VOD networks are cable-affiliated programming networks that are demanded by MVPD subscribers and for which there are no adequate substitutes.' (22 FCC Rcd. 17791, 17816 (2007)).
33. '[W]e find that the exclusive contract prohibition continues to be necessary to preserve and protect competition and diversity in the distribution of video programming, and accordingly, retain it again for five years, until October 5, 2012.' (22 FCC Rcd. 17791, 17792 (2007)).
34. 'What is most significant to our analysis is not the percentage of total available programming that is vertically integrated with cable operators, but rather the popularity of the programming that is vertically integrated and how the inability of competitive MVPDs to access this programming will affect the preservation and protection of competition in the video distribution marketplace. While there has been a decrease since 2002 in the percentage of the most popular programming networks that are vertically integrated, we find that the four largest cable MSOs (Comcast, Time Warner, Cox, and Cablevision) still have an interest in six of the Top 20 satellite-delivered networks as ranked by

subscribership, seven of the Top 20 satellite-delivered networks as ranked by prime time ratings, almost half of all RSNs, popular subscription premium networks, such as HBO and Cinemax, and video-on-demand ('VOD') networks, such as iN DEMAND.' (22 FCC Rcd. 17791, 17814-5 (2007)).

35. 'An exclusive arrangement between a cable-affiliated programmer and its affiliated cable operator will reduce the number of platforms distributing the cable-affiliated programming network and thus the total number of subscribers to the network. This results in a reduction in potential advertising or subscription revenues that would otherwise be available to the network. In the long term, however, the cable-affiliated programmer would gain from an increased number of subscribers as customers switch to the affiliated cable distribution service in order to receive the exclusive programming. Thus, an exclusive contract is a kind of 'investment,' in which an initial loss of profits from programming is incurred in order to achieve higher profits later from increased cable distribution. This type of arrangement is most profitable when the costs of the investment are low and its benefits are high.' (22 FCC Rcd. 17791, 17821 (2007)).
36. 'We find that access to vertically integrated programming is essential for new entrants in the video marketplace to compete effectively. If the programming offered by a competitive MVPD lacks 'must have' programming that is offered by the incumbent cable operator, subscribers will be less likely to switch to the competitive MVPD. We give little weight to the claims by cable operators that recent entrants, such as telephone companies, have not experienced 'any trouble' to date in acquiring access to satellite-delivered vertically integrated programming.' (22 FCC Rcd. 17791, 17819 (2007)).
37. '[W]e conclude that there are no good substitutes for some satellite-delivered vertically integrated programming and that such programming therefore remains necessary for viable competition in the video distribution market.' (22 FCC Rcd. 17791, 17810 (2007)).
38. 'The exclusive contract prohibition in Section 628(c)(2)(D) [of the Communications Act] and the implementing rules pertain to all satellite-delivered programming networks that are vertically integrated with a cable operator, regardless of their popularity.' (22 FCC Rcd. 17791, 17839 (2007)). 'One of the key anti-competitive practices that the exclusive contract prohibition addresses is the practice of leveraging cable's market power collectively by withholding affiliated programming from rival MVPDs while selling the affiliated programming to other cable operators which do not compete with one another. A cable operator may gain by weakening a current or potential rival (such as a DBS operator) even in markets that the cable operator itself does not serve. Thus, proposals to narrow the exclusive contract prohibition by allowing exclusive arrangements outside of the footprint of the affiliated cable operator or with cable operators whose networks pass only a small number of households throughout the nation will impede competition in the video distribution marketplace. We similarly find that allowing exclusive arrangements for affiliated cable operators that face competition from both DBS and telephone companies would harm competition in the video distribution marketplace. We conclude herein that a cable operator will not lose the incentive and ability to enter into an exclusive arrangement in a given geographic area simply because it faces competition from both DBS operators and telephone companies in that area.' (22 FCC Rcd. 17791, 17814 (2007)).
39. 'Section 628 makes no distinction among MVPDs of the kind suggested by these commenters. Moreover, we find that adopting such restrictions on the entities that can benefit from the prohibition will limit competition in the video distribution market and will result in no discernible public interest benefits.' (22 FCC Rcd. 17791, 17842 (2007)).
40. Public Law, 102-385, 106 STAT. 1460, *codified at* 47 U.S.C. § 543(80(A) (2006). 'A cable operator may not require the subscription to any tier other than the basic service tier required by paragraph (7) as a condition of access to video programming offered on a per channel or per program basis. A cable operator may not discriminate between subscribers to the basic service tier and other subscribers with regard to the rates charged for video programming offered on a per channel or per program basis.'
41. 'The tier buy-through prohibition of the 1992 Cable Act prohibits cable operators from requiring subscribers to purchase a particular service tier, other than the basic service tier,

in order to obtain access to video programming offered on a per-channel or per-program basis.' ('Sections of the Cable Television Consumer Protection and Competition Act of 1992: Rate Regulation Buy-Through Prohibition, Third Order on Reconsideration', 9 FCC Rcd. 4316, para. 25 (1994)). See also, Federal Communications Commission, Fact Sheet, Consumer Options for Selecting Cable Channels and the Tier Buy-Through Prohibition, (Feb. 2003), available at: http://fjallfoss.fcc.gov/edocs_public/attachmatch/DOC-231469A1.pdf.

42. See Letter from FCC Chairman Kevin Martin to representatives of several minority public advocacy organizations August 22, 2007, available at: http://www.fcc.gov/commissioners/previous/martin/alacarte-ltr-082207.pdf.
43. 'Implementation of Section 304 of the Telecommunications Act of 1996, Commercial Availability of Navigation Devices, CS Docket No. 97-80, Second Report and Order', 20 FCC Rcd. 6794 (2005).
44. 'At the heart of a robust retail market for navigation devices is the reliance of cable operators on the same security technology and conditional access interface that consumer electronics manufacturers must rely on in developing competitive navigation devices. We conclude that a software-oriented conditional access solution may provide a 'common reliance' standard capable of both reducing the costs for set-top boxes and adding significantly to the options that equipment manufacturers now have in using the CableCARD. In balancing our specific statutory requirement to assure commercial availability of navigation devices and our general obligation to facilitate and promote the DTV transition, we conclude that a further extension of the effective date of the prohibition on integrated devices will permit the development of the statutorily required competitive market for navigation devices, with the potential benefit of reducing costs to consumers.' (20 FCC Rcd. 6794, 6807-8 (2005)).
45. '[A] CableCARD . . . plugs into a slot in a host navigation device, permitting the device to perform both the security and non-security functions.' Charter Communications, Inc. v. Federal Communications Commission, 460 F.3d 31, 34 (D.C. Cir. 2006), available at: http://www.cesweb.org/shared_files/edm/2006/govalert/DCCircuitAdvanceNewhousevFCCOrder081806.pdf. [hereinafter cited as CableCard Affirmance].
46. See 'Implementation of Section 304 of the Telecommunications Act of 1996' (20 FCC Rcd. 6794 (2005)), 'Comcast Corporation Request for Waiver of Section 76.1204(a)(1) of the Commission's Rules, Memorandum Opinion and Order' (CSR-7012-Z, 22 FCC Rcd. 228, *rev. den.*, 22 FCC Rcd. 17,113 (2007) *pet. for rev. den.*, Comcast Corp. v. F.C.C., 526 F.3d 763, 381 (D.C. Cir. 2008)).
47. 'Until recently, providers have generally required customers to sign a one- or two-year agreement in order to take advantage of the various types of calling plans discussed above. As a rule, providers have also required customers to pay early termination fees ('ETFs') when they cancel their wireless service before the expiration of these agreements.' ('Implementation of Section 6002(B) of the Omnibus Budget Reconciliation Act of 1993 Annual Report and Analysis of Competitive Market Conditions With Respect to Commercial Mobile Services', WT Docket No. 08-27, DA 09-54, Thirteenth Report, 2009 WL 151633, 113 (rel. Jan. 16, 2009), available at: http://hraunfoss.fcc.gov/edocs_public/attachmatch/DA-09-54A1.pdf).
48. 'As a rule, providers have also required customers to pay early termination fees ("ETFs") when they cancel their wireless service before the expiration of these agreements. Fixed-term service contracts and ETFs are part of a traditional industry business model in which providers use handset subsidies to offer consumers a discount on the upfront price of handsets and thereby promote the sale of mobile telephone services.' (DA 09-54, para. 113 (2009)).
49. For a more comprehensive examination of this topic, see Frieden (2008b).
50. See Hush-a-Phone v. United States, 238 F.2d 266, 269 (D.C. Cir. 1956) (ordering the FCC to eliminate telephone company tariff restrictions on customers' right to attach non-electronic acoustic devices to telephones). In 1968 the FCC extended the right to include

attachment of electronic devices. Use of the Carterfone Device in Message Toll Telephone Service, 13 FCC 2d 420 (1968), *recon. denied*, 14 FCC 2d 571 (1968).

51. See Frieden (2008c).
52. The Carterfone policy established by the FCC in 1968 requires all wireline telephone companies to allow subscribers to attach any technically compatible device. Consumers take for granted the right to attach any device to a network that is 'privately beneficial without being publicly harmful.' (See 'Use of the Carterfone Device in Message Toll Telephone Service, Decision', 13 FCC 2d 420, 423 (1968), *recon. denied,* 14 FCC 2d 571 (1968); Telerent Leasing Corp. et al., 45 FCC 2d 204, 205 (1974), *aff'd sub nom.* North Carolina Utilities Commission v. FCC, 537 F.2d 787 (4th Cir. 1976), *cert. denied,* 429 U.S. 1027 (1976); Mebane Home Telephone Co., 53 FCC 2d 473, 477 (1975), *aff'd sub nom.* Mebane Home Telephone Co. v. FCC, 535 F.2d 1324, 1329 (D.C. Cir. 1976). See also, Public Utility Comm'n of Texas v. FCC, 886 F.2d 1325, 1329 (D.C. Cir. 1989)) (noting long established FCC policy that carriers and non-carriers alike have a federal right to interconnect to the public telephone network in ways that are privately beneficial if they are not publicly detrimental).
    Previous FCC opposition to this principle failed to pass muster with a reviewing court that interpreted the Communications Act as mandating the right of consumers to attach equipment to the network in ways that were privately beneficial but not publicly harmful. Hush-A-Phone Corp. v. US, 238 F. 2d 266 (D.C. Cir. 1956). 'The intervenors' tariffs [prohibiting the use of plastic device to enhance privacy and low volume conversations], under the Commission's decision, are in unwarranted interference with the telephone subscriber's right reasonably to use his telephone in ways which are privately beneficial without being publicly detrimental.' (238 F. 2d 266, 269 (D.C. Cir. 1956)).
53. 'If you own an iPhone and you're fairly technical, then you've no doubt gone through the steps necessary to 'jailbreak' your iPhone - the process that opens up the phone to allow for the installation of unapproved third-party applications'. [J]ailbreaking is a straightforward process that allows you to install unapproved third-party applications on your device. It is sometimes confused with 'unlocking' - the process that makes the phone capable of working on other carriers besides AT&T (in the US, that is)' (Perez, 2009).
54. See Cauley (2007). The top four carriers control 88.1 per cent of the wireless telecommunications market and that figure will near 90 per cent upon completion of Verizon's acquisition of Alltel.
55. Digital subscriber lines provide Internet access via copper wires initially used solely to provide narrowband telephone service. Telephone companies retrofit the wires to provide medium speed broadband services by expanding the available bandwidth by about 1500 kiloHertz. The FCC provides the following definition: 'Digital Subscriber Line is a technology for bringing high-speed and high-bandwidth, which is directly proportional to the amount of data transmitted or received per unit time, information to homes and small businesses over ordinary copper telephone lines already installed in hundreds of millions of homes and businesses worldwide. With DSL, consumers and businesses take advantage of having a dedicated, always-on connection to the Internet.' Federal Communications Commission, FCC Consumer Facts, Broadband Access for Consumers, available at: http://www.fcc.gov/cgb/consumerfacts /dsl2.html.
56. '[T]raditional phone companies that are primed to offer a 'triple play' of voice, high-speed Internet access, and video services over their respective networks.' ('Exclusive Service Contracts for Provision of Video Services in Multiple Dwelling Units and Other Real Estate Developments, Notice of Proposed Rule Making', 22 FCC Rcd. 5935, 5938 (2007)).
57. The quadruple play refers to the combination of 'video, broadband Internet access, VoIP and wireless service . . .' ('AT&T Inc. and Bellsouth Corporation, Application for Transfer of Control, Memorandum Opinion and Order', 22 FCC Rcd. 5662, 5735 (2007)).
58. 'Internet Policy Statement' (2005).
59. 'Internet Policy Statement' (2005, p. 14988).

60. Comcast Corp. v. F.C.C., __F.3d __, slip op. (D.C. Cir. April 6, 2010) (No. 08-1291); available at: http://pacer.cadc.uscourts.gov/common/opinions/201004/08-1291-1238302.pdf. [hereinafter Comcast Corp. v. FCC].
61. Peer-to-peer file transfers involve the transfer of content between two or more participants. With the use of software, such as BitTorrent, files can arrive in a timely manner by subdividing content into smaller units that are routed simultaneously via any participating network subscriber.
62. 'Comcast Internet Order' (2008).
63. 'Comcast Internet Order' (2008, p. 13028).
64. 'Deep packet inspection uses specialized high-speed hardware and software that can identify packets in real-time. A service provider could use deep packet inspection to distinguish peer-to-peer traffic or even just traffic from a single peer-to-peer file-sharing application and either block it or reduce its available bandwidth. Without deep packet inspection, service providers and others could only resort to crude application-level techniques, such as cutting off all streaming video clips using standard formats after a certain time.' (Werbach, 2005).
65. 'When Comcast judges that there are too many peer-to-peer uploads in a given area, Comcast's equipment terminates some of those connections by sending RST packets. In other words, Comcast determines how it will route some connections based not on their destinations but on their contents; in laymen's terms, Comcast opens its customers' mail because it wants to deliver mail not based on the address or type of stamp on the envelope but on the type of letter contained therein. Furthermore, Comcast's interruption of customers' uploads by definition interferes with Internet users' downloads since "any end-point that is uploading has a corresponding end-point that is downloading." Also, because Comcast's method, sending RST packets to both sides of a TCP connection, is the same method computers connected via TCP use to communicate with each other, a customer has no way of knowing when Comcast (rather than its peer) terminates a connection. This practice is not "minimally intrusive" but invasive and outright discriminatory.' ('Comcast Internet Order', 2008, p. 13051) (citations omitted).
66. 'When an Internet user opens a webpage, sends an email, or shares a document with a colleague, the user's computer usually establishes a connection with another computer (such as a server or another end user's computer) using, for example, the Transmission Control Protocol (TCP). For certain applications to work properly, that connection must be continuous and reliable. Computers linked via a TCP connection monitor that connection to ensure that packets of data sent from one user to the other over the connection "arrive in sequence and without error," at least from the perspective of the receiving computer. If either computer detects that "something seriously wrong has happened within the network," it sends a "reset packet" or "RST packet" to the other, signalling that the current connection should be terminated and a new connection established "if reliable communication is to continue."' ('Comcast Internet Order', 2008, p. 13051, para. 41) (citations omitted).
67. 'Comcast's practice is over inclusive for at least three independent reasons. First, it can affect customers who are using little bandwidth simply because they are using a disfavored application. Second, it is not employed only during times of the day when congestion is prevalent . . . And third, its equipment does not appear to target only those neighborhoods that have congested nodes – evidence suggests that Comcast has deployed some of its network management equipment several routers (or hops) upstream from its customers, encompassing a broader geographic and system area. With some equipment deployed over a wider geographic or system area, Comcast's technique may impact numerous nodes within its network simultaneously, regardless of whether any particular node is experiencing congestion.' ('Comcast Internet Order', 2008, p. 13056) (citations omitted).
68. 'The Associated Press (AP) subsequently conducted several nationwide tests to investigate the allegations that Comcast was interfering with its customers' use of peer-to-peer applications, including BitTorrent. On October 17, 2007, the AP reported the results of these tests: It concluded that Comcast "actively interferes with attempts by some of its

high-speed Internet subscribers to share files online." "Comcast's interference affects all types of content, meaning that, for instance, an independent movie producer who wanted to distribute his work using BitTorrent and his Comcast connection could find that difficult or impossible." The AP found that Comcast's conduct had a "drastic effect . . . on one type of traffic - in some cases blocking it rather than slowing it down."' ('Comcast Internet Order', 2008, p. 13031).

69. 'Comcast Internet Order' (2008, p. 13032).
70. 'Following these tests, Comcast changed its account and admitted that it targets peer-to-peer traffic for interference.' (23 FCC Rcd. 13028, 13031 (2008)).
71. 'Comcast Internet Order' (2008, p. 13031).
72. 'Comcast Internet Order' (2008, p. 13052) (citations omitted).
73. 'Comcast Internet Order' (2008, p. 13030).
74. 'Comcast Internet Order' (2008). After receiving Comcast's explanations for how it will treat subscriber traffic in a non-discriminatory manner, the FCC expressed concerns that Comcast's network management tactics might favour the company's telephone service offering *vis a vis* Internet telephone services of unaffiliated ventures. (See 'Letter from Dana R. Shafer, Chief Wireline Competition Bureau and Matthew Berry, General Counsel to Katheryn A. Zachem, Vice President Regulatory Affairs, Comcast Corp.' (Jan. 18, 2009), available at: http://hraunfoss.fcc.gov/edocs_public/attachmatch/DOC-288047A1.pdf) [hereinafter cited as Comcast VoIP Letter]. Comcast's response is available at: http:// gullfoss2.fcc.gov/prod/ecfs/retrieve.cgi?native_or_pdf=pdf&id_document=6520194593.
75. 'Comcast Internet Order' (2008, p. 13051–3).
76. 'Comcast Internet Order' (2008, p. 13058–9).
77. 'Comcast Internet Order' (2008, p. 13058).
78. 'Comcast Internet Order' (2008, p. 13034) (quoting 2005 Internet Policy Statement, 20 FCC Rcd. 14988, para. 5).
79. In re 'Appropriate Framework for Broadband Access to the Internet Over Wireline Facilities' (20 FCC Rcd. 14853, 14904 (2005)), *rev. denied*, Time Warner Telecom, Inc. v. FCC, 507 F.3d 205 (3d Cir. 2007).
80. The Commission also invoked the following statutory provisions as further justification for its decision to assume jurisdiction and to order a remedy: Section 1 of the Communications Act, 47 U.S.C. § 151, Section 201, 47 U.S.C. § 201, Section 256, 47 U.S.C. §256, Section 257, 47 U.S.C. § 257 and Section 601(4), 47 U.S.C. § 601(a) (2006). [There is only 601(a) and the Commission may have erred in the citation].
81. 'Comcast Internet Order' (2008, p. 13035, 13048).
82. 47 U.S.C. § 152(a).
83. 'Comcast Internet Order' (2008, para. 39) (citations omitted).
84. 'Comcast Internet Order' (2008, para. 38), *citing* CBS, Inc. v. FCC, 629 F.2d 1, 26–7 (1980) (reasoning that the Commission had, in the context of an adjudication, reasonably construed its ancillary authority to encompass television networks), *aff'd*, 453 U.S. 367 (1981); 'Complaint of Carter-Mondale Presidential Committee, Inc. against The ABC, CBS and NBC Television Networks, Memorandum Opinion and Order' (74 FCC 2d 631, para. 25 n.9 (1979)) ('Our power to adjudicate complaints involving requests for access to the networks is surely "reasonably ancillary to the effective performance of the Commission's various responsibilities."' (quoting United States v. Southwestern Cable Co., 392 U.S. 157, 178 (1968)); see also New York State Comm'n on Cable Television v. FCC, 749 F.2d 804, 815 (D.C. Cir. 1984) (upholding adjudicatory decision that pre-empted certain state and local satellite television regulations under Commission's ancillary authority); Negrete-Rodriguez v. Mukasey, 518 F.3d 497, 503-4 (7th Cir. 2008) ('An agency is not precluded from announcing new principles in an adjudicative proceeding rather than through notice-and-comment rule-making.').
85. Comcast Corp. v. FCC (2010).
86. Comcast Corp. v. FCC (2010, p. 3) *citing* Am.Library Ass'n v. F.C.C., 406 F.3d 689, 692 (D.C. Cir. 2005).

87. The court does not interpret the Brand X case as precedent for the imposition of plenary authority over any matter involving cable TV company provided Internet access. 'By leaping from *Brand X*'s observation that the Commission's ancillary authority may allow it to impose *some* kinds of obligations on cable Internet providers to a claim of plenary authority over such providers, the Commission runs afoul of *Southwestern Cable* and *Midwest Video I*.' (Comcast Corp. v. FCC at 14). 'The Commission's exercise of ancillary authority over Comcast's network management practices must, to repeat, "be independently justified."' (Comcast Corp. v. FCC, 2102, p. 16), *citing* National Ass'n of Regulatory Utility Commissioners v. FCC, 533 F.2d 601, 613 (D.C. Cir. 1976) (rejecting the FCC's pre-emption of state and local regulation of two-way, intrastate, non-video cable transmissions).
88. 'The Commission therefore rests its assertion of authority over Comcast's network management practices on the broad language of section 4(i) of the Act: "The Commission may perform any and all acts, make such rules and regulations, and issue such orders, not inconsistent with this chapter, as may be necessary in the execution of its functions,"' (Comcast Corp. v. FCC, 2010, p. 6), *citing* 47 U.S.C. § 154(i) and In 're Formal Compl. of Free Press & Public Knowledge Against Comcast Corp. for Secretly Degrading Peer-to-Peer Applications', 23 FCC Rcd. 13028, 13036 (2008).
89. United States v. Southwestern Cable Co., 392 U.S. 157 (1968), United States v. Midwest Video Corp., 406 U.S. 649 (1972) (Midwest Video I), and FCC v. Midwest Video Corp., 440 U.S. 689 (1979) (Midwest Video II).
90. Comcast Corp. v. FCC (2010, p. 6).
91. Comcast Corp. v. FCC (2010, p. 7).
92. The court noted that Comcast had conceded 'that the Commission's action here satisfies the first requirement because the company's Internet service qualifies as "interstate and foreign communication by wire" within the meaning of Title I of the Communications Act.' (Comcast Corp. v. FCC, 2010, p. 7–8, *citing* 47 U.S.C. § 152(a)). The court also rejected the Commission's claim that because Comcast had used the existence of FCC jurisdiction in another case the company should be judicially stopped from challenging the Commission's jurisdiction now. The court interpreted Comcast's position in the other case as simply acknowledging the FCC's jurisdiction over wire and radio services, which includes what Comcast offers. 'Because Comcast never clearly argued in the California litigation that the Commission's assertion of authority over the company's network management practices would be "reasonably ancillary to the Commission's effective performance of its statutorily mandated responsibilities" (*American Library*'s second requirement), 406 F.3d at 692, that question remains for us to answer.' (Comcast Corp. v. FCC, 2010, p. 12).
93. The Commission cited to Secs. 1, 230(b), 706, 257, 201 and 623 of the Communications Act.
94. Comcast Corp. v. FCC, 2010, p. 23.
95. 'Were we to accept that theory of ancillary authority, we see no reason why the Commission would have to stop . . . [at imposing regulation of Internet Service Providers' rates] for we can think of few examples of regulations that apply to Title II common carrier services, Title III broadcast services, or Title VI cable services that the Commission, relying on the broad policies articulated in section 230(b) and section 1, would be unable to impose upon Internet service providers.' (Comcast Corp. v. FCC, 2010, p. 23–4).
96. See In the Matter of Implementation of Section 6002(b) of the Omnibus Budget Reconciliation Act of 1993, Annual Report and Analysis of Competitive Market Conditions With Respect to Commercial Mobile Services, Twelfth Report, FCC 08-28 (rel. Feb 4, 2008), available at: http://wireless.fcc.gov/index.htm?job=cmrs_reports#d36e145.
97. 23 FCC Rcd. 13028 (2008), para. 49.
98. See Ammori (2009), Frieden (2007a, b), Schewick (2007), Schejter (2007), Wu and Yoo (2007), Cherry (2006), Herman (2006), McTaggart (2006), Wu (2003), Sidak (2006), Yoo (2006), Thierer (2005); Yoo (Fall 2005), Yoo (2004), Lemley and Lessig (2001).

REFERENCES

Ammori, M. (2009), 'Beyond Content Neutrality: Understanding Content-based Promotion of Democratic Speech', *Federal Communications Law Journal*, **61**, 273–324.

Cauley, L. (2007, May 21), 'AT&T Eager to Wield Its iWeapon', *USA Today*. Retrieved from: http://www.usatoday.com/tech/wireless/2007-05-21-at&tiphone_N.htm.

Cherry, B. (2006), 'Misusing Network Neutrality to Eliminate Common Carriage Threatens Free Speech and the Postal System', *Northern Kentucky Law Review*, **33**, 483–511.

'Comcast Internet Order' (2008), 'Formal Complaint of Free Press and Public Knowledge Against Comcast Corporation for Secretly Degrading Peer-to-Peer Applications', File No. EB-08-IH-1518, Memorandum Opinion and Order, 23 FCC Rcd. 13028 (2008).

Frieden, R. (2006), 'What Do Pizza Delivery and Information Services Have in Common? Lessons from Recent Judicial and Regulatory Struggles with Convergence', *Rutgers Computer and Technology Law Journal*, **32**, 247–96.

Frieden, R. (2007a), 'Internet 3.0: Identifying Problems and Solutions to the Network Neutrality Debate', *International Journal of Communication*, **1**, 461–92.

Frieden, R. (2007b), 'Network Neutrality or Bias? Handicapping the Odds for a Tiered and Branded Internet', *Hastings Communications* and *Entertainment Law Journal*, **29**, 171–216.

Frieden, R. (2008a), 'Neither Fish Nor Fowl: New Strategies for Selective Regulation of Information Services', *Journal on Telecommunication & High Technology Law*, **6**, 373–423.

Frieden, R. (2008b), 'Hold the Phone: Assessing the Rights of Wireless Handset Owners and Carriers', *University of Pittsburgh Law Review*, **69**, 675–725.

Frieden, R. (2008c), 'Wireless Carterfone - A Long Overdue Policy Promoting Consumer Choice and Competition', Working paper, New America Foundation Wireless Future Program. Retrieved from: http://www.newamerica.net/files/Wireless_Carterfone_Frieden.pdf

Herman, B. (2006), 'Opening Bottlenecks: On Behalf of Mandated Network Neutrality', *Federal Communications Law Journal*, **59**, 107–59.

'Internet Policy Statement' (2005), 'Appropriate Framework for Broadband Access to the Internet over Wireline Facilities, Policy Statement', 20 FCC Rcd 14986 (2005).

Lemley, M. and Lessig, L. (2001), 'The End of End-to-End: Preserving the Architecture of the Internet in the Broadband Era', *UCLA Law Review*, **48**, 925–72.

McTaggart, C. (2006), 'Was The Internet Ever Neutral?' presented at the 34th Research Conference on Communication, Information and Internet Policy, George Mason University School of Law, Arlington, Virginia.

Mossberg, W. (2007, Oct 21), 'Free My Phone', All Things Digital Blog. Retrieved from: http://mossblog.allthingsd.com /20071021/free-my-phone/.

Perez, S. (2009, Jan 12), 'Why You Have to Jailbreak the iPhone', *The New York Times*. Retrieved from: http://www.nytimes.com/external/readwriteweb/2009/01/12/12readwriteweb-why_you_have_to_jailbreak_the_iphone.html.

Rosenberg, E. (2007), 'Assessing Wireless and Broadband Substitution in Local Telephone Markets', *The National Regulatory Research Institute*. Retrieved from: http://nrri.org/pubs/telecommunications/07-06.pdf.

Schejter, A. (2007), '"Justice, and Only Justice, You Shall Pursue": Network Neutrality, the First Amendment and John Rawls's Theory of Justice', *Michigan Telecommunications and Technology Law Review*, **14**, 137–74.

Schewick, B. (2007), 'Towards an Economic Framework for Network Neutrality Regulation', *Journal on Telecommunications and High Technology Law*, **5**, 329–91.

Sidak, J. (2006), 'A Consumer-Welfare Approach to Network Neutrality Regulation of the Internet', *Journal of Competition Law and Economics*, **2**, 349–474.

Thierer, A. (2005), 'Are "Dumb Pipe" Mandates Smart Public Policy? Vertical Integration, Net Neutrality, and the Network Layers Model', *Journal on Telecommunications and High Technology Law*, **3**, 275–308.

Werbach, K. (2005), 'Breaking the Ice: Rethinking Telecommunications Law for the Digital Age', *Journal on Telecommunications and High Technology Law*, **4**, 59–92.

Wingfield, N. (2008, Oct 27), 'Time to Leave the Laptop Behind', *The Wall Street Journal*. Retrieved from: http://online.wsj.com/article/SB 12247776388426 2815.html.

Wu, T. (2003), 'Network Neutrality, Broadband Discrimination', *Journal on Telecommunications and High Technology Law*, **2**, 141–79.

Wu, T. and Yoo, C. (2007), 'Keeping the Internet Neutral? Tim Wu and Christopher Yoo Debate', *Federal Communications Law Journal*, **59**, 575–92.

Yoo, C. (2004), 'Would Mandating Broadband Network Neutrality Help or Hurt Competition? A Comment on the End-to-End Debate', *Journal on Telecommunications and High Technology Law*, **3**, 23–68.

Yoo, C. (2005), 'Beyond Network Neutrality', *Harvard Journal of Law & Technology*, **19**, 1–76.

Yoo, C. (2006), 'Network Neutrality and the Economics of Congestion', *Georgetown Law Journal*, **94**, 1847–908.

4. Incentive regulation, investments and technological change

Ingo Vogelsang

INTRODUCTION

This chapter is about network industries, which are characterized by nontrivial investment challenges. They generally exhibit economies of scale persisting over a wide range of output and leading to lumpiness of investments. Lumpiness refers to the large size of capacity increments, which can be associated with capacity shortages, excess capacity and (wasteful) duplicate investments. Furthermore, lumpiness refers to long lead times and durability of the investments. A common feature of network investments is sunkness, which implies risks associated with real options. Both the option to delay investment and thereby learn about the future and the option to have capacity available when it is needed can be valuable and thereby influence investment risk. In addition, competitive risks, for example from duplicative investment, play a major role in investment decisions. Examples of regulated network industries with (currently) weak competitive risks include electricity transmission and distribution networks, while strong competitive risks characterize broadband telecommunications access and backhaul and next-generation networks (NGN).

In the 1970s the main problem tackled by industrial organisation literature was that of regulatory incentives for excessive investment under rate-of-return regulation (Averch-Johnson effect). The incentive-regulation movement of the 1980s and 1990s was a reaction to this type of rate-of-return regulation tradition (Vogelsang, 2002). In contrast to the previous emphasis on potentially excessive investment, incentive regulation put the emphasis on (short-term) productive efficiency and low consumer prices. Has therefore investment been neglected? What about the over-investment in telecommunications fibre networks before 2000/2001? Today regulated incumbents in the same industry complain that regulation stifles their investment incentives. Their lobbying resulted, e.g., in a heavily contested German telecommunications law[1] that provides a regulatory holiday for innovative investment as does current practice of the US Federal Communications Commission. Such legal and regulatory measures derive their justification from the presumption that they increase (innovative) investment and that the resulting additional benefits from (innovation and) investment are going to be high relative to benefits foregone from short-term cost reductions and/or price reductions. This brief characterization suggests that regulation can have ambivalent investment effects.

For at least two basic reasons regulation can enhance and accelerate investment. First, by helping to lower the price of the output, regulation increases the demanded output quantity and consequently the capacity required to produce this output. Second, successful competition-enhancing regulation fires up the race for new bottleneck investment between incumbent and entrants (by creating entrants with less of a cannibalization problem than the incumbent).

For at least two other reasons regulation can reduce and retard investments. First, regulation lowers the expected investment returns, going along with increases or decreases in risks. This works via the truncation of uncertain investment outcomes that are caused by price constraints. Investment risks are thereby shifted from consumers and the access seekers to the regulated firm. The second reason for reduced or delayed investment is the regulator's lack of commitment leading to a fear of regulatory expropriation.

Depending on their purpose, investments may be affected differently by regulation in general and by incentive regulation in particular. Investment in cost reduction and replacement investment, e.g., may be positively affected by price-cap or yardstick regulation (Borrmann and Brunekreeft, 2009). This would hold to the extent that regulated firms can keep the benefits from cost reductions in the form of higher profits. In contrast, investment in quality improvements may suffer under these types of regulation because lower quality is a substitute for price increases above the cap or benchmark (Armstrong et al., 1994; Kwoka, 2009). However, quality improvements may increase sales so that empirical effects tend to be inconclusive. For example, Banerjee (2003) finds neutral or positive quality effects from moving to price-cap regulation in telecommunications retail markets.[2]

Investment in new products and services can be particularly characteristic of some network industries, such as the telecommunications sector (in the time of digital convergence). Regulation here constrains the upside opportunities necessary to take on the additional risks associated with innovation. In contrast, incentive regulation may be more compatible with legacy infrastructure investment by an incumbent. This chapter contrasts expansion investment and investment in new types of infrastructures, leaving out quality regulation in particular.

The following section provides a review of the academic literature about the relationship between price regulation and investment. Next policy proposals are developed on pricing, based on an idiosyncratic reading of the surveyed literature and based on the assumption that regulators can commit to incentive regulation. This assumption, however, is not trivial. Almost always regulators want investment, but they also want low prices. Because prices are set after investment, the wish for lower prices creates an ex-post conflict with the ex-ante desire for high investment (Brito et al., 2008). Lack of commitment then leads to ex-post policies detrimental to investment. Anticipating such policies, the regulated firm will refrain from investing. The following section therefore introduces the regulatory commitment issue. It shows the potential tension between the inability of regulators to commit over the long time horizon of infrastructure investments and the provision of cost-reducing incentives. This leads to policy proposals balancing the investment and incentive aspects. A penultimate section takes up the difference between ordinary and innovative investments as a potential reason for abandoning regulation altogether. This section develops a framework for identifying characteristics of markets that should be regulated versus those that should not. A final section concludes.

LITERATURE REVIEW ON INVESTMENT EFFECTS OF PRICE REGULATION

In this chapter, the focus is on regulated prices as the main regulatory incentive variables. Price regulation has effects, among others, on investments in cost reduction, replacement, expansion, new products and quality of service. In principle, the regulator can address these effects directly, for example, through direct regulation of quality or of expansion investment. While using a second instrument besides price has the potential of improving investment effects, I am here neglecting this possibility.

As shown in the following literature survey the power of incentives and tightness of regulation play major roles for investment incentives. The strength or power of incentives is measured by the percentage of cost reductions the firm may keep, or of cost increases that it may have to suffer (Laffont and Tirole, 1993). Under strong incentives, the firms keep/suffer a high percentage, while under weak incentives they keep/suffer a low percentage. The power of incentives is quite separate from the tightness of regulation (which is more related to the participation constraint for the firm). Tightness refers to the (economic or excess) profit rate that the regulator concedes to the firm in case normal expectations are fulfilled. Tight regulation refers to a low or zero expected profit rate and usually a low regulated price. Conversely, soft regulation refers to a high expected profit rate and usually a high regulated price. Intermediate regulation would lie between tight and soft regulation.

The power of incentives is closely related to the risk that the regulated firm is bearing. Different types of price regulation can with some caution be ranked by the risks/incentives they provide for the firm. Rate-of-return regulation and other cost-plus regulations generally provide low risk and weak incentives. Profit-sharing regulation is associated with medium risk/incentives. Price-cap regulation as the next step carries medium to high risk/incentives. In the list, yardstick/benchmarking regulation (including engineering cost models) comes up with the highest risk/strongest incentives. While these are ranked from low risk/weak incentives to high risk/strong incentives, the regulator can make compensating adjustments through incentive-mitigating measures, such as true-ups from time to time.

End-User Regulation

A growing literature has emerged recently on the relationship between investment and regulation. This has, however, not yet led to very clear results.[3] Unsurprisingly, the early work concentrated on rate-of-return regulation, while the newer work emphasizes incentive regulation, price caps in particular, and sometimes compares rate-of-return regulation (or other types of cost-based regulation) with price caps. Beginning with end-user regulation of dominant incumbents the concentration here is more on theoretical than empirical contributions.[4]

While according to conventional wisdom rate-of-return regulation is likely associated with excessive investment, the literature is actually more differentiated. First, it has been known since Averch and Johnson (1962) that the excessive investment result only holds for an allowed rate of return s between the monopoly rate m and the cost of capital r ($r < s < m$). In the more realistic model formulation of Bawa and Sibley (1980) a higher allowed rate than m would lead to no change in investment compared to no regulation or even to reduced investment. Similarly, a rate of return at $s = r$ would lead to efficiency and $s < r$ would lead to underinvestment. The original results of Averch and Johnson are qualified by:

- considerations of regulatory lag (Baumol and Klevorick, 1970; Bailey and Coleman, 1971). Such lags generally reduce the overcapitalization bias but could also lead to undercapitalization (Joskow and MacAvoy, 1975). With an endogenous lag that decreases in the deviation between actual and allowed rate of return efficiency can be reached even if the allowed rate exceeds the cost of capital (Bawa and Sibley, 1980);
- different valuations of the rate base (largely historical costs versus

replacement costs). Evans and Guthrie (2005, 2006) note that replacement cost valuation can expose the regulated firm to asset price risks; and

- addressing a used-and-useful criterion for investments to be included in the rate base. Gilbert and Newbery (1994), in particular, argue that rate-of-return regulation with a used-and-useful criterion is likely to lead to an efficient amount of investment. In contrast, Égert (2009) argues that the used-and-useful criterion introduces uncertainty into the regulatory process that would lead to underinvestment or a biased type of investment. This is also implied by Evans' and Guthrie's (2005, 2006) critique of the use of optimized replacement costs that do not include excess capacity for the case of demand uncertainty. Such excess capacity would not appear to be 'used and useful' in states of low demand and would therefore be disqualified for inclusion in the rate base by regulators (Baumol and Sidak, 2002).

Thus, it appears from the literature that the effects of rate-of-return regulation on investment would heavily depend on the way it is actually handled by regulators and courts.

A positive relationship between price-cap regulation and investment is established early by Cabral and Riordan (1989) for the case of cost-reducing investments. This is, however, limited to the full commitment case (infinite time horizon) and to a specialized type of investment. Later work came to much more qualified conclusions, finding that positive investment effects would depend on the length of commitment (Biglaiser and Riordan, 2000) and on the level of the cap (Nagel and Rammerstorfer, 2008; Roques and Savva, 2006 and 2009). These latter works use a real-option approach so that the price cap triggering optimal investment is highly dependent on sunkness and uncertainty. Generally, overestimating the cap seems to have less dire consequences for investment than underestimating it. Dobbs (2004) finds that, because of the truncation problem inherent in capped prices, underinvestment would arise even under optimal price caps and would lead to non-price rationing (deteriorated quality). All this work, just like in the case of rate-of-return regulation, strongly suggests that the investment effects of price-cap regulation clearly depend on the way the regulation is handled in practice.

Sobel (1999) finds that yardstick regulation, by using information on low-cost firms (ex-post), may prevent optimal investment (ex-ante) of regulated firms. Borrmann and Brunekreeft (2009), in a sunk-cost model under certainty, show that yardstick regulation leads to postponement of expansion investment (relative to the social optimum, though not necessarily relative to unconstrained profit maximization), while it accelerates replacement investment.

The work on the relationship between profit-sharing regulation and investment seems to be restricted to Panteghini and Scarpa (2003) and

Moretto et al. (2008).[5] They find that under uncertainty straightforward RPI-X price caps lead to higher investment than profit-sharing regulation. While insightful these papers seem to derive their results from their asymmetric definition of profit-sharing, where 'sharing' only occurs if the profits exceed a certain level. Thus, profit-sharing does not reduce the firm's risk because it only happens in the good states of the world. Rather, it prevents the firm from reaping the upside potential in the good states that would be necessary for compensating downside risks in bad states. This result has potential practical importance, because asymmetric profit-sharing is actually used by some regulators. It is also highly intuitive but it says very little about the effect of real, i.e., symmetric, profit-sharing, where the firm would have some downside protection. Such symmetric profit-sharing would include price caps and rate-of-return regulation as polar cases with price caps as zero sharing and rate-of-return regulation as 100 per cent sharing.

Interestingly, the two main empirical papers on the relationship between different types of regulation and investment in telecommunications network modernization show larger investments in incentive regulation regimes (price caps in particular) compared to rate-of-return regulation (Greenstein et al., 1995; Ai and Sappington, 2002). This may be due to the fact that, in its practical application, incentive regulation in the US is quite soft.[6]

Access Price Regulation

The network investment relevant for this chapter can concern competitive bottlenecks (low replicability) or complementary infrastructure downstream or upstream of the bottleneck (high replicability). In both cases, the investor can either be the regulated incumbent or unregulated competitors. The term 'bottleneck' is used in the sense of an essential facility, which is a necessary input (fixed proportions) that is owned by an incumbent and cannot be duplicated economically by potential entrants (natural monopoly property). Examples of such bottlenecks include transmission and distribution networks in electricity that are necessary for competing electricity generators to reach potential customers. They also include local loops in fixed telephone networks that local and long-distance carriers need in order to originate and terminate calls. Bottleneck regulation concerns access of alternative competitors to such bottleneck facilities owned by dominant incumbents.

In contrast to end-user regulation that tries to prevent exploitation of consumers and shall lead to competitive prices bottleneck regulation tries to enhance competition. The main investor types are the dominant incumbent and the entrants or alternative competitors. To the extent that competition-enhancing regulation is successful, it may increase investment by alternative competitors at the expense of the incumbent. Total investment may thereby diminish or increase depending on which effect is larger.

The theoretical literature on the relationship between access price regulation for monopolistic bottlenecks and investment is quite diversified regarding the issues addressed.[7]

Effects of regulation on incumbent bottleneck investment

A sizeable part of the literature is mainly concerned with the effect of the regulated access price on the incentive of the bottleneck owner/incumbent to invest in new or expanded infrastructure, independent of the effect on potential alternative competitors. The concern here is predominantly with access prices based on TELRIC/LRAIC.[8] The main argument is that access prices (and prices for unbundled network elements) that do not cover all costs of investment would stifle investments. Proponents of the TELRIC/LRAIC approach argue that by definition these two cost concepts include all costs of expansion investments in new infrastructure. Thus, any shortfall in (expected) coverage of investment costs would have to come from cost measurement errors or mistakes in the underlying models. Potential errors could come: (a) from measurement of the required capacities under lumpiness paired with uncertain/fluctuating demand,[9] and (b) from measurement of the weighted average cost of capital (WACC) under sunkness. Opponents of the TELRIC/LRAIC approach argue that regulators systematically err by not including enough reserve capacities and by making no WACC adjustments for real options. Comacho and Menezes (2009) show that failure to include real options of delay (under an ECPR approach) leads to suboptimal investments. In contrast, their alternative of using an Option to Delay Pricing Rule (ODPR) essentially requires the regulator to be fully informed about market conditions and thereby be able to implement the optimal end-user prices directly. In my view, regulators probably err in the wrong direction by not including the value of real options in the calculations for costs of capital (WACC) for TELRIC/LRAIC.

Effects of bottleneck regulation on bypass investment

A second large part of the access-related literature addresses the incentive effects of unbundling obligations and their prices on competitors' investments. This literature specifically centres on the stepping-stone or ladder-of-investment hypothesis (partially due to Cave and Vogelsang, 2003). The ladder-of-investment hypothesis claims that entry by alternative providers in a market dominated by an incumbent is hindered by the necessity to acquire assets with a range of bottleneck properties. As time goes by, as entrants learn and as they grow in size (thereby availing themselves of economies of scale), they can climb an investment ladder with increasing bottleneck properties. Foreseeing that development the regulator should begin by forcing the incumbent to make all bottleneck inputs available at attractive prices thereby enabling entry. However, the regulator should commit to reducing the attractiveness of regulated access over time, beginning with inputs with less bottleneck properties. This is meant to increase incentives for alternative providers to actually invest in assets with increasing bottleneck properties because regulated access becomes less and less attractive.

The ladder-of-investment hypothesis has been embraced by European telecommunications regulators but has been criticized in the literature. Bourreau and Doğan (2006) point out in a theoretical model that with increasing availability of alternative or bypass infrastructure the incumbent bottleneck owner would voluntarily provide bottleneck access at increasingly attractive terms for the alternative competitors, thereby retarding bypass. Thus, according to them, instead of increasing regulated access prices as bypass becomes more and more available, the regulator should prohibit unbundled access, once bypass becomes economical because otherwise bypass would come too late. The authors claim that, for the same reason, regulatory sunset clauses would not help.[10] However, a major problem with both an application of the ladder-of-investment approach and with the Bourreau and Doğan suggestion is that the regulator will generally not know, when bypass is sufficiently feasible and that this feasibility will differ locally across the country.

A further counter-argument to the ladder-of-investment approach can be derived from the inclusion of real options in the incumbent's access costs. Accordingly, for sunk bottleneck access the risk of bypass would justify initial surcharges on conventional TELRIC/LRAIC calculations but these would no longer be feasible, once bypass occurs, thus leading to a declining path of access prices.

The ladder-of-investment approach assumes that bypass is based on an extension of investments in the same legacy technology of the incumbent. In reality, however, it usually occurs through a new technology or improvement of another technology that is different from the legacy infrastructure of the incumbent. Examples of the former could be FTTH or VDSL,[11] through which the bypass opportunities may deteriorate. An example of the latter is a cable TV network that competes with the telephone/DSL network of the incumbent and of entrants using the incumbent's technology. The ladder-of-investment approach does not work here because: (a) entrants cannot effectively duplicate the incumbent's local loops; and (b) the cable TV company investments may be jeopardized by any boost given to the incumbent by selling access to the entrants (Pindyck, 2007).

Overall, the working of the ladder-of-investment approach appears to be strongly dependent on the circumstances of the industry as well as on the way it is implemented by the regulator.[12]

Effects on incumbents and entrants

A third part of the access-related literature concentrates on the interaction of the regulatory effects on incumbents and entrants. Gans (2001), for example, suggests an optimal two-part access tariff that ensures optimal investment of a regulated firm that has to immediately grant access to this new infrastructure to rivals. Thus, the formula both provides for the optimal timing of investment and helps pre-empt competing investments by potential rivals.

Several papers deal with incumbent and entrant investment in models that capture a new industry, in which two firms have to decide, which one will invest first and in which access regulation has been established before (Hori and Mizuno, 2006; Vareda and Hoernig, 2007). Here, low access charges usually (but not always) retard both the incumbent's (initial) and the entrant's investments, while high access charges lead to pre-emptive strategies.

The empirical literature on both incumbent and entrant investment includes Grajek and Röller (2009), whose estimations relate to telecommunications investments in fixed networks. They find a negative relationship between access regulation and individual incumbents' and entrants' investments, although total entrants' investments increase. In addition, incumbents invest more in response to entrants' investment increases. The effect of regulation is found only, when controlling for the endogeneity of access regulation. In particular, regulators are found to tighten regulation in response to increased investments by incumbents.

PRICE REGULATION FOR EXPANSION INVESTMENT UNDER FULL COMMITMENT

The Case for Intermediate Regulation

The literature on the relationship between regulation, investments and innovation suggests many different case-specific outcomes. Keeping the cases apart and deriving case-specific regulations is highly information-intensive and may be subject to moral hazard and adverse selection on the side of the regulators. Nevertheless, there are things that regulators cannot and probably should not do. Among them is taking responsibility for infrastructure investment decisions and for innovations. The approach here is to use simple economics and insights from the literature for extracting some fairly general properties and to come up with a few rough-and-ready rules.[13] They may do injustice to the individual case but are more likely to be feasible for implementation and less subject to commitment problems than more specific case-dependent rules.

Consider first the relationship between the regulated (bottleneck) price and the incumbent's infrastructure investment, as depicted in Figure 4.1. The simplified view illustrated by the investment function combines two constraints on investment. The shape of the function is assumed to be affected by cost and demand risks. In particular, the risk results in a thick corridor in the horizontal portion. This leads to asymmetric effects of tight versus soft regulation. Tight regulation can lead to high investment, due to the implied large demand. However, it could also imply zero investment if the regulated firm (or the capital market) views the investment as too risky at that price. In contrast, a price increase to the level of soft regulation implies no regulatory risk (under full commitment), but leads to small investment. Intermediate regulation leads to substantially higher investment that is also virtually assured. The view exposed in this argumentation contrasts with most, which largely neglects any demand-side effects from lower prices.

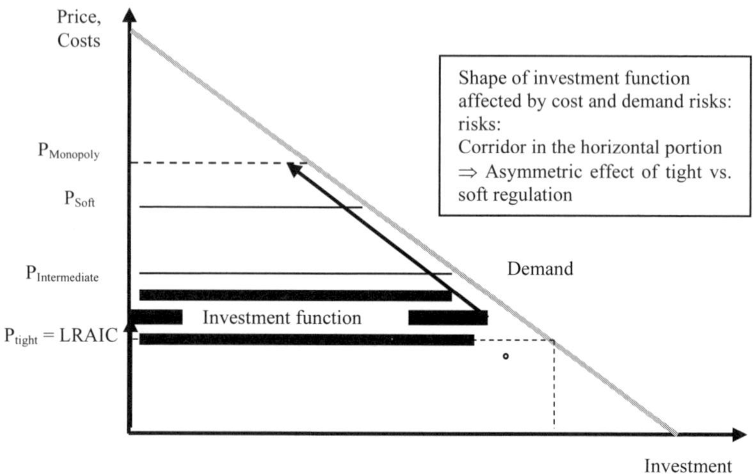

Figure 4.1 Infrastructure investment and price: Soft vs. tight regulation

In Table 4.1, a distinction is made between types of infrastructure for investment purposes. Bottleneck infrastructure (to which the access is regulated) could either be legacy and innovative infrastructures of incumbent (Column 1) or bypass infrastructure by competitors (Column 2). The latter would not strictly represent bottlenecks, which by definition could not economically be duplicated. However, the regulatory restructuring and reform movement is based on the premise that new technical and market developments can potentially abolish or reduce bottlenecks over time and that this can be helped by regulation. A low regulated price for bottleneck access could have facilitated competitive entry. However, a continued low access price can discourage entrants from investing in bottleneck bypass, while an increased access price could induce bypass investment. This is the ladder-of-investment aspect (Cave and Vogelsang, 2003; Cave, 2006). In addition, the entrants may be more likely to invest in new types of bottleneck infrastructure, while the replacement effect of such infrastructure may prevent the incumbent from doing so (Bourreau and Doğan, 2004; Hori and Mizuno, 2009). Low access prices may therefore initially increase both competition for the market and competition in the market. However, the increased competition in the market will make competition for the market unattractive. The next type of infrastructure concerns investments downstream or upstream of the bottleneck and is generally not regulated. This infrastructure can again be that of a vertically integrated incumbent (Column 3) or it could be alternative competitors' infrastructure (Column 4). The infrastructure downstream or upstream of the bottleneck is by assumption no bottleneck (otherwise it would be included there).

Table 4.1 Effects of tightness of bottleneck regulation on infrastructure investment in the absence of retail regulation

Investment Type Regulation	Incumbent Bottleneck	Competitive Bypass (Make or Buy)	Incumbent Downstream	Competitive Downstream
Tight	- (+)	- Sappington: 0	- (+)	+
Intermediate	+	0 Sappington: 0	+	0
Soft	+ (-)	+ (-) Sappington: 0	+ (-)	-

Figure 4.1 provides the basis for the 'Incumbent Bottleneck' column in Table 4.1. Accordingly, tight regulation can only have a positive effect on investment if there is no cost uncertainty. Otherwise, tight regulation would choke investment. In contrast, soft regulation has a positive effect at high uncertainty and inelastic demand, but could have substantial negative effects if uncertainty were less and demand more elastic. Intermediate regulation would balance the two tendencies.

The second column indicates that competitive bypass investment is discouraged by tight bottleneck regulation, because access to the incumbent's bottleneck is then cheaper than bypass. In contrast, soft regulation makes bypass attractive if bypass is fully possible. Intermediate regulation makes bypass attractive if bypass is partially possible. This line of reasoning about bypass investment is questioned by Sappington (2005b), who shows in theoretical models that the tightness of bottleneck regulation is just compensated by the incumbent's competitive reactions downstream. This means that tight regulation is accompanied by aggressive downstream competition, while soft regulation would be accompanied by more collusive behaviour. As a result, the alternative competitors only invest in bottleneck bypass if they can do so more cheaply than the incumbent and that will be independent of the regulated bottleneck access charge. The question if this behaviour is restricted to Sappington's model assumptions or if it holds more generally has been analysed by Mandy (2009), who finds that input prices generally do matter for the efficient make-or-buy decision and that efficient decisions can be induced by pricing the input access at the entrant's marginal cost (of bypass). This may, however, leave the entrants out in the cold if they cannot economically duplicate the bottleneck facility.

Because of mostly fixed proportions between bottleneck and complementary investments, tight bottleneck regulation increases downstream output and downstream investment overall. The distribution of investment between incumbent and competitors, tentatively shown on Columns 3 and 4, depend on their relative efficiency downstream and on the amount of bypass investment.

Table 4.2 displays effects of the tightness of end-user regulation on infrastructure investments. Here the results for competitive bypass and downstream investments are opposite to the case of bottleneck regulation, because – in contrast to the latter – end-user regulation does not benefit but rather tends to handicap competitors. Tight end-user regulation of the incumbent acts like increased competition in the market and therefore makes competition for the market less attractive. As a result, entry will be reduced and exit increased. There is a possibility though that (in an oligopolistic setting) alternative competitors already in the market may expand when end-user regulation tightens up. The effects of soft end-user regulation would then just be the reverse.

The effects of tightness of end-user regulation on the incumbent's investment are quite similar to those of bottleneck regulation except that there are additional effects from the way end-user regulation affects alternative competitors. The negative effect of tight regulation on the incumbent's investment may therefore be buffered by the reduction in the number of competitors and the positive effect of soft regulation may be somewhat neutralized by increased competition.

Table 4.2 Effects of tightness of end-user regulation on infrastructure investment

Investment Type Regulation	Incumbent Bottleneck	Competitive Bypass (Make or Buy)	Incumbent Downstream	Competitive Downstream
Tight	-/+	- (+)	-/+	- (+)
Intermediate	+	0	+	0
Soft	+/-	+ (-)	+/-	+ (-)

On the bottleneck level, tight regulation is best for upstream/downstream investment and soft regulation best for bottleneck and bypass investment. The best overall approach to end-user regulation depends on the relative weight and relative sunkness of bottleneck infrastructure vs. other infrastructure. Intermediate regulation appears to be the generally best compromise. On the end-user level soft/intermediate regulation virtually dominates for all types of investment. Soft regulation enhances competition as long as foreclosure can be avoided via bottleneck regulation. Soft bottleneck regulation can therefore increase price-squeeze problems. This assessment is in line with the view that end-user markets should be deregulated first.[14]

Intermediate Regulation as Incentive Regulation

Intermediate or soft regulation seems to provide better investment incentives than tight regulation. Incentive regulation, however, seems to call for a tight approach. How then can soft regulation provide efficiency incentives?[15] Consider different types of incentive regulation.

Soft profit-sharing regulation could mean:

1. Soft definition of (excess) profits. Such an approach to softness would preserve incentives, because it would preserve the extent to which the regulated firm remains a residual claimant;
2. More (higher percentage of) sharing. This means a move in the direction of rate-of-return regulation. Such a move reduces incentives; and
3. Asymmetric sharing in favour of the regulated firm, meaning that the firm suffers a smaller share of any losses and gains a larger share of any profits.[16] Such softness would likely lead to overinvestment, because the firm would face reduced risks.

Soft price-cap regulation means a higher cap. Generally, the cost-reducing incentives are deemed largely independent of the price-cap level so that incentives are preserved. In contrast, investment incentives are increased (Roques and Savva, 2006, 2009; Nagel and Rammerstorfer, 2008).[17] There is an allocative inefficiency, though. Under end-user regulation part of this inefficiency is (in the long run) balanced by increased competitive pressure. Under bottleneck regulation part of the reduced downstream competition would be balanced by bypass incentives.

Regulation based on analytical cost models (LRAIC or TELRIC) provides intrinsic efficiency incentives if the models are independent of the incumbent's actual costs. Soft regulation here could be implemented via a higher built-in rate of return (which could be more than a simple risk surcharge). In particular, regulators could include a surcharge for real options in case of sunk assets (err in favour of including real options). There could be additional uncertainty from the replacement cost approach used in such models (Evans and Guthrie, 2005).

Benchmarking (yardstick) regulation is usually applied in reference to an actual efficiency frontier provided by a set of firms. While regulated rates on the frontier would represent tight regulation, intermediate or soft regulation could allow for a pre-set distance from the efficiency frontier. Also, under soft regulation the rate could be based on the cost average of the firms rather than on the frontier. Efficiency would be preserved to the extent that the benchmark is independent of the particular regulated firm's behaviour.

Thus, with the exception of some forms of profit-sharing soft/intermediate regulation appears to be fully compatible with providing cost-reducing/productivity-enhancing incentives.

However, what is the yardstick for intermediate regulation and how can it be implemented? Criteria for tight regulation can usually be established with some precision and therefore be framed in regulatory rules/laws. In contrast, soft/intermediate regulation may require regulatory discretion.[18] Verifiable criteria for 'intermediate' are hard to come by. One could therefore establish a two-step procedure.

Step 1 involves establishing and applying criteria for applicability of tight versus soft/intermediate regulation, keeping in mind that soft/intermediate resembles light regulation and can therefore be viewed as a step in the direction of deregulation. For example, under the ladder-of-investment approach, soft/intermediate regulation may be inappropriate in markets with routine (small, short-run) investments without bypass opportunities. In such markets, any move towards deregulation would be unwarranted, and surcharges on the firm's cost of capital would be unnecessary for triggering investments. In contrast, softer regulation would be justified under increased uncertainty, increased sunkness and increased bypass possibilities.

Step 2 then involves choosing a specific type of soft/intermediate regulation, given that it is first established as necessary/appropriate. Examples of intermediate regulation that have been codified include a combination of ex-post regulation and the application of competition law criteria in the German Telecommunications Act of 2003. This approach gives the incumbent some flexibility because it does not have to get permission before setting prices. At the same time, the criterion for regulatory intervention is not based on efficient costs (which are the criterion for ex-ante regulation in the same law) but rather on non-abusive prices.[19] Another approach that would be applicable in case of reasonable downstream competition is the ECPR.[20] Benchmarking based on averages rather than on frontier costs would be another example for intermediate regulation. This would be a pricing approach where clear differentiation of criteria is possible. A radical approach on the governance level would be the choice of a pro-industry regulator (Evans et al., 2008).

As a general rule, at the same expected returns, the stronger the power of incentives, the greater the risk that the firm faces.[21] As a result, regulatory mechanisms with stronger incentives will be associated with higher costs of capital for the regulated firm. In that sense, regulation may have to be softer for inducing investments the stronger the incentives the regulation provides. The empirical and theoretical literature suggests that, initially, the move from rate-of-return regulation to incentive regulation or from state-owned (unregulated) to privatised incentive-regulated enterprises involved quite soft regulation. This happened both because of inexperience and cautiousness of the regulators, who are highly afraid of service interruptions, and because of large potentials for efficiency improvements. After some time, this cautiousness and potential productivity improvements wear out so that regulation becomes tighter. That may be the reason why Greenstein et al. (1995) and Ai and Sappington (2002) found positive relationships between the introduction of incentive regulation and investment. It may also be the reason why incumbents today complain about the lack of investment incentives. This would suggest a return to 'softer' regulation.

LONG-TERM INVESTMENT AND VARIABLE COMMITMENT

A Two-Period Framework

The importance of commitment for incentive regulation is emphasized in the literature. In particular, Laffont and Tirole's (1993) long treatise of incentive regulation provides for extensive analysis of conflicts between the strength of incentives and the strength of commitment.[22] Under lack of commitment productivity gains from incentives would be punished by tighter incentives, which leave the firm with less profits. Knowing or expecting this, firms would refrain from productivity improvements. In principle, the same holds for investments that lead to cost reductions or are sunk. Thus, commitment appears to be valuable.[23]

However, there is a widespread inability to commit. Regulators face legal constraints on commitment. Changes in regulatory personnel hinder personal commitments by previous regulators. There is an impossibility to write complete regulatory contracts.[24]

Commitment can be good for investment to the extent that it provides a reliable basis for the investment decisions and overcomes dynamic inconsistency of the regulators. It also prevents any ex-post regulatory bias against profits. This is particularly relevant for infrastructure innovations with their potential for high profits or high losses.

At the same time, it can often be suboptimal to exercise commitment. Flexibility may be highly valuable in a changing environment. This not only holds for learning from mistakes but also for the inability under commitment to adapt to new situations.

The effects of a lack of commitment depend on the political/legal environment ('institutional endowment'). In a culture of symmetric fairness, regulated firms may be shielded against large losses even if there is no commitment. In particular, the lack of commitment can deal with unexpected technological/market changes and can correct mistakes.

As a result, commitment needs balancing with sensible flexibility/incentives (Levy and Spiller, 1996). The ability to achieve that is the strength of due process (the US approach). Due process rules themselves can be quite stable, depending on a country's legal traditions. At the same time, they allow for flexibility but generally make it hard to implement sudden policy changes.

In general, the longer the time horizon of a regulatory decision the less regulators can commit. Infrastructure investments have long lead times and long lives. As a result, full regulatory commitment for the time horizon of an investment is not possible. A general result of the literature on Bayesian incentive regulation is that the less the regulator can commit to incentives (and the associated profits and losses) the weaker should incentives be. The compatibility of incentive regulation and efficient investment is therefore in doubt.

Based on this insight a two-period framework is proposed (based on Vogelsang, 2006), distinguishing a short period and a long period.

The short period typically coincides with the length of a regulatory lag, or of (RPI-X)-type adjustments or adjustments from profit-sharing. During a short period, the firm makes and executes decisions on operations, repairs and maintenance costs. For the time of a short period, full regulatory commitment and steep incentives for cost reductions are feasible.

The long (commitment) period corresponds to the time for revisions of (RPI-X)-adjustments and of incentive mechanisms at the end of each long period. It could also correspond to the length of long-term contracts. Almost full commitment to incentives is feasible inside a long period. However, beyond the long period such commitment is generally not feasible.

Infrastructure investments go beyond several long periods so that only very basic regulatory commitment is possible for the time horizon of such investments. Consequently, little or no cost-reducing regulatory incentives are feasible over the time period relevant for infrastructure investment.

How is the above discussion of the tightness of regulation affected by the two-period framework? First, too soft regulation is likely to lead to excess profits over time. Since such profits tend to be unacceptable to the public and hence to regulators, they reduce the length of the commitment period. Second, conversely, too tight regulation is likely to lead to losses over time. Since losses are also unacceptable to regulators, they also reduce the length of the commitment period. In contrast to both, intermediate regulation is less likely to lead to either excessive profits or excessive losses and is therefore more likely to be viable for longer than either soft or tight regulation. As a consequence, intermediate regulation enhances the commitment power and investment incentives. Intermediate regulation is compatible with short-term incentive regulation and extends the length of the short period. However, how can regulators commit to 'intermediate regulation' in the first place?

The following considers several approaches to intermediate regulation with some commitment power.

A Variant of Rate-of-Return Regulation

In the US rate-of-return regulation has provided strong commitment for many decades and was generally associated with an allowed rate of return ≥ cost of capital (Evans and Garber, 1988).[25] In practice, rate-of-return regulation (intermediate to soft regulation) has been combined with a used-and-useful criterion for including assets in the rate base. This may counter any Averch-Johnson type overcapitalization tendencies. As mentioned above, according to Gilbert and Newbery (1994) it provides for an efficient approach to investing. At the same time, in the US, rate-of-return regulation represents a credible commitment because of Supreme Court decisions ('Hope'). And the used-and-useful criterion has been subject to extensive court review there. It may, however, introduce new regulatory uncertainties that could reduce investment incentives / increase the cost of capital (Baumol and Sidak, 2002; Égert, 2009).[26] State-of-the-art cost models may reduce this uncertainty but increase the costs and (initially) time lag due to regulation.

How can the rate-of-return regulation with used-and-useful criterion be combined with incentive regulation for cost reduction (and efficient pricing)? Price-cap regulation has been described as rate-of-return regulation with a pre-specified, long regulatory lag (Liston, 1993). Using this insight, rate-of-return regulation only needs to be applied at RPI-X updates.[27] This provides for some incentives and flexibility. Investment risks can further be reduced through the use of historic cost standards (Égert, 2009). Further downward flexibility through price caps could reduce any inefficiencies stemming from out-of-date historic costs.

While at first blush this suggestion appears to be tailor-made for the US only, it has to be kept in mind that current updates of price-cap regulation outside the US also rely very heavily on rate-of-return criteria (in the form of actual and permissible WACC).

Infrastructure Sharing and Long-Term Contracts

Two approaches for facilitating bottleneck infrastructure investments that are associated with some commitment are infrastructure sharing and long-term contracts (for access or unbundled network elements) between incumbent and alternative competitors. In both cases, the investment risk is shared between incumbent and alternative competitors. The basic question in these cases is, to what extent does the type of regulation of infrastructure access change the overall risk of innovative infrastructure investments (rather than only its distribution)? Is some version of the Modigliani-Miller theorem applicable here?

Infrastructure sharing between incumbent and access seekers can take the form of joint ownership so that infrastructure sharing commitments can cover the investment period. In this case, there is genuine risk sharing ex-ante. Additionally, there are real effects because the infrastructure sharing reduces ex-ante (first-mover) competition and affects competition ex-post (which can be softer or fiercer, see Ilic et al., 2009). Infrastructure sharing involves complex, long-term transactions with monitoring and collusion problems.

Long-term contracts (ex-ante) between incumbent and access seekers move away from the customary mandated short-term access, which provides a risk-free option for access seekers (Hausman, 1997; Pindyck, 2007). In contrast, long-term contracts would be desirable and there should be a surcharge for short-term access that equals the value of the option. From a commitment perspective and because they tend to be incomplete, long-term supply contracts probably cannot cover the entire investment period.

Repair Models for Insufficient Investments under Regulation

There exist a number of repair models for insufficient investments under regulation. They have in common that they only cover specific types of investment or that they apply only to specific industries.[28]

Widespread universal service subsidies in telecommunications, now under discussion for broadband access, typically have one part of an industry or class of consumers subsidize another. Most such mechanisms introduce some allocative inefficiency in the course of financing, e.g., rural infrastructure. Public subsidies are the source of 2009 stimulus packages for broadband access in several countries.[29]

Regulators have extorted investment commitment by regulated telecommunications carriers in exchange for favourable regulation, for example, in New York state around 1990.

Generation resource adequacy regulation is introduced in several US states to compensate investment disincentives from regulated electricity generation spot pricing.[30]

It appears that repair models for lack of investment can be most appropriate if the output produced with such investments has strong public goods properties and therefore cannot efficiently be sold in markets (like, e.g., electricity reliability). They may also be called for if quality of service is jeopardized by incentive regulation. As Kwoka (2009) points out, quality may involve costs that were not contemplated in incentive regulation.

REGULATION AND ORDINARY INVESTMENTS VERSUS INNOVATIVE INVESTMENTS

Regulation versus Competition Policy

The next section contrasts the effects of regulation on ordinary investments versus on innovative (infrastructure) investments, which are particularly relevant for the telecommunications sector.[31]

Ordinary investments concern maintenance, replacement or expansion of legacy infrastructure. From a regulatory perspective, they are characterized by fairly well known costs and well known demands so that (analytical) cost models developed in the past could be fully applicable. Nevertheless, some problems of sunk costs remain so that a surcharge for real options may need to be added to the WACC. Unbundling and competitive network access is feasible (e.g., in telecommunications), leading to sufficient downstream competition and downstream deregulation.

In contrast, innovative investments concern new types of infrastructure. The costs are little known and highly uncertain. Because they are usually also associated with new end-user products (at least in telecommunications) their demand is hard to assess and there is a risk of low penetration and capacity utilization. Initially, there will be high average costs based on the large sunk costs of getting the incumbent started. Penetration pricing below costs can help the start but may be hard to distinguish from foreclosure and predation. Unbundling and access regulation are inherently difficult because of the lack of experience with the new technology (Faulhaber, 2003). At the same time, innovative infrastructure is more likely a case of symmetry in starting positions between incumbent and other market players so that a possible race for investment could ensue.

The question arising from all of this is if innovative investments should be a case for deregulation (or for lack of regulation to begin with). This begs the further question how the decision between regulation and no regulation should be made. Since the regulation in question is based on bottleneck/essential facilities properties and therefore market power, deregulation or no regulation means that the particular market would be governed solely by competition policy. From a normative perspective, deregulation is therefore appropriate if competition policy (alone) is providing a higher level of welfare than regulation (with or without additional competition policy).

The decision between regulation and competition policy requires a comparative evaluation in solving the (bottleneck) problem at hand. This in turn requires an assessment of the main properties of regulation and competition policy. Table 4.3 provides the characteristic properties of regulation with their advantages and drawbacks.[32] All three specific characteristics (ex-ante remedies, specialized agency and prescriptive intervention) tend to lead to strong and preventative interventions that can potentially prevent large damages from anti-competitive behaviour. At the same time, those characteristics reduce the freedom of the incumbent to compete and discover new possibilities.

Table 4.3 Properties of regulation

Properties of regulation	Advantages	Drawbacks
Ex-ante remedies	Immediacy, precision, dependability, prevention	Reduction of freedom to compete, too much intervention
Specialized agency	Specialized knowledge, speed of intervention	Influence of interest groups, (too little or) too much intervention
Prescriptive intervention (affirmative duties) Pricing Quality	Strong influence on desired behaviour, precision	Reduction of freedom to compete, inefficient prescriptions because of asymmetric information; too much intervention

The contrasting characteristics of general competition law are named in Column 1 (Table 4.4). The requirement to show a violation before action is taken makes competition law (alone) inappropriate if violations: (a) result in large, irreparable damages; (b) are hard to prove; and (c) they occur frequently and repeatedly.

In principle, competition law could remain appropriate even under such circumstances if penalties and compensation payments for violations were large enough to prevent such violations and damages (Shavell, 1984). In practice, penalties and compensations are limited and uncertain and therefore insufficient to prevent such violations and damages. Competition policy remedies can also be insufficiently tailored to pricing situations and quality-related violations and can be hard to maintain over time. These properties largely disqualify sole reliance on competition law in situations where incumbents own monopolistic bottlenecks that cannot reasonably be duplicated by alternative competitors and that are necessary for competing in the end-user markets served by the bottlenecks.

As Tables 4.3 and 4.4 show the choice between sector-specific regulation and general competition policy always involves tradeoffs. These tradeoffs may be strongly affected if investments by an incumbent involve technological change. In particular, the advantages of regulation and disadvantages of competition policy will become less relevant if the alternative under regulation is no or insufficient innovation.

There are two arguments for deregulation of or regulatory holidays for innovative infrastructure. First, the patent argument states that you get more innovation from the additional freedom and lack of profit constraint provided by an extended period of no regulation, and that this additional innovation is more valuable than the potential deadweight loss from monopoly pricing. Second, the error argument states that regulation of innovative infrastructure is inherently more complicated than regulation of legacy infrastructure. Also, potential benefits from innovation are much higher than benefits from regulation. The error from false and distorting regulation is therefore more likely and more severe than in the case of legacy infrastructure. These arguments do not mean that the potential for innovation automatically calls for the absence of regulation.[33] However, the cards would be more heavily stacked against regulation the more important innovation becomes.

Table 4.4 Inappropriateness of general competition law

Property of competition law	Competition law inappropriate if ...	Relevant for ...
Requirement to show violation	Large, irreparable damages (compensated by large penalties?) Difficult to prove abuses, e.g. Denial of access hidden by slowing down negotiations Frequent and repeated abuses	Access to monopolistic bottlenecks Predation against competitors
Inability to set prices	Lack of comparable markets Economies of scale and scope Long duration of intervention in a changing environment	Access to monopolistic bottlenecks Market dominance in access market Monopoly in end-user market
Inability of supervision	Considerable information requirements Continuous supervision requirements	Access requirements Price regulation

Thus, how can one distinguish ordinary from innovative investments? One potentially workable approach is the notion of 'emerging markets' under the EU communications framework. This notion is based on the property that 'the three-criteria test cannot be applied'. The three-criteria test stipulates that a dominant firm in a market defined by competition law criteria should be regulated if: (a) there are high and stable barriers to entry; (b) competition is not expected to increase in the foreseeable future; and (c) the first two market failures cannot be adequately dealt with through competition policy instruments. These last three criteria have to be met cumulatively (i.e., all have to hold together). The non-applicability of the three criteria test essentially means that either a market cannot (yet) be defined for the product in question or that one cannot measure if there are high and enduring entry barriers or if competition is likely to be effective or if competition policy could effectively deal with those entry barriers or lack of competition. This notion of emerging markets takes an extremely narrow view of innovations and, to the best of the author's knowledge, has as of yet not shown any innovation to qualify as an emerging market. A weaker concept might be the creation of a new market in the competition policy sense.

Regulatory Holidays

Regulatory holidays are a wait-and-see approach, under which regulation only begins with a lag after conditions for regulation (regulatory requirement) have been met.[34] Gans and King (2002 and 2003) establish conditions under which access holidays can increase investment incentives for innovative infrastructure. The lag before regulation sets in can be viewed as a short period, for which commitment is feasible. In that case, the holiday is unlikely to be long enough for financing large sunk investments. Baake et al. (2005) therefore describe a scheme for establishing a longer regulatory holiday. At the same time, a commitment to such a long holiday for, say, 10-15 years may not really be credible. However, breaking this kind of commitment and installing regulation may itself take time so that the 'long period' in this case is likely to be longer than ordinary long periods.

Unless they provide an incumbent with an insurmountable lead, regulatory holidays could be combined with intermediate regulation (based on the rate-of-return regulation variety discussed in the previous section) after the holidays expire. A combination of intermediate regulation with regulatory holidays could then spur investment.

A major problem of regulatory holidays is that verifiable standards are needed to determine under which conditions regulatory holidays would be warranted. An example could be the very narrow definition of innovation under the EU approach, i.e., the non-applicability of the EU communications framework three-criteria test mentioned above. A somewhat wider criterion would be the creation of a new market, independent of the applicability of the three-criteria test. However, defining a new market poses itself severe difficulties, because the hypothetical monopoly test is usually hard to adapt to this case (Gual, 2003).

Stronger than regulatory holidays is full and therefore (initially) unlimited deregulation of innovations and particularly risky infrastructure investments. The problem in both cases is that of finding criteria for such deregulation, which would have to be at least as strict as those for a regulatory holiday.[35] Deregulation does not necessarily include a credible commitment against re-regulation. However, a long lag is likely before re-regulation becomes feasible. The FCC has some discretion of regulatory forbearance under the US Telecommunications Act of 1996. It can refrain from regulation that reduces investment incentives. An example has been the lifting of unbundling requirements for the UNE-P (Platform of unbundled network elements) in 2004. In contrast to regulatory forbearance the FCC can actually exercise deregulation as a more credible commitment. This option has been exercised by the FCC for new fibre lines and it is claimed by proponents to have increased fibre deployment.

Some countries have sunset clauses, under which regulation would end after a pre-specified period of time. However, for example in Canada, they have raised commitment issues through extension of the sunset period (Beaudry, 2010).

CONCLUDING REMARKS

This chapter takes a fairly general rather than case-specific approach to the relationship between regulation and investment. Nevertheless, the regulator will have to determine if investment problems and/or innovations play a major role in the particular industry. If that is the case then there are two main regulatory concerns for investment/innovation. They are uncertainty and the lack of regulatory commitment over the long time horizon associated with investment.

Uncertainty leads to the truncation issue and thereby to an asymmetric error distribution that favours intermediate over tight and soft regulation. The regulatory commitment problem also favours intermediate regulation. In addition, it favours a regulatory review cycle with true-ups based on actual costs and based on rate-of-return criteria. Genuine innovations should not be regulated. However, strict and verifiable standards are needed for deregulation and for regulatory holidays based on the 'innovation' argument. Under weaker criteria innovative infrastructure should be regulated lightly.

ACKNOWLEDGEMENT

The author would like to thank John Kwoka for insightful comments.

NOTES

1. On December 3, 2009, the German § 9a TKG, effective February 24, 2007, was declared incompatible with European Community law by the Court of Justice of the European Communities.
2. The survey by Sappington (2005a) on regulation of service quality cites mixed results from the empirical literature, but is itself largely restricted to theoretical findings.
3. For reviews of the literature on regulation and investment see Guthrie (2006) and, specifically for the case of broadband investment, Cambini and Jiang (2009).
4. Cambini and Jiang (2009) have only found two papers on end-user regulation and telecommunications infrastructure investment (Greenstein et al., 1995; Ai and Sappington, 2002). In contrast, they list 23 works on access regulation and infrastructure investment,

but quite a few of these are either not really empirical (simulations and numerical examples) or financed by incumbents or organizations of alternative competitors. Cambini and Jiang note that 'the lack of reasonable time-series data weakens the robustness of empirical analysis'.

5. In addition, Weisman (2005) considers the relationship of profit-sharing regulation with investments in quality.
6. Compatible with this are the results of Cambini and Rondi (forthcoming) for European energy utilities, who find more investment under price caps than under rate-of-return regulation.
7. 2-way interconnection regulation is omitted here, which seems to be restricted to telecommunications. This neglects, in particular, the termination monopoly issue. See Vogelsang (2003).
8. TELRIC stands for 'Total Element Long-Run Incremental Cost', while LRAIC stands for 'Long-Run Average Incremental Cost'. Both of these are usually measured in analytical cost models and are therefore independent of the firm's actual costs. While in addition price caps, benchmarking and the efficient component pricing rule (ECPR) have been used or suggested for bottleneck pricing, there appears to be little specific literature linking them to investment.
9. Mandy and Sharkey (2003) provide correction factors for the use of current equipment values when TELRIC/LRAIC is recomputed at shorter intervals than investment lives.
10. Avenali et al. (2010), in what appears to be the first theoretical model of the ladder-of-investment hypothesis, show that under their assumptions the Bourreau and Doğan assessment of the ladder-of-investment approach and of sunset clauses would not hold.
11. FTTH stands for 'Fiber To The Home', while VDSL stands for 'Very-High-Data-Rate Digital Subscriber Line' and can usually be seen as 'Fiber To The Neighborhood'.
12. The empirical literature on this subject appears to be fairly blind to subtle aspects of this approach. If, for example, Hazlett and Bazelon (2005) find that low UNE-P rates in the US are associated with a decrease in CLEC-owned telephone lines that does not contradict the ladder-of-investment approach. Because a large part of the network elements covered by UNE-P are clearly replicable they should actually be priced highly to spur CLEC investment. In contrast, unbundled loops should be priced low. UNE-P stands for the platform of unbundled network elements that allow entrants to offer network services almost without having any own network infrastructure.
13. There are two distinct methodological approaches to incentive regulation, the Bayesian and non-Bayesian approaches. The non-Bayesian approach to price regulation goes back to Baumol (1968, 1982), Vogelsang and Finsinger (1979) and Littlechild (1983). It is based on the aims for welfare improvement, not optimization. It is geared for application, but investments have generally not been addressed explicitly in this literature. In contrast, the Bayesian approach, initiated by Baron and Myerson (1982) and Laffont and Tirole (1986) uses a principal-agent framework that allows for full-constrained welfare optimization. It is in general not directly applicable, but addresses investment incentives via commitment. The qualitative insights of this approach are usable for the non-Bayesian approach taken in this paper. For penetrating surveys of the Bayesian approach see Laffont and Tirole (1993) and Armstrong and Sappington (2007), who also survey non-Bayesian mechanisms. For a critique, see Vogelsang (2006).
14. This simple analysis has not considered any interactions between bottleneck regulation and end-user regulation.
15. It is assumed throughout that firms are maximizing profits and therefore fully respond to incentives instead of incurring X-inefficiency.
16. This is the opposite of the sharing studied in Panteghini and Scarpa (2003) and Moretto et al. (2008), which led to underinvestment.
17. The strongest empirical evidence for this hypothesis is Cambini and Rondi (forthcoming), who find (while controlling for endogeneity of the tightness of regulation) that infrastructure investments in European electric and gas utilities decrease in the X-factor

used for deriving price caps and that investments increase in the WACC used for rate-of-return regulation.

18. The commitment problem is treated extensively below.
19. Non-abusive prices include normal (workably-competitive) mark-ups on the firm's actual costs (rather than prices equal efficient costs).
20. Another concern for investment incentives of the incumbent could come from spillover effects of the incumbent's investment on the demand for entrants' services. Technology upgrades, from which entrants would benefit, would fall under such spillovers. Kotakorpi (2006) argues those incumbents' investments in infrastructure with such demand spillovers to entrants would only be efficient if the incumbent can earn as much from selling access as from selling downstream. This would suggest using the ECPR but may, at the same time, favour some downstream regulation.
21. Risk may also have increased through other aspects of regulatory restructuring, such as vertical separation or pro-competitive policies (Kwoka, 2009).
22. For other relevant work see Baron and Besanko (1987), Gilbert and Newbery (1994) and Levy and Spiller (1996).
23. Commitment appears to be particularly valuable, when it comes to investments. Innovations not based on investments but rather on learning by doing may be achievable without commitment. See Lewis and Yildirim (2002).
24. A lack of commitment can be exogenous, reflecting a change in outside variables, such as inflation or political elections. It can also be endogenous, reflecting a change in regulatory variables, such as profit or investments (Grajek and Röller, 2009).
25. See, however, Joskow and MacAvoy (1975), for a period, where electricity rates were not cost covering.
26. Égert (2009) also points out that the regulated firm may choose projects that will have a lower variance of expected outcomes if the investments will be judged with ex-post information.
27. Similarly, it can be applied to other incentive-regulation updates, such as new profit-sharing formulas or benchmark updates.
28. Kwoka (2009) discusses several approaches in this area.
29. For the contrasting effects of fiscal versus regulatory measures see Bauer (2009).
30. For an extensive critique and literature review of generation adequacy, see Roques (2008).
31. Kwoka, in a mail to the author, points out that the quality may be more important than innovation for the functioning of incentive regulation. Both quality and innovation appear to be problems that incentive regulation cannot easily deal with. For innovation the question is if deregulation is called for or if WACC adjustments suffice. For quality the question is if incentive regulation of prices has to be complemented by specific quality regulation. For more on the latter see Kwoka (2009).
32. This and the following table are adapted from Holznagel and Vogelsang (2009).
33. Competition policy has to deal with its own potential error costs. For the case of innovations, see Manne and Wright (2009).
34. During a discussion in Peru on regulatory holidays the chief regulator of Osiptel, Guillermo Thornberry, asked the author: What is that? I have not had a holiday in 2 ½ years!
35. Of course, the usual criteria for deregulation, which were established for legacy markets, would continue to hold for innovative markets. This would include the non-fulfilment of the three-criteria test to the extent that it can be measured.

REFERENCES

Ai, C. and Sappington, D. (2002), 'The Impact of State Incentive Regulation on the US Telecommunications Industry', *Journal of Regulatory Economics,* **22**, 133–60.

Armstrong, M. and Sappington, D. (2006), 'Regulation, Competition and Liberalization', *Journal of Economic Literature,* **44**, 325–66.
Armstrong, M. and Sappington, D. (2007), 'Recent Developments in the Theory of Regulation', in Armstrong, M. and Porter, R. (eds), *Handbook of Industrial Organization* (Volume 3), Amsterdam: North Holland.
Armstrong, M., Cowan, S. and Vickers. J. (1994), *Regulatory Reform – Economic Analysis and British Experience*, Cambridge, Mass., and London: MIT Press.
Avenali, A., Matteucci, G. and Reverberi, P. (2010), 'Dynamic Access Pricing and Incentives to Invest in Alternative Infrastructures', *International Journal of Industrial Organization,* **28**, 167–75.
Averch, H. and Johnson, L. (1962), 'The Behavior of the Firm Under Regulatory Constraint', *American Economic Review*, **52**, 1052–69.
Baake, P., Kamecke, U. and Wey, C. (2005), 'A Regulatory Framework for New and Emerging Markets: Dynamic Solutions to Policy Failures', *Communications & Strategies,* **60**, 123–36.
Bailey, E. and Coleman, R. (1971), 'The Effect of Lagged Regulation in an Averch-Johnson Model', *Bell Journal of Economics and Management Science,* **2**, 278–92.
Banerjee, A. (2003), 'Does Incentive Regulation "Cause" Degradation of Retail Telephone Service Quality?', *Information Economics and Policy,* **15**, 243–69.
Baron, P. and Besanko, D. (1987), 'Commitment and Fairness in a Dynamic Regulatory Relationship', *Review of Economic Studies,* **54**, 413–36.
Baron, P. and Myerson, R. (1982), 'Regulating a Monopolist with Unknown Costs', *Econometrica,* **50**, 911–30.
Bauer, M. (2009), 'Regulation, Public Policy, and Investment in Communications Infrastructure', SSRN Working Paper. Retrieved from: http://papers.ssrn.com/sol3/papers. cfm?abstract_id=1339043.
Baumol, J. (1968), 'Reasonable Rules for Rate Regulation: Plausible Polices for an Imperfect World', in Phillips, A. and Williamson, O. (eds), *Prices: Issues in Theory, Practice, and Public Policy*, Philadelphia: University of Pennsylvania Press, 101–23.
Baumol, J. (1982), 'Productivity Adjustment Clauses and Rate Adjustment for Inflation', *Public Utilities Fortnightly*, **110**, 11–18.
Baumol, J. and Klevorick, A. (1970), 'Input Choices and Rate-of-Return Regulation: An Overview of The Discussion', *Bell Journal of Economics and Management Science,* **1**, 162–90.
Baumol, J. and Sidak, J. (2002), 'The Pig in the Python: Is Lumpy Capacity Investment Used and Useful?', *Energy Law Journal,* **23**, 383–458.
Bawa, S. and Sibley, D. (1980), 'Dynamic Behavior of a Firm Subject to Stochastic Regulatory Review', *International Economic Review,* **21**, 627–42.
Beaudry, P. (2010), 'Wireline deregulation: The Canadian experience', *Telecommunications Policy*, **34**, 606–15.
Biglaiser, G. and Riordan, M. (2000), 'Dynamics of Price Regulation', *RAND Journal of Economics*, **31**, 744–67.
Borrmann, J. and Brunekreeft, G. (2009), 'The Effect of Monopoly Regulation on the Timing of Investment', Bremen Energy Working Papers No. 01, Bremer Energie Institut.
Bourreau, M. and Doğan, P. (2004), 'Service-Based versus Facilities-Based Competition in Local Access Networks', *Information Economics and Policy,* **16**, 287–306.

Bourreau, M. and Doğan, P. (2005), 'Unbundling the Local Loop', *European Economic Review,* **49**, 173–99.

Bourreau, M. and Doğan, P. (2006), 'Build-or-Buy Strategies in the Local Loop', *American Economic Review,* **96**, 72–6.

Brito, D., Pereira, P. and Vareda, J. (2008), 'Can Two-Part Tariffs Promote Efficient Investment on Next Generation Networks?', Working Paper 34, Portuguese Competition Authority.

Cabral, L. and Riordan, M. (1989), 'Incentives for Cost Reduction under Price Cap Regulation,' *Journal of Regulatory Economics,* **1**, 93–102.

Cambini, C. and Jiang, Y. (2009), 'Broadband Investment and Regulation: A Literature Review', *Telecommunications Policy,* **33**, 559–74.

Cambini, C. and Rondi, L. (2010), 'Incentive Regulation and Investment: Evidence from European Energy Utilities', *Journal of Regulatory Economics*, **38**, 1–26.

Cave, M. (2006), 'Encouraging Infrastructure Investment via the Ladder of Investment', *Telecommunications Policy,* **30**, 223–37.

Cave, M. and Vogelsang, I. (2003), 'How Access Pricing and Entry Interact', *Telecommunications Policy,* **27**, 717–27.

Comacho, T. and Menezes, M. (2009), 'Access Pricing and Investment: A Real Options Approach', *Journal of Regulatory Economics,* **36**, 107–26.

Dobbs, I. (2004), 'Intertemporal Price Cap Regulation under Uncertainty', *Economic Journal*, **114**, 421–40.

Égert, B. (2009), 'Infrastructure Investment in Network Industries: The Role of Incentive Regulation and Regulatory Independence', Working Paper No. 688, OECD Economics Department.

Evans, J., Levine, P. and Trillas, F. (2008), 'Lobbies, Delegation and the Under-Investment Problem in Regulation', *International Journal of Industrial Organization,* **26**, 17–40.

Evans, T. and Garber, S. (1988), 'Public Utility Regulators are Only Human: A Positive Theory of Regulatory Constraints,' *American Economic Review,* **78**, 444–62.

Evans, T. and Guthrie, G. (2005), 'Risk, Price Regulation, and Irreversible Investment', *International Journal of Industrial Organization,* **23**, 109–28.

Evans, T. and Guthrie, G. (2006), 'Incentive Regulation of Prices when Costs are Sunk', *Journal of Regulatory Economics,* **29**, 239–64.

Faulhaber, R. (2003), 'Policy-Induced Competition: The Telecommunications Experiments', *Information Economics and Policy,* **15**, 73–97.

Gans, J. (2001), 'Regulating Private Infrastructure Investments: Optimal Pricing for Access to Essential Facilities', *Journal of Regulatory Economics,* **20**, 167–89.

Gans, J. and King, S. (2002), 'Access Holidays and the Timing of Infrastructure Investment', Working Paper No. 2002-14, Melbourne Business School. Retrieved from: http://ssrn.com/sol3/papers.cfm?abstract_id=361500.

Gans, J. and King, S. (2003), 'Access Holidays for Network Infrastructure Investment', *Agenda,* **10**, 163–78.

Gilbert, R. and Newbery, D. (1994), 'The Dynamic Efficiency of Regulatory Constitutions', *RAND Journal of Economics,* **25**, 538–54.

Grajek, M. and Röller, L. (2009), 'The Effect of Regulation on Investment in Network Industries: Evidence from European Telecoms', Working Paper 09-004, ESMT. Retrieved from: http://papers.ssrn.com/sol3/papers.cfm?abstract_id=14486 66.

Greenstein, S., McMaster, Y. and Spiller, P. (1995), 'The Effect of Incentive Regulation on Infrastructure Modernization: Local Exchange Companies' Deployment Of Digital Technology', *Journal of Economics & Management Strategy,* **4**, 187–236.

Gual, J. (2003), 'Market Definition in the Telecoms Industry', Discussion Paper Series No. 3988, Centre for Economic Policy Research. Retrieved from: http://www.iese.edu/research/pdfs/DI-0517-E.pdf.

Guthrie, G. (2006), 'Regulating Infrastructure: The Impact on Risk and Investment', *Journal of Economic Literature,* **44**, 925–72.

Haucap, J., Heimeshoff, U. and Uhde, A. (2007), 'Credible Threats as an Instrument of Regulation for Network Industries', in Welfens, P. and Weske, M. (eds), *Digital Economic Dynamics Innovations, Networks and Regulations*, Berlin: Springer Verlag, 171–202.

Hausman, J. (1997), 'Valuing the Effect of Regulation on New Services in Telecommunications', *Brookings Papers on Economic Activity. Microeconomics, 1997*, 1–54.

Hazlett W. and Bazelon, C. (2005), 'Regulated Unbundling of Telecommunications Networks: A Stepping Stone to Facilities-Based Competition?', presented at the Telecommunications Policy Research Conference, September 23-25. Retrieved from: http://mason.gmu.edu/~thazlett/pubs/Stepping%20Stone%20TPRC.10.04.05 %20.pdf.

Holznagel, B. and Vogelsang, I. (2009), 'Weiterentwicklung der TK-Regulierung im Lichte neuer Herausforderungen und ökonomischer Erkenntnisse', in J. Haucap and J. Kuehling (eds), *Effiziente Rahmenbedingungen für Telekommunikations-märkte in der Zukunft: Kartellrecht, Netzneutralität und Preis-Kosten-Scheren*, Baden-Baden: Nomos Verlag, 13–114.

Hori, K. and Mizuno, K. (2006), 'Access Pricing and Investment with Stochastically Growing Demand', *International Journal of Industrial Organization,* **24**, 795–808.

Hori, K. and Mizuno, K. (2009), 'Competition Schemes and Investment in Network Infrastructure under Uncertainty', *Journal of Regulatory Economics,* **35**, 179–200.

Ilic, D., Neumann, K. and Plückebaum, T. (2009), 'The Economics of Next Generation Access – Addendum', WIK-Consult GmbH. Retrieved from: http://www.wik.org/content/ecta_study_addendum_2009.pdf.

Joskow, L. and MacAvoy, P. (1975), 'Regulation and the Financial Conditions of the Electric Power Companies in the 1970s', *American Economic Review,* **65**, 295–311.

Kotakorpi, K. (2006), 'Access Price Regulation, Investment and Entry in Telecommunications', *International Journal of Industrial Organization,* **24**, 1013–20.

Kwoka, J. (2009), 'Investment Adequacy under Incentive Regulation', Working paper, Northeastern University.

Laffont, J. and Tirole, J. (1986), 'Using Cost Observation to Regulate Firms', *Journal of Political Economy,* **94**, 614–41.

Laffont, J. and Tirole, J. (1993), *A Theory of Incentives in Procurement and Regulation*, Cambridge, MA: MIT Press.

Levy, B. and Spiller, P. (eds) (1996), *Regulation, Institutions, and Commitment*, Cambridge: Cambridge University Press.

Lewis, T. and Yildirim, H. (2002), 'Learning by Doing and Dynamic Regulation', *RAND Journal of Economics,* **33**, 22–36.

Liston, C. (1993), 'Price-Cap versus Rate-of-Return Regulation', *Journal of Regulatory Economics,* **5**, 25–48.
Littlechild, S. (1983), *Regulation of British Telecommunications' Profitability*, Report to the Secretary of State, Department of Industry, London: Her Majesty's Stationery Office.
Mandy, D. (2009), 'Pricing Inputs to Induce Efficient Make-or-Buy Decisions', *Journal of Regulatory Economics,* **36**, 29–43.
Mandy, D. and Sharkey, W. (2003), 'Dynamic Pricing and Investment from Static Proxy Models', *Review of Network Economics,* **2**, 403–39.
Manne, G. and Wright, J. (2009), 'The Limits of Antitrust in the New Economy'. Retrieved from: http://papers.ssrn.com/sol3/papers.cfm?abstract_id=1490849.
Moretto, M., Panteghini, P. and Scarpa, C. (2008), 'Profit Sharing and Investment by Regulated Utilities: A Welfare Analysis', *Review of Financial Economics,* **17**, 315–37.
Nagel, T. and Rammerstorfer, M. (2008), 'Price Regulation and Investment Behavior – How Real Options can Explain Underinvestment', Vienna University of Economics and Business Administration. Retrieved from: http://ssrn.com/abstract =1009123.
Panteghini, P. and Scarpa, C. (2003), 'Irreversible Investment and Regulatory Risk', Working Paper No. 934, CESifo. Retrieved from: http://ssrn.com/abstract=401 581.
Pindyck, R. (2007), 'Mandatory Unbundling and Irreversible Investment in Telecom Networks', *Review of Network Economics,* **6**, 274–98.
Roques, F. (2008), 'Market Design for Generation Adequacy: Healing Causes rather than Symptoms', ERPG Working Paper 0810 & CWPE Working Paper 0821, May. Retrieved from: http://www.eprg.group.cam.ac.uk/wp-content/uploads/ 2008/11/nts0810.pdf.
Roques, F. and Savva, N. (2006), 'Price Cap Regulation and Investment Incentives Under Demand Uncertainty', CWPE 0636 and EPRG 0616 Working Papers, May. Retrieved from: http://www.eprg.group.cam.ac.uk/wp-content/uploads/2008/11/epr g0616.pdf.
Roques, F. and Savva, N. (2009), 'Investment under Uncertainty with Price Ceilings in Oligopolies', *Journal of Economic Dynamics and Control,* **33**, 507–24.
Sappington, D. (2005a), 'Regulating Service Quality: A Survey', *Journal of Regulatory Economics,* **27**, 123–54.
Sappington, D. (2005b), 'On the Irrelevance of Input Prices for Make-or-Buy Decisions', *American Economic Review,* **95**, 1631–38.
Shavell, S. (1984), 'Liability for Harm versus Regulation of Safety', *Journal of Legal Studies*, **13**, 357–74.
Sobel, J. (1999), 'A Reexamination of Yardstick Competition', *Journal of Economics & Management Strategy,* **8**, 33–60.
Vareda, J and Hoernig, S. (2007), 'The Race for Telecoms Infrastructure Investment with Bypass: Can Access Regulation Achieve the First Best?', CEPR Discussion Paper No. DP6203.
Vogelsang, I. (2001), 'Price Regulation for Independent Transmission Companies', *Journal of Regulatory Economics,* **20**, 141–65.
Vogelsang, I. (2002), 'Incentive Regulation and Competition in Public Utility Markets: A 20-Year Perspective', *Journal of Regulatory Economics,* **22**, 5–28.

Vogelsang, I. (2003), 'Price Regulation of Access to Telecommunications Networks?', *Journal of Economic Literature*, **41**, 830–62.
Vogelsang, I. (2006), 'Electricity Transmission Pricing and Performance-Based Regulation', *The Energy Journal,* **27**, 97–126.
Vogelsang, I. and Finsinger, J. (1979), 'A Regulatory Adjustment Process for Optimal Pricing by Multiproduct Monopoly Firms', *Bell Journal of Economics,* **10**, 157–71.
Weisman, D. (2005), 'Price Regulation and Quality', *Information Economics and Policy,* **17**, 165–74.

5. Policy and regulation for next generation networks

Martin Cave

INTRODUCTION

For over 100 years fixed telecommunications networks have relied on copper to deliver calls to customers' premises. This imposed a limit on capacity, which hardly bit in the days when voice calls were the only traffic. Now is a different world, where (predominantly) data traffic is mingled with voice. Increasingly the two are indistinguishable under IP transmission procedures. As a result, of this change, even the theoretical limits of copper will be breached by the requirements placed on it, particularly by peer-to-peer video transmissions.

As a result, an historic shift is occurring in the telecommunications infrastructure, which extends the replacement of copper with fibre, long ago accomplished within the 'core' inter-exchange network, to the local loop, connecting customers to the network. What is needed is a next generation access network (NGA). It is needed to permit the development of high-speed (superfast) broadband. Current generation broadband has already transformed the communications possibilities of many households. High-speed broadband will accelerate this process. But the effects on production are quite as wide ranging. Broadband is a key general-purpose technology that can transform the operations of business. NGAs increase speeds by an order of magnitude and are easily capable of providing the symmetrical upstream and downstream services which businesses typically want and which current generation broadband is less suited to provide.

Inevitably, what is happening is not as sudden and dramatic as the above account might suggest. First, many consumers already have access to cable networks, based on fibre/co-axial technologies which are already some way towards fibre in capacity. Secondly, some network modernisations will not take the fibre fully to the premises, but will rely on the copper for the last few metres. Thirdly, the process described above may be geographically restricted, take decades, and may still be incomplete. While estimates of the capital cost of building an NGA to pass all homes in the United States (US) or in the European Union (EU) amount to hundreds of billions of US dollars, actual spending on a partial deployment to 2020 is likely to be substantially less, perhaps one tenth of this. Nonetheless, the implications of NGAs for industry structure, the mix of wire-based and wireless service, the regulatory regime and the digital divide have yet to be worked out.

This chapter focuses on the policy and regulatory challenges posed by the introduction of NGAs. Notably in developed countries with ubiquitous networks for the first time in decades government and regulators are not facing operators with fully sunk costs in the most monopolised part of the network, the local loop.[1] Thus their problems have increasing similarity with those faced by regulators of other infrastructures seeking to elicit efficient investment decisions, except that telecommunications have the extra complication, or benefit, of operating in an environment where no element of the value chain is conclusively a natural monopoly. However, a faster pace of technological change entails a greater risk of obsolescence than is present in the case of many infrastructures.

The next section describes the underlying technologies and summarises the spread of current and next generation broadband to date. The following section sets out the regulatory approaches to NGAs being adopted in various jurisdictions. The penultimate section turns to the role of central government in promoting high-speed broadband, as part either of a long-term policy or of a recovery plan. A final section contains conclusions.

BROADBAND TECHNOLOGIES AND THE SPREAD OF BROADBAND

Current and Next Generation Broadband

Broadband is a general-purpose technology providing high-speed transfer of information (voice and data) between fixed and mobile devices, using a wide range of technologies, wireline and wireless. It can support a range of business, household and user services. In particular, when combined with collateral investment in human capital, broadband can transform business processes, leading to different spatial organisation of production, new logistical processes, and new (decentralised) forms of business organisations.

The capability of a broadband service depends on a variety of characteristics of the data transfer: its symmetry (equality of domestic and upstream speeds); latency; and other characteristics. However, the most widely used description is download speeds, in megabits per second (Mbps). Since 1996, this variable has increased by a factor of 10 roughly every four years – implying by extrapolation speeds of 100 Mbps in 2013 (Lewin et al., 2009).

Current generation broadband is provided by a number of wireline and wireless technologies of which the most prominent are copper-based ADSL (asymmetric digital subscriber line), cable and 3G mobile networks.

Panel A of Figure 5.1 shows how ADSL is provided.[2] The end user premises are connected to the line exchange by a copper wire; backhaul takes the data to a core exchange, where access is available via international backbone networks to the World Wide Web (WWW).

Competition has been inserted into this structure by erecting access points for competitors to buy components of the incumbents' networks. In 2008, 44 per cent of retail ADSL connections in the EU were provided by competitors (EC, 2009a). Three main access opportunities are available: (a) the competitor can resell the incumbent product; (b) can connect at the core exchange; or (c) buy bitstream service from the incumbent, including electronic ('active') elements, or install own electronics in the local exchange and rent a 'passive' asset, typically the copper line or unbundled local loop (ULL), from the incumbents. The thrust of regulation within the EU is to promote in particular the last form of access, which maximises the degree of infrastructure competition.

The remaining panels of Figure 5.1 show how this architecture is changed by NGAs. Panel B shows the variant known as fibre to the node (FTTN) or cabinet (i.e., a piece of street furniture connected to say 200 premises rather than, say, the 5,000 connected to the local exchange[3]); the link from the cabinet to the premises continuing to be copper. Panel C illustrates fibre to the home or premises (FTTP). Different variants are available: either a partially shared regime in which 32 or 64 end users share the split ends of a single fibre, or a dedicated fibre to each user.

The choice between FTTN and FTTP is complex. The final copper link imposes a practical speed limit of about 50 Mbps on FTTN; the capacity of FTTP is at least 100 Mbps. This makes FTTN appear a transitional technology. However, the capital cost of FTTP is about five times that of FTTN (ERG, 2009), and moving to FTTP via FTTN is also costly.

In relation to FTTN, the access points are beside sub-loop unbundling, bitstream, and sharing a duct to the sub-loop. In relation to FTTP, the access points are bitstream, a shared fibre, or a shared duct. Note that there is no natural access point at the local exchange, leaving current users of unbundled local copper loops in a dilemma whether to go forward to customers via duct-sharing or sub-loop unbundling, or whether to retreat to bitstream.

While much current discussion implicitly restricts NGAs to be developments of the telecommunications supplier's copper network, this is mistaken. The primitive concept here is the retail service, such as broadband,

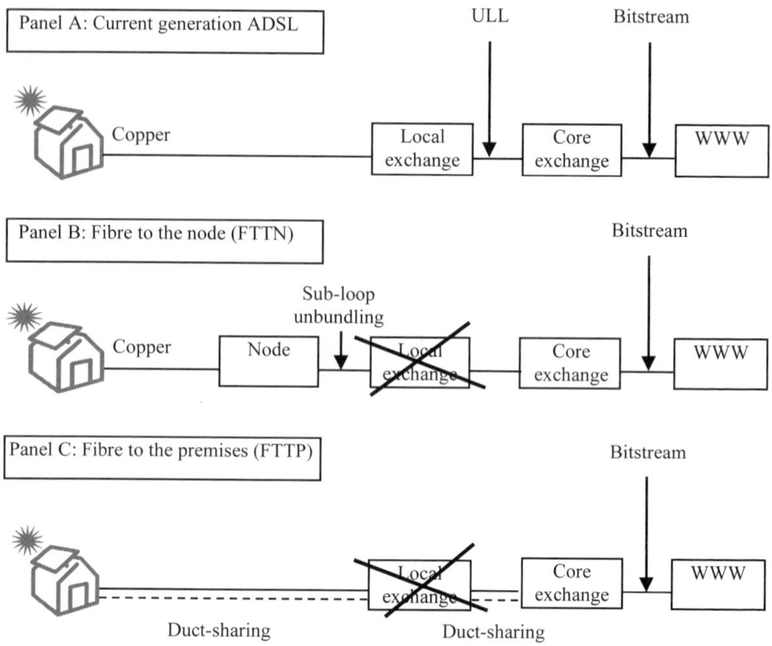

Figure 5.1 *Network architectures*

which end users may require; the demand for wholesale broadband network services flows from this, and any technology that meets that demand should count as an NGA. Upgraded cable networks (using the DOCSIS 3.0 standard) can demonstrably match and exceed the speeds of FTTN, and the services they supply thus fall into the same retail and wholesale market as fibre-based networks. Mobile technologies present a different picture.

The past trajectory of 'fastest commercially available' fixed and mobile technologies suggests the persistence of a ten-fold gap between fixed and mobile speeds, with a lag of about 4 years.[4] If this continues, it is questionable whether a sufficient number of end users, taking all price and non-price characteristics of the services into account, currently regard fixed and mobile high speed broadband as substitutes to place them in the same market. However, these relationships may change over the physical lives of NGAs.

The Spread of Fibre

The main features of adoption of broadband can be captured easily. Table 5.1 shows for a number of countries the number of fixed and fixed wireless broadband subscribers per 100 inhabitants in December 2009, together with the number of fibre subscribers.[5, 6]

The most notable features of these data are the relatively good performance of certain European countries, the middling performance of the US, which is the cause of considerable national angst, and, most important for current purposes, the very large variation in the speed of fibre, with Korea and Japan considerably in advance of the best European performer.

Table 5.1 Fixed and fixed wireless broadband subscribers per 100 persons

	Total	Fibre
Denmark	37.5	4.2
Netherlands	37.1	0.8
Korea	33.5	16.4
Sweden	32.4	7.4
France	30.4	0.1
Germany	30.4	0.2
UK	29.5	0.0
US	26.9	1.3
Japan	24.8	13.5
Australia	24.3	0.0
OECD	23.3	2.6

Source: OECD (2010).

Data on mobile broadband are less readily available.[7] At the start of 2009, there were 5.2 dedicated data service cards/modems/keys per 100 inhabitants of the EU, compared with 24.8 fixed broadband subscriptions per 100 (EC 2010, p. 3-4).

REGULATION

Investment in NGAs

This section discusses how regulators deal with NGAs. It does so primarily within the context of the European regulatory regime. The EU contains areas where cable networks currently compete with telecommunications operators and others where there is a single fixed network. The diffusion within the EU is very limited, except in Sweden. Both casual observation and preliminary econometric work suggest that competitive dynamics in some areas appear to lead to a race to deploy NGAs. In other areas, including those that lack a cable or other infrastructure-based competitor using an earlier technology than fibre, deployment is slow or non-existent.

Underlying this is a key difference in the application of NPV methods to appraise investment in monopoly and competitive environments. In a monopoly, replacement of an existing technology is governed by the condition that additional costs (fixed and variable) of the new technology must be less than the sum of the variable cost of the old technology and incremental revenues that the new technology brings.[8] If this condition is not fulfilled, the monopolist may choose to 'sweat the existing assets'. In the context of the replacement of copper by fibre in an access network, this relation is expressed in static form as:[9]

$$\text{Annualised full fibre cost} < \text{copper operating cost} + \text{incremental fibre revenue}$$

In a competitive market, the right-hand side is augmented by: (a) revenue gained from competitors as a result of the investment; and (b) revenue protected from competitors by the investment.

Regulation in Competitive NGA Areas

In areas where an investment race is in process or could be stimulated, what regulatory policies are available? The answer, of course, depends on the geographical market definition. A national market definition is first more likely to produce a dominant operator than a geographical market confined to competitive areas.[10] In the latter case single firm dominance may or may not be found. If such dominance is not found (and the stringent conditions for finding of collective dominance are not satisfied), then under the European regulatory framework regulation is not permitted.

Who in practice are the suppliers of NGA? Although, most fibre connections are provided by firms other than the telecommunications incumbent, the breakdown of supply differs considerably by country.

A major category is cable companies. As noted, cable networks using the DOCSIS 3.0 standard are capable of matching FTTN technologies, and even some FTTP ones. The penetration of cable (not all of it upgraded) varies from above 90 per cent in Netherlands and the US to virtually zero in Mediterranean members of the EU. However, European cable companies, unlike their US equivalents, tend to be financially vulnerable.

A second category consists of telecommunications firms competing with the incumbent. Examples are Fastweb in Italy, and Iliad (Free) and SFR in France. In other countries, especially in Eastern Europe where regulations permit the aerial delivery of services (fibre strung from poles rather than buried underground), independent fibre networks flourish.

Finally, public firms and bodies have constructed NGAs. Some have been independent initiatives by, e.g., Swedish municipally owned electricity companies. Head-to-head competition of this kind is distinct from but related to direct interventions by municipalities to provide on an open access basis assets which can used by others to provide retail services. It is natural to ask whether such investment crowds out or crowds in private sector investment. A country where local and regional public authorities played a particularly active role is France. In 2008, the French regulator ARCEP undertook an impact analysis of public investment amounting to approximately €1 billion, concluding that it enhanced private investment, fostered local operators and reduced the price of rural coverage (ARCEP, 2008).

In the EU, all public investment is subject to state aid rules. A large number of cases have been examined by the Commission, applying the 'market economy investor principle', which asks whether an equivalent investment would be made by the private sector.[11] The Commission for the purpose of its decisions identifies white areas, where there are no networks available, grey areas, where there is only one, and black areas, where there are at least two infrastructures. In the first two areas, State intervention might be legitimate in the pursuit of public policy goals. In practice, almost no broadband project is found to breach the rules[12]. In 2009, the Commission published its Guidelines on the application of EU state aid rules to public funding of broadband networks (EC, 2009b). These explicitly discuss application of the rules to NGAs. A key question is how to treat areas with two or more current generation broadband infrastructures but an uncertain number of competing NGAs. The document opens a loophole for state subsidy if there is evidence of an unsatisfactory historical pattern of investment in network upgrades. The general tenor of the document is hospitable to state support for the deployment of NGAs.

In most jurisdictions, regulators found the level of competition inadequate to be effective and to make regulation unnecessary. In such cases the regulator can rely on whatever competitive pressure is available to encourage build out of fibre, and simultaneously adopt one of the forms of access regulation described below.

Regulating a Monopoly NGA

It is almost inevitable that many premises are served by a single wireline NGA. Their extent may diminish over time, but the population residing there will still be significant. What regulatory regime in such areas will promote the replacement of copper with fibre where it is commercially viable to do so?

The problem is that, absent competitive pressure, operators may choose to delay the installation of fibre even when investment in a fibre network has a positive expected NPV as compared with maintaining the legacy copper network. This is because delaying the fibre until uncertainties are removed has an option value to the investor from which it has to be bought out for the investment to proceed.

The regulator's access regime has two effects on an access provider's profit: a low access price restricts its revenues directly, and it puts a squeeze on retail prices generally, as access-based competitors compete away retail margins. If the regulator wishes to encourage investment, what approach would be suitable?

The possibilities, in decreasing order of severity, are:

- No imposition of mandatory access, and leave end users at the mercy of a dominant or monopoly firm;
- Restrict mandatory access to fibre to specified wholesale products, e.g., those capable of speeds currently available using DSL technologies. This approach gives the installer of fibre exclusive access to higher speeds, unless it agreed commercial terms with access seekers. In one possible consequence of this approach, access is mandated to a current generation broadband at a price which maintains its existing retail price, thus protecting existing customers of unbundlers from any price consequence of the introduction of fibre to replace copper;
- Impose mandatory access obligations, but at prices which are more generous than cost-based prices;
- Incorporate a risk-related element in the cost of capital when settling access prices, (this approach is set out in detail in the Commission's NGA Recommendation (EC, 2009a); or
- Apply the normal approach to cost-oriented pricing at the standard cost of capital.

Separation and Co-investment Issues and NGAs

Debate concerning whether, and how, vertical integrated telecommunications networks should be separated into network and retailing activities, or into the (monopoly) local loop and the rest, has raged for the past five years. The acknowledged goal of such separation is to prevent monopoly power in one level being leveraged into other parts of the value chain by price or non-price discrimination. Accounting separation and use of margin squeeze type tests (ex-ante by regulators and ex-post by competition authorities[13]) are seen as a remedy for price discrimination, but ensuring treatment by the network of its own affiliate and competitors which is identical in non-price terms has sometimes found to require 'deeper' separation. The main candidates are: functional or operational separation, and structural or ownership separation. The former is imposed on the incumbent in Australia, Italy, New Zealand and the UK. It is adopted as a remedy, within the European regulatory framework, subject to strict conditions which will limit its application. A vertical ownership or structural separation is not imposed on an existing major telecommunications company since the break-up of the Bell System in the USA in 1985.

The construction of NGAs raises the issue again in a different form, sharpened by the possibility of co-investment. The cost of constructing even the least costly version of an NGA encourages consideration of ways of sharing the cost, which can take the forms:

- Vertical: retailers of services provided over NGA contribute to the cost of construction, either via a joint venture or through contractual commitment;
- Horizontal: operators could share the costs of building the NGA. This could be a group of fixed operators, mobile operators or a mixed group. In the case of mobile operators, the NGA does not replace the wireless 'last mile', but provides the backhaul from base stations which will be required if mobile broadband takes off; or
- Government: the government as co-investor places public funds into NGA investment, and in return receives some control over the organisation, structure and implementation of the project. This aspect is considered below.

While technical aspects of the operational or structural separation of the 'local' NGA from either the core network or retailing are beyond the scope of this article, it is clear that while copper networks were designed and built for operation by an integrated monopoly, an NGA could be designed and built from scratch with a view to facilitating access by several firms. This approach tends to lower the cost of separation of both the operational and the structural kinds.

There are, however, economic issues at stake.[14] Structural separation of NGAs creates a transaction boundary with all retailers – as distinct from current arrangements in which the local loop operator typically provides retail services to a large proportion (45 per cent on average in the EU) of retail customers. If extended to the next generation, this would partially internalise co-ordination of investment in, say, the construction of the NGA and the marketing of the new retail services it supports. With complete separation, the spectre of the 'hold-up' problems is raised – that the network is not built as a result of the operator's fear that after it has made the NGA, retailers will reduce the price they offer to pay for it to provide service to their own customers. The problem can in principle be solved by writing a long-term contract of the 'take or pay' kind, which effectively makes the two parties co-investors, but the retailer might be able to evade the contractual commitment by choosing bankruptcy, or by other means.

Horizontal co-investment seems commercially more feasible. Network sharing is already a feature of the mobile sector especially in more remote areas, and European competition authorities have approved certain variants, especially those which involve the sharing of passive elements alone (masts, antennae, even spectrum) rather than the active or electronic elements which support product differentiation. It is conceivable that a group of mobile networks or a combination of one or more fixed networks and mobile networks could co-invest in an NGA.

In one variant, an operator would install not a single fibre, but several in the expectation of leasing them to competitors. More narrowly, the French regulator will require operators in certain circumstances to share the costs of installing an in-building multi-fibre, to prevent a bottleneck from being created (ARCEP, 2009).

It would, however be important to prevent such arrangements acting as a barrier to subsequent entry. The co-owners of the networks would assume risks which would not be borne by later comers seeking to buy access; price differentiation would be justified, but calculating a legitimate limit would be problematic. The opportunity for collusive exclusionary or exploitative conduct would be increased.

Migration Issues

The architecture of fibre networks differs from that of copper networks. Current generation broadband in Europe is often supplied by competitors who have built out to the incumbent's local exchange, where they rent local loops. That point may disappear in a fibre network, being replaced in a fibre-to-the-cabinet (FTTC) variant by the possibility of interconnection at the sub-loop, a point of access which is technically and commercially more difficult than at the local exchange. If the network is of a fibre-to-the-home (FTTH) kind, in the version known as point-to-multipoint, unbundling the fibre is difficult, but if a single fibre goes to each home (point-to-point) it can be leased to a competitor.

This approach causes problems for competitors currently relying on LLU (Cave, 2010). That is, they may be forced to revert to use of bitstream. This prospect may deter switching to the fibre network, and prolong the era of inefficient simultaneous operation of both the old and the new networks. Regulators need to devise strategies that permit the transition to proceed.

Box. 1

Finland: a fibre network will be constructed to within 2 km of population points; local communities will then decide how to build a subsidised local loop, which, given users' heavy reliance on wireless technologies, may not be fibre-based.

France: the French regulator is among the first to mandate duct access, which is utilised by telecommunications competitors to France Telecom. A special law was passed requiring an operator arriving first at a multi-dwelling unit to make that building's internal wiring available on a shared-cost basis to competitors; such regulation of the 'terminating segment' is likely to be copied more generally.

Spain: after interactions with the EC, the Spanish regulator imposed on its incumbent an obligation to make available a wholesale broadband product capable only of speeds of up to 30Mbps.

The Netherlands: the incumbent KPN faced with strong cable competition began early deployment of FTTN connections. In 2008, it merged with Reggiefiber, a fibre network specialist, to provide FTTH connection. The combined entity is subject to price control on the mandatory provision of passive assets, including unbundled fibre.

The UK: high-speed broadband is offered to about half the population by the cable operator, and the incumbent BT announced plans to provide mostly FTTN connections to 40 per cent of homes. In early 2009, Ofcom issued a statement indicating its intention to mandate access to passive assets at cost-oriented prices; in the case of wholesale products with active components, access would be mandated but prices are unconstrained.

The US: access to fibre networks is not mandatory since 2004. As a result, competitive pressures arise largely within a duopoly formed by the local telecommunications and the cable company.

Japan: access to NTT's fibre network, currently with a fibre market share of over 70 per cent, is mandated since 2001; end-to-end fibre competition is present in some areas.

Korea: access regulation has generally been eschewed in favour of the promotion of end-to-end network competition. An FTTH access obligation is restricted to facilities built before 2004.

Lessons of Experience

Regulators adopted a variety of approaches towards NGAs, even within the EU where a certain commonalty of approach is imposed by a common set of Directives. The range is illustrated in Box. 1, which summarises features of special interest in several countries.

In relation to current generation broadband, the data provide a basis for testing the impact of alternative regulatory interventions on outcomes.[15] Grajek and Röller (2009) analysed the impact of access regulation on investment undertaken by 70 European telecommunications firms over a ten-year period. In the model, with the form of regulation endogenous, they conclude that stronger access regulation reduces total industry and individual carrier investment. Moreover, higher infrastructure investment by the incumbent elicits tougher regulation, creating a negative feedback. Bacache et al. (2010), using European data, find no link between competitors' record in ULL and their propensity to install fibre connections to customers.

Summary of NGA Regulation

It is necessary to ask if there is a 'right way' to regulate NGAs, or if each country is unique. The point of view adopted here is that generalisation is feasible in principle, but that, as well as being evidence-based, it has to take account of the potential for competition (itself influenced by past, present and expectations of future regulation). It is clear from the above account that the regulators are struggling to devise instruments to combine timely investment in NGAs and efficient use of the networks once built. Where NGA competition exists, the investment incentives are sharpened, but regulators are still faced with the dilemma of 'how many are enough'. In the US, two networks (and wireless technologies) are considered enough to obviate the need for access regulation. This is not the general view in Europe, where access is mostly mandated in some form to the telecommunications incumbent's NGA, even in cabled areas.

However, the scope and form of access regulation vary considerably in markets characterised by both duopoly and monopoly. In particular, access to passive assets is more heavily regulated than to active assets, which are either not mandated at all or are subject to looser pricing rules. Or (as in Spain) access providers may not be required to allow competitors to replicate all the services they can produce. Both developments of traditional access regulation of copper networks are intended to bring forward investment. It is, however, too soon to identify what works and what does not.

A second development is the increasing impetus behind separation, driven in part by a desire to avoid the harmful effects of integration in the copper world, but more strongly by the increasing role of co-investment. The latter effect is seen most strongly where the government becomes a co-investor, and imposes open access and separation as contractual commitments.

GOVERNMENT POLICY TOWARD NGAs

The received wisdom of a decade ago in liberal economic circles is that the telecommunications sector permanently escaped, to its great benefit, from reliance on public finances and its inevitable accompaniment – subjection to the 'dead hand' of government control, which often had anti-competitive consequences. The sector was rich enough to fend for itself; privatisation gave it access to private capital; and governments saw it largely as a source of rather than a sink for public funds. This view even survived the dot.com crash of year 2000.

What a difference a few years make! Faced with the enormity of expenditure on NGAs, the earlier view is virtually reversed itself. Some form of public funding is now seen as necessary and appropriate almost everywhere, not simply as an aberrant feature of Asian economies. This reflects the fact that advanced countries with ubiquitous fixed-copper networks enjoy essentially a 'free ride' on the copper access network. Regulators are confronting incumbent operators with a sunk and largely depreciated asset which they could price almost at will.[16] However, the costs of NGAs are not sunk. Operators must see the prospect of a return and if there are uncertainties, they may exercise the option of delay even in undertaking apparently profitable investments. The sheer scale of investments, especially on FTTP variants of access networks is daunting. The fibre pathfinders in Asia relied on more or less transparent public subsidies to install the fibre. Their followers elsewhere now seek to copy this.[17]

Why Intervene?

There are several motives for public investment in telecommunications at national, regional or municipal level.[18] Broadly:

(a) *Equity motive*: Where public spending is justified by the need to provide otherwise disadvantaged population groups or regions with services deemed necessary to permit full participation in economic, political and social life. This aim goes a long way back in the history of telecommunications to the foundation of a universal telephone service at the start of the 20th century by AT&T under Theodore Vail, through policies of cross subsidies of line rentals by call prices (to encourage adoption), and to equalisation of prices through universal service obligations. This tradition is maintained in the EU via a universal service obligation for broadband which guarantees access to a particular quality and speed of service at a maximum price throughout a territory. It is envisaged that this will be accomplished by 2013.

Precedent suggests that making a service which is adopted spontaneously by 70-80 per cent of the population is quite feasible. However, the passage of time and the development of competition will complicate its implementation. In a competitive world it should ideally be achieved by a means which does not distort competition between providers. This also implies a competitive and technologically neutral process, including wireless technologies. Second, it is generally recognised that providing access to broadband is not enough. People need assistance in adoption too, including the acquisition of suitable device and instruction in the necessary skills.

Is a policy of near universal access to high-speed broadband based on NGAs feasible? In some small island states and Japan and Korea, it is either accomplished or being accomplished. Finland and Sweden within the EU adopted such an objective. In other Member States, attempts to devote economic resources to a universal NGA within a similar time frame are likely to prove disproportionately expensive.

(b) *Industrial policy*: The motive is to construct high-speed networks as an instrument for the provision of what the OECD describes as a faster and more powerful general purpose technology – broadband – used both in production (by SMEs for example) and in consumption. Public intervention is designed to solve the underlying market failure flowing from the presence of network externalities: a critical mass of high-speed broadband users can galvanise an economy, just as the World Bank data suggest current generation broadband has in the recent past.

This approach underlies many regional and national approaches. At the regional or municipal level, the concern is often to avoid being 'left behind' by neighbours, or alternatively, to 'get ahead'. Clearly, not every locality can succeed in this endeavour, but the fear of being left behind is a powerful means of generating the local resources. A study by the French regulator (ARCEP, 2008) suggested that investment by local authorities in France has extended and quickened the availability of broadband, promoted competition and encouraged rather than discouraged private investment.

(c) *Economic Recovery*: In countries which have been hit hardest by the recession, especially the UK and the USA, unprecedented deficits are being run to avoid further output declines. At the same time, a significant percentage of GDP has been lost, probably permanently, which reduces the return to NGA investment. The macro-economic situation opens a window of opportunity for NGA investment which may close as policies to reduce the deficit take over.

Data on planned government expenditure have been collated by Qiang (2009). Figure 5.2 shows the share of the total stimulus package (in US$bn) accounted for by broadband in selected countries.

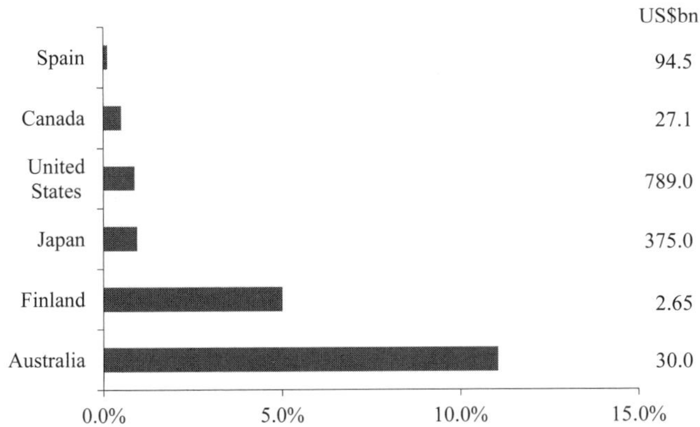

Figure 5.2 *Broadband components as percentage of stimulus plans*

Assessment of the usefulness of expenditure on communications networks is embedded in a wider debate about the size of the multiplier for government spending, including on infrastructures, as opposed to multipliers associated with tax cuts, and Barro (2009) warns against the application of large 'voodoo multipliers'. To be useful as part of a recovery plan, expenditure must also be timely.[19] It is doubtful whether NGA projects meet this criterion. Above all, to justify infrastructure expenditure on NGAs rather than on energy grids, railways or housing (to name but three competitors), it must be shown that the expenditure not only yields positive benefits, but greater benefits than alternatives.

Public investment in high-speed broadband has advantages over the caricature of Keynesian public spending policies, which involves the digging and filling in of holes in the road, in every respect except one crucial one. Unfortunately, constructing an advanced local telecommunications network cannot be accomplished without considerable planning; as a project, it is anything but 'shovel-ready'. This is part of the reason for the relatively small showing of broadband projects in national recovery plans. Even in Australia, with high government commitment to public investment in communications, the first version of the national broadband plan pre-dated the current financial crisis, and the build-out of the subsequent version is occurring as the economy's growth returned to normal. As the focus switches to reducing deficits, the recovery motive waned.

Clarity as to which, or which combination, of the three above-noted motives is being pursued is fundamental to the development of good public policy. It is commonly believed that outside countries which have high levels of NGA installation or those prepared to make large investments in it, separate but overlapping stages of public policy are required: first, policy to achieve universal access to current generation broadband (with speeds of, say, 2 Mbps), and, second, a plan to accelerate the spread of next generation broadband (with speeds, say, of 50-100 Mbps), with a view to achieving near universal coverage in the medium to long term.

It must be recognised that the second objective, unlike the first, will require massive investments on a scale beyond the scope of public funding. Accordingly, such investments should be planned within the framework of a public/private partnership in which the government plays a co-ordinating and a partial financing role; the latter being designed to crowd in rather than crowd out public investment.

Where to Intervene

As noted, investment in fibre-access networks is costly, and takes place against a background of financial stringency. This is reason enough to focus on where returns are greatest. However, there are other reasons too. Countries and regions differ in the degree of competition they have exhibited in current generation broadband. In some areas there are competing end-to-end networks, normally areas with a telecoms and a cable network. Where both are in place, the potential is there for upgrading the former to a FTTC or a FTTH NGA, and the latter to high-speed network based on the DOCSIS 3.0 standard. These data suggest that an investment race between the operators can occur, and has occurred in countries such as the US, Sweden and the Netherlands, and cities such as Paris. Such examples form a useful competitive benchmark for evaluating the desirability of investment in NGAs. Introducing public subsidies in such a context incurs the risks both of replacing private investment and of distorting competition between the networks.[20] This suggests that public investment should steer clear of competitive areas.

This does not mean any government or regulatory involvement. It will be essential to maximise regulatory certainty by specifying the access regime (if any) for both networks. It may be necessary to prevent the emergence of bottlenecks.[21] And deployment in competitive areas can be a component of an indicative plan for all areas.

The second category comprises areas where there is only one fixed existing network. The problem of promoting investment in NGAs here is particularly acute. In the first place, a clear access regime is required to create regulatory certainty; dithering by the regulator can discourage investment. Secondly, the operator has to be bought out of the option of not investing in NGAs until demand and execution uncertainties are resolved, in circumstances where by definition there is no rival able to get to market first.

It is argued that, absent public funding, there exists an irreconcilable conflict between the goals of bringing NGA investment forward and maintaining a regulatory regime for open access-based entry. Regulators responded in various ways by: granting partial 'holidays' from access regulation; limiting the range of access products available; adopting more generous access pricing rules for certain access products; or interpreting existing access pricing rules based on cost-based pricing in ways which are more generous to the access provider. It is here that public investment delivered (for example) within the contractual framework of a private/public partnership can, in principle, break the logjam and elicit the required investment.

Finally, there are areas where investment in a wireline NGA is unlikely ever to be commercially viable. These areas are likely to be similar in composition to areas which current generation broadband does not reach. In due course, the question of providing universal next generation access must be faced. Wireless technologies may provide the answer in a sparsely populated area where problems of contention caused by spectrum shortage are limited (although the backhaul problems remain a factor). The predictable conclusion of the discussion is to focus public funding on the intermediate area. This creates a 'boundary problem' with competitive areas. Is there a risk of discouraging the extension of network coverage and of entrenching existing cable areas? Given the high costs of cable rollout and its limited extent in recent years, this is probably a risk worth taking.

How to Intervene

Following this provisional answer to the 'where' question, the next question is 'how?' The issue here is that public involvement can take many forms. Some of the options are noted and the discussion then turns to particular cases, to see what lessons can be learnt. The first and most fundamental question is whether public investment should impact on the costs or the revenue side of the NGA investment project. Most of the discussion is about the public sector providing a capital input of some kind. But the government could equally influence private or public demand.

It could do the latter by subsidies or taxes. For example, it could provide vouchers to firms and businesses which they could use to purchase services relying on next generation access networks. There is, however, little certainty about what effect this would have; and, for reasons given above, it might have to be geographically specific. The alternative tax-based approach is more practicable. Thus a tax could be imposed on non-NGA network services, which would encourage substitution in favour of NGAs.[22]

Increasing public demand is a more plausible alternative. The delivery of public services by electronic means is an objective of most governments: both to save costs and to improve services. However, it may be unrealistic to rely too heavily on such expenditures on improved services to elicit demand for NGAs and with it the necessary private sector investment.

Another implementation question concerns the conflict between the width and the depth of a NGA investment project with public involvement. Suppose that the cost per line of a FTTH deployment is three or four times that of a FTTC alternative. Should limited public funds cover a larger area more with a slower and possibly interim network or smaller areas with FTTH?

The equity issue bound up in this question is further complicated by its link to the sequencing of a partly publicly funded deployment. The largest commercial returns to NGA investment are likely to be found in more heavily populated, often more affluent areas, where costs are lower and willingness to pay is probably higher. In some countries, this will be politically acceptable only within the context of a national plan to complete a wider (but not necessarily a fibre) roll out fairly quickly.

A more technical issue to be resolved is whether the network built out should be asymmetrical, like current xDSL networks and current and prospective mobile networks, or symmetric, like FTTH networks. It is likely that services will increasingly require symmetric capabilities, either because they will involve file sharing or because public services such as health and education delivered by broadband will impose increasing requirements of this kind.

Additionally, there is a fundamental question of the level at which public investment should be co-ordinated. Consider two polar alternatives. In one, there is a national plan, probably covering several years, for construction of a high-speed broadband network with a wide coverage. This is implemented by public subsidy or via a public/private investment vehicle, with the proportions between the two forms of ownership changing over time. In the second, regional or local branches of government make uncoordinated investments, e.g., in a specific network asset, such an unlit fibre network covering a particular area.

The second variant is more flexible. It does not require an overarching plan, and can be done by a government authority at any level. However, the absence of an overall plan is a potential disadvantage, as isolated implementation of particular technologies risks limiting the range of services available to NGA customers, as well as systematic attainment of equity goals.

Finally, however the above issue is resolved, there is the choice of the investment in which the public sector participates. Such investment could be the NGA as a whole, including backhaul, the last mile and connections to public bodies such as schools and hospitals and to the premises of firms and households. Or it could be particularly focussed on individual assets. The choice should be made on the basis of the return generated not by the public investment but by the sum of the public investment and the private investment which it elicits. Thus it may be desirable to focus public investment on particularly risky assets, as is done in one of the illustrations considered below. If the NGA is constructed on a separated basis, with different organisations running different 'layers', such as passive assets, active assets and retailing, then, as in another illustration, public investment can be specialised in one or another layer.

So far there has been little analysis of how choices relating to the above dimensions of intervention should be made. A valuable exception is the OECD (2009a). This concentrates on investment in communications as part of a recovery plan, and offers a useful analysis of the goals of connectivity, open access, innovation and growth and social benefits. The OECD also emphasises that the project must have long-term viability, to ensure that it can be transferred to the private sector in due course without continuing large subsidies.

There has been, however, a dearth of more empirical analysis, partly made up in the case of the US by the publication of comprehensive policy statement on broadband known as the national broadband plan (FCC, 2010).[23]

Examples

The two OECD countries with the highest levels of deployment of fibre networks are Japan and Korea. The Korean government implemented a comprehensive plan for the provision of broadband, known as the Korean Information Infrastructure (KII) since 1995. It involved government subsidies to competitive private investors initially in a variety of technologies, and latterly in fibre. The task is simplified by the high proportion of the population residing in multi-dwelling units. The current goal is to build a FTTB Broadband Convergence Network (BcN) providing service to 12 million households by 2010.

The same broad approach, under the title 'Next Generation Broadband Strategy 2010' was adopted in Japan (Ida 2009). Competition in the supply of ADSL, driven by low unbundling charges, followed by fibre competition, allowed high-fibre penetration rates to be established without government subsidy; such subsidies are largely confined to taking high-speed broadband to rural areas. The goal of making fibre access available to 90 per cent of households is already achieved.

Another interesting example is Singapore. In December April 2007 and April 2008, the Singapore government issued a request for proposals to build and operate its proposed next generation national broadband network (Next Gen NBN)[24]. This will offer competitively priced ultra-high speed broadband (100 Mbps downstream, 50 Mbps upstream) to all homes, businesses, schools and other premises. The government was prepared to invest up to S$5 billion (€2.4 billion) in the project, but after a competitive tendering process, a subsidy of only S$1 billion (€0.5 billion) was required. The structure of the NBN is shown in Table 5.2.

The contract for NetCo was issued in 2008, and that for OpCo in May 2009. OpCo will offer a wholesale service of 100Mbps for S$21 (€10) per month and a 1Gbps for S$121 (€59) per month. Enterprise customers pay between four and seven times as much. The total public subsidy required is significantly less than the maximum provided, demonstrating in this case, but not in others, the ability of a well-designed tendering process to remove rents.

Table 5.2 Structure of the Singaporean NBN

Layer	Infrastructure	Operation
1	Passive	NetCo: design, build and operate the network passive infrastructure
2 / 3	Active	OpCo: design, build and operate the network active infrastructure
Retail		Retail service providers: purchase services from OpCo and provide to end users

The key separation requirement relates to links between the OpCo and downstream affiliated units. The OpCo must: operate as a standalone basis: be located in separate premises, make own decisions on assets and commercial policy. OpCo directors must not have responsibility for an affiliated operator, nor can their remuneration be linked to an affiliated company's performance. This is supplemented by a requirement for structural separation between NetCo, the passive network operator (expected to be a monopoly) and downstream operators. In this context, structural separation means 'no effective control'.

In Australia, the government issued a request for proposals to construct a FTTN network capable of providing 12 Mbps to at least 90 per cent of Australian homes, for which government funding of up to A$4.7 billion (€2.9 billion) is available. Several competing bids are submitted, but Telstra's, the incumbent, was disqualified. In 2009, the Government announced that none are satisfactory, and announced a plan to create a company in majority public ownership which would spend A$43 billion on a FTTH network providing speeds of at least 50 Mbps to 90 per cent of homes (Australian Government 2010). This is by far the largest government project noted here, in relative terms. It is unusual also in involving majority public ownership as a key feature, although the plan involves drawing down the public investment after five years. It is not clear, however, how it will be implemented, in particular what role will be played by Telstra's existing network.

In New Zealand, the government published a consultation document in March 2009 which has as its objective to deploy fibre to 75 per cent of homes within 10 years (New Zealand Government 2009). It will invest NZ$ 1.5 billion (€0.7 billion) to create a Crown Fibre Investment Co, which, together with private co-investors, will form local fibre companies (LFCs) to construct and provide access to fibre-optic network infrastructure in the target areas. The LFCs will provide open access to the network on equivalent terms, provide wholesale access to dark fibre on the network, and be prohibited from providing retail services. The government recently announced that the LFCs will have an access holiday for ten years, in the course of which competition will be provided by the legacy copper network (New Zealand Government 2010).

In Europe, government subsidy is more 'low key', and a mixture of local and national initiatives. France is particularly active in promoting regional plans, but other countries have made considerable strides, within the constraints of their financial situations.[25]

CONCLUDING REMARKS

Providing high-speed broadband requires the replacement in the local loop of copper with fibre, and a major change in network architecture. This imposes substantial demands on regulators, given the dominance of the historical monopolist in the local loop. In the US, where there is potential for competition between NGAs, regulators decided not to mandate access to fibre infrastructure. Other regulators sought forms of co-investment which generate a structure which facilitates competition. However, the approach lacks credibility in Europe, where regulators are under a statutory duty to intervene if they encounter significant market power when every three years they review major markets (which include copper and fibre infrastructure). Achieving an agreed co-investment solution for the whole local loop (as opposed to in-building wiring alone) presents significant difficulties.

Accordingly, it is likely that some form of behavioural or access regulation will be imposed. The recognition that this profoundly affects investment incentives for the incumbent has led regulators to devise ways of adapting conventional cost-based access pricing. This involved amending the way in which access is mandated, by altering the range of access points or access services available and by changing the basis on which access seekers pay for access to the incumbent's facilities. However, it is not possible for a regulator in Europe credibly to commit to such a policy over the medium term, and this puts a limit on the effectiveness of the more radical proposals.

These policies represent different choices in the trade-off between building the new networks, and promoting competition on them once built. It is not yet possible to say which approach works. The preliminary evidence suggests (unsurprisingly) that competitive pressures are successful in bringing investment forward, but novel regulatory interventions are as yet untested. This is no reason for not trying, and mechanisms which entail some form of commitment may be the most effective. On this basis, it might be better to offer a higher cost of capital in a cost-based pricing formula than to seek to encourage investment with different forms of regulatory holiday.

The terms of the regulatory trade-off can be more favourable if the government is prepared to subsidise spending on NGAs, in a way which does not have the effect of distorting competition. A range of examples of such interventions are described above. NGAs among infrastructure projects competing for funds, and the short-term pay-off to the economy is unfortunately diminished by the recession. This suggests that the case for intervention requires a longer term, rather than a purely cyclical justification.

It is important to make the objectives of public funding clear. Industrial policy seems the strongest motive, but maintaining regional balance and preventing continuation of the digital divide in the fibre age are also strongly present. In some models with public funding, competition is sacrificed to bring investment forward. This carries dangers, both for the efficiency of network design and operation and for the maintenance of an innovative environment.

ACKNOWLEGEMENTS

This chapter draws on Cave and Hatta (2009), Huigen and Cave (2008), Lewin et al. Cave (2009), Cave (2010) and Cave and Martin (2010). The author expresses sincere gratitude to his co-authors.

NOTES

1. It is thus important to distinguish innovative investment in the 'monopolistic' local loop from similar developments over past decades in the 'competitive' core network, including the installation of digital switches in exchanges and the replacement of copper with fibre for transmission.
2. ADSL comes in several varieties, including ADSL2+, which has higher speed but a lower geographical coverage than the original.
3. Countries differ considerably in the detailed architectures of their copper networks.
4. Moreover, mobile speeds depend upon the availability of sufficient spectrum - a key shared input for all users; whereas with FTTH, each user id is served with a dedicated (and hence guaranteed) local loop.
5. The most accessible broadband data are available from the OECD Internet Portal, covering 30 countries, and in periodic reports from the European Commission, covering 27 Member States.
6. For accounts of the development of broadband, see Huigen and Cave (2008), and Fransman (2006).
7. See also OECD (2009b).
8. The incremental cost of a fibre network is of course, substantially reduced where an operator inherits physical assets and customers from a pre-existing copper network.

9. Regulation of broadband prices (normally at the wholesale level) influences the scale of the revenue increment. The lower the price of ADSL, the greater the incremental revenue associated with a customer switching to fibre, but the smaller the number of customers who will choose to switch.
10. Of course, if different operators are dominant in different geographical areas, the number of individual geographical markets grows correspondingly.
11. In the well-known *City of Amsterdam* case, the principle was taken to justify participation by the municipality, jointly with private investors, in the construction of a fibre ring throughout the city.
12. An exception is the *Appingedam* case, where state subsidies were applied in an area with several private operators.
13. In the US, two recent Supreme Court judgments (*Trinko* and *Linkline*) made it clear that a margin squeeze conducted by a regulated telecommunications firm cannot be impugned under US competition law.
14. The empirical literature on the effects of vertical integration and separation is reviewed in Lafontaine and Slade (2007), who conclude: '[the weight of the evidence] says that, under most circumstances, profit-maximising vertical integration decisions are efficient, not just from the firms' point of view, but also from the consumers' point of view.' (p. 680).
15. For a recent survey, see Cambini and Jiang (2009).
16. A good illustration is the manner in which OFTEL/Ofcom in the UK changed the valuation method of the local loop from historic cost to current cost and back again within the space of ten years, in pursuit of its variable pricing objectives.
17. See Huigen and Cave (2008).
18. See Gomez-Barroso and Feijoo (2010).
19. A fuller list of possible criteria is provided in OECD (2009a).
20. However, existing operators may not plan to invest. Thus in Australia a dispute between the incumbent and the government led to the cancellation of plans for fibre investment. In New Zealand, on the other hand, the incumbent was already planning to invest in a fibre to the cabinet network when the government announced plans for FTTH.
21. An example of the latter is action taken by the French government, in the form of specific legislation, to specify the terms on which competing operators can co-invest in in-building wiring, and thereby all gain access to customers in multi-dwelling units.
22. The former UK government's proposal to impose a 'line tax' of £6 (€7) per year on non-fibre fixed lines is an example of this approach. Moreover, the proceeds are intended for use to subsidise NGA construction (Digital Britain, 2009).
23. The work by ARCEP (2008), already cited, is an important exception.
24. IDA Press Releases, 4 April 2008 and 4 May 2009.
25. For a useful comparison of policies in France, Italy and Portugal, see Bourreau et al. (2010).

REFERENCES

ARCEP (2008), *Etude sur l'Intervention des Collectivités Territoriales en Matière de Points Hauts*. Paris: Autorité de Régulation des Communications Electroniques et des Postes.

ARCEP (2009), *Présentation des Projets de Décisions et de Recommandations Soumis à Consultation Publique par l'ARCEP*. Paris: Autorité de Régulation des Communications Electroniques et des Postes.

Australian Government (2010), *NBN Implementations Plan,* May.

Bacache, M., Bourreau, M. and Gaudin, G. (2010), 'The Ladder of Investment Approach and the Development of New Access Infrastructures: Which Empirical Evidence?'. Retrieved from: http://www.eurocpr.org/prs/Germain%20Gaudin.pdf.
Barro, R. (2009), 'Demand Side Voodoo Economics', *The Economists' Voice*, **6**, 1–4.
Bourreau, M., Cambini, C. and Hoernig, S. (2010), 'National FTTH plans in France, Italy and Portugal', *Communications and Strategies*, **87**, 107–26.
BSG (2008), 'A Framework for Evaluating the Value of Next Generation Broadband', Broadband Stakeholders Group. Retrieved from: http://www.broadbanduk.org/component/option,com_docman/task,doc_view/gid,1009/Itemid,63/.
Cambini, C. and Jiang, Y. (2009), 'Broadband Investment and Regulation', mimeo, Politecnico di Torino.
Cave, M. (2006), 'Six Degrees of Separation', *Communications and Strategies*, **67**, 89–104.
Cave, M. (2010), 'Snakes and Ladders: Unbundling in a Next Generation World', *Telecommunications Policy*, **34**, 80–5.
Cave, M. and Hatta, K. (2009), 'Transforming Telecommunications Technologies-Policy and Regulation', *Oxford Review of Economic Policy*, **25**, 488–505.
Cave, M. and Martin, I. (2010), 'Motives and Means for Public Investment in Nation Wide Next Generation Networks', *Telecommunications Policy*, **39**, 505–12.
Digital Britain (2009), *Digital Britain - Final Report*, Department for Culture, Media and Sport and Department for Business, Innovation and Skills, Cm 7650.
EC (2009a), *Draft Commission Recommendation on the regulated access to Next Generation Access Networks (NGA),* June.
EC (2009b), *Community Guidelines for the application of State aid rules in relation to rapid deployment of broadband networks,* September.
EC (2010), *Progress Report on the Single European Electronic Communications Market 2009, 5th Report*, COM(2010)253 final, May.
ERG (2009), *Report on Next Generation Access - Economic Analysis and Regulatory Principles*, ERG(09) 17.
Federal Communications Commission (2010), *The National Broadband Plan.*
Fransman, M. (ed.) (2006), *Global Broadband Battles: Why the US and Europe Lag while Asia Leads*, Palo Alto, CA: Stanford University Press.
Gomez-Barroso, J. and Feijoo, G. (2010), 'A Conceptual Framework for Public-Private Interplay in the Telecommunications Sector', *Telecommunications Policy*, **34**, 487–95.
Grajek, M. and Röller, L-H. (2009), 'The Effect of Regulation on Investment in Network Industries: Evidence from the Telecommunications Industry', European School of Management and Technology Working Paper #09-004.
Huigen, J. and Cave, M. (2008), 'Regulation and the Promotion of Investment in Next Generation Networks: A European Dilemma', *Telecommunications Policy*, **28**, 713–21.
Ida, T. (2009), *Broadband Economics: Lessons from Japan,* London: Routledge.
IDATE (2007), *Digiworld Presentation*, Montpellier. IDATE Consultancy and Research.
Lafontaine, F. and Slade, M. (2007), 'Vertical Integration and Firm Boundaries: the Evidence', *Journal of Economic Literature*, **45**, 629–85.
Lewin, D., Williamson, B. and Cave, M. (2009), 'Regulating Next-Generation Fixed Access to Telecommunications Services', *INFO*, **11**, 3–18.

New Zealand Government (2009), *Broadband Investment Initiative*, Draft Cabinet paper for consultation, March.

New Zealand Government (2010), *Ultra-fast Broadband Initiative – Overview of Amendments,* July.

OECD (2009a), *The Role of Communication Infrastructure Investment in Economic Recovery*, DSTI/ICCP/CISP(2009)1/FINAL, Paris, OECD.

OECD (2009b) *Mobile Broadband: Pricing and Services*, DSTI/ICCP/CISP(2008)6/FINAL, Paris, OECD.

OECD (2010), OECD Broadband Portal. Retrieved from: http://www.oecd.org/sti/ict/broadband.

Qiang, C. (2009), *Broadband Infrastructure in Stimulus Packages: Relevance for Developing Countries*, World Bank.

6. Sector regulation and investment incentives: The European experience

Harald Gruber

INTRODUCTION

This study looks at the track record of open access regulation in the European Union (EU) and relates it to investment behaviour. Regulatory reform in the sector is inspired by the notion of providing access to bottleneck elements in infrastructure precisely to induce further investment by new entrants. This is supposed to accelerate investment in the sector, which is traditionally determined by incumbent operators. The sector liberalisation programmes of the 1990s often also entailed the privatisation of incumbents (Newberry, 1999). Thus access to capital markets became easier for incumbents as they did not have to cope with any budget constraints of government.

There is an ample economic literature that assesses the impact of regulation and investment behaviour (for a survey see Guthrie, 2006). For instance, Alesina et al. (2005) show that market entry regulation does have an important impact on investment. This is of relevance as investment crucially affects future prices, quantity and quality of products and services, whereas delays in investment may lead to substantial welfare costs. As an example, Hausman (1997), for the United States (US), showed that regulatory delays in introducing mobile telecommunications services in the early-1980s cost up to US$50 billion per annum (at 1994 values). Thus overall magnitudes involved with the telecommunications sector, which according to OECD (2009) accounts typically for 3-5 per cent of GDP can be quite substantial. The design of sector regulation for telecommunications, as for any other infrastructure sector, needs very careful weighting of factors that are influenced by industry-specific technology features, firm behaviour and regulatory incentives (Armstrong and Sappington, 2006). Regulatory reform in telecommunications during the 1990s, like in other network industries such as electricity, is inspired by the concept of open access regulation to bottleneck elements of vertically integrated providers of infrastructure services. Competitive access is seen as the means to eliminate the 'deadweight loss' from monopoly, and to establish efficient service provision. Cost-based access pricing regimes are adopted mainly to favour competitive entry. Local loop access products allow entrants to offer services with reduced upfront investment, while relying on the existing networks of the incumbent. Entrants are then expected to successively invest to an increasing degree in own infrastructure. While successful in attracting entrants, the pricing regime seems to negatively affect long-term incentives for investment for both the incumbent and new entrants. This is in line with theoretical predictions (Bourreau and Doğan, 2006) and consistent with empirical findings (Gruber, 2010). Certain provisions of access regulation, such as mandatory unbundling at the local loop, seem to have become rather a substitute for investment by new entrants than a complement. The conflict between regulation, competition and investment in broadband telecommunications is also emphasised the survey of Cambini and Jiang (2009).

Regulation also has strong effects in the mobile telecommunications sector. There is a distinction between pre-entry regulation, which effectively determines the number of spectrum licences and hence the number of network based firms to compete, and post-entry regulation, which is essentially regulation on pricing. More entry typically effects (greater) investment and (more rapid) subscriber take-up (Gruber and Verboven, 2001). For post-entry regulation such as price regulation the interaction with investment incentives is much more complex. It can be seen as an optimisation exercise of a multiproduct firm with market power. Deviations from single mark-up pricing may be entirely efficient when the firm has to recoup large sunk costs. Striking deviations can be observed in roaming markets and mobile termination pricing. Regulatory interventions such as orienting wholesale prices to cost with the intent of enforcing single margins across all service markets can be problematic. Though this is made with the intent of ensuring competition can hence be seen as a break of an implicit regulatory contract (Haucap, 2003) and thus deter investment. So both types of regulation can induce a greater degree of pricing competition but may have profoundly different effects on investment incentives.

Overall, the challenge for regulatory authorities therefore is to reconcile investment incentives with the aim of creating competitive conditions in the sector. This debate is renewed in the context of widespread calls for enhanced roll out of next generation broadband networks. There is a consensus that this will require large investments and that market forces may not be able to ensure a level of investment commensurate with the political goals bridging any 'digital divide'. Next generation networks should be open to allow equal access, but firms that have the resources such as the incumbent fixed-line operators may not be prepared to invest under this premise. This incentive problem is compounded by highly uncertain revenue streams from next generation networks. Hence new regulatory approaches are required, to which the European Commission has already responded with a revision of the regulatory framework.

The chapter is arranged as follows. The following section briefly sketches the main policy and regulatory developments in the telecommunications sector in the EU. Next, the interaction between regulation and investment incentives is described by looking at the fixed-line local loop access and inter-carrier compensation mechanisms in the mobile telecommunications sector. A penultimate section outlines the future policy and regulatory challenges. A final section concludes.

PAST REGULATORY DEVELOPMENTS IN EUROPE

In assessing regulatory developments in Europe institutional settings of the EU and the power that has been delegated to the European Commission for addressing the regulatory concerns in the telecommunications sector must be taken into account. The power to intervene in the telecommunications sector originated in the European Commission's mission to promote economic integration and to remove obstacles to the functioning of markets. EU-wide sector liberalisation is formally established in 1998, when all telecommunications markets are in principle opened to competition. While some Member Countries already had some experience in introducing competition before that date, for most countries it is a major change. Though some countries such as Greece and Luxembourg are granted derogations for a couple of years, they eventually had to fall in line. The 1998 regulatory framework segmented the telecommunications sector into four markets: fixed, mobile, leased lines and cable TV. Firms trespassing a market share of 25 per cent are designated as firms with significant market power (SMP), and hence subject to regulation by national regulatory authorities. This meant that in the fixed-line markets the incumbent firm is regulated as it typically had a market share close to 100 per cent. In the mobile markets there are typically at least two firms fulfilling the criterion of SMP. The regulations however are still a patchwork and are missing provisions that are considered important to achieve competition in the market, such as the requirement of unbundling. Moreover, there is much fragmentation in telecommunications markets across the EU, with substantial heterogeneity in the enforcement of regulatory obligations as regularly pointed out in the annual implementation reports compiled by the European Commission services. Following a number of complaints, the European Commission made major enquiries on services such as access to local loops and roaming services. Moreover, a major review is launched in 1999 with a view of reforming this regulatory framework, which is in effect closely tied to technologies and did not respond any more to a world of convergence of the different communication technologies.

The ensuing new regulatory framework of 2002 is a more consistent and also a much more comprehensive regulatory framework on 'Electronic Communications', closely related to competition policy methodologies (Nihoul and Rodford, 2004). The notion of electronic communications extended the scope of regulation to the broader market of telecommunications including also transmission of broadcasting signals. This entailed, among other things, the definition of 18 relevant markets using competition policy criteria of determining the relevant market and by adopting antitrust criteria for the determination of firms with significant market power. Ex-ante regulation would only become necessary in those markets where competition law (i.e., ex-post) remedies would be insufficient. Implicitly the threshold level market share for SMP increased from 25 per cent to 40 per cent.

This new framework needs to be seen in the context of the 'Lisbon Strategy', the institutional answer provided by the EU leaders in Lisbon in the year 2000 as an answer to the economic policy debate in Europe on improving productivity growth performance by meeting a number of ambitious quantitative goals by 2010. The telecommunications sector, in particular broadband communications, has an important role in this (European Commission, 2003).

The EU's regulatory framework on electronic communications, though providing a harmonised set of regulatory measures across member states, also leaves some room for discretion for national policies in implementing the relevant directives. These policies can take account of the different national setting and points of departure, with emphasis either on service-based competition or on facility-based competition. The different options also entail different investment incentives. For instance, there are considerably different approaches regulating the incumbent's wholesale access products such as bitstream access (Baake and Preissl, 2006). Sweden uses a retail-minus approach for setting the wholesale access price, while Italy uses historic costs for this. In the Netherlands it is not regulated at all, with the justification that there is already a sufficient degree of competition in the market due to alternative platforms for broadband access.

With respect to mobile telecommunications, the regulatory focus is on providing an environment conducive to competition. This is pursued by increasing the number of licences over time. Prices have seen strong declines as a result of infrastructure competition and subscriber growth is very strong. Indeed, Gruber and Verboven (2001) show that increased inter-platform competition leads to faster diffusion of mobile telecommunications. Nevertheless, regulatory challenges persist also in this sector, but on mostly other issues than in the fixed-line sector. This is in particular the case for the interconnection rate regime used for inter-carrier compensation. Europe chose the calling party pays principle as the scheme to charge customers for calls, where operators compensate one another by paying interconnection (or termination) rates for connecting with customers on their network. Mobile firms may use termination rates as a device for tacit collusion with the intent of keeping retail prices high, especially when combined with imperfect tariff information by consumers (Gans and King, 2000). Consumer information asymmetry is exacerbated in the case of international roaming, because consumers have difficulty getting information on prices adopted by the host network firm. Moreover, national competition authorities have a limited legal basis to intervene as the prices applied in any case concern foreign consumers. Because of this lack of market integration across EU Member States, the European Commission had a legal basis to intervene on clearly national regulatory failures by setting a cap on roaming tariffs in 2007. Following the success of this roaming regulation, the European Commission intervened also on mobile termination rates. It has instructed national regulatory authorities to set a glide-path regime toward cost-based termination rates. Market power on call termination for own customers may require continuous regulation, as do other services such as international roaming.

The 2002 regulatory framework for electronic communications is revised in 2009, with changes concerning the definition of relevant markets by reducing the number from eighteen to seven. The European Commission wanted also to set up a European regulatory authority, but this aim is opposed by the Member States. Thus the revision compromised by creating the Body of European Regulators for Electronic Communications (BEREC), which has a coordinating role of the national regulatory authorities and functions as advisor to the European Commission. As a complement to remedies for non-price discrimination in the access to network elements, the revised regulatory framework provides also for the possibility of imposing structural separation for vertically integrated incumbent firms with SMP in access markets. This measure is not yet applied in practice, but the threat of application has induced in some countries, like the UK, 'voluntary' arrangements to separate wholesale from retail activities.

The revised regulatory framework takes account of the way in which network access products priced at a wholesale level influence investment incentives. The regulatory framework declares itself supportive for investments by both incumbents and new entrants. The regulatory framework stays firmly based on the notion of access-price regulation and non-discriminatory access to infrastructure elements. But there is also provision for the conditions of access to newly built network elements. Differently from before, firms now can also make an allowance in the access cost calculation for market risk. This is meant to offset the risk firms run when investing in new types of infrastructure compared to the access seekers that have the advantage of asking for access only after they observe how the new assets perform in the marketplace. This position signals the awareness of the tension between open-access provision and incentives to invest.

REGULATION AND THE IMPACT ON INVESTMENT INCENTIVES

The economic literature extensively covered the interdependency between regulation and investment incentives. Rate-of-return regulation may have a strongly positive effect on investment if the warranted rate of return for the regulated firm is sufficiently high. There are clearly welfare considerations that induce regulators not to concede excessive rates of return. On the other hand, alternative forms of adopted incentive regulation are shifting market risks by varying degrees to owners of infrastructure, and may adversely affect investment incentives. In fact, incentive regulation induces forms of mark-up pricing along long-run incremental cost. But uniform profit margins across different services may be difficult to justify for a firm that must recover predominantly sunk costs, as there are good efficiency arguments that suggest that prices deviating from cost are socially optimal. Likewise multiproduct firms, such as vertically integrated telecommunications firms with market power, are subject to constraints in some product markets but not in others, and changes in regulations in some markets could spill over to other markets. These propositions on regulation and incentives for investment are illustrated with the case of unbundling of the local loop and inter-operator compensation in mobile telecommunications sectors.

Unbundling of Network Elements in Fixed-Line Markets

The mitigants for market power entailed by the 2002 regulatory framework included the requirement of unbundling of network elements, in particular at the local loop, at cost-based prices. As in most regulatory schemes, also in Europe, access prices for network elements are based on some kind of forward-looking long run incremental cost. This implies that the rental price for each network element is equal to the incremental cost of creating and supplying that leased element if the incumbent is designing and constructing a completely new, optimally configured network with state-of-the-art technology. Such a setting for telecommunications provides clear advantages to new entrants as equipment prices are declining substantially over time and hence forward-looking prices tend to underestimate the effective costs incurred in the past by the incumbent. Moreover, such a pricing rule under-compensates incumbents for the risks in making irreversible investments (Pindyck, 2007). In other words, this asymmetry in network costs gives the new entrant an option that the incumbent does not have: to enter only when market trends appear favourable. If this option is properly included into the lease price, the latter underestimates the true economic cost to the incumbent.

If access prices are too favourable to the new entrant, the incentives of the incumbent to invest in new infrastructure are reduced. This may be accepted temporarily if the new entrants eventually invest on their own. The 'ladder of investment' theory (Cave and Vogelsang, 2003; Cave, 2006) postulates that initially new entrants use the facilities of the incumbent for service-based competition and later invest in own infrastructure, i.e., assets with increasing difficulty to replicate. This approach is notionally adopted in the Netherlands with an increasing time profile for access prices (Rood and te Velde, 2003). However this concept of dynamic access prices with a sunset clause for regulation is not implemented (Poel, 2006).

Using forward-looking costs for determining access prices without considering a sufficiently high adjustment for market risk may have negative effects on infrastructure investment by the firm with upstream market power. This is in particular the risk when regulators cannot ex-ante commit to specific ex-post prices. This however is only one side of the coin. The other is the incentives for investment of alternative operators. Bourreau and Doğan (2006) show that low access prices provide a disincentive for investment in own facilities by new entrants. They can have access to the incumbent's infrastructure at lower cost than building infrastructure on their own. Moreover, incumbents have an incentive to provide access because this allows them to deter entry in infrastructure competition.

This regulatory framework thus gives incentives to increased competition on the DSL platform, but it has provided relatively limited incentives for infrastructure competition. Table 6.1 shows that the retail market share of incumbents is declining. But looking at the market shares of the different broadband access technologies in the EU, it also shows that the trend is heavily tilted towards DSL technology, which by 2010 still accounts for 77.9 per cent of the broadband access lines, almost the same as in 2004. The focus on a single-access technology may have two fundamental drawbacks for the diffusion of broadband access. First, the investment level is crucially affected by the incentive for the incumbent public switch telephone network (PSTN) operator. Second, the benefits of inter-platform competition are foregone. Cable modem, which used to be the most important alternative broadband platform is losing share.

The prevailing regulatory concept seems successful in attracting entry on the DSL platform, but it is less effective inducing inter-platform competition. But inter-platform competition seems a major driving force for broadband penetration (Gruber and Denni, 2007) and appears also to be the only credible way of creating the premise for rolling back regulation in the fixed line broadband sector. Mandatory local loop unbundling seems rather a substitute

Table 6.1 Shares of broadband access technologies in EU (%)

	2004	2006	2008	2010
Incumbent's market share in DSL market		57.2	55.9	55.0
Market share of broadband technology				
DSL	77.8	81.8	79.9	77.9
Cable	20.0	15.9	15.2	15.6
Other	2.2	3.3	4.9	6.5
Total	100.0	100.0	100.0	100.0

Source: Author from European Commission data.

than a complement for investment in alternative broadband infrastructure. Gruber (2010) illustrates how it could actually reduce incentives to invest in both DSL technology by the incumbent and alternative platforms such as cable TV networks by new entrants. As speeding up the roll-out of broadband infrastructure is still among the key items on the Europe 2020 strategy for creating Europe as the most advanced economic region in the world, this suggests that there are considerable regulatory challenges for Europe in the field of legacy networks such as DSL facing the transition to next generation networks.

Interoperator Compensation in Mobile Networks

The mobile telecommunications market is the first of the telecommunications markets to be liberalised in many countries during the first half of the 1990s through the concession of licences for radio spectrum, leading to a market structure of typically three to four firms (Gruber, 2005). It thereby achieved a market structure which delivered several features of a competitive industry. Nevertheless pricing structures persisted that would indicate a continuation of market power. In fact, the mobile telecommunications industry is a network industry where different networks compete for customers. Hence pricing decisions depend on interaction with other networks and are also constrained by regulatory decisions. The theoretical and practical foundations of pricing in telecommunications changed strongly along the technological trajectory of the industry and its market structure. With the rolling back of monopolies, pricing became strongly influenced by compensation mechanisms set up for interconnected traffic among networks. In contrast with many other network industries, the mobile telecommunications industry is less subject to specific price regulations. This reflects the idea that facility based network competition is sufficient to restrain retail prices. Nevertheless consumers and policy makers complain about several market distortions, such as high termination and roaming prices, as well as the presence of firms with apparently strong market power. Hence regulatory challenges of redressing market failures that relate to the abuse of market power appear far from being resolved. This will be dwelled upon in more detail with the examples of international roaming and national mobile termination payments.

International roaming occurs when a mobile phone subscriber is abroad and uses the network of foreign firms. This is the most important exception in a home network functioning under the traditional principle of Calling Party Pays (CPP), as for all inbound calls the mobile subscriber roaming abroad has to pay a fee as well. The pricing of roaming services is undertaken in a two-step procedure. The first is wholesale inter-operator tariff (IOT) at which the visited network firm charges the user's home network firm for the call, usually by adding a mark-up of 15 per cent on the normal network tariff. The second stage is retail pricing where the home network firm sets the price for the subscriber, normally by adding a 10 to 35 per cent margin on top of the wholesale price set in the first stage. The roaming price to the final customer thus obtained therefore involves double marginalisation. Technical constraints make it difficult to escape this mechanism. Visited mobile firms have no incentive to lower the wholesale prices because their counterparts cannot guarantee traffic redirection to their network. This inability to direct traffic to the cheapest of parallel networks in a visited country makes it difficult to apply competitive pressure. Moreover, mobile users typically shows ignorance about roaming costs charged by visited networks and this induces an absence of price competition at the retail level. The European Commission (2006) found in its impact assessment on roaming charges that at €1.15 per minute, the average retail charge for a roamed call (residential) is more than five times higher than the actual cost of providing wholesale service and 50 per cent higher than the average IOT. Retail roaming charges are roughly four times higher than domestic tariffs. Though roaming traffic is generally quite a small percentage of the total traffic of a firm, it is estimated that roaming accounts for 5.7 per cent of revenues. For the Commission this is clear evidence of abuse of market power, and hence as remedy established EU voice call roaming regulation in 2007, by capping the retail charge at €0.50. This measure was presented as transitory (for a three year period) and possibly to be replaced by voluntary industry measures. This, however, was not effective and the Commission further reduced roaming charges to €0.39 in 2010, and this measure is complemented by price caps on data roaming charges. Again the roaming price caps are for a three year period with an objective to lower it to €0.15 in 2012. Also with this objective roaming rates are a multiple of national call rates and hence the Commission is seeking a 'structural solution' which removes the price discrimination between roaming and non-roaming users and could involve abandoning the roaming regime altogether.

Mobile termination is particularly important early in evolution of the industry, as mobile telecommunications firms in most countries had a special regime to determine their access prices. Frequently they are not bound to cost-based prices and large asymmetries in interconnection charges can occur between fixed and mobile networks. Initially they are justified by the fact that mobile networks are newly built, whereas fixed-line networks are much older and hence already amortised to a much larger extent. However, these arguments have lost appeal over time. Anyway, a mobile network is in a monopoly position for providing access to any of its customers. High interconnection charges also function as a device for collusion (Armstrong, 1998). With the pervasiveness of the mobile networks, regulators started to insist on cost-based prices for interconnection, though strong asymmetries persisted and are justified by the higher operating cost of new mobile networks compared to older fixed-line networks. For instance, according to EU regulations, only mobile firms with SMP status as defined by the national regulator must publish non-discriminatory cost-based interconnection offerings.

A special position is access charges in the case of fixed-to-mobile calls. Armstrong (2001) refers to this as 'competitive bottleneck'. In this market there are several networks competing vigorously for the same pool of subscribers, but these networks have a monopoly position in providing services to their subscribers. The termination charge set by a mobile firm does not affect directly the customers of its own network, but the price set for the fixed-line subscriber. As before, the market power of the mobile firm provides the incentive for setting termination charges above termination costs. This extra profit can be used to subsidise the acquisition of new subscribers, while locking them in through devices such as handset subsidies. Mobile firms offer new subscribers handsets below cost in exchange for a minimum subscription period. However, in this case the cost of the handset subsidy is not covered by the airtime payments of the mobile subscriber, but by the fixed-line subscribers calling the mobile network. Mobile subscribers benefit from this pricing policy, but their benefit is more than outweighed by the cost it imposes on fixed-line subscribers. The rapid expansion of the mobile subscriber base therefore is subsidised by the fixed-line network (Wright, 2000). High fixed-to-mobile prices induce an inefficiently low traffic from fixed-to-mobile networks. To redress this situation, regulatory action is required to lower mobile termination charges to marginal cost (Armstrong, 2001; Gans and King, 2000) and possibly to increase mobile retail charges to cover common and fixed costs (Hausman, 2000).

In Europe the theoretical debate (Armstrong and Wright, 2009) whether fixed-to-mobile calls should be regulated or whether there are countervailing mechanisms that could relax the requirement for regulation is decided for the former. However, differently from the case of roaming where a directive is issued, the Commission issued a recommendation for regulating the fixed and mobile termination rates in 2009. The Commission indicated that termination rates should be oriented by forward-looking long-run incremental cost, should be symmetric and any asymmetries be adequately justified (and phased out). Figure 6.1 shows the evolution of average mobile termination rates in the EU. The rates steadily declined from Euro cents 12.65 (2005) to Euro cents 6.71 (2009). The Commission expects further decline to Euro cents 1.5 by 2012.

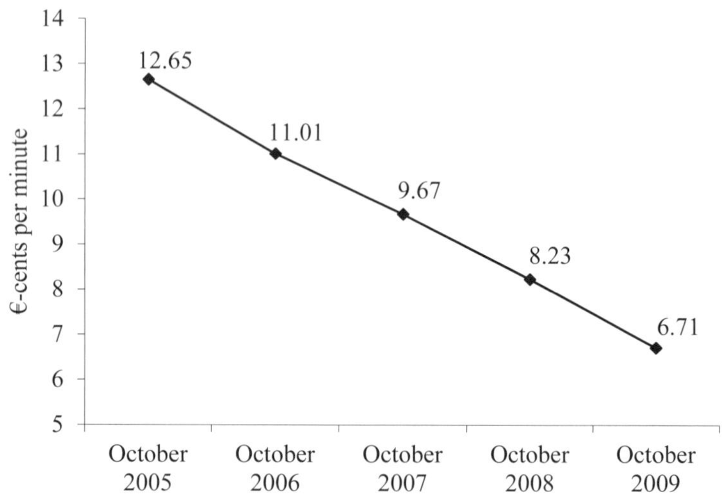

Source: European Commission (2010a).

Figure 6.1 *EU average interconnection charges for call termination on mobile networks (fixed-to-mobile interconnection rates)*

For multiproduct firms with market power such as mobile telecommunications firms, regulatory intervention may have knock-on effects on other markets. Genakos and Valletti (2007) assessed the effect of a reduction in mobile termination rates on retail prices. They find that retail prices for mobile services increase as a result, though not to the full extent. Some of the reduction in termination prices could therefore not be passed on to the consumer. The reduction in termination rates is thought to have led to a reduction in the profit margins of mobile operators and thus to a more intensive use of infrastructure (infrastructure sweating). Clearly the value of a subscriber in attracting (high margin) incoming calls is strongly reduced as a result, and led to a reassessment of the role of expanding the subscriber base which ultimately is also the driver for network investment. As the attention is focussing on the traffic pattern of existing subscribers, infrastructure investment is likely to lose priority. Moreover, with the increase of flat fee pricing schemes the performance of individual calls is becoming less relevant which again allows for infrastructure saving. Overall investment incentives thus could be diminished, though in presence of market power the case could be made that it induces more efficient investment.

The increasing importance of mobile broadband is expected to make the traditional charging principle to voice traffic not sustainable. Mobile voice traffic, which accounts for some 90 per cent of revenues, is charged according to time. But this is no longer realistic in a technological context where traffic is delivered over an all IP network and mobile broadband services are becoming pervasive. The introduction of flat rates and bundles is an important driver of the development of mobile broadband, but this pricing approach often leads to reduced average revenue streams per user. It is estimated that in comparison with voice, mobile broadband subscribers are creating on average 130 times more traffic while paying only 1 per cent of the price per MB (Markendhal et al., 2009). To summarise, price regulation oriented to cost reduces the scope of firms for price flexibility and, together with technological pressures that undermine the traditional time-based voice pricing model, reduce the scope of firms to raise resources for investment, as acknowledged by the European Commission (2010a).

NEW REGULATORY CHALLENGES

The economic policy debate in Europe is centred on improving productivity growth performance, trying to meet the ambitious quantitative goals set out in 2000 in the Lisbon Agenda aimed at making Europe the most competitive region in the world. The telecommunications sector, in particular broadband communications, is attributed an important role in this (European Commission, 2003). Though countries are struggling with implementing the declared targets during the decade, this commitment is renewed in 2009 with the launch of the Europe 2020 strategy. This strategy outlines the development of broadband networks as a key component enabling further growth in Europe. Under the 'Smart Growth' priority aiming at the development of an economy based on knowledge and innovation, the European Commission (2010b) formulated a 'Digital Agenda for Europe' (DAE) initiative that proposes very concrete targets for broadband network roll-out. Among the objectives is that by 2020 there should be high-speed broadband access (i.e., in excess of 30 Mbit/s) to all and at least 50 per cent of households should subscribe to Internet services in excess of 100 Mbit/s.

The latter objective is achievable mainly by fibre to fibre-to-the-home (FTTH) networks, or under certain conditions by upgraded cable TV networks. DSL networks will not have the capacity for such performance. This requires telecommunications firms select the optimum time for switching to fibre technology. Currently most are pursuing a gradual strategy in pushing fibre closer to the customer by creating intermediary branching units to reduce the length of the local loop. However, such GPON (Gigabit Passive Optical Network) technologies, which share the fibre capacity, have inherent limits and are inferior to point-to-point (P2P) solutions, where the local loop is entirely fibre. The owners of copper lines therefore must in principle replace the whole local loop with fibre, and thus the incremental revenue from the shift to fibre may not warrant this investment that makes the copper infrastructure obsolete. There is, however, the incentive to do it if a competitor is threatening to build a fibre network. In general, there may be differences in the preferred technological design of the next generation access architecture, depending on whether the firm has a legacy network. In the former case the preference would be rather for GPON and in the latter for P2P technology. Upgraded cable networks appear the only technological alternative for next generation broadband access. Wireless technologies, though expected to increase their transmission capacity significantly, are also unlikely to achieve that of 100 Mbit/s needed to qualify for next generation access. Figure 6.2 shows the diffusion of the different broadband platforms across EU Member States. Geographically large countries like Italy do not have cable networks at, or like Germany and France, they are only a small fraction of the total broadband access paths. Only in a very few, mostly geographically smaller, countries is there significant presence of cable networks. Ultimately, the most likely scenario is that in many countries or regions there will be at most one network providing the transmission capacity of at least 100 Mbit/s. This also means that this could have features of a natural monopoly; there would be a need for a utility type of access regulation of this network to avoid the abuse of dominant position.

Estimates of the total investment cost required to achieve the DAE broadband targets are quite high. The problem is that with current expectations of revenues from broadband access a large part of these investments is financially not profitable and significant public support is required to fulfil the Digital Agenda broadband targets. The key issue behind hindering market driven investments into next generation networks in particular lies in the high cost of deployment and long payback periods. Deploying FTTH networks in areas with a low population density carries a high cost. Therefore it is unlikely that covering such areas can be financed purely through market mechanisms and that telecommunications operators will possibly be able to raise the financial resources needed to implement the broadband targets. Accordingly, it is safe to say that the ambitious broadband development targets of the Digital Agenda will fall short without large scale

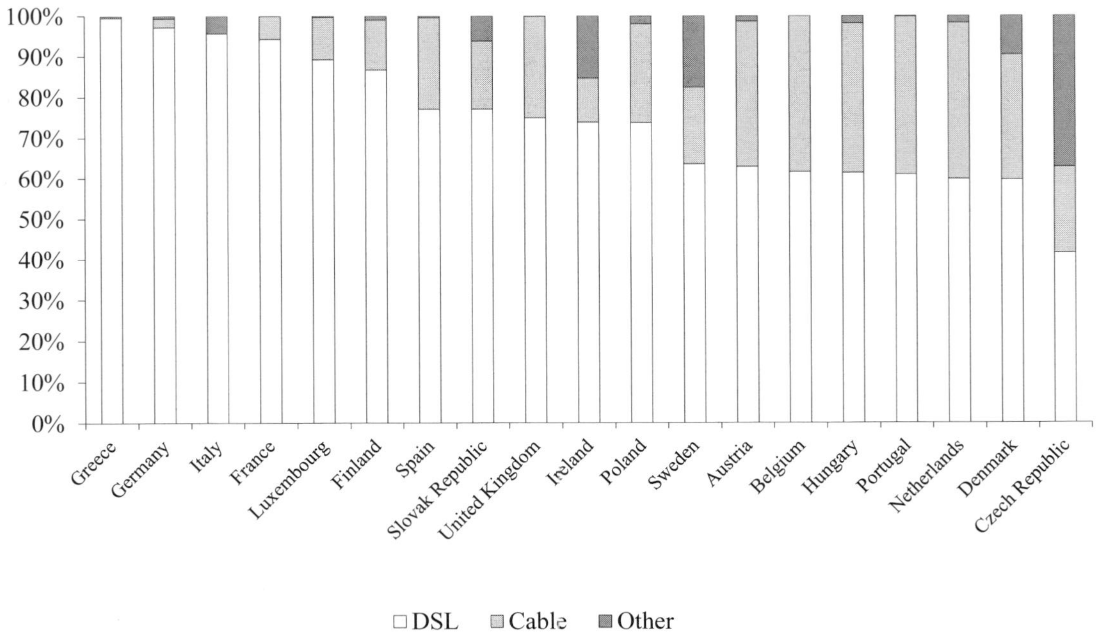

Source: OECD (2009).

Figure 6.2 Shares of broadband access technologies for EU Member States (June 2006)

government intervention. One of the options is to raise investment incentives, as in the US, by foregoing access regulation for next generation access. In the aftermath, the incumbent Verizon made substantial investment in fibre access infrastructure. The situation in the US, however, is facilitated by the fact that there is already widespread cable TV infrastructure, thus ensuring some form of platform competition. Such a position of regulatory forbearance is, however, currently not tenable in Europe, where cable networks are much less pervasive or non-existent in many countries. The investment ladder concept seems to be successful in attracting entry on the fixed-line telecommunications platform, but it is less so for inducing inter-platform competition and investment. It seems that the revised EU regulatory framework will remain firmly based for the foreseeable future on the notions of access price regulation and unbundling.

CONCLUDING REMARKS

Regulatory reform in telecommunications in Europe, like in other network industries, is inspired by the concept of open access regulation to bottleneck elements in the customer access infrastructure. Competitive access is seen as the means for eliminating the deadweight loss from monopoly and to establish efficient service provision in fixed-line telecommunications. Cost-based access pricing regimes are introduced in Europe to favour competitive entry, at least for intra-platform competition. In this sense the ladder of investment concept worked to illustrate the entry mode with increasing own facilities over time. However, it failed to deliver significant investment for inter-platform competition. This issue is now compounded by the fact that FTTH becomes in many contexts the only option for high-speed broadband access. This therefore requires a stepping up of regulation towards a utility style regulation with warranted rates of return for providers of open access fibre networks. The implicit rate of return should provide for sufficient incentives to invest, but there remains the problem that competitive pressure may not be as high as desired by policy makers. This therefore requires substantial public support to the roll out of NGA networks. In the context of mobile telecommunications, it is shown that price regulation oriented to cost reduced the flexibility of firms in setting price. Together with technological pressures this is challenging the traditional time-based voice pricing model to generate revenues. As a consequence, mobile firms reduced scope to raise resources for investment from current business, as noted also by the European Commission (2010a). This is a relatively new aspect for the mobile telecommunications industry which is used to relatively high profitability and in that sense regulatory policy very much aligned to consumer interest in achieving low prices. A further issue for regulatory policy is to create incentives for dynamic efficiency in terms of the sector pursuing innovation in technology and services.

ACKNOWLEDGEMENT

The views expressed are personal and need not necessarily reflect those of the EIB.

REFERENCES

Alesina, A., Ardagna, S., Nicoletti, G. and Schiantarelli, F. (2005), 'Regulation and Investment', *Journal of the European Economic Association*, **3**, 791–825.
Armstrong, M. (1998), 'Network Interconnection in Telecommunications', *Economic Journal*, **108**, 545–64.
Armstrong, M. (2001), 'The Theory of Access Pricing and Interconnection', MPRA Paper 15608, University Library of Munich, Germany.
Armstrong, M. and Sappington, M. (2006), 'Regulation, Competition and Liberalisation', *Journal of Economic Literature*, **44**, 325–66.
Armstrong, M. and Wright, J. (2009), 'Mobile Call Termination', *Economic Journal*, **119**, F270–F307.
Baake, P. and Preissl, B. (2006), *Local Loop Unbundling and Bitstream Access in Europe and the US*, Politikberatung Kompakt 20, DIW: Berlin.
Bourreau, M. and Doğan, P. (2006), 'Build-or-Buy Strategies in the Local Loop', *American Economic Review*, **96**, 72–6.
Cambini, C. and Jiang, Y. (2009), 'Broadband Investment and Regulation: A Literature Review', *Telecommunications Policy*, **33**, 559–74.
Cave, M. (2003), 'Remedies for Broadband Services', Warwick Business School. September.
Cave, M. (2006), 'Encouraging Infrastructure Competition via the Ladder of Investment', *Telecommunications Policy*, **30**, 223–37.
Cave, M. and Vogelsang, I. (2003), 'How Access Pricing and Entry Interact', *Telecommunications Policy,* **27**, 717–27.
European Commission (2003), 'Electronic Communications: The Road to the Knowledge Economy', COM (2003) 65 final.
European Commission (2006), 'Roaming on Public Mobile Networks within the Community', COM(2006) 382 final.
European Commission (2010a), 'Progress Report on the Single European Electronic Communications Market', 15th Implementation Report, COM(2010) 630.
European Commission (2010b), 'A Digital Agenda for Europe', COM(2010) 245 final/2.
Gans, J. and King, S. (2000), 'Mobile Network Competition, Customer Ignorance, and Fixed-to-Mobile Call Prices', *Information Economics and Policy*, **12**, 301–28.
Gans J. and King, S. (2004), 'Access Holidays and the Timing of Investment', *Economic Record*, **80**, 89–100.

Genakos, C. and Valletti, T. (2007), 'Testing the "Waterbed" Effect in Mobile Telephony', CEPR Discussion Paper 7611.

Gruber, H. (2005), *The Economics of Mobile Telecommunications*, Cambridge: Cambridge University Press.

Gruber, H. (2010), 'European Sector Regulation and Investment Incentives for Broadband Communication Networks', in Falch, M. and Markendahl, J. (eds) *Promoting New Telecom Infrastructures*, Cheltenham: Edward Elgar.

Gruber, H. and Denni, M. (2007), 'The Diffusion of Broadband Telecommunications in the US: The Role of Different Forms of Competition', *Communications & Strategies*, **4**, 139–57.

Gruber, H. and Verboven, F. (2001), 'The Diffusion of Mobile Telecommunications Services in the European Union', *European Economic Review*, **45**, 577–88.

Gryseels, M. and Begonha, D. (2010), 'Fiber: The Future of Fixed in Europe', presentation at the FTTH Council Europe Conference, Lisbon, 25 February.

Guthrie, G. (2006), 'Regulating Infrastructure: The Impact on Risk and Investment', *Journal of Economic Literature*, **44**, 925–72.

Haucap, J. (2003), 'The Economics of Mobile Telephone Regulation', University FAF Economics Working Paper No. 4.

Hausman, J. (1997), 'Valuing the Effect of Regulation on New Services in Telecommunications', *Brookings Papers on Economic Activity: Microeconomics*, 1–38.

Hausman, J. (2000), 'Efficiency Effects on the US Economy from Wireless Taxation', *National Tax Journal*, **53**, 733–42.

Jorde,T., Sidak, J. and Teece, D. (2000), 'Innovation, Investment and Unbundling', *Yale Journal on Regulation*, **17**, 1–37.

Markendhal, J., Mölleryd, B., Mäkitalo Ö. and Werding, J. (2009), 'Business Innovation Strategies to Reduce the Revenue Gap for Wireless Broadband Services', *Communications & Strategies*, **75**, 35–56.

Newberry, D. (1999), *Privatisation, Restructuring and Regulation of Network Utilities*, Cambridge: MIT Press.

Nihoul, P. and Rodford, P. (2004), *EU Electronic Communications Law: Competition and Regulation in the Telecommunications Market*, Oxford: Oxford University Press.

OECD (2009), *Communications Outlook*, Paris: Organisation for Economic Co-operation and Development.

Pindyck, R. (2007), 'Mandatory Unbundling and Irreversible Investment in Telecom Networks', *Review of Network Economics*, **6**, 274–98.

Poel, M. (2006), 'Regulation of the Local Loop in the Netherlands' in P. Baake and B. Preissl (eds) *Local Loop Unbundling and Bitstream Access: Regulatory Practice in Europe and the US*, Politikberatung Kompakt 20, DIW: Berlin.

Rood, H. and te Velde, R. (2003), 'Investment Strategies in the Netherlands,' *Telecommunications Policy*, **27**, 701–15.

Wright, J. (2000), 'Competition and Termination in Cellular Networks', mimeo, University of Auckland.

7. Pricing of complements and network effects

Nicholas Economides and Brian Viard

INTRODUCTION

This study examines a monopolist of a base good that benefits from a complementary good provided by either it or another firm. Use of the complementary good requires the base good, but not the reverse. The model assesses and calibrates the extent of the positive influence on the base good profits that is created by the existence of the two sources (internal or external) of the complementary good. An equivalence between a model of a base and complementary good, and a reduced-form model of the base good where network effects are assumed in the utility function as a surrogate for the presence of direct network effects (i.e., a consumer's utility directly increases in the number of users) or indirect network effects (i.e., arising from increased variety of complementary goods produced by other firms) is established. This allows us to examine the pricing of the complementary good under different market structures and in the context of the effect of other complementary goods via the network effects. Additionally, the study assesses and calibrates the influence of the intensity of network effects and quality improvements in the complementary good on profits from the base good. Also evaluated is the incentive that a monopolist has to improve the quality of the base good rather than that of a complementary good that it produces.

The model has implications for the base good monopolist's trade off in improving the quality of its own complementary good versus subsidizing increases in other network effects. The monopolist could subsidize increases in other network effects by, e.g., taking actions to increase sales of the base good thereby increasing consumers' utility directly (direct network effects) or facilitating or subsidizing increased variety of other complementary goods available (indirect network effects). The base good monopolist prefers that an independent firm offer an additional complementary good rather than improve the quality of an extant complementary good by the same amount as the quality offered by the new good, assuming the costs of the two are the same. This results from the complementary goods firm's incentive to restrict output more at higher quality levels, limiting the increase in base good sales via sales of the complementary good. Importantly, the base good monopolist gains more from adding a complementary good to its portfolio of products than increasing the quality of an existing portfolio product by the same quality as that of the new good if the costs of doing so are the same. The effect is stronger than if an independent firm produces the complementary good. This is because adding a complementary good increases sale of the base good because of the complementarities, but an increase in the quality of the complementary good does not affect sales of the base good because the monopolist can fully adjust the price of the complementary good to capture profits from its increased quality.

The model also has implications for the base good monopolist's incentives to invest in improving the base and complementary goods under different market structures and in making them compatible. An independent base good monopolist has a greater incentive to invest in improving the quality of the base good (at the margin) than a joint monopolist who produces both the base and complementary good. Improvements in the base good increase its price and therefore the effective price to use the complementary good. A producer of both internalizes this and has less incentive to improve the base good, while an independent monopolist does not. Conversely, a monopolist who produces both the base and complementary goods has a greater incentive to improve the complementary good (on the margin) than an independent firm would have to improve it. Improvements in the complementary good's quality increase sales of the base good, which the joint monopolist internalizes but the independent firm does not. Finally, if a single firm owns both the base and complementary goods it has a greater incentive to make them compatible than if separate firms offered the two products because increasing compatibility improves sales of both. The base good benefits directly from a more compatible product and the complementary good benefits indirectly because it requires purchase of the base good. A joint monopolist internalizes this feedback while independent firms do not.

Based on these results, a possible explanation of the fact that Microsoft Office is significantly more expensive than Microsoft Windows is discussed. Microsoft has approximately the same market share (over 90 per cent) in the market for operating systems for personal computers as in the market for 'Office applications' (a bundle of word processing, spreadsheet, presentation and database software). However, Microsoft charges a price for its Windows operating system that is significantly lower than the price of its office suite. Although the model does not address the level of prices for Windows and

Office, it can explain this difference in relative prices for Windows and Office. A joint monopolist, such as Microsoft, has two price instruments, the base good and complementary good price. It is optimal to keep the operating system price low even if Office is quite valuable because some users buy Windows for use with other complementary goods. Raising the price of Office but keeping the price of Windows low allows the joint monopolist to capture some of the value provided by Office while not pricing users of other goods complementary to Windows out of the market.

The model of a base and a complementary good is similar to models of 'mix and match,' where consumers assemble systems in fixed proportions, but differs from typical assumptions in these models because the base good in the model is valuable without use of the complementary good. In mix and match models typically neither good is valuable without the other. Mix and match models originated from Matutes and Regibeau (1988) and Economides (1989).[1, 2]

The reduced-form model of the base good in which network effects are summarized by a term that influences utility positively and is increasing in sales, derives from Katz and Shapiro (1985) and Farrell and Saloner (1986). The network effects summarized in the utility function can result from either direct or indirect network effects. In the former case, a consumer benefits directly from the number of individuals adopting the base good (e.g., because there is a larger network to exchange files with) while in the latter case a consumer benefits indirectly from the number of individuals adopting the base good through the increased availability of software variety. Both of these effects are summarized by a term in consumers' utility functions, which is increasing in total sales of the base good.[3]

There has been little attempt to calibrate the size of the network effect used in reduced-form models. Exceptions are Economides (1996b) and Clements (2004). Economides (1996b) calibrates the size of the network effect in the context of measuring the incentive of a patent-holding monopolist who also sells a complementary good to invite competitors in the complementary goods market so as to maximize the network effects. Clements (2004) evaluates the effect of the strength of network effects, degree of compatibility and the density of consumers in the market on standardization under oligopolistic competition. The objective of these papers is different from our objective of providing an equivalence of these modelling approaches and evaluating the incentives of the base good provider to innovate, promote other complementary products and set compatibility standards.

The rest of this chapter starts by setting up the basic framework of the research. The five models used are then developed and discussed. These models differ in the way that network effects and inherent product quality are modelled. The equilibria of these models is then considered. A discussion of the incentives to invest in quality in either the base good or the complementary good in different ownership structures and under different intensities of network effects follows and compatibility decisions made by the base good monopolist are examined. Next, there is a discussion of the explanation of Microsoft's relative pricing provided by the analysis. To conclude, the results are compared with the empirical literature on network effects.

BASIC FRAMEWORK

Assume that consumers are differentiated by their preferences for quality of the base good (B) and quality of the complementary good (C). The second good requires the first good to provide positive utility.[4] For example, think of the Windows operating system as the base good, and an office suite (such as Microsoft Office) as the complementary good, not necessarily produced by the same company. Let the marginal utility of quality of the base good be θ and the marginal utility of quality of the complementary good be ϕ. The pair (θ, ϕ) defines a consumer type. Also, assume that both θ and ϕ are distributed independently and uniformly on [0, 1].

Assumed network effects could be direct effects that result from a consumer's utility directly increasing in the number of other users of the base good or indirect effects that result from other complementary goods whose existence positively influences consumers' willingness to pay for the base good via economies of scale in production. Assume for this study the latter case that the positive consumption effects between the base good and the complementary goods reinforce each other. These effects are summarized by adding a term proportional to sales of the base good in the utility function of a typical consumer.

When consuming one unit of the base good and possibly one unit of the complementary good, consumer (θ, ϕ) receive utility

$$U = \theta q_B - p_B + \alpha x_B + \delta V ,$$

where q_B is the quality of the base good, p_B is the price of the base good, V is the utility from the consumption of the complementary good, x_B is the sales of the base good, α measures the intensity of the network effects and δ is an indicator variable taking the value one if the complementary good is bought and zero otherwise. Thus, network effects arising out of direct or indirect network effects are summarized by an additive term in the utility function proportional to sales.[5] Consumers not purchasing receive zero utility. The utility from the consumption of the complementary good is

$$V = \varphi q_C - p_C ,$$

where q_C is the quality of the complementary good and p_C is the price of the complementary good.

The first model has a base good monopolist in a market where network effects are summarized in the utility function of consumers as proportional to sales. The second model has two monopolists (independent firms), one for the base good and one for the complementary good, and assumes no network effects. The third model adds network effects to the independent firms in Model 2. The fourth model has a single monopolist (joint monopolist) producing both the base and the complementary good. The fifth model adds network effects to the joint monopolist considered in Model 4.

MODELS

Model 1: Single Good Monopolist in a Market with Network Effects

First consider a model of a single good monopolist selling the base good with network effects arising from direct or indirect effects due to the presence of other complementary goods produced with increasing returns to scale. In this case, $\delta = 0$ and consumer θ who buys one unit of the base good of quality q_B at price p_B receives utility of

$$U = \theta q_B - p_B + \alpha x_B , \qquad (7.1)$$

where $\alpha > 0$ measures the intensity of the network effect (marginal utility of network expansion). All consumers of type $\theta > \theta_B$ buy the good, where the marginal consumer is

$$\theta_B = \frac{(p_B - \alpha x_B)}{q_B} . \qquad (7.2)$$

Sales are

$$x_B = (1 - \theta_B) = 1 - \frac{(p_B - \alpha x_B)}{q_B} . \qquad (7.3)$$

Inverting the demand gives

$$x_B = \frac{(q_B - p_B)}{(q_B - \alpha)}, \ \Pi_B = p_B x_B = \frac{p_B(q_B - p_B)}{(q_B - \alpha)}.^{6} \tag{7.4}$$

Assuming zero costs, maximizing profits implies:[7]

$$p_B^* = \frac{q_B}{2}, \ x_B^* = \frac{q_B}{2(q_B - \alpha)} \text{ and } \Pi_B^* = \frac{q_B^2}{4(q_B - \alpha)}.^{8} \tag{7.5}$$

In the case of no network effects, i.e., when $\alpha = 0$, the demand without network effects is a pivot of the demand with network effects through the point $(0, q_B)$. It is well known that such pivots of linear demands lead to the same monopoly price. Thus, the equilibrium price is unaffected by network effects, while sales and profits are higher with them. Using the subscript 0 for the variables with no networks effects $(\alpha = 0)$, gives

$$x_B^* = x_{B0}\left[\frac{q_B}{(q_B - \alpha)}\right]; \ p_B^* = p_{B0}, \text{ and } \Pi_B^* = \Pi_{B0}\left[\frac{q_B}{(q_B - \alpha)}\right]. \tag{7.6}$$

Model 2: Independent Firms without Network Effects

This model considers two independent monopolists, one for the base good and another for the complementary good, and no network effects are allowed. Comparing the equilibrium of Model 2 to that of Model 1, enables calibration of the intensity of network effects necessary to generate base good profits equivalent to those generated by sales of a complementary good.

There are two groups of purchasers to consider (see Figure 7.1). First, consumers of type $\theta > \theta_B$, $\phi < \phi_{B,BU}$ buy the base good only, where θ_B is the marginal consumer indifferent between buying the base good and buying nothing, i.e.

$$\theta_B = p_B / q_B, \tag{7.7}$$

and $\phi_{B,BU}$ is the marginal consumer indifferent between buying only the base good and buying both the base and complementary goods, i.e.

$$\varphi_{B,BU} = p_C / q_C. \tag{7.8}$$

Second, consumers of types $\varphi > \varphi_{B,BU}$, $\theta > \theta_B$, as well as of types $\varphi > \varphi_{BU}(\theta)$, $\theta < \theta_B$, buy both, where $\varphi_{BU}(\theta)$ is the marginal consumer of

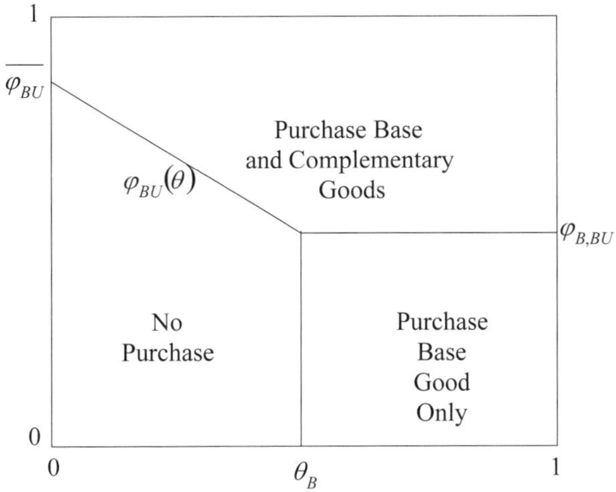

Figure 7.1 *Independent firm with no network effects*

type θ indifferent between buying both goods and buying nothing, i.e.

$$\varphi_{BU}(\theta) = (p_B + p_C - \theta q_B)/q_C \, . \tag{7.9}$$

The profits for the base good monopolist are

$$\Pi_B = \left[(1-\theta_B)\varphi_{B,BU} + \left(1-\varphi_{B,BU} - (\overline{\varphi_{BU}} - \varphi_{B,BU}\right)/2\right] p_B \, , \tag{7.10}$$

where $\overline{\varphi_{BU}} = (p_B + p_C)/q_C$ is the consumer of type $\theta = 0$ who is indifferent between buying both goods and nothing. The profits for the complementary good monopolist are

$$\Pi_C = \left[(1-\varphi_{B,BU}) - (\overline{\varphi_{BU}} - \varphi_{B,BU})\theta_B/2\right] p_C \, . \tag{7.11}$$

At the Nash equilibrium in a price-setting game, the first-order conditions for the two monopolists are

$$p_B(3p_B + 4p_C) - 2q_B q_C = 0 \text{ and } p_B^2 - 2q_B(q_C - 2p_C) = 0 \, . \tag{7.12}$$

Since the first-order conditions are nonlinear they are solved numerically to find the equilibrium.[9] The analysis restricts $q_C \geq q_B$ since only interior solutions and for $q_C > q_B$, $\overline{\varphi_{BU}} > 1$ are considered.[10]

Model 3: Independent Firms with Network Effects

In Model 3, we incorporate network effects arising from direct consumption externalities or other complementary goods into Model 2. The utility function of consumers (eq. 7.1) now has a positive α capturing the network effects. The same regions of consumer types buy as in Model 2, but some margins now depend on α. We use superscript n to denote the presence of network effects

$$\theta_B^n = (p_B - \alpha x_B)/q_B\,,\ \varphi_{B,BU}^n = \varphi_{B,BU}\,, \tag{7.13}$$

$$\varphi_{BU}^n = (p_B + p_C - \theta q_B - \alpha x_B)/q_C,\ \overline{\varphi_{BU}^n} = (p_B + p_C - \alpha x_B)/q_C\,. \tag{7.14}$$

Demand for the base good is given by solving for x_B in

$$x_B = 1 - \theta_B^n(x_B) + \left[1 - \left(\overline{\varphi_{BU}^n}(x_B) - \varphi_{B,BU}^n(x_B)\right)\theta_B^n / 2\right]. \tag{7.15}$$

Since θ_B^n and φ_{BU}^n are both linear functions of x_B, this is a quadratic equation. Using the positive root, x_B^*, that solves this equation, the profit function for the base good monopolist is

$$\Pi_B^n = \left[\left(1 - \theta_B^n(x_B^*)\right)\varphi_{B,BU}^n + \left(1 - \varphi_{B,BU}^n - 1/2\left(\overline{\varphi_{BU}^n}(x_B^*) - \varphi_{B,BU}^n\right)\theta_B^n(x_B^*)\right)\right]p_B \tag{7.16}$$

and for the complementary good monopolist is

$$\Pi_C^n = \left[(1 - \varphi_{B.BU}^n) - 1/2\left(\overline{\varphi_{BU}^n}(x_B^*) - \varphi_{B,BU}^n\right)\theta_B^n(x_B^*)\right]p_C \tag{7.17}$$

The first-order conditions for the two firms are nonlinear functions of the prices and so are solved numerically.[11]

Model 4: Joint Monopolist without Network Effects

In Model 4, the joint monopolist sells both the base and complementary goods. The marginal consumers are defined in the same manner as in Model 2, and the profit function for the joint monopolist is

$$\Pi_B + \Pi_C = (1-\theta_B)\varphi_{B,BU} p_B + \left(1-\varphi_{B,BU} - 1/2\left(\overline{\varphi_{BU}} - \varphi_{B,BU}\right)\theta_B\right)(p_B + p_C) \tag{7.18}$$

The joint monopolist chooses both prices to maximize its profits. The first-order conditions are

$$3p_B(p_B+2p_C) - 2q_B q_C = 0 \text{ and } 3p_B^2 - 2q_B(q_C - 2p_C) = 0\,. \tag{7.19}$$

These can be solved to get the equilibrium prices, quantities, and profits:

$$p_B = \frac{2q_B}{3},\ p_C = \frac{q_C}{2} - \frac{q_B}{3}, \tag{7.20}$$

$$x_B = 1 - \frac{p_B(p_B+2p_C)}{(2q_B q_C)} \text{ and } x_C = 1 - \frac{(p_B^2 + 2p_C q_B)}{(2q_B q_C)}.\text{[12]} \tag{7.21}$$

Notice that the price of the base good is independent of the quality of the complementary good. This is true for general demand functions, since the marginal revenue of the joint monopolist from sales of the base good is independent of the quality and price of the complementary good, at the optimal complementary good price. To see this, consider general demand functions for the base and complementary goods, $D_B(p_B)$ and $D_C(p_B+p_C)$ respectively. Then profits are:

$$\Pi_B = p_B\left[D_B(p_B) + D_C(p_B+p_C)\right] \text{ and } \Pi_C = p_C D_C(p_B+p_C), \tag{7.22}$$

and joint profits are $\Pi = \Pi_B + \Pi_C$ so that the first-order conditions are (where primes denote derivatives):

$$\begin{aligned} D_B + p_B D_B' + D_C + (p_B+p_C)D_C' &= 0, \\ D_C + (p_B+p_C)D_C' &= 0. \end{aligned} \tag{7.23}$$

These conditions imply that $D_B(p_B)+p_B D_B'(p_B)=0$. Therefore, for the joint monopolist the choice of price for the base good is independent of the choice of price and quality of the complementary good.

The joint monopolist completely internalizes in the complementary good price any changes in the quality of the complementary good, and therefore the price of the basic good remains unaffected by such quality changes.[13] In the analysis only positive prices are considered for the complementary good and therefore restrict $q_C > 2q_B/3$.[14]

Model 5: Joint Monopolist with Network Effects

Model 5 incorporates network effects for the base good into Model 4. The marginal consumers are defined in the same manner as in Model 3 and the profit function for the joint monopolist is

$$\Pi_B^n + \Pi_C^n = \left(1-\theta_B^n\left(x_B^*\right)\right)\varphi_{B,BU}^n p_B$$
$$+\left(1-\varphi_{B,BU}^n - \frac{1}{2}\left(\overline{\phi_{BU}^n}\left(x_B^*\right)-\varphi_{B,BU}^n\right)\theta_B^n\left(x_B^*\right)\right)\left(p_B+p_C\right). \tag{7.24}$$

The first-order conditions for the firm are nonlinear functions of the prices and are solved numerically.[15]

EQUIVALENCE RESULTS

In this section, the size of network effects necessary to achieve the same base good profits as those arising from sales of the complementary good are calibrated. This is possible since the models explicitly allow for positive effects of the complementary good sales as well as models that allow for network effects that are summarized in the utility function. Thus, establishing equivalence between the network effects (defined as added profits to a base good monopolist) created by the presence of a complementary good and those summarized in the utility function is done for the various industry structures and for quality levels. This equivalence is used in base good profits to analyse the incentive of the base good monopolist to offer its own complementary good, improve the quality of a complementary good that it offers, and subsidize an independent firm so that it offers or increases the quality of a complementary good it provides.

The focus is on a particular type of equivalence, in base good profits, because the primary interest is in the incentives of the base good monopolist. This equivalence, of course, does not ensure that consumer welfare is equated. Doing so requires determining how to weight the utility of consumers with high versus low valuations of base and complementary goods since purchasing patterns vary across different equilibria. In addition, profits could not be equilibrated at the same time as consumer welfare. One could also calibrate equivalence in total profits across both firms. However, this is an inappropriate comparison to make when comparing models with and without network effects. Similarly, calibrating the equivalence in total (base and complementary good) profits for the base good monopolist is inappropriate when comparing models in which the base good firm controls the complementary good to those in which it does not. Accordingly, the focus is on equivalence in base good profits as the goal is to evaluate the incentives of the base good monopolist.[16]

An important property of all the models is scalability. It is easy to check that the equilibrium sales x_B and x_C are unaffected by a common scaling (up or down) of q_B, q_C, and α by the same coefficient $\lambda > 0$. Additionally, the equilibrium prices p_B and p_C are proportional to the common scaling factor λ of q_B, q_C, and α, and therefore their ratio (p_C / p_B) is unaffected by scaling. It follows that equilibrium profits are also proportional in the scaling factor λ. Thus, all variables are scaled (normalized) in terms of the quality of the base good q_B, defining the normalized quality of the complementary good as $\tilde{q}_C = q_C / q_B$, the normalized α or normalized network effects as $\tilde{\alpha} = \alpha / q_B$, the normalized prices of the goods as $\tilde{p}_B = p_B / q_B, \tilde{p}_C = p_C / q_B$, the normalized relative price of the complementary good in relation to the base good as $\tilde{R}_{CB} = \tilde{p}_C / \tilde{p}_B = p_C / p_B$, the normalized base good profits as $\tilde{\Pi}_B = \Pi_B / q_B$, and the normalized complementary good profits as $\tilde{\Pi}_C = \Pi_C / q_B$. All normalized variables remain unaffected by the common scaling of q_B, q_C, and α. Below, are reported results for all models in terms of normalized variables.

Equivalence of Network and Complementary Good Effects Produced by an Independent Firm

The demonstration begins with a model of two independent monopolists, one producing the base good and another producing a complementary good (Model 2). This situation is compared with a model of a single base good monopolist with network effects summarized in their utility function (Model 1). Equivalence between the two models is established by equating the normalized base good equilibrium profits. An independent firm selling the complementary good results in increased sales of the base good. The equivalence finds the network effects (αx) in the utility of individual consumers, where $\tilde{\alpha}$ measures the intensity of the network effect necessary to equate base good profits.

Table 7.1 Independent firms: Equivalence of quality and network effects

Normalized Complementary Good Quality $(\tilde{q}_C = q_C / q_B)$	Normalized Relative Complementary Good Price $(\tilde{R}_{CB} = p_C / p_B)$	Normalized Base Good Profits $(\tilde{\Pi}_B = \tilde{\Pi}_B / q_B)$	Normalized Equivalent α $(\tilde{\alpha} = \alpha / q_B)$
1	0.7071	0.3431	0.2714
2	1.2291	0.4003	0.3755
3	1.7375	0.4273	0.4149
5	2.7441	0.4532	0.4484
10	5.2481	0.4755	0.4743

Notes: (a) in this and all subsequent tables, results are to 4 d.p. unless otherwise noted. (b) these are equilibrium prices under presence of the complementary good but no network effects.

Table 7.1 shows the normalized network effects, $\tilde{\alpha}$, required to obtain equivalent normalized base good profits in the absence of the complementary good. For example, line three of the table indicates that a base good monopolist in the absence of a complementary good but with an $\tilde{\alpha}$ of 0.4149 earns the same normalized base good profits as a base good monopolist with an $\tilde{\alpha}$ of zero in the presence of an independent monopolist producing a complementary good of normalized quality $\tilde{q}_C = 3$. In this and all following analyses $q_C \geq q_B$ is chosen to ensure an interior solution for the independent firm's market structure and to ensure a positive price for the complementary good in the joint monopolist market structure as described earlier.

Equivalence of Network and Complementary Good Effects Produced by a Joint Monopolist

The base good sales of the joint monopolist increase when it also sells the complementary good. Normalized network effects, $\tilde{\alpha}$, are required to obtain equivalent normalized base good profits by a monopolist providing only the base good. The results are summarized in Table 7.2. This is equivalent to Table 7.1 but for a joint monopolist rather than for two independent firms. For example, line three of the table indicates that a monopolist producing a base good in the absence of a complementary good with an $\tilde{\alpha}$ of 0.4375 earns the same normalized base good profits as a monopolist selling a base and a complementary good of normalized quality $\tilde{q}_C = 3$ with an $\tilde{\alpha}$ of zero.

Table 7.2 Joint monopolist: Equivalence of quality and network effects

Normalized Complementary Good Quality $(\tilde{q}_C = q_C / q_B)$	Normalized Relative Complementary Good Price $(\tilde{R}_{CB} = p_C / p_B)$	Normalized Base Good Profits $(\tilde{\Pi}_B = \tilde{\Pi}_B / q_B)$	Normalized Equivalent α $(\tilde{\alpha} = \alpha / q_B)$
1	0.2500	0.4444	0.4375
2	1.0000	0.4444	0.4375
3	1.7500	0.4444	0.4375
5	3.2500	0.4444	0.4375
10	7.0000	0.4444	0.4375

Note: These are equilibrium prices under presence of complementary good but no network effects.

The results in Table 7.2 are presented in numerical form for easy comparisons with other tables. They can also be presented in algebraic form using equations (7.20) and (7.21) as: $\tilde{R}_{CB} = 3\tilde{q}_C / 4 - 1/2$ and $\tilde{\Pi}_B = 4/9$. Equating $\tilde{\Pi}_B$ to the normalized base good profits from Model 1 (single good monopolist with network effects) gives (from equation 7.5) the equivalent $\tilde{\alpha}$ of $\tilde{\alpha} = 7/16$.

Comparing Table 7.1 and Table 7.2, we observe that, while normalized base good profits are sensitive to the normalized quality of the complementary good for the independent monopolist, they are not for the joint monopolist. For the joint monopolist, all the variation in the normalized quality of the complementary good is reflected in the normalized complementary good price and the normalized base good price is unaffected (i.e., $\tilde{p}_B = 2/3$ while $\tilde{p}_C = (\tilde{q}_C / 2) - 1/3$).[17] This follows from the fact that the joint monopolist is able to adjust the price of the complementary good to fully reflect its adjustment in quality. Since it has both price instruments available, the joint monopolist can adjust the complementary good price so that the margin for consumers buying only the base good (the θ_B margin in Figure 7.1) is not distorted by the change in complementary good quality. The joint monopolist does not want to alter the base good price because consumers who buy only the base good may be priced out of the market since they do not benefit from complementary good quality improvements. In contrast, the independent monopolist of the base good, in a Nash equilibrium framework, changes its price in the direction of changes in the quality of the complementary good. Thus, base good prices and profits are sensitive to quality changes of the complementary good when independent firms produce the two goods separately but not when the same firm produces them. As a result, the strength of the network effects (as measured by the $\tilde{\alpha}$ needed to equate the normalized base good profits) is not sensitive to changes in the normalized quality for the joint monopolist but is for the equilibrium of independent firms.[18]

Table 7.1 and Table 7.2 are used to assess the base good monopolist's incentive to invest in improving the quality of the complementary good when it owns the complementary good versus when an independent firm owns it. Microsoft in effect subsidizes compatible applications that it does not sell by including in Windows various functions that are useful to applications developers and which applications developers would have to develop by themselves if they were not available in Windows.[19] As noted, the base good monopolist does not benefit (in terms of base good profits) from improvements in the complementary good quality when it owns both products, but does when an independent firm controls the complementary good. Therefore, the base good monopolist has a greater incentive to invest in improving the complementary good when an independent firm controls it. Of course, as a joint monopolist, there might be separate incentives provided by the complementary good profits that it would benefit from.

Equivalence of Low-Quality Good with Network Effects and a High-Quality Good for an Independent Firm

Next the effect of increasing the normalized quality of the complementary good when independent firms produce the base and complementary goods is analysed. An increase in the degree of normalized network effects equivalent to an increase in the normalized quality of the complementary good is found. In particular, increases in the normalized quality of the complementary good in Model 2 are compared to an increase in normalized network effects (an increase in $\tilde{\alpha}$ from 0) in Model 3 with a fixed normalized quality of $\tilde{q}_C = 1$. In Table 7.3, e.g., row three considers a base good monopolist in the presence of an independent complementary good monopolist with normalized relative quality $\tilde{q}_C = 1$. If the normalized quality of the complementary good is increased to $\tilde{q}_C = 5$ this is equivalent (in normalized base good profits) to increasing $\tilde{\alpha}$ from zero to 0.2792.

These results can be used to assess the incentive of the base good monopolist to subsidize an increase in the quality of an independent firm's complementary good versus subsidizing an additional complementary good offered by an independent firm. As shown, an independent monopolist who produces the base good has normalized profits of $1/4$ when there is no complementary good and no network effects (Model 1). So an independent monopolist producing a base good in the absence of a complementary good and with no network effects earns normalized base good profits of 0.25. From

Table 7.3 Equivalence of quality increases and network effects, independent firms

Increase in Normalized Complementary Good Quality $(\tilde{q}_C = q_C / q_B)$	Normalized Relative Complementary Good Price (High Quality) $(\tilde{R}_{CB} = p_C / p_B)$	Normalized Base Good Profits (High Quality) $(\tilde{\Pi}_B = \tilde{\Pi}_B / q_B)$	Equivalent Increase in Normalized α $(\tilde{\alpha} = \alpha / q_B)$
$1 \to 2$	1.2291	0.4003	0.1591
$1 \to 3$	1.7375	0.4273	0.2230
$1 \to 5$	2.7441	0.4532	0.2792
$1 \to 10$	5.2481	0.4755	0.3242

Notes: These are equilibrium prices and profits under the higher normalized complementary good quality.

row one of Table 7.1 a base good monopolist in the presence of an independent complementary good monopolist offering normalized complementary good quality $\tilde{q}_C = 1$ earns base good profits of 0.3431. Thus, adding one complementary good of quality $\tilde{q}_C = 1$ increases normalized base good profits by approximately 0.0931. This is larger than the normalized base good profits increase precipitated by a normalized quality increase from $\tilde{q}_C = 1$ to 2 in the complementary good (which, by comparing the base good profits in row one of Table 7.3 to base good profits in row one of Table 7.1, is approximately 0.0572).

Thus, a monopolist of the base good prefers that the independent firm add a complementary good of normalized quality 1 rather than increase the normalized quality of a complementary good from 1 to 2 if the costs of both changes are the same. Adding a complementary good expands the market for the base good more than an equivalent increase in the normalized quality of the complementary good increases the market for the base good because the elasticity of demand for the complementary good is declining in its quality so that the producer of the complementary good restricts output more per incremental increase in quality as the quality rises. This can be seen by computing the elasticity of demand for the complementary good from (7.11), which yields $-p_C / (q_C - p_C - 0.5\theta_B p_B)$.[20] Demand for the complementary good becomes more inelastic at higher quality levels because the market becomes saturated. Thus at increasingly higher quality levels of the complementary good, the complementary good firm restricts output more and the base good monopolist benefits less from market expansion of the base good. The complementary goods firm does not internalize the profits from the market expansion of the base good and at increasingly higher quality levels the market for the complementary good becomes saturated (the marginal consumer approaches $\theta = 0$) so it is optimal to raise price and limit output. This would imply that Microsoft prefers to subsidize a greater number of applications that are independent goods with respect to each other (neither substitutes nor complements to each other) but are complementary goods to its Windows operating system (base good) rather than a few such applications of higher quality.

Equivalence of a Low-Quality Good with Network Effects and a High-Quality Good for a Joint Monopolist

Next, the effect of increasing the normalized quality of the complementary good when a joint monopolist produces the base and complementary goods is analysed. Increases in the normalized quality in Model 4 are compared to increases in normalized network effects (an increase in $\tilde{\alpha}$, starting from 0) in Model 5 with fixed normalized quality equal to $\tilde{q}_C = 1$. The results are reported in Table 7.4. For example, row three of Table 7.4 considers a joint monopolist producing base and complementary goods of normalized quality $\tilde{q}_C = 1$. If the normalized quality of the complementary good is increased to $\tilde{q}_C = 5$ no increase in $\tilde{\alpha}$ is required to maintain the same normalized base good profits. The base good profits are invariant to the complementary good quality. As noted earlier, the joint monopolist can adjust the price of the complementary good to fully reflect changes in its quality so it does not need to change the base good price. The zero $\tilde{\alpha}$ increases in Table 7.4 mean that the joint monopolist does not get any benefits in its normalized base good profits from increases in the normalized quality of the complementary good that it produces.

Comparing Table 7.3 and Table 7.4, we observe that normalized profits for the base good are sensitive to improvements in the normalized quality of the complementary good for the independent firms but not for the joint monopolist. As discussed earlier, this follows from the fact that the joint monopolist is able to adjust the price of the complementary good to fully reflect its change in quality. In contrast, the independent monopolist of the base good, at the Nash equilibrium, changes its price in the direction of changes in the quality of the complementary good. Thus, to improve base good profits the joint monopolist should subsidize independent complementary goods but not its own, whilst an independent firm producing the base good benefits from both.

Table 7.2 and Table 7.4 can also be used to assess the incentive of the joint monopolist to invest in increasing the quality of its complementary good versus adding a complementary good. From Model 1 a monopolist producing only a base good and with no network effects earns normalized base good profits of $1/4$. So a monopolist producing a base good in the absence of a

Table 7.4 Equivalence of quality increases and network effects, joint monopolist

Increase in Normalized Complementary Good Quality $(\tilde{q}_C = q_C / q_B)$	Normalized Relative Complementary Good Price (High Quality) $(\tilde{R}_{CB} = p_C / p_B)$	Normalized Base Good Profits (High Quality) $(\tilde{\Pi}_B = \tilde{\Pi}_B / q_B)$	Equivalent Increase in Normalized α $(\tilde{\alpha} = \alpha / q_B)$
$1 \rightarrow 2$	1.0000	0.4444	0.0000
$1 \rightarrow 3$	1.7500	0.4444	0.0000
$1 \rightarrow 5$	3.2500	0.4444	0.0000
$1 \rightarrow 10$	7.0000	0.4444	0.0000

Notes: (a) these are equilibrium prices and profits under the higher normalized complementary good quality. (b) increase is from zero.

complementary good and with no network effects earns normalized base good profits of 0.25. From row one (Table 7.2) a joint monopolist offering a base good along with a complementary good of normalized quality $\tilde{q}_C = 1$ earns normalized base good profits of $4/9$. Thus, adding one complementary good of normalized quality $\tilde{q}_C = 1$ increases normalized base good profits by $7/36$. From row one of Table 7.4, increasing the normalized quality level of the complementary good has no effect on normalized base good profits, because the joint monopolist has both price instruments available and can adjust the complementary good price optimally without distorting the margin for consumers buying only the base good. This implies that the joint monopolist has an incentive to add a complementary good of minimal quality but not invest in its improvement based on its effect on base good profits only.[21]

EFFECT OF QUALITY LEVEL AND NETWORK EFFECTS ON PROFITS

An important question frequently posed in the network effects literature concerns the incentive to improve the quality of products and how this is affected by the presence of complementary goods and network effects. In this section the incentive for firms to invest in quality at the margin under different market structures (joint monopoly versus independent firms) and different levels of network effects are assessed. Although not explicitly modelled an investment stage can assess the incentives to invest at the margin by considering the marginal effects of quality improvements on base good profits.

First, the effect on profits of quality changes in the base and complementary goods in the presence of varying levels of network effects is assessed. Also contrasted are the effects of quality changes when independent firms produce the two products to those when a joint monopolist produces both.

Next, consider the effect of changes in base good quality on the normalized base good profits of the base good monopolist with an independent monopolist providing a complementary good. The results on $d\tilde{\Pi}_B / dq_B$ are reported in column 1 of Table 7.5 for different combinations of normalized network effects and normalized complementary good quality levels.[22]

Second, the effect of changes in the complementary good quality on the normalized base good profits of the base good monopolist with an independent monopolist providing a complementary good is assessed. The results on $d\tilde{\Pi}_B / dq_C$ are reported in column 2 of Table 7.5.

Third, the effect of changes in the base good quality on the normalized complementary good profits of the complementary good monopolist with an independent monopolist providing the base good is assessed. The results on $d\tilde{\Pi}_C / dq_B$ are reported in column 3 of Table 7.5.

Fourth, the effect of changes in the complementary good quality on the normalized complementary good profits of the complementary good monopolist with an independent monopolist providing the base good is assessed. The results on $d\tilde{\Pi}_C / dq_C$ are reported in column 4 of Table 7.5.

Fifth, the effect of changes in base good quality on the normalized base good profits (Column 5) and normalized complementary good profits (Column 7) of the joint monopolist is examined. The total effect of the change in base good quality on the joint monopolist is the sum of the two columns.

Sixth, the effect of changes in complementary good quality on the normalized base good profits (Column 6) and normalized complementary good profits (Column 8) of the joint monopolist is considered. Again, the total effect of the change in the complementary good quality on the joint monopolist is the sum of the two columns.

Each row of Table 7.5 provides the effects at a given combination of normalized network effects and normalized quality levels. For example, row two shows that for an $\tilde{\alpha}$ of zero and $\tilde{q}_C = 2$, a marginal increase in base good quality increases the normalized profits of the independent base good monopolist by 0.3270, decreases the normalized profits of the independent complementary good monopolist by 0.0571, increases the joint monopolist's normalized base good profits by 0.4444 and decreases the joint monopolist's normalized complementary good profits by -0.1482. At the same level of normalized network effects and quality levels, a marginal increase in complementary good quality increases the normalized profits of the independent base good monopolist by 0.0366, normalized profits of the independent complementary good monopolist by 0.2194, increases the joint monopolist's normalized complementary good profits by 0.2593 and does not affect the joint monopolist's normalized base good profits.

Note that increasing the quality of the base good decreases normalized profits for the complementary good ($d\tilde{\Pi}_C / dq_B < 0$), when independent monopolists produce the two goods. Since the base good is required for consumers to value the complementary good, an increase in the base good's quality increases price sufficiently that the complementary good firm's profits are squeezed. Conversely, $d\tilde{\Pi}_B / dq_C > 0$ when an independent monopolist produces the second good. Improving the complementary good increases complementary good consumers' willingness to pay for the base good, which complementary good consumers must purchase, thus allowing the base good monopolist to increase the price of the base good. Because of the increased base good price, the monopolist loses some sales to base-good-only consumers, but not enough to offset the increased revenues from complementary good consumers.

For the joint monopolist, $d\tilde{\Pi}_C / dq_B$ is also negative because the joint monopolist finds it optimal to raise the price of the base good sufficiently that it sacrifices some sales of the complementary good because some potential consumers find it too expensive to buy along with the base good. The results for $d\tilde{\Pi}_B / dq_C$ differ from that for independent firms. When $\tilde{\alpha} = 0$ base good profits are unaffected by changes in q_C because the joint monopolist has two price instruments and can adjust p_C without pricing any base-good only customers out of the market. When $\tilde{\alpha} > 0$, otherwise, $d\tilde{\Pi}_C / dq_B < 0$ because the joint monopolist does not have two prices it can set independently. The two prices are linked through the network effects. Each base good customer cares about how many other consumers buy the base good (the network effects) and buyers of the complementary good must also buy the base good affecting its installed base. As a result, adjusting $\tilde{p}_C$ affects x_B through $\tilde{\alpha}$.

Comparing columns 1 with 5 and 7 of Table 7.5, increases in the quality of the base good have a smaller positive effect on the total (base and complementary good) normalized profits of the joint monopolist than on the normalized profits of the base good monopolist when there are independent monopolists. Thus, an independent base good monopolist has a greater marginal incentive to improve the base good than a joint monopolist. This is because the independent monopolist does not internalize the negative effect that a higher base good price has on the profits of the complementary good (as reflected in the negative values of $d\tilde{\Pi}_C / dq_B$ in column 3), while the joint monopolist does (as reflected in the negative values of $d\tilde{\Pi}_C / dq_B$ in column 7).

Comparing column 4 with columns 6 and 8 of Table 7.5, increases in the quality of the complementary good have a greater positive effect on the total (base and complementary good) normalized profits of the joint monopolist than on the normalized profits of the complementary good monopolist when there are independent monopolists. Thus, the joint monopolist has a greater marginal incentive to improve the complementary good than an independent monopolist selling the complementary good in the presence of an independent base good monopolist. This is because the joint monopolist can adjust the complementary good price fully (partially) to reflect the complementary good quality increase without affecting sales of the base good (as much) when $\tilde{\alpha} = 0$ ($\tilde{\alpha} > 0$). The independent complementary good monopolist, on the other hand, has to share some of the benefits of the complementary good improvement with the independent base good monopolist as reflected in the positive values of $d\tilde{\Pi}_B / dq_C$ in column 2.

Also, note that $d\tilde{\Pi}_B / dq_B + d\tilde{\Pi}_C / dq_B$ is greater for the joint monopolist than for the independent firms, which means that the effect on the joint monopolist's normalized profits from an increase in the base good quality is greater than the effect on the combined normalized profits of the independent firms. This is because the joint monopolist is better able to capture the benefits of increasing the base good quality by adjusting the complementary good price optimally.

The model can be used to assess the marginal incentive to increase compatibility between the base good and complementary goods. Firms in markets with network effects, like software, often face decisions about the degree to which their product should be made compatible with other products or conform to industry standards. In our model, this is equivalent to determining the effect on profits of an increase in normalized network effects ($\tilde{\alpha}$). Comparing this incentive at different normalized quality levels and for different market structures (independent firms versus a joint monopolist) shows the effect of increasing network effects on the normalized profits of independent base good and complementary good monopolists. Values of $d\tilde{\Pi}_B / d\alpha$ are in column 1 of Table 7.6 and values of $d\tilde{\Pi}_C / d\alpha$ in column 2.[23] Second, the effect of increasing normalized network effects on the normalized profits of the joint monopolist is assessed. Values of $d\tilde{\Pi}_B / d\alpha$ are in column 3 and values of $d\tilde{\Pi}_C / d\alpha$ are in column 4 of Table 7.6 and the effect on the total normalized profits of the joint monopolist is the

Table 7.5 Effect of quality increases on profits

		1	2	3	4	5	6	7	8
Normalized α	Normalized Complementary Good Quality	IF	IF	IF	IF	JM	JM	JM	JM
$\left(\tilde{\alpha} = \frac{\alpha}{q_B}\right)$	$\left(\tilde{q}_C = \frac{q_C}{q_B}\right)$	$\frac{d\tilde{\Pi}_B}{dq_B}$	$\frac{d\tilde{\Pi}_B}{dq_C}$	$\frac{d\tilde{\Pi}_C}{dq_B}$	$\frac{d\tilde{\Pi}_C}{dq_C}$	$\frac{d\tilde{\Pi}_B}{dq_B}$	$\frac{d\tilde{\Pi}_B}{dq_C}$	$\frac{d\tilde{\Pi}_C}{dq_B}$	$\frac{d\tilde{\Pi}_C}{dq_C}$
0	1	n.a.	n.a.	n.a.	n.a.	0.4444	0.0000	-0.1852	0.2870
0	2	0.3270	0.0366	-0.0571	0.2194	0.4444	0.0000	-0.1482	0.2593
0	3	0.3675	0.0199	-0.0816	0.2298	0.4444	0.0000	-0.1358	0.2541
0	4	0.3934	0.0124	-0.1030	0.2357	0.4444	0.0000	-0.1296	0.2523
0	5	0.4110	0.0084	-0.1193	0.2394	0.4444	0.0000	-0.1259	0.2515
0.4	1	0.2302	0.0587	-0.0441	0.2203	0.4603	-0.0335	-0.2282	0.3061
0.4	2	0.3065	0.0259	-0.0796	0.2306	0.4343	-0.0083	-0.1676	0.2641
0.4	3	0.3472	0.0142	-0.1061	0.2368	0.4259	-0.0037	-0.1475	0.2563
0.4	4	0.3724	0.0089	-0.1262	0.2405	0.4218	-0.0021	-0.1376	0.2535
0.4	5	0.3894	0.0060	-0.1418	0.2429	0.4193	-0.0013	-0.1316	0.2523

Notes: (a) n.a. means at the corner solution derivatives not defined. (b) IF = Independent Firms, JM = Joint Monopolist.

sum of the two columns. Each row of Table 7.6 provides the effect at a given combination of normalized network effects and quality levels. For example, row two of Table 7.6 indicates that at normalized complementary good quality of $\tilde{q}_C = 3$ and normalized network effects of $\tilde{\alpha} = 0.2$, a marginal increase in compatibility (normalized network effects) increases the normalized profits of the independent base good monopolist by 0.3644, the independent complementary good monopolist by 0.1853, the normalized base good profits of the joint monopolist by 0.3939 and the normalized complementary good profits of the joint monopolist by 0.1284.

Comparing the sum of columns 3 and 4 to columns 1 and 2 of Table 7.6, observe that normalized profits are more sensitive to normalized network effects for a joint monopolist than for either independent monopolist. When network effects are greater, the value goes up both to consumers of the base good and to consumers of the complementary good. The value of the base good goes up directly because of the network effects. The value to complementary goods consumers goes up because they must buy the base good to use the complementary good and therefore also benefit indirectly from the increased network effects. This is why $d\tilde{\Pi}_B / d\alpha$ and $d\tilde{\Pi}_C / d\alpha$ are both positive for the independent monopolists (columns 1 and 2 of Table 7.6). In fact, the complementary good monopolist receives substantial benefits from the increase of network effects. However, because each of the independent firms does not take fully into consideration the effect they have on each other, their individual incentives to make their products more compatible are lower than the incentive of the joint monopolist to make its two products more compatible with other firms' goods. Since consumers of both the base and complementary goods benefit, the joint monopolist captures both benefits, while in the case of the independent monopolists this benefit is shared between the two firms.

Table 7.6 Effects of the intensity of network effects on profits

		1	2	3	4
Normalized α	Normalized Complementary Good Quality	IF	IF	JM	JM
$\left(\tilde{\alpha}=\frac{\alpha}{q_B}\right)$	$\left(\tilde{q}_C=\frac{q_C}{q_B}\right)$	$\frac{d\tilde{\Pi}_B}{d\alpha}$	$\frac{d\tilde{\Pi}_C}{d\alpha}$	$\frac{d\tilde{\Pi}_B}{d\alpha}$	$\frac{d\tilde{\Pi}_C}{d\alpha}$
0.1	3	0.3260	0.1776	0.3606	0.1214
0.2	3	0.3644	0.1853	0.3939	0.1284
0.3	3	0.4089	0.1900	0.4301	0.1352
0.4	3	0.4620	0.1892	0.4698	0.1415
0.5	3	0.5255	0.1807	0.5145	0.1461
0.6	3	0.6024	0.1615	0.5666	0.1470
0.7	3	0.6941	0.1300	0.6304	0.1412
0.8	3	0.7979	0.0879	0.7131	0.1231
0.9	3	0.9045	0.0416	0.8266	0.0831
0.1	5	0.3116	0.1999	0.3475	0.1319
0.2	5	0.3461	0.2098	0.3820	0.1354
0.3	5	0.3866	0.2170	0.4207	0.1380
0.4	5	0.4347	0.2199	0.4641	0.1393
0.5	5	0.4931	0.2158	0.5137	0.1386
0.6	5	0.5651	0.2009	0.5716	0.1343
0.7	5	0.6541	0.1714	0.6413	0.1242
0.8	5	0.7613	0.1249	0.7282	0.1042
0.9	5	0.8815	0.0644	0.8419	0.0673

Notes: IF = Independent Firms, JM = Joint Monopolist.

PRICING OF WINDOWS AND OFFICE

A puzzle of the Microsoft antitrust case is that Microsoft was charging a price for its Windows operating system significantly lower than most economic models predict (e.g., Direct Testimony of Schmalensee in *United States v. Microsoft* (1999) at paragraph 163). At the same time, Microsoft was selling the Microsoft Office suite of applications[24] at a significantly higher price than Windows, even though Microsoft's market share was comparable in the Windows and Office markets.[25] At the time of the antitrust trial, Microsoft sold the majority of Windows and Office units through original equipment manufacturers (OEMs). While precise OEM price data is proprietary and difficult to obtain, estimates of the Office to Windows price ratio are in the range of 1.4 to 3.75.[26] Explanations of the price difference do not explain the low relative Windows price except for the possibility of very strong potential competition in the operating systems market (see Economides 2001).

Four main failing explanations have been offered. The first explanation is that Microsoft was keeping the price of Windows low to increase network effects, allowing it to possibly increase its price in the future. This explanation is unsatisfying given that Microsoft continued pricing Windows low even after it had gained a very high market share. A second possible explanation is that the existing installed base of Windows constrained Microsoft's pricing because consumers who bought a new computer would uninstall Windows from their old computer and install it on the new one. However, Microsoft's licensing requirements and the sheer complexity of uninstalling the operating system make it almost impossible for a user to uninstall a Windows operating system that was pre-installed by a computer hardware manufacturer and move it to a different (presumably new) computer. Moreover, typically, US users who buy Windows pre-installed on their new computer are not given software that would allow them to install Windows to a different computer.[27] So it is unlikely that the Windows installed base constrained the Windows price. A third possible explanation is that since computer systems (hardware and software) are durable, pricing of new versions of Windows is constrained by the availability of old computer system versions (including Windows). However, very rapid technological change in hardware has prompted consumers to buy new computers much faster than traditional obsolescence rates would imply and Windows was only a small part of the price of a new personal computer. Thus, it is unlikely that durability was a significant factor constraining the price of Windows. A fourth possible explanation is that the price of Windows is constrained by the possibility of consumers pirating the software. Although pirating of both Microsoft Office and Windows would have the same effect, it is more difficult to pirate Windows. Therefore, piracy issues do not explain the price difference between Windows and Microsoft Office.

Another explanation that has been proposed and dismissed in the context of pure monopoly models for Windows and Microsoft Office (see Economides 2001) is that Microsoft kept the price of Windows low because this allowed Microsoft to charge more for complementary goods, such as Microsoft Office, that it produces. In the context of pure monopoly models for Windows and Microsoft Office, this explanation was insufficient to explain the very different prices charged for Windows and Office. In contrast, the model, in which a joint monopolist sets prices of the base and complementary goods in the presence or absence of network effects from direct consumption externalities or other complementary goods, is able to explain the relative prices of Windows and Office.

Model 4 is applied, with Windows as the base good and Microsoft Office as the complementary good.[28] Using equations (7.20) and (7.21), the ratio of prices in Model 4 can be expressed analytically as

$$\tilde{R}_{CB} = \frac{p_C}{p_B} = \frac{3q_C}{4q_B} - \frac{1}{2}. \tag{7.25}$$

Ratios of the price of Office to the price of Windows reported during the Microsoft antitrust trial can be explained as equilibrium of the model. Ratios of 1.4 to 3.75 for the price of Office relative to Windows reported in the Microsoft antitrust trial require $\frac{76}{30} \le \frac{q_C}{q_B} \le \frac{17}{3}$.[29] The equilibrium of Model 4 also implies

$$\frac{x_C}{x_B} = \frac{3}{4} + \frac{q_B}{6q_C}, \tag{7.26}$$

from (7.20) and (7.21). The actual relative sales ratio of Microsoft Office and Windows can be used to infer the underlying relative qualities of the two goods and the equilibrium price ratio they imply. To determine the relative sales of Word and Office we obtained survey data from the Current Population Survey (CPS) Supplement on Computer and Internet Use from September 2001.[30] The survey asked the following questions about spreadsheet and word processors for both home and office use: (a) Do you use the computer at home (at the office) for word processing or desktop publishing?; or (b) Do you use the computer at home (at the office) for spreadsheets or databases?

It is assumed that respondents answering 'yes' to using a word processor or spreadsheet at either at work or at home (there are no questions relating to use of presentation software) owned an office suite.[31] Since only respondents who owned a computer answered either of these two questions, dividing the number of respondents we defined as owning an office suite by the number of respondents would yield office suite owners as a fraction of operating system (OS) owners (since computers and operating systems are purchased in fixed proportions) or:

$$\frac{\text{Office owners}}{\text{OS owners}} = \frac{\text{Microsoft Office} + \text{non-Microsoft Office Owners}}{\text{Windows OS} + \text{non-Windows OS Owners}}. \tag{7.27}$$

From the survey, we obtained a fraction of 0.82 for this ratio. Since,

$$\frac{x_C}{x_B} = \frac{\text{Microsoft Office owners}}{\text{Windows OS owners}} \tag{7.28}$$

the numerator of (7.27) must be adjusted by Microsoft's share in the Office suite market and the denominator of (7.27) by Microsoft's share in the operating system market so that to obtain:

$$\frac{x_C}{x_B} = 0.82 * \frac{\text{Microsoft Office share}}{\text{Windows OS share}}. \tag{7.29}$$

At the time of the antitrust trial, the market share of Windows among personal computers was estimated to be between 95 per cent and 97 per cent, while Microsoft Office's share among office suites was estimated to be 95 per cent. This implies the ratio of Microsoft Office to Microsoft Windows sales in (7.29) is between 0.80 and 0.82. Using (7.26) this yields a normalized quality ratio of between 2.38 and 3.14 and, using (7.25) a price ratio of between 1.29 and 1.85, which is at the lower end of the range estimated during the trial.

It is interesting to compare the ratios of these prices under the two different market structures. Table 7.7 displays the normalized relative complementary good price obtained at given normalized quality levels for the joint monopolist (Model 4) versus independent firms (Model 2). Since Model 2 cannot be solved analytically, we have displayed these results numerically. Except at low normalized quality levels of Office, a joint monopolist (such as Microsoft) has a higher normalized relative complementary good price than if an independent firm controlled Office. Microsoft, as a joint monopolist, internalizes the complementary good profits and therefore prefers to keep the price of the base good low so as to not choke off the positive feedback with those complementary goods that Microsoft does not produce, while pricing the complementary good relatively high to benefit from sales to those with high demand for Office. If, on the other hand, an independent firm were to sell Office, Microsoft can only benefit from sales of those with high demand for Office by increasing the price of Windows. If the normalized quality of Office is sufficiently low, then it is more important for the joint monopolist to capture profits from the base good and it is priced relatively high, but for reasonably high-normalized quality levels of the complementary good, the base good monopolist has an incentive to keep the base good price relatively low.

Davis et al. (1999) show that a monopolist selling a base and complementary good can have an incentive to price the complementary good lower than the base good. They assume a linear demand function for each good and that each product's demand depends negatively on the other good

Table 7.7 Complementary to base good price ratio, joint monopolist versus independent firms

Normalized Complementary Good Quality $\left(\tilde{q}_C = \frac{q_C}{q_B}\right)$	Normalized Relative Price of Complementary Good $\left(\tilde{R}_{CB} = \frac{p_C}{p_B}\right)$	
	JM	IF
1	0.2500	0.7071
2	1.0000	1.2292
3	1.7500	1.7375
4	2.5000	2.2417
5	3.2500	2.7439
6	4.0000	3.2455
7	4.7500	3.7465
8	5.5000	4.2472
9	6.2500	4.7477
10	7.0000	5.2482

price. The goods have symmetric demand except for the intercept and the base good has the bigger demand. Given this setup, the monopolist prices the base good higher than the complementary good, the opposite of the current finding. The intuition for the Davis et al. result is that the monopolist wants to price the base good relatively high to garner greater demand while pricing the complementary good relatively low so as to not choke off demand for the good. In current modelling, the monopolist is not concerned about choking off demand for the base good if it sets a relatively high price for the complementary good as consumers who place a low value on the complementary good simply purchase only the base good. The monopolist can set the price instruments independently. Davis et al., on the other hand, can be viewed as a representative agent model. Since the representative consumer purchases units of both goods, demand for the base good is always negatively affected by the price of the complementary good.

RELATION TO THE EMPIRICAL LITERATURE

This section demonstrates that the model can be used to simulate and calibrate results from the empirical literature estimating pricing effects of complementary goods and network effects. The model could thus be used to estimate counterfactuals in these situations, sometimes with extensions to our model. To allow calibration to the empirical data, we introduce an intercept term into the utility consumers obtain from the base and complementary goods. Specifically:

$$U = k_B + \theta q_B - p_B + \alpha x_B + \delta V$$

and

$$V = k_C + \varphi q_C - p_C,$$

where k_B and k_C are constants and represent the baseline utility that the lowest type consumer obtains from purchasing the goods. Thus, our earlier theoretical results assume that the baseline utility obtained from each good is zero for both goods.

Gandal et al. (2000) estimate a structural model of adoption of CD players and complementary CD titles to determine the magnitude of network effects. Using data on the number of titles and CD players sold between 1985 and 1992, the authors find that the elasticity of the number of CD titles with respect to CD player sales is 0.56 while the elasticity of CD player sales with respect to the number of CD titles available is 0.033. This does not exactly correspond to the current setup since there are multiple complementary goods; however, total sales of CDs can be treated as a composite good to apply this framework.

Model 2 is calibrated to these results, as Model 2 is appropriate since firms selling CD players generally differ from those selling CD titles. Assuming that the base good corresponds to CD players and the complementary good to CD titles, the equilibrium quantities of the base (x_B) and complementary (x_C) goods are found at given normalized quality level $(\tilde{q}_C)$ and normalized utility intercepts[32] (defined as $\tilde{k}_C = k_C / q_B$ and $\tilde{k}_B = k_B / q_B$). Increasing the complementary good normalized utility intercept to $\tilde{k}'_C$ results in the equilibrium quantity of the complementary (x'_C) and base goods (x'_B). Also, increasing the complementary good normalized utility intercept simulates an increase in sales of the complementary good. Computing the elasticity of base good sales with respect to complementary good sales: $\varepsilon_{BC} = (x'_B - x_B)x_C / ((x'_C - x_C)x_B)$, provides the elasticity of complementary good sales with respect to base good sales in a similar manner by increasing the base good normalized utility intercept to $\tilde{k}'_B$ (while holding $\tilde{k}_C$ constant) and calculating $\varepsilon_{CB} = (x'_C - x_C)x_B / ((x'_B - x_B)x_C)$.

At $\tilde{k}_B = 0.3$, $\tilde{k}_C = 0.1$, and $\tilde{q}_C = 2$, $\varepsilon_{BC} = 0.018$ and $\varepsilon_{CB} = 0.319$ are obtained (which are close to the empirical results). At these values,

$\tilde{R}_{CB} = 1.071$, normalized profits of the base good monopolist are 0.587 and normalized profits of the complementary good monopolist are 0.462. Once calibrated, various counterfactuals can be performed. For example, the sales, prices and profits of CD players and CD titles resulting from a merger of CD player and CD title manufacturers could be simulated by evaluating Model 4 at these parameter values. The effect of increased title variety could be examined by increasing $\tilde{\alpha}$ and solving for the new equilibrium, while increases in CD player quality (relative to CD quality) could be simulated by decreasing $\tilde{q}_C$ and solving for the new equilibrium.

Gandal (1995) estimates a hedonic model of personal computer database management systems (DBMS) software pricing. Using data on all major products offered from 1989 to 1991, Gandal estimates the value of a DBMS being compatible with the Lotus spreadsheet, the dominant spreadsheet at the time. Compatibility with the Lotus standard meant that the DBMS could export files in a Lotus-compatible format. Gandal finds that DBMS products compatible with the Lotus standard had a 31 per cent higher price relative to incompatible DBMS's, controlling for other quality variables.

To simulate this using again Model 2 (since the DBMS's and Lotus spreadsheet were produced by separate firms) and assume that the base good is a DBMS and the complementary good is the Lotus spreadsheet. First, the equilibrium normalized relative complementary price $(\tilde{R}_{CB})$ is found at a given normalized quality level $(\tilde{q}_C)$. Then increasing the normalized quality to $\tilde{q}'_C$ the new equilibrium normalized relative complementary good price $(\tilde{R}'_{CB})$ allowing the quantity to adjust optimally is obtained. Finally, the elasticity of the complementary good price with respect to the complementary good quality is: $\varepsilon_{Pq} = (\tilde{R}'_{CB} - \tilde{R}_{CB})\tilde{q}_C / ((\tilde{q}'_C - \tilde{q}_C)\tilde{R}_{CB})$. The mode is not calibrated to the empirical results in this case since the quality improvement equivalent to compatibility with the Lotus standard cannot be measured. However, at $\tilde{k}_B = \tilde{k}_C = 0$ and $\tilde{q}_C = 2$, $\varepsilon_{Pq} = 1.075$.

There are several papers which estimate the pricing effects of complementary goods and network effects but would require incorporating dynamic effects in the model. Brynjolfsson and Kemerer (1996) estimate a hedonic model of personal computer spreadsheet pricing on products sold between 1987 and 1992. The authors estimate the elasticity of the spreadsheet price with respect to the size of the spreadsheet's installed base. Ohashi (2003) uses a random-coefficients discrete choice model to estimate the importance of indirect network effects in the standards battle between the Beta and VHS formats in the US videocassette recorder market between 1978 and 1996. Ohashi estimates elasticities of market share with respect to the installed base of recorders. Park (2003) estimates indirect network effects in the VCR market. The author estimates the response of one format's network 'advantage' (relative strength of its network) to relative sales in each period.

Application to two other papers would involve extending the model to consider multiple competing base goods. Dranove and Gandal (2003) test for indirect network effects in the DVD market and the extent to which pre-announcement of the competing DIVX technology slowed adoption. Since the DVD format was an open standard, multiple studios were deciding whether to issue films in the DVD format. Nair et al. (2004) estimate indirect network effects in the market for personal digital assistants (PDAs). In this case, the market includes two competing base good (PDA) firms and many software (complementary) good providers. Finally, Rysman (2004) uses a structural model to estimate the indirect network effects between consumer usage (measured by number of references per household per month from surveys) and quantity of advertisements in the yellow pages directory market. Approximately 41 per cent of these markets have a single publisher so that the model can be calibrated in these monopoly markets. However, to do so would require a model of advertising demand to appropriately model the price of consumer advertising usage.

CONCLUDING REMARKS

A model is solved with two goods, a base good and a complementary good whose use requires the base good, for two alternative industry structures, joint monopoly and two independent monopolists. This is related to a model with network effects summarized in the consumers' utility functions and the appropriate parameter values are found for network effects that produce the same equilibrium results. The effect of changes in the inherent quality of the base and complementary goods are assessed and equated to increases in the intensity of network effects required to maintain the same base good profits. Also, the incentive to invest, in either the base or complementary good quality and product compatibility is evaluated. Finally, an economically rational explanation of Microsoft's relative pricing of Windows and Office is provided with a demonstration of how the model can be calibrated to empirical network effects studies to perform counterfactuals.

ACKNOWLEDGEMENTS

Ravi Mantena and Andy Skrzypacz are thanked for useful comments. Brian Viard acknowledges financial support from the Fletcher Jones Foundation.

NOTES

1. The model is an example of a micro model as defined by Economides (1996a) or the components approach as defined by Shy (2001).
2. The approach does not consider the more distantly related effect of changes in software variety considered in Church and Gandal (1992) or Chou and Shy (1990). The former evaluate how the compatibility decisions of software firms affect the degree of standardization in the hardware market, while the latter demonstrate that increasing returns in the production of complementary goods can substitute for the assumption of network effects. This paper attempts to take network effects and a complementary good as given and evaluate their equivalence.
3. This is an example of a 'macro' model as defined by Economides (1996a) or the 'network externalities approach' as defined by Shy (2001).
4. Since the complementary good requires the presence of the base good but not conversely, it is expected that the equilibria in terms of prices and quantities will be asymmetric across firms.
5. Assume that that the influence of positive consumption (network) effects on the willingness to pay for the base good can be summarized by an additive term which is proportional to sales of the base good. This assumes that higher sales of the base good are reflected in higher sales of other complementary goods and vice versa.
6. This specification requires $\alpha < q_B$ for demand to be downward sloping.
7. While the model assumes zero costs, positive costs could easily be added. That is, $d\Pi_B / dp_B = (q_B - 2p_B)/(q_B - \alpha) = 0$ and $d^2\Pi_B / dp_B^2 = -2/(q_B - \alpha) < 0$ since $q_B > \alpha$.
8. Also the model requires that everyone does not buy the good which implies $x_B^* < 1$ or $2(q_B - \alpha) > q_B$, i.e., $\alpha < q_B / 2$.
9. The second-order conditions are $-(3p_B + 2p_C)/q_B q_C < 0$ and $-2/q_C < 0$ respectively, both of which are met for all parameter values.
10. Note that the first-order conditions place no restrictions on the relative qualities. The positive root of the first first-order condition is $1/3(-2p_C + \sqrt{4p_C^2 + 6q_B q_C})$ which is always positive. Solving the second first-order condition for p_C gives $q_C / 2 + p_B^2 / 4q_B$ which is always positive.
11. Also verified numerically is that the nonlinear second-order conditions hold and that $\Pi_B^n(p_B; p_C^*)$ is quasi-concave in p_B and $\Pi_C^n(p_C; p_B^*)$ is quasi-concave in p_C .
12. The second-order condition is met as the Hessian is negative definite for all parameter values.
13. Also notice that, for independent firms, the first-order conditions cannot be decomposed as in joint monopoly, and therefore the equilibrium prices of both the base and complementary good do depend on the quality levels of both goods. For independent firms, the first-order conditions are:

    (A) $D_B + p_B D_B' + D_C + p_B D_C' = 0$,

    (B) $D_C + p_C D_C' = 0$.

    Substitution from (B) into (A) cannot accomplish decomposition as in joint monopoly. Of course, comparison of (B) with equation (7.22) confirms Cournot's result that the total price $p_B + p_C$ is lower under joint monopoly.
14. Although in principle the joint monopolist could choose to sell the complementary good below cost, such action could raise serious antitrust concerns.

15. Also verified is that the second-order conditions are met. The conditions are solved over a grid of possible prices to ensure that the global maximum is obtained.
16. The possibility of anti-competitive leveraging of monopoly power from the base to the complementary good is not discussed.
17. As shown in general in Note 13, the sum of the prices $p_B + p_C$ is lower for the joint monopolist than for the independent monopolists.
18. Also observed is that the $\tilde{\alpha}$'s are neither consistently higher nor lower for the joint monopolist relative to the independent firms. At high levels of complementary good quality the independent firms' $\tilde{\alpha}$ -equivalent is greater, while at low quality levels the opposite is true.
19. All modern computer operating systems contain functions useful to applications developers but typically not directly useful to end-users. For example, Windows has timing functions that are useful to applications developers and have no direct functional value to end-users and built-in abilities to print to a variety of printers, a necessary capability for applications.
20. The demand equation for the complementary good firm simplifies to $x_C = 1 - p_C / q_C - \theta_B p_B / 2q_C$.
21. The base good monopolist's incentives could be evaluated by total rather than marginal profits but this would require specifying the cost structure for quality improvements. The results would thus depend arbitrarily on the functional form of the cost function. Also the base good monopolist's incentives could be evaluated based on base and complementary goods profits rather than just base good profits. However, the objective is instead to assess the base good monopolist's incentive beyond that provided by complementary good profits alone since these incentives would be the same for both a joint monopolist and an independent firm facing the same cost structure and in the absence of complementarities.
22. Derivatives are calculated using Richardson extrapolation (see, Acton 1990, p. 106) with a step-size of one per cent of q_B or q_C .
23. Derivatives are calculated using Richardson extrapolation with step-size of one per cent of $\tilde{\alpha}$.
24. Microsoft Office typically includes Word (word processor); Excel spreadsheet; PowerPoint presentations tool; Outlook personal information management tool; and Access database.
25. The marginal cost of Windows and Office are near zero and almost the same since neither ships with paper manuals, and are generally preloaded by OEMs on computers at this time.
26. See e.g., 'Some Experts Blame Rising Software Prices on Microsoft,' *PCWorld.com.* Retrieved from: http://www.cnn.com/TECH/computing/9901/11/microrise.idg/.
27. US users are typically given a recovery CD that allows them to restore the particular computer model they own, including Windows, to the original condition when it was shipped from the factory. Such a CD is unable to install Windows on any other computer model.
28. The case of zero network effects $\alpha = 0$ is presented for brevity. The same result holds for positive network effects $(\alpha > 0)$ using Models 3 and 5.
29. See Direct Testimony Schmalensee in *United States v. Microsoft* (1999) at paragraph 163 and footnote 164.
30. See http://www.bls.census.gov/cps/ for details.
31. Although consumers could have purchased stand-alone word processor or spreadsheet software this was rare by 2001.
32. Model 2 is 'scalable' in k_B, k_C, q_B and q_C in the sense that multiplying all four by a factor λ leaves sales of both goods unaffected and the normalized price unchanged.

REFERENCES

Acton, S. (1990), *Numerical Methods that Work*, 2nd, Washington DC: Mathematics Association of America.

Brynjolfsson, E. and Kemerer, C. (1996), 'Network Externalities in Microcomputer Software: An Econometric Analysis of the Spreadsheet Market', *Management Science*, **42**, 1627–47.

Chou, C. and Shy, O. (1990), 'Network Effects without Network Externalities', *International Journal of Industrial Organization*, **8**, 259–70.

Church, J. and Gandal, N. (1992), 'Network Effects, Software Provision and Standardization', *The Journal of Industrial Economics*, **40**, 85–103.

Clements, M. (2004), 'Direct and Indirect Network Effects: Are they Equivalent?', *International Journal of Industrial Organization*, **22**, 633–45.

Davis, S., MacCrisken, J. and Murphy, K. (1999), 'The Evolution of the PC Operating System: An Economic Analysis of Software Design', Working paper, University of Chicago.

Dranove, D. and Gandal, N. (2003), 'The DVD vs. DIVX Standard War: Empirical Evidence of Network Effects and Preannouncement Effects', *Journal of Economics and Management Strategy*, **12**, 363–86.

Economides, N. (1989), 'Desirability of Compatibility in the Absence of Network Externalities', *American Economic Review*, **79**, 1165–81.

Economides, N. (1996a), 'The Economics of Networks', *International Journal of Industrial Organization*, **14**, 673–99.

Economides, N. (1996b), 'Network Externalities, Complementarities, and Invitations to Enter', *European Journal of Political Economy*, **12**, 211–32.

Economides, N. (2001), 'The Microsoft Antitrust Case', *Journal of Industry, Competition and Trade: From Theory to Policy*, **1**, 7–39.

Farrell, J. and Saloner, G. (1986), 'Installed Base and Compatibility: Innovation, Product Preannouncements, and Predation', *American Economic Review*, **76**, 940–55.

Gandal, N. (1995), 'Competing Compatibility Standards and Network Externalities in the PC Software Market', *The Review of Economics and Statistics*, **77**, 599–608.

Gandal, N., Kende, M. and Rob, R. (2000), 'The Dynamics of Technological Adoption in Hardware/Software Systems: The Case of Compact Disc Players', *RAND Journal of Economics*, **31**, 43–61.

Katz, M. and Shapiro, C. (1985), 'Network Externalities, Competition and Compatibility', *American Economic Review*, **75**, 424–40.

Matutes, C. and Regibeau, P. (1988), 'Mix and Match: Product Compatibility without Network Externalities', *Rand Journal of Economics*, **19**, 221–34.

Nair, H., Chintagunta, P. and Dubé, J. (2004), 'Empirical Analysis of Indirect Network Effects in the Market for Personal Digital Assistants', *Quantitative Marketing and Economics*, **2**, 23–58.

Ohashi, H. (2003), 'The Role of Network Effects in the US VCR Market', *Journal of Economics and Management Strategy*, **12**, 447–94.

Park, S. (2003), 'Quantitative Analysis of Network Externalities in Competing Technologies: The VCR Case', *Review of Economics and Statistics*, **86**, 937–45.

Rysman, M. (2004), 'Competition between Networks: A Study of the Market for Yellow Pages', *Review of Economic Studies*, **71**, 483–512.

Schmalensee, R. (1999), Direct Testimony of Richard L. Schmalensee in United States v. Microsoft.

Shy, O. (2001), *The Economics of Network Industries*, New York: Cambridge University Press.

8. Spillovers and network neutrality

Christiaan Hogendorn

INTRODUCTION

In September 2009, FCC Chairman Julius Genachowski proposed two new principles for Internet policy, non-discrimination and transparency. Non-discrimination is the key element of the policy known as 'network neutrality' and declares that the telephone and cable companies (Internet service providers or ISPs) that provide local broadband Internet service may not 'block or degrade lawful traffic' or 'pick winners'. The ensuing rule-making process[1] has brought forth vigorous debate. A prominent economic issue in that debate is the nature and extent of spillovers or externalities that come from household broadband Internet service.

If positive spillovers are large and can cause market failure they become an important underlying economic justification for network neutrality regulation. Spillover benefits do not accrue to those making the decisions, and thus the decisions may not be optimal from society's point of view. If ISPs begin new types of discriminatory practices, this would be a significant, discrete change in the economic configuration of the Internet. Among other things, this would cause large changes in the spillovers emanating from the Internet.

The nature of Internet spillovers is not that different from the spillovers arising from many older infrastructure services. Telecommunications and other networks have been regulated as common carriers to prevent their private interests of discrimination hurting their public benefits from spillovers (Noam, 1994). The relationship of open access and network neutrality regulations to common carriage is complex (Hogendorn, 2005), but the basic purpose is to prevent discrimination.

The practices addressed by network neutrality include an: (i) ISP offering content providers the ability to have their traffic prioritized over other providers' traffic; (ii) ISP preferring one service or one set of applications over others; or (iii) ISP choosing to block or slow a service or set of services. Clearly any of these would be a large change from current practice, but the question is why that should be a public policy concern? The reason is that the ISP would choose preferred services or differential prices based on private valuations of those services. That is, the ISP will base its preferred services and fees on what it can privately appropriate from content provider's revenue (e.g., advertising revenue or subscription or product prices to consumers).

Many standard economic results suggest such preferences and pricing are efficient, but they require that private values be consistent with public values. That is, the preferences and prices set by the ISP would have to include any public values beyond the pure private revenue of the content provider including the future potential of the content.

This chapter suggests three main reasons for divergence. First, the Internet is a general purpose technology (GPT), which means that it is an input into a wide range of uses across the economy. This means that the applications of content providers often have public values in excess of their private value. Second, the Internet, as the name suggests, is a network of networks, which means that network effects are rampant throughout all Internet-associated products. These take time to grow and they accrue to users beyond the content provider, so the dynamic, public value is likely to be higher than the static, private value. Third, the Internet is an innovation-spawning technology, so that most of its content is rapidly changing and developing, adding new value. This means that the static value of content may be much less than the dynamic value, since successful development causes future increases in value.

The chapter is organized as follows. Next, the relevant economic concepts of surplus and externalities, paying particular attention to the difference between marginal and inframarginal externalities, which have sometimes been confused in the network neutrality debate, are discussed. The following three sections respectively address the main sources of spillovers that are relevant: GPT, network effects and innovation. Each of the sections establishes that the spillovers are: relevant to the Internet, likely to be large, and most important, that there is an inverse relationship between privately appropriable surplus and public benefits through spillovers. A penultimate section discusses whether competition between ISPs ameliorates these market failures. A final section concludes.

ECONOMIC APPROACHES TO EFFICIENCY

In this section, there is a brief discussion of some standard terminology and approaches to whether market outcomes produce the highest possible social welfare.

Efficiency – Marginal and Inframarginal

The case for government policy-making that affects markets often rests on spillovers, generally some type of direct effect of economic actions that is not mediated through the price system.

An externality usually refers to an exception to the marginal efficiency result. It is a case where, on the margin, too much or too little of an activity is undertaken in a private market because the price of the good signals only the private marginal benefit or private marginal cost and not some additional social benefit or cost.[2] The concept of externality is usually taken to imply that an agent does indeed have control over the activity, but that 'the effect produced is not a deliberate creation but an unintended or incidental by-product of some otherwise legitimate activity' (Mishan, 1971, p. 2).

In the Internet context, externalities are often positive: e.g., the contributors to Wikipedia create positive externalities to other Internet users by providing useful information, but do not receive monetary compensation for their efforts. In some cases, it is possible to internalize an externality by finding a way to charge for a service that would otherwise be available for free. The most common method on the Web is to sell advertising; another, less-common method is to charge subscription fees and protect the Website with a password. Usually when an externality is internalized, it is then simply referred to as an effect (see Liebowitz and Margolis (1994) for discussion of this in the network context).

In most economic literature, an externality only creates an inefficient market outcome if it meets two conditions. First, it must be possible to find an alternative pricing or advertising scheme that fixes the externality without prohibitively high transactions costs. Second, the pricing must actually change behaviour on the margin relating to the externality (Papandreou, 1994). For example, computer networks may increase employee productivity at a firm, but a system for ISPs to charge for these effects would have prohibitively high transactions costs. Also, given limits in individual employees' ability to discern how the network affects productivity, it is not clear that such a system could be behaviour affecting.

Nonetheless, there is a strand of economic thinking on this type of spillover effect that is important for understanding policies like network neutrality. This thinking goes back to Dupuit (1844) who was looking at indivisible decisions such as whether or not to build a bridge. He noted that while bridge tolls might be efficient on the margin, the large inframarginal surplus created by a bridge might make it socially desirable even if the tolls did not cover the cost.

An important implication of such inframarginal externalities, or more simply, complementarities, is that certain configurations of economic activity may be more desirable for an industry or nation than others. This logic is used with respect to both individual industries and whole economies of developing countries – for early and more recent reviews see Scitovsky (1954) and Azariadis and Stachurski (2005).

Another area where complementarities are important is innovation. Arrow (1962) emphasized that innovators often create large surplus (on both the margin and inframarginally) that is not easily appropriable. Since the surplus accrues to those other than the innovator, there is not enough incentive to create the innovation in the first place. More recently, Lipsey et al. (2005) emphasize that the majority of spillovers caused by GPTs are not marginal positive externalities but are what they term technological complementarities. The important difference between externalities and complementarities is that externalities can create inefficient prices, whereas complementarities only matter when considering discrete policy changes or outright prohibitions of certain activities. If, e.g., an ISP decides to disable e-mail service, then all the complementarities that come from people using e-mail are lost, and this would be a cost of the change in policy.

Because inframarginal externalities and technological complementarities are both very important in the Internet context, in addition to marginal externalities, the term ‘spillovers’ is used throughout this chapter to denote the sum of all these types of effects. Thus, the use of the word spillover is completely synonymous with the way ‘externality’ is used in some economic studies but is broader than the way externality is used in others.

The following sections identify three main reasons why these effects may be large for the Internet: the fact that the Internet is a GPT, the presence of network effects, and the importance of innovation.

Internalizing Complementary Externalities

Since Internet access causes such large spillovers, it might be asked whether ISPs would do everything they could to stimulate the spillovers in an attempt to capture at least some of the surplus for themselves – Farrell and Weiser (2003) call this ‘internalizing complementary externalities’ or ICE. ICE is clearly relevant to the arguments made here, but there are two separate reasons to be concerned that ICE may not hold in this case.

First, there are a set of circumstances under which ICE will not hold that Farrell and Weiser detail in their paper. If at least one of these conditions exists, then the private interests of an ISP will not be fully consonant with the public interests of maximizing total welfare. Among the reasons Farrell and Weiser give that an ISP might block or degrade certain services in violation of ICE include: (i) it aids the ISP in charging different prices to different customers in order to increase profits; (ii) it may make it harder for other firms to enter the market, either as ISPs or as application providers; (iii) there may be bargaining problems that prevent internalization; (iv) firms may not fully realize the benefits of all externalities; and (v) if Internet applications have other spillover benefits, it may make it easier to capture (but in the process reduce) those spillovers.

The second reason relates to appropriable versus non-appropriable spillovers. All of the value discussed in Farrell and Weiser is at least potentially appropriable, since the whole premise of their paper is to ask why there might be exceptions to the idea that a monopolist will naturally try to appropriate the entire surplus it creates. However, this chapter emphasizes that there is in addition a great deal of non-appropriable spillover from the Internet, non-appropriable because it occurs either generally across the economy, or as network effects, or as innovation spillovers. All of these non-appropriable spillovers are beyond what is included under ICE. Thus, it is completely consistent for an ISP to follow ICE and nonetheless reduce non-appropriable spillovers. All this requires is that the ISP simultaneously increases appropriable spillovers while (inadvertently) decreasing non-appropriable spillovers.

GENERAL PURPOSE TECHNOLOGY

Internet as a GPT

Certain technologies, called GPTs by Bresnahan and Trajtenberg (1995), are used widely throughout the economy and thus have extraordinary impact. In their book *Economic Transformations: General Purpose Technologies and Long Term Economic Growth*, Lipsey, Carlaw and Bekar (2005, abbreviated 'LCB') discuss the nature of GPTs and their effects. They provide a list of GPTs that includes electricity, railroads, the internal combustion engine and the Internet.

LCB define a GPT as 'a single generic technology, recognizable as such over its whole lifetime that initially has much scope for improvement and eventually comes to be widely used, to have many uses, and to have many spillover effects'. The chapter deals with the 'scope for improvement' in the Innovation section below. In this section, the concern is with the 'widely used' issue, and the resultant spillover effects. OECD (2009) gives a listing of the various uses of the Internet and associated spillover benefits.

GPTs are inputs into many further activities which themselves create value. If those follow-on opportunities create value as producer surplus, it may be possible to appropriate it (at least partially) by charging the producers for use of the GPT. However, if the follow-on value occurs as consumer surplus, it is typically not possible to appropriate it (unless the downstream firms are able to practice very effective price discrimination). Frischmann and Lemley (2006, p. 117) put it this way: 'If there is consumer surplus in the second transaction – and there always is – that consumer surplus is external to the original transaction, because neither the original buyer nor the original seller can capture it'.

The implication is that allowing a GPT provider to discriminate between applications tends to favour those applications that create more appropriable surplus, regardless of the level of total surplus.

Magnitude of GPT Spillovers

Several studies find that spillovers from GPTs and from information technology (IT) in particular, are very large and affect entire economies. Jorgenson and Stiroh (1999) estimate that one sixth of the United States' productivity growth from 1990-1996 is attributable to IT. Röller and Waverman (2001) find that almost one third of OECD economic growth 1970-1990 is attributable to telecommunications infrastructure. Czernich et al. (2009) find that an increase of 10 per cent in broadband penetration increases annual GDP growth by 0.9-1.5 percentage points. Jorgenson et al. (2008) show that US productivity growth in the early-2000s is based on a wide variety of industries adopting new forms of IT in production. Indeed, most research on economic growth and GPTs suggests that economies need GPTs in order to grow (LCB, Jovanovic and Rousseau 2005).

Appropriable versus Non-appropriable GPT Spillovers

A wide range of GPTs creates large inframarginal complementarities because GPTs create new markets, and these new markets create value for both consumers and producers. Bresnahan and Trajtenberg (1995, p. 84) say that 'GPT's play the role of "enabling technologies", opening up new opportunities rather than offering complete, final solutions'.

Since it is in the nature of a GPT to create new markets, they will be created whether the GPT producer is discriminating between different users or not. The question is whether total welfare is higher with the set of markets created by a technology whose providers discriminate versus the set of markets created by non-discriminatory providers. A numerical measure is not possible, since the counterfactuals are unknown – neither can the future path of the Internet be known, nor is the historical path-not-taken of unregulated and discriminating railroads or electricity providers knowable.

The thrust of the literature on GPTs is that their widespread and not very appropriable benefits are the source of their influence on economic growth. Studies of GPTs often conclude with warnings that measures to increase appropriability may actually reduce the value of a GPT (Bresnahan and Trajtenberg, 1995, p. 94; LCB, p. 519). The International Telecommunication Union (ITU) makes a similar point in their *World Telecommunication/ICT Development Report 2006* (p. 40): 'both ICTs and electricity are "enabling" or "General Purpose Technologies", which means their use and their impacts, are ubiquitous yet difficult to measure because they are mainly indirect. It is not electricity or ICTs as such that make the (bulk) impact on economy and society but how they are used to transform organisation, processes and behaviours'.

Mowery and Simcoe (2002) point to several open and non-discriminatory features of the early Internet that allowed it to become a GPT and they contrast these with efforts at computer networking in the UK and France that are more closed. Among the features they cite are neutrality with respect to commercial applications, liberal licensing and diffusion of AT&T technologies – especially UNIX, non-discriminatory treatment of dial-up ISPs by local telephone companies, and significant use of public domain technology – especially TCP/IP and HTTP/HTML.

NETWORK EFFECTS

Network Effects on the Internet

For many technologies, and especially for the Internet, the value of the network as a whole rises as the number of users increases. Furthermore, this is also true of many applications on the Internet, which are themselves networks that connect users – whether for e-commerce, socializing, information retrieval, and so forth. Katz and Shapiro (1985) identified two ways this could happen, either a direct effect from user to user or an indirect effect operating through complementary goods.

When an effect is direct, the consumers receive value directly from communicating with one another. The most famous early example is the telephone network, and many of the basic Internet protocols also involve direct communication – e-mail and chat, for example. There has been a resurgence of Internet applications designed to create direct network effects, often under the label 'Web 2.0'. These allow users to directly share profiles and pictures (Facebook), current activities (Twitter), favourite news stories (Digg), speak to each other (Voice over IP, e.g., Skype), and so on.

With an indirect network effect, users also value the system more as the total number of users rises, but through a different mechanism. Content providers offer various products on the system, and these are what users want. The more users, the more content providers will provide the products and therefore the more value to the users.

Indirect network effects occur at several levels in the Internet. At the broadest level, the more Internet users there are, the more Internet-related applications are developed, but this is more of an innovation effect which we discuss below. At a narrower level, many of the applications developed for the Internet are themselves platforms with their own user and content provider communities. For example, standards like html and xml have this property – the more users with Web browsers or other applications that use the latest versions of these standards, the more incentive for programmers to develop new applications that use them. The same is true for some Websites, e.g., the more users of Facebook, the more incentive for developers to create new Facebook applications.

A cross-platform indirect network effect is a type of indirect network effect that happens through the (partial) compatibility of different platforms (Hogendorn and Yuen, 2009). For instance, suppose another Internet user joins a Web-based financial information service like Pageonce. This increases the incentive for Pageonce to improve all of its product offerings, including the one available on the Apple iPhone, since the protocols used to provide the Web-based service are partially compatible with those used to provide the iPhone service. The improved iPhone version of Pageonce generates additional value for iPhone users. Thus, an indirect network effect creates a positive spillover for iPhone users even though it originated with a Web-based user.

Magnitude of Network Effects

No one knows the total value of network effects emanating from the Internet. Since the Internet is a network of networks, and since many of the applications that run on the Internet are themselves networks, the total number of networks is huge. There is a well-developed body of research that estimates the value of network effects on just one network. A summary of this work, which is surveyed in Birke (2009), is presented in Table 8.1.

Several of the papers study how consumers value a 10 per cent increase in the installed base of compatible users of a network. While the methods used vary, it seems that consumers typically equate this to about a 5 per cent decrease in price of the network good. Thus, e.g., a fall in the compatible installed base by 30 per cent would harm a consumer the same as if the networked good (say, a social network website) raised its price by 15 per cent.

Only one of the studies directly measures uninternalized network externalities from compatibility. Ohashi (2003) examined the well-known example of VHS and Betamax video cassettes in the 1980s. He estimated that if, hypothetically, these had been compatible in 1986 there would have been indirect network externalities equal to almost $10 per US household.

Table 8.1 Empirical research on network effects

Authors	Topic	Spillover
Pashigian, Gould (1998)	Shopping mall rents	72–87% reduction in rent for large stores in shopping malls, controlling for sales per square foot.
Rauch (1993)	Industrial park land prices	417–947% greater price appreciation in successful industrial parks compared with surrounding land.
Brynjolfsson, Kemerer (1996)	Spreadsheet software	10% increase in installed base associated with a 7.5% increase in price.
Gandal, Kende, Rob (2000)	CD titles and player sales	10% increase in CD titles is equivalent to a 5% price cut in CD player prices.
Madden, Coble-Neal, Dalzell (2004)	Mobile phone adoption	10% increase in subscribers associated with 1.5% to 3.3% increase in growth rate of subscriptions.
Ohashi (2003)	VHS versus Betamax VCRs	10% increase in installed base associated with a 9.6% increase in market share of one type of VCR. 1986 value of network externalities: $29 per US household. 1986 value of having VHS and Betamax is hypothetically compatible: $9.73 per US household.
Gowrisankaran, Stavins (2004)	Banks adopting ACH electronic payments	10% increase in share of banks adopting ACH associated with approximately 4–9% higher probability of a bank adopting ACH.
Miller, Tucker (2007)	Electronic health records	State privacy laws associated with 25% reduction in probability of a hospital adopting electronic records.
Prieger, Hu (2006)	Video game adoption	10% increase in game titles equivalent to a 10% decrease in console price.
Clements, Ohashi (2005)	Video game adoption	10% increase in game titles equivalent to a 3.6% decrease in console price.

Appropriable versus Non-appropriable Network Effects

There has been some controversy as to whether network effects create market failures (Liebowitz and Margolis, 1994). Direct network effects are widely accepted as a potential cause of market failure. All direct networks share the feature that users desire to communicate with one another, and the more possible pairs or groups of users, the more value the entire system has. Thus, when a new user joins such a network, all of the other users receive a positive spillover. Sometimes the network can encourage joining with introductory pricing or other incentives, but it is rare for all of the surplus to be appropriable in prices, so typically the network remains too small from a social point of view. Indirect network effects are more complicated, since the pricing of the complementary products may make the effects fully price-mediated. However, Church et al. (2008) show that under reasonable conditions there can be adoption externalities in the indirect case too.

The reverse of a network effect can be called a nonuser negative network effect, so that when a user either leaves or does not join a network, there is a loss of what would otherwise be the positive network effect (Nagler, 2009). Any impediment to a user joining the network therefore has a nonuser negative effect on all users. For example, suppose an ISP introduces a traffic management practice that forces users to pay extra for a voice application like Skype. Then some users will not feel the benefits of joining are sufficient to justify paying the fee, and they will not join. But this does not create a loss for that consumer alone. All of the other users of the network will also receive less value, even if they choose to pay the fee, because the direct network effect has been reduced.

Because the Internet is at the heart of a constellation of information and communication technologies, cross-platform indirect network effects are also quite important. They suggest a further cost to traffic management that differentially affects certain types of services. If these services are partially compatible across platforms, then there could be a nonuser negative effect outside of the Internet on other ICT platforms. In addition, both network effects are often embroiled with the issue of compatibility, where two or more networks may not allow full interconnection. The theoretical literature is close to unanimous that competing platforms will not privately choose to be compatible with one another as much as socially optimal (e.g., Farrell and Saloner, 1985; Chou and Shy, 1993; Crémer et al., 2000). In the case of network neutrality, measures such as blocking Websites and applications, degrading Websites, or offering multiple classes or types of services are all forms of 'virtual incompatibility' that could reduce social surplus.

INNOVATION

Innovation Spillovers from the Internet

Of the sources of spillovers discussed in this chapter, innovation most captures the imagination. Firms and other types of users throughout the economy make the Internet an input into new activities, and these in turn add value for society. Innovation spillovers fall into the general categories. Ordered from least to most dramatic are the adoption of existing technologies, increases in productivity, and new applications.

The simple use of existing Internet applications by new business and consumers does not involve creation of new technology, but it is important for increasing productivity. Every time a firm or consumer adopts an existing

Internet technology, it faces its own unique problems and develops its own unique solutions. For example, a firm may adopt an Internet-based travel expense voucher system for its employees. Obviously many other firms have already done this, but since each firm has slightly different needs, flexible technologies are important to a successful adoption. LCB note that just because there is a 'blueprint' for implementing a technology, this does not include all the 'tacit knowledge' that goes with the blueprint. Thus, adoption of existing Internet technologies becomes a form of innovation, where each firm has to solve its own problems and implement the technology in its own way. The ability of a firm to accept and implement spillovers from another firm is called absorptive capacity (Cohen and Levinthal, 1989), and firms that are more open to new technology and more experienced in developing it themselves are generally better at absorbing these spillovers.

In absorbing an Internet application, firms face risks relating to the costs and benefits of the project, and the ongoing value of the application in relation to other Internet applications. This relation to other applications is important because most firms try to reuse their applications to perform multiple tasks; this is called technological convergence by Rosenberg (1976).

Other innovative uses of the Internet are to increase the productivity of activities that already exist. This diffusion of the Internet throughout the economy takes time, as firms alter their production methods, using the Internet as an input. A bank, e.g., can offer financial services with Web-based or cell-phone-based updates. A trucking firm can use online GPS tracking to improve scheduling and delivery times. A firm like eBay may take a very old activity – running an auction house – and completely redefine it by using the Internet as an input. These are examples of extended technological complementarities of the Internet, where the Internet is the key driver, but the spillover takes place in another industry, like trucking or auctions. Diffusion like this is common with all GPTs – electricity for instance, took a long time to fully penetrate the economy, reorganizing everything from factory floor layouts to the hours of shopping and working (David, 1990).

Finally, the Internet gives rise to new innovations. Some innovations involve the Internet, such as developing new protocols and capabilities, while many involve new applications which usually back onto another. In other words, the Internet is a platform for many innovations, some of which are platforms for innovations. For instance, the WWW is an innovation built on the Internet that in turn ushered in additional technologies – first Websites themselves, then search engines, social networking, and so on. Some of these tools might also be platforms for follow-on innovation; for instance, a firm like Zillow uses Microsoft mapping technology to provide real estate searching. In this way, innovation online is often 'recursive' (Zittrain, 2009).

Magnitude of Innovation Spillovers

The size of spillovers from innovation in general (and in a few cases from the Internet in particular) is studied by several authors. Table 8.2, drawn partly from Frischmann and Lemley (2006) presents selected results.

Table 8.2 Empirical research on innovation spillovers

Authors	Topic	Spillover
Mansfield et al. (1977)	Survey firms, use results to estimate demand curve	25% private return, 56% social return.
Deng (2008)	Patent citations	Spillover value of $0.6 to $1.2 million per citation.
Jones, Williams (1998)	Average of 6 other studies of social return to R&D	Social return 27% within industry, 100% across whole economy.
Goto, Suzuki (1989)	Data on Japanese R&D	Return from spillovers 3.14 times larger than return within an industry.
Bernstein, Nadiri (1989)	Data on US industries	Social rate of return 1.30–2.23 times private rate of return.
Bloom et al. (2005)	Data on US firms	Social rate of return 3.5 times private rate of return.

Generally the findings are that innovators do earn high returns to the capital they invest, which is not surprising since innovation is a very risky activity. The estimated spillover returns to society as a whole are much higher, in many studies 2 or 3 times higher. The fact that these social returns are so much higher than most financial returns should not be surprising, since the financial returns to any investment only reflect the surplus the investor can appropriate to himself or herself, whereas the returns to society reflect all the spillovers discussed above.

Appropriable versus Non-appropriable Innovation Spillovers

The question of whether innovators can appropriate the full surplus of their innovations and whether they receive optimal incentives to innovate has been studied much more extensively than GPT complementarities and network effects. Arrow (1962) first noted the extensive appropriation problems in settings like this. The chain of innovation is so extensive that it is very unlikely that the owner of any one innovation fully appropriates its entire surplus.

As in the previous two cases, the difference between externalities and complementarities is important. In many cases, innovation may not involve an externality on the margin. Probably more common, there are discrete innovation decisions that are indivisible. Either the innovator has access to crucial inputs or access to the market, or not. If not, then potential inframarginal surplus is lost since the innovation is not created. LCB say that these 'technological complementarities' are myriad and go far beyond most definitions of externality. Relating this to overall economic growth, they claim that total factor productive (TFP) growth measures changes in surplus from adopting new technologies, so those which simply earn a normal profit do not appear in TFP growth. Nevertheless, these new technologies are technological change, and they do prevent diminishing returns from setting in and causing a fall in productivity. So relative to the counterfactual, they produce an unobserved gain.

LCB's policy conclusions regarding innovation emphasize the difficulty of appropriating or even perceiving where the gains will come from. They conclude that

> . . . any measure that slows diffusion will also slow the rate at which related downstream innovations occur. Thus, strengthening property rights does not unambiguously accelerate invention. Because it slows diffusion of any pre-existing set of inventions, its effects on future inventions, many of which depend on the diffusion of existing inventions, cannot be determined in the absence of detailed, case-by-case knowledge. (LCB, p. 519)

Bresnahan and Trajtenberg (1995) also note that not only do appropriation problems exist, but that some types of appropriation may actually make things worse. In their model, there are 'vertical externalities' between the providers of technology and the providers of applications, but there are also 'horizontal externalities' between the various application providers. Strengthening the extent of vertical appropriation can actually lower growth because it can lessen the horizontal externalities.

COMPETITION

It is often suggested that robust competition between ISPs, and ideally facilities-based competition, will solve any market failures and reduce the need for government regulation (see especially Yoo, 2005). This may be true for traditional antitrust concerns related to market power. However, it is not clear that competition does much to alleviate the spillovers issues discussed above (Brennan, 2010 also makes the points discussed here).

The positive effect of competition on spillovers is that competitive markets generally have a higher level of output than less competitive markets. In this case, it could be expected that a competitive market would result in more households subscribing to broadband Internet, and for those households to consume more hours of service due to lower prices. To the extent that the spillovers discussed above are related to underuse, the market failure is thus ameliorated by competition.

But this chapter is primarily concerned with the relationship of spillovers to discrimination, since preventing discrimination is the main goal of network neutrality. There the relationship of competition to spillovers is less clear.

In the first place, it is not clear that competition reduces the amount of discrimination – see Prescott (1975) and Dana (1999). Many industries, particularly in transportation, see extensive price discrimination even though there is also competition. Retail chain stores also practice extensive third-degree price discrimination by offering different products that appeal to different groups of consumers.

Second, competitive firms are typically more concerned with appropriable surplus, because competitive pressure forces them to seek out every source of profit. To the extent that there are spillovers, they are usually less appropriable in a competitive market because spillovers typically accrue to the system as a whole rather than to one supplier. For example, in Bresnahan and Trajtenberg's (1995) model of GPTs, they specifically say that 'monopoly pricing by the GPT is not the villain;' it is instead the fact that a prisoner's dilemma game is being played where the GPT and the various applications are complements. This is not to say that monopoly pricing does not cause conventional deadweight losses, but that it is not the only cause of market failure in GPT settings.

Competition has many benefits, and there are probably many reasons for policy to encourage competition in broadband. However, the amount of competition seems to be largely unrelated to the amount or type of spillovers coming from household broadband Internet access.

CONCLUDING REMARKS

The Internet's benefits to society and to economic growth are enormous, and this chapter has emphasized that most of these benefits come in the form of spillovers – benefits that accrue to third parties in the rest of the economy rather than directly to the ISP or its customers. Spillovers occur beyond the standard buyer-seller transaction represented by a consumer subscribing to an ISP. The essential question with respect to network neutrality policy is whether appropriable spillovers are related to non-appropriable spillovers, and there are several reasons to think they are not. The relationship between competition and spillovers is also not robust. All of this suggests a role for government policy in preserving the spillovers from Internet access.

NOTES

1. Federal Communications Commission, In the Matter of Preserving the Open Internet and Broadband Industry Practices, Notice of Proposed Rulemaking, GN Docket No. 09-191; WC Docket No. 07-52, October 2009.
2. This approach, pioneered by Pigou (1924), is taught in most economic textbooks.

REFERENCES

Arrow, K. (1962), 'Economic Welfare and the Allocation of Resources for Invention', in R. Nelson (ed.), *The Rate and Direction of Inventive Activity*, Princeton: Princeton University Press.

Azariadis, C. and Stachurski, J. (2005), 'Poverty Traps', in P. Aghion and S. Durlauf (eds), *Handbook of Economic Growth*, Amsterdam: Elsevier North-Holland.

Bernstein, J. and Nadiri, M. (1989), 'Research and Development and Intra-industry Spillovers: An Empirical Application of Dynamic Duality', *Review of Economic Studies*, **56**, 249–67.

Birke, D. (2009), 'The Economics of Networks: A Survey of the Empirical Literature', *Journal of Economic Surveys*, **23**, 762–93.

Bloom, N., Schankerman, M. and Reenen, J. (2005), 'Identifying Technology Spillovers and Product Market Rivalry', CEP Discussion Paper No. 67.

Brennan, T. (2010), 'Net Neutrality or Minimum Quality Standards: Network Effects vs. Market Power Justifications'. Retrieved from: http://ssrn.com/abstract=1622226.

Bresnahan, T. and Trajtenberg, M. (1995), 'General Purpose Technologies: "Engines of Growth"?', *Journal of Econometrics*, **65**, 83–108.

Brynjolfsson, E. and Kemerer, C. (1996), 'Network Externalities in Microcomputer Software: An Econometric Analysis of the Spreadsheet Market', *Management Science*, **42**, 1627–47.

Chou, C. and Shy, O. (1993), 'Partial Compatibility and Supporting Services', *Economics Letters*, **41**, 193–97.

Church, J., Gandal, N. and Krause, D. (2008), 'Indirect Network Effects and Adoption Externalities', *Review of Network Economics*, **7**, 337–58.

Clements, M. and Ohashi, H. (2005), 'Indirect Network Effects and the Product Cycle: Video Games in the US, 1994-2002', *Journal of Industrial Economics*, **53**, 515–42.

Cohen, W. and Levinthal, D. (1989), 'Innovation and Learning: The Two Faces of R&D', *Economic Journal*, **99**, 569–96.

Crémer, J., Rey, P. and Tirole, J. (2000), 'Connectivity on the Commercial Internet', *Journal of Industrial Economics*, **48**, 433–72.

Czernich, N., Falck, O. and Kretschmer, T. (2009), 'Broadband Infrastructure and Economic Growth', CESifo Working Paper No. 2861. Retrieved from: http://www.cesifo.de/DocCIDL/cesifo1_wp2861.pdf.

Dana, J. (1999), 'Equilibrium Price Dispersion under Demand Uncertainty: The Roles of Costly Capacity and Market Structure', *RAND Journal of Economics*, **30**, 632–60.

David, P. (1990), 'The Dynamo and The Computer: An Historical Perspective on the Modern Productivity Paradox', *American Economic Review*, **80**, 355–61.

Deng, Y. (2008), 'The Value of Knowledge Spillovers in the US Semiconductor Industry', *International Journal of Industrial Organization*, **26**, 1044–58.

Dupuit, J. (1844), 'De la mesure de l'utilité des travaux publics', *Annales des Ponts et Chaussées*, s. II, 2nd semester, 332–375, translated by R. Barback (1952), 'On the Measurement of the Utility of Public Works', *International Economic Papers*, **2**, 83–110.

Farrell, J. and Saloner, G. (1985), 'Standardization, Compatibility, and Innovation', *Rand Journal of Economics*, **16**, 70–83.

Farrell, J. and Weiser, P. (2003), 'Modularity, Vertical Integration, and Open Access Policies: Towards a Convergence of Antitrust and Regulation in the Internet Age', *Harvard Journal of Law and Technology*, **17**, 85–134.

Frischmann, B. and Lemley, M. (2006), 'Spillovers', *Columbia Law Review*, **100**, 101–43.

Frischmann, B. and Schewick, B. (2007), 'Network Neutrality and the Economics of an Information Superhighway: A Reply to Professor Yoo', *Jurimetrics*, **47**, 383–428.

Gandal, N., Kende, M. and Rob, R. (2000), 'The Dynamics of Technological Adoption in Hardware/Software Systems: The Case of Compact Disc Players', *RAND Journal of Economics*, **31**, 43–61.

Goto, A. and Suzuki, K. (1989), 'R & D Capital, Rate of Return on R & D Investment and Spillover of R & D in Japanese Manufacturing Industries', *Review of Economics and Statistics*, **71**, 555–64.

Gowrisankaran, G. and Stavins, J. (2004), 'Network Externalities and Technology Adoption: Lessons from Electronic Payments', *RAND Journal of Economics*, **35**, 260–76.

Hogendorn, C. (2005), 'Regulating Vertical Integration in Broadband: Open Access versus Common Carriage', *Review of Network Economics*, **4**, 19–32.

Hogendorn, C. and Yuen, S. (2009), 'Platform Competition with "Must-Have" Components', *Journal of Industrial Economics*, **57**, 294–318.

ITU (2006), *World Telecommunication/ICT Development Report 2006*. Retrieved from: http://foss.org.my/projects/us-my-free-trade-agreement-ssues/resources/wtdr 2006-e.pdf.

Jones, C. and Williams, J. (1998), 'Measuring the Social Return to R&D', *Quarterly Journal of Economics*, **113**, 1119–35.

Jorgenson, D. and Stiroh, K. (1999), 'Information Technology and Growth', *American Economic Review*, **89**, 109–15.

Jorgenson, D., Ho, M., Samuels, J. and Stiroh, K. (2008), 'Industry Origins of the American Productivity Resurgence', *Interdisciplinary Information Sciences*, **14**, 43–59.

Jovanovic, B. and Rousseau, P. (2005), 'General Purpose Technologies', *Handbook of Economic Growth*, 1181–224.

Katz, M. and Shapiro, C. (1985), 'Network Externalities, Competition, and Compatibility', *American Economic Review*, **75**, 424–40.

Liebowitz, S. and Margolis, S. (1994), 'Network Externality: An Uncommon Tragedy', *Journal of Economic Perspectives*, **8**, 133–50.

Lipsey, R., Carlaw, K. and Bekar, C. (2005), *Economic Transformations: General Purpose Technologies and Long-Term Economic Growth*, Oxford, NY: Oxford University Press.

Madden, G., Coble-Neal, G. and Dalzell, B. (2004), 'A Dynamic Model of Mobile Telephony Subscription Incorporating a Network Effect', *Telecommunications Policy*, **28**, 133–44.

Mansfield, E., Rapoport, J., Romeo, A., Wagner, S. and Beardsley, G. (1977), 'Social and Private Rates of Return from Industrial Innovations', *Quarterly Journal of Economics*, **91**, 221–40.

Miller, A. and Tucker, C. (2007), 'Privacy, Network Effects and Electronic Medical Record Technology Adoption', Proceedings of WEIS. Retrieved from: http://idei.fr/doc/conf/sic/papers_2007/tucker2.pdf

Mishan, E. (1971), 'The Postwar Literature on Externalities: An Interpretative Essay', *Journal of Economic Literature*, **9**, 1–28.

Mowery, D. and Simcoe, T. (2002), 'Is the Internet a US Invention? – An Economic and Technological History of Computer Networking', *Research Policy*, **31**, 1369–87.

Nagler, M. (2009), 'Network Externalities, Mutuality, and Compatibility', NET Institute Working Paper No. 08-37. Retrieved from: http://ssrn.com/abstract =1303641.

Noam, E. (1994), 'Beyond Liberalization II: The Impending Doom of Common Carriage', *Telecommunications Policy*, **18**, 435–52.

OECD (2009), 'Network Developments in Support of Innovation and User Needs', OECD Working Party on Communication Infrastructures and Services Policy. Retrieved from: http://www.broadbandcommission.org/resources/network_develop ment.pdf.

Ohashi, H. (2003), 'The Role of Network Effects in the US VCR Market, 1978-1986', *Journal of Economics & Management Strategy*, **12**, 447–94.

Papandreou, A. (1994), *Externality and Institutions*, Oxford, NY: Oxford University Press.

Pashigian, B. and Gould, E. (1998), 'Internalizing Externalities: The Pricing of Space in Shopping Malls', *Journal of Law and Economics*, **41**, 115–42.

Pigou, A. (1932), *The Economics of Welfare*, Library of Economics and Liberty. Retrieved from: http://www.econlib.org/library/NPDBooks/Pigou/pgEW8.html.

Prescott, E. (1975), 'Efficiency of the Natural Rate', *Journal of Political Economy*, **83**, 1229–36.

Prieger, J. and Hu, W. (2006), 'An Empirical Analysis of Indirect Network Effects in the Home Video Game Market'. NET Institute Working Paper No. 06-25. Retrieved from: http://ssrn.com/abstract=941223.

Rauch, J. (1993), 'Does History Matter Only When It Matters Little? The Case of City-Industry Location', *Quarterly Journal of Economics*, **108**, 843–67.

Röller, L. and Waverman, L. (2001), 'Telecommunications Infrastructure and Economic Development: A Simultaneous Approach', *American Economic Review*, **91**, 909–23.

Rosenberg, N. (1976), *Perspectives on Technology*, Cambridge, UK: Cambridge University Press.

Scitovsky, T. (1954), 'Two Concepts of External Economies', *Journal of Political Economy*, **62**, 143–51.

Yoo, C. (2005), 'Beyond Network Neutrality', *Harvard Journal of Law & Technology*, **19**, 1–77.

Zittrain, J. (2009), *The Future of the Internet – And How to Stop It*, New Haven, US and London, UK: Yale University Press.

9. Network neutrality and sector performance: Exploring policy options with simulation methods

Kurt DeMaagd and Johannes M. Bauer

INTRODUCTION

The main concern of the network neutrality debate is a clarification of the principles that ought to govern the relations between network operators and providers of applications and content. In this discussion, a broad range of economic and non-economic goals is advanced by stakeholders. Important economic concerns are the efficient use of network capacity and the creation of incentives that support investment and innovation in network infrastructure and advanced communication services. Whether, and which types of, legal and regulatory intervention can enhance sector performance is subject to considerable controversy. Vertical relations between network operators and content providers can be structured differently. Conceivable arrangements span a spectrum from reliance on ex-post antitrust to ex-ante rules and detailed regulation. Bringing clarity to this important policy discourse is complicated by the complexity of the issues, which are difficult to model analytically. Because the institutional design problem is relatively new, historical evidence that could be used to test alternative theories, or that could serve as a precedent to assess specific courses of actions, is fairly limited. Focusing on economic issues, this chapter explores the contribution of computational methods to develop a richer understanding of the potential effects of alternative approaches.

The network neutrality debate is part of a broader overhaul of the legal and regulatory rules governing the information and communication industries. An increasing number of countries are revisiting the prevailing frameworks, which had been put into effect since the 1980s to facilitate the liberalisation of telecommunications. These reforms unleashed technological and economic changes which instigated further adjustments of the institutional environment. In spite of considerable uncertainty as to the effects of specific types of regulation, few policy-making bodies have adopted rules or advanced broad principles. In September 2010, the Council of Europe passed a declaration supporting network neutrality, broadly circumscribed as a fundamental human right in the information age.[1] Three months later, in December 2010, the United States Federal Communications Commission (FCC) promulgated an Order specifying three principles of an open Internet.[2]

Not only is the need for mandated network neutrality rules contested in the political realm, where broader political objectives also are deliberated; it is far from being settled theoretically and empirically within the community of economic researchers. Considerable progress has been made in a short period of time, but theoretical explorations have yielded a broad range of possible outcomes, contingent on specific model assumptions and theoretical frames. Consequently, much uncertainty prevails about the implications of alternative policy regimes for sector performance. Of course, this is true for many policy problems and does not necessarily imply inaction. However, it has consequences for the design of good policies and should also be an encouragement to dedicate additional efforts to improve understanding of the problem space.

This chapter explores whether progress in addressing these questions can be made by means of simulation methods, which have been useful in informing other policy issues. Evolutionary computational methods, capable of coevolving populations of heterogeneous agents, are used to study the effects of policy interventions in communications systems. Contributions to information and communications policy research are made in three areas. First, simulation methods help to alleviate some of the information constraints of the present network neutrality discussion. Second, a framework is developed which allows examination of a wide range of issues related to network neutrality and network management. Third, the chapter familiarizes the community of information and communications policy researchers with computational techniques that have potentially much broader uses in the field.

The following section synthesizes selected contributions to the literature. Next, a description of the conceptual model that is at the heart of the genetic programming model is provided, which is thereafter detailed. The following section documents selected findings. A final section lists key lessons.

THE STATE OF NETWORK NEUTRALITY RESEARCH

The network neutrality debate illustrates both the achievements and frustrations of public policy research. On the one hand, the gravity of issues stimulated a vigorous research agenda that, within a rather short timeframe, deepened the understanding of the issues considerably. At the same time, given the pressures of a policy agenda that moves at its own timescale and is strongly influenced by partisan interests, many of the issues are not yet analysed and tested in ways that are both rigorous and reflect realistic conditions well. As in earlier liberalisation discussions, gaps in knowledge are overcome with educated guesses and beliefs about the effects of policy instruments on system performance. This is probably unavoidable given the rapidity of technological change and the complexity of the interrelations between players. Prospects and limits of actual policy instruments will only become more transparent as time passes and empirical evidence becomes available that allows a better assessment of their impacts.

Regulatory theory and practice has only paid scant attention to the interrelations between alternative forms of regulation and innovation (Bauer, 2011). During liberalisation, a working assumption is that compared to past monopoly organization, competition would support all the main objectives of reform (e.g., increased efficiency and diffusion of services). However, insights in industrial organization and innovation research suggest that investment in new network infrastructure and innovation in new applications and services may require deviations from the competitive model used as a blueprint to design these earlier regulatory interventions. Dynamic efficiency is stimulated by temporary, contestable market power. These issues now have to be addressed in the context of network neutrality. Digitization and convergence have greatly expanded the space of possible innovations in advanced communications systems. Present and future network platforms are general-purpose technologies that support broad ranges of services and applications. Innovation and value generation in these systems often requires the co-operation between complementary components (e.g., network services, devices, applications, and services). Competition unfolds in more dimensions than price, including inter-modal rivalry, between bundles of services, and between systems of suppliers rather than between individual firms.

Network neutrality rules interact with this system and affect various performance characteristics. The discussion continues to be strongly shaped by two incompatible views, each claiming that the favoured solution is most conducive to innovation: open networks and end-to-end connectivity on the one hand; unfettered markets on the other. An initial clarification emanating from recent research is that these are special scenarios that describe the situation in advanced communication networks under some but not all conditions. The scientific dialog has, second, contributed to a better understanding of the meaning of 'net neutrality' by charting how vertical rules could be specified. No generally shared convention has yet emerged from these efforts, however. Several authors equate network neutrality with a zero-price rule that prevents network operators from charging content and application providers (Krämer and Wiewiorra, 2010; Lee and Wu, 2009). Alternatives to that rule are then seen as 'deviations' from network neutrality. Although this use is crisp, it is somewhat misleading as it does not take into consideration that different rules span a continuum that are 'more' or 'less' neutral. For example, non-discrimination is a specification that constrains network operators less than a zero-price rule while retaining certain protections for content and application providers. It essentially allows price differentiation for some platform services as long as the services are offered to all third parties. An even less restrictive specification would allow full price differentiation, as long as it is not abused to achieve unfair competitive advantage. Other aspects of network neutrality such as no blocking and transparency complement these rules.

Early policy debates were based on detailed, but qualitative, explorations of the advantages and disadvantages of alternative policy designs. Network neutrality was typically framed as a dichotomous choice (Ganley and Allgrove, 2006). Pundits either supported (Wu, 2003; Windhausen, 2006; Herman, 2007; van Schewick, 2007) or opposed it (Yoo, 2005; Dixon et al., 2006; Ford et al., 2006; Hahn and Wallsten, 2006). This discussion generated many claims and counterclaims as to the nature of the policy problem and design of 'good' approaches, but many did not survive more rigorous analysis. For example, some opponents have asserted that net neutrality would eliminate incentives to innovate and to invest. Proponents of net neutrality, on the other hand, painted a grim future in which the absence of net neutrality would seriously impede Internet-based innovation. This stalemate was gradually overcome as insights became more nuanced and the contingencies of regulatory intervention in vertically related markets were worked out in more detail (Farrell and Weiser, 2003; Felten, 2006; Bauer, 2007; Frieden, 2010).

Additional rigor was added with the introduction of formal models (Kocsis and de Bijl, 2007; Beltrán and Sharkey, 2009). Recent theoretical advances have further refined these findings by examining short- and long-term efficiency aspects of vertical regulation in greater detail. In short-term perspectives, the efficiency of different network neutrality rules in allocating scarce network capacity is studied. The addition of investment and innovation decisions allows examining the consequences of these rules for long-term performance. Papers using industrial organization models and game theory have added considerable depth and analytical precision to the analysis of policy options. Several contributions to this stream of literature are discussed in a recent survey (Schuett, 2010), so that it is not necessary to repeat findings in detail. Table 9.1 summarizes key assumptions and conclusions.

The papers synthesized in Table 9.1 take a zero-price rule imposed on network operators as the baseline scenario and then investigate the effects of deviations from this strict form of network neutrality, most often, quality-of-service-tiering (QoS-T), on short- and long-term outcomes. The models differ in their assumptions regarding the allocation of network capacity, structure of network and content/application provider markets, and whether they examine investment and/or innovation decisions. Three papers use M/M/1 queueing models to address the allocation of network capacity. One model considers competitive ISPs whereas five papers assume that network provision is a monopoly. Three papers model competition in content and application. The majority of the papers explore the effects of different regulatory regimes on short-term resource allocation and long-term decisions. Outcomes are, to a degree, contingent on specific model assumptions. This is particularly true for short-term effects. Several papers find that network neutrality is welfare-enhancing (e.g., Economides and Hermalin, 2010) but others conclude that it is welfare-reducing (e.g., Krämer and Wiewiorra, 2010). Findings are more consistent with regard to investment and innovation implications, where a recurring finding is that network differentiation facilitates innovation and investment. With the exception of Shrimali (2008) all other authors find this outcome is likely but contingent on specific conditions. For example, in the model presented by Choi and Kim (2010) a trade-off exists between access fees that an ISP can charge from consumers and priority fees that it can charge from content providers. As the value of priority service diminishes with the available capacity, the incentive of the ISP to invest under a discriminatory regime may be lower than under a network neutrality regime. A limitation of these papers is the reliance on simple assumptions that may not capture the situation in any particular country or location. Broadband access markets rarely are pure monopolies. Characterized by 'high' sunk and 'low' incremental costs, once network investment is committed they may exhibit intense rivalry in the presence of duopoly or a small competitive fringe. With the emergence of wireless broadband, there is a substitute available for many of the services accessible via fixed broadband. Furthermore, the papers could be expanded using theory incorporating richer theories of innovation. Third, to remain tractable analytical methods have to ignore many of the aspects that are relevant in technologically dynamic industries. Such environments are difficult to comprehend by players, who often will not be able to identify the best strategy. Decisions will thus be based on much simpler heuristics that may be adapted if the outcomes are not as anticipated. As agents have different abilities to make sense of their environment and respond differently to similar sets of circumstances, reliance on representative agents may cause additional limitations. Innovation is propelled by differences in perceptions of agents and their willingness to take risk. To capture it, agent heterogeneity must be considered.

Table 9.1 Recent research on the effects of different vertical regulation regimes

	Hermalin & Katz (2007)	Shrimali (2008)	Cheng et al. (2010)	Choi & Kim (2010)	Economides & Hermalin (2010)	Krämer & Wiewiorra (2010)
Vertical regulation regimes	Zero price versus quality of service tiering (QoS-T)	Zero price versus pride differentiation for network services	Zero price versus quality of service tiering	Zero price versus quality of service tiering	Zero price versus quality of service tiering	Zero price versus quality of service tiering
Allocation of network capacity	Independent	Independent	M/M/1 queueing	M/M/1 queueing	ISPs subdivide bandwidth and sell priority service	M/M/1 queueing
ISP market structure	Competition	Monopoly	Monopoly	Monopoly	Monopoly	Monopoly
Content provider market structure	Monopoly	Monopoly or duopoly	Competition	Competition	Monopoly	Competition
Investment by ISPs	No	Yes	Yes	Yes	Yes	Yes
Innovation by content providers	Yes	Yes	No	No	Yes	Yes
Selected findings	Restricting a platform to a single product constrains application providers seeking lower and higher-than-average quality platform services; allows those in middle to use higher quality; likely negative welfare effects	Zero price rule maximizes social surplus in the short-run; in the long-run, ability of network operators to price differentiate facilitates innovation	In the short-run, network operators gain, and content providers lose, if QoS-T is permitted. Incentives for ISPs to expand network capacity are generally higher if QoS-T is prohibited (i.e., zero prices rule is enforced)	It cannot be excluded that zero price rule results in higher network investment	In the short-run, network neutrality superior to subdivision but investment incentives are highest if price discrimination is permitted. Net effect a priori unclear	In the short-run, QoS-T is welfare superior if the same number of content providers (CPs) are active; QoS-T creates stronger incentives for broadband investment if and only if competition between CPs for ad revenue is not too strong

Sources: Valletti (2010); Krämer (2011); own research.

A STYLISED MODEL OF VERTICALLY RELATED COMMUNICATION MARKETS

An assessment of the performance effects of alternative rules governing vertical relations between market players requires a model of dynamic competition in vertically related, concentrated markets. Except in cases of fully-modular services, where the degree of interdependence is minimal, resource allocation decisions of players with a presence in only one layer (e.g., network operators, application and content providers) are usually influenced by the conditions in the related market (Bauer, 2007; DeMaagd and Bauer, 2010). For example, the value of Internet access services supplied by network operators will also depend on the variety and quantity of content and applications that are available. Conversely, the value of content will, to a certain degree, depend on attributes of the network, such as download speed and jitter, used to access it. Vertically integrated players similarly need to take the economic conditions at multiple layers into account.

The many possible strategies open to stakeholders in this dynamically interrelated system are difficult to model analytically. Researchers have therefore tried three other avenues to augment, or in lieu of, game-theoretic approaches. One path is the use of scenario techniques (e.g., Friederiszick et al., 2011). Another is reliance on system dynamic models (Vaishnav, 2010). A third approach, which is detailed here, is the use of evolutionary computational methods. Bauer and DeMaagd (2008) and DeMaagd and Bauer (2010) have outlined the contours of such a program and the remainder of this chapter draws on that research. The models developed in these papers capture the decisions of key players, each trying to optimize their own objective functions, subject to the conditions in vertically related markets and the strategies of players operating in these markets.

In the specification discussed here, three types of agents are distinguished: network operators (telcos), application providers, and consumers. Although agents of the same type share generic objective functions, every agent has a different strategy. Thus, types of heterogeneous agents interact in a co-evolutionary game, whose outcomes are computed. (The section below discusses the computational approach in more detail.) A telco seeks to maximize profits, equal to the revenues generated by the sale of its service less the cost of building capacity. The profit for the ith telco is:

$$\Pi_{t,i} = p_{t,i} \sum_{c \in C_{t,i}} c - r_t K_i \tag{9.1}$$

where $\Pi_{t,i}$ is profitability of the ith telco, $p_{t,i}$ is the price charged by the ith telco to the consumers, $c \in C_{t,i}$ represents the capacity purchased from the ith

telco, r_t is the cost of building capacity, and K_i is the amount of capacity built by the ith telco. Note that $p_{t,i}$ and K_i are the two decision variables for the telco operators.

The profit maximization condition for application providers is:

$$\Pi_{a,j} = p_{a,j} \sum_{c \in C_{a,j}} c - r_a Q_j \tag{9.2}$$

Application providers also maximize the difference between revenues and costs. In equation (9.2), $\Pi_{a,j}$ is profitability of the jth application provider, $p_{a,j}$ is the price charged by the jth application provider to consumers, $c \in C_{a,j}$ represents the quantity purchased from the jth application provider, r_a is the cost of quality, and Q_j is the investment in quality by the jth application provider. Application providers' decision variables are $p_{a,j}$ and Q_j.

Consumers' utility is increased by using more applications of a high quality, it is decreased by network congestion, the price paid for the application, and the price paid for network access. The utility realized by the kth consumer is:

$$\Pi_k = Q_j^{\alpha} C_{c,k}^{\beta} - \gamma \left(\frac{\sum_{c \in C_{t,i}} c}{K_i} \right) - p_{t,i} Q C_{c,k} - p_{a,j} C_{c,k} \tag{9.3}$$

Parameters α, β are exogenously defined with $0 \le \alpha \le 1$, $0 \le \beta \le 1$ to assure that a solution to the maximization problem exists. γ represents the disutility from congestion, the term in parentheses. Congestion is defined as the ratio of the total use of the ith telco's capacity versus its total network capacity. As utilization approaches the capacity limit, congestion gets worse, reducing the total utility. The final two components of the equation represent the expenses of consumers for a telco's network capacity and for services bought from application providers. Since high quality applications use more resources, it is assumed that the amount of the network operator's capacity used is equal to the units of the application consumed times the quality of that application. Consuming a high-quality application has two counteracting effects: it increases the overall value of the consumption, but it also increases network congestion, which, *ceteris paribus*, lowers the utility. For simplicity, the model assumes that a consumer only uses one application provider and network provider. This assumption reflects a scenario with a level of sunk or transaction costs that renders using multiple service providers uneconomic.

THE GENETIC PROGRAMMING APPROACH

Within each of these classes of agents, types with differing characteristics exist. Each agent has a strategy, which is played with the goal of maximizing an agent's profits or utility. The approach used for this study has two main components: the simulation and the evolutionary algorithm. The simulation represents the actual game played by the telcos, application providers, and consumers. In the simulation, each agent plays its strategy in an effort to maximize its individual objective function. The evolutionary algorithm is responsible for creating and evolving new strategies for the agents. Like in biological evolution, the fittest agents – in other words, those with the highest profit or utility – survive, reproduce, and evolve. Agents with poor strategies 'die out', making room for new and better strategies. Although the simulation also computes the total welfare of the system to understand the global effects of different strategies, the individual agents are selfish.

To test these strategies, the simulation uses a set of telcos, application providers, and consumers. Each agent in the simulation plays against the other agents to determine its individual utility. The following sequence describes the process by with the simulation computes the utilities for the telcos. A corresponding process is repeated for each application provider and for each consumer:

For each telco in the set of telcos

1. Select $T-1$ other telcos, where T is an exogenously defined parameter determining the number of telcos per simulation. For example, T could be set to unity to represent a monopolist, or to a value greater than one to test various states of competition.
2. Select A application providers, where A is an exogenously defined parameter determining the number of application providers per simulation. Like T, A is set to represent different levels of competition.
3. Select C consumers, where C is an exogenously defined parameter determining the number of consumers per simulation. Setting $C=1$ effectively represents a homogeneous set of consumers in which they all have the same consumption strategy. Setting $C>1$ represents a heterogeneous set of consumers.
4. The telcos each determine their prices and level of infrastructure investment (capacity), based on their individual strategies.
5. The application providers determine their quality and prices based on their individual strategies.
6. The consumers determine their consumption level based on their individual strategies.

7. The profit/utility is computed. This value is then used later by the evolutionary algorithm to determine the fitness of the given telco.
8. Go to the next telco.[3]

For the above system to work, the computer needs a system to represent each strategy. Each strategy is essentially an equation, though the precise representation in the computer is designed to specifically support the genetic program. Each of these equations is built from two types of components: operators and terminals. The operators consist of common mathematical functions, such as addition, subtraction, multiplication, division, powers, roots, logs, and so on. The terminals consist of numbers and variables. The variables can be values that are predefined at run time (e.g., number of consumers) or a function of other agents' decisions (e.g., congestion on the network). These equations are represented using a tree structure. There is no requirement that the agents have a reasonable strategy. In fact, during the early stages of the simulation, most agents have poor strategies. Yet over time, the strategies coevolve to find profitable responses to the other players.

The evolutionary algorithm is responsible for taking an existing pool of strategies and generating a new set of strategies. This consists of two general steps. First, it selects a 'good' strategy from the current pool of strategies. Then, using that strategy, it generates a new strategy. These two steps are repeated until a new population of strategies is formed. The first step is to pick 'good' strategies from the set of current strategies. This simulation uses fitness proportionate selection to make its choices. Each strategy has a profitability score as described in the previous section. This is its 'fitness'. Then the system computes the ratio of the individual agent's fitness to the total (sum of) fitness of all agents. This number is the probability that the strategy is selected by the genetic program. The genetic program has three tools by which it can take the old set of strategies and evolve (hopefully) better solutions: (1) replication takes a 'good' strategy and reuses it, (2) mutation changes a part of the strategy randomly, and (3) crossover combines two strategies to generate a new one.

Players' strategies coevolve until profitable ones are found in response to the other players. Strategies that outperform others are retained and further refined whereas weaker strategies are discarded. Thus, the fitness score is a joint outcome of the agent's decisions and those of others. Whether a player will change strategy depends on how well the agent does relative to the fitness of the system. In contrast to game theory, where a solution is determined analytically, the approach runs a simulation to find the best decisions for agents given specific parameters (e.g., number of competitors, the sensitivity of users to quality changes, and the cost of investment into network infrastructure). Each agent attempts to maximize its own objective function; there is no social planner seeking to optimize an objective function for the system.

The evolutionary algorithm finds 'good' strategies for the agents based upon parameter choices and agent interactions. As specified, the simulation contains five exogenously determined variables: cost of telecommunications infrastructure (r_n), cost of application quality (r_a), a factor reflecting how utility responds to quality (α), an adjustment factor for the utility of using telecommunications services (β), and an adjustment factor that captures the disutility from congestion (γ). To reduce the chances of a bias from specific numerical values, the system is run over ranges of the variables. Because the combinatorial complexity from simulating many values and combinations of these exogenously determined variables increases dramatically, each is tested at two levels (resulting in $2^5 = 32$ possible constellations). Low and high values for the cost of infrastructure and of application quality are determined experimentally. The range of values for the adjustment factors, which are in essence elasticities, is constrained to values contained in $[0,1]$.

The evolutionary algorithm is run to explore different competitive scenarios. Two levels are used for each class of agents: monopoly or competition (operationalized as three players). Similarly, suppliers could face one homogeneous set of consumers or a situation where different consumer classes pursued different strategies. This yielded $2^3 = 8$ scenarios. As the effect of rules that limit the network operator to differentiate prices is the primary concern, one scenario is defined in which price differentiation is not allowed and another in which the network operators are free to differentiate if it is profitable. Note, that price differentiation for services sold to consumers and not quality-of-service tiering for content and application providers are examined. Each of the 32 simulations is run for all eight competitive scenarios and the two regulatory scenarios, yielding a total of 32*8*2 = 512 simulations.[4]

FINDINGS FROM APPLICATION OF THE EVOLUTIONARY ALGORITHM

The 512 simulations generated a rich set of data that allows studying the effects of economic conditions and regulatory choices on outcomes and performance using standard regression methods. In a previous study the effects of competition and discriminatory pricing on agents' profitability and utility were examined (DeMaagd and Bauer, 2010, reported in summary fashion in Table 9.2). This chapter examines four additional questions that are at the heart of the network neutrality debate (see Table 9.3): (1) whether price differentiation alleviates congestion, (2) whether the ability of telcos to price discriminate increases network investment, (3) whether this effect is related to the costs of upgrading the network, and (4) whether telco's ability to price discriminate affects the distribution of wealth generated in the system.

The findings reported in Table 9.2 allow insights into a complicated interdependent system. First, the number of competitors shows the anticipated sign with regard to network operator profits (–), application provider profits (+), and consumer utility (+). More interestingly, the number of application providers is negatively related to network operator profits and consumer utility. Somewhat surprisingly, if network operators are permitted to price discriminate, their own profits are negatively affected. Likewise, telco price differentiation is negatively related to consumer utility. However, price discrimination is positively related to application provider profits (see DeMaagd and Bauer 2010, for a more detailed discussion).

Table 9.2 Determinants of player's profits and utility

Independent variable	Dependent variables		
	Network provider profits	Application provider profits	Consumer utility
Number of network operators (*n*)	-0.011 *	0.065 **	0.128 **
Number of application providers (*a*)	-0.020 *	0.001	-0.043 **
Ability to price differentiate	-0.194 ***	0.744 ***	-0.239 ***
R^2	0.30	0.55	0.63
N	512	512	512
F	3.229 **	135.069 ***	5.833 ***

Notes: * significant at 90% level, ** significant at 95% level, *** significant at 99% level.

Source: Bauer and DeMaagd (2008).

A related question is how discriminatory pricing is linked to consumers' valuation of the network good. Two contradictory forces affect consumers' utility. The first-order effect of charging discriminatory prices should result in higher prices for some end users, thereby reducing total consumer utility. However, as a secondary effect, if a user is 'very sensitive' to congestion, this may actually be a positive result. Although the individual user reduces consumption in the face of higher prices, other users will too. This will reduce the extent to which the network is congested. If a user sufficiently values an uncongested network, the reduced total consumption could be offset by the improvement in congestion. In other words, if a user values the quality of congestion over the raw quantity of congestion, discriminatory pricing may in fact improve the user's utility.

The data analysis shows that, in general, discriminatory pricing does in fact reduce consumer utility as expected. However, there is an interaction effect between the disutility from congestion (γ) and discriminatory pricing. When both the disutility is high and the network provider levies the additional fees, consumer utility actually increases. Hence, when dealing with a congested network and consumers with a strong distaste for congestion, the consumers actually benefit from the discriminatory access.

Compared to other factors, the magnitude of this effect is relatively small. It also has a relatively weak statistical significance, especially compared with the effect for general use of the network. As a result, it is important not to give disproportionate weight to the link with congestion. Nonetheless, certain consumers benefit when the total use and congestion on the network decreases.

Table 9.3 Effects of discriminatory pricing

Independent variable	Determinants of			
	consumer utility	infrastructure investment	infrastructure investment under high cost	share of telco wealth
Network price	-29.604 *	11.98 ***	11.91 ***	0.016 ***
Application price	-2.932 *			-0.003 ***
Network consumption	15.818 **			
Congestion disutility	-3.162 *	12.38 *	12.39 *	
Discriminatory price	-8.090 ***	-0.576		0.000
Interaction discrimination + congestion disutility	3.451 *			
Interaction cost + discriminatory prices			5.87 ***	
N	512	512	512	512
R^2	0.30	0.667	0.673	
F	6.18 ***	33.41 ***	45.29 ***	1172 ***

Notes: * significant at 90% level, ** significant at 95% level, *** significant at 99% level.

One of the standard arguments behind discriminatory pricing is that it increases network investment. Because of the high costs of networks, the additional revenues should result in greater investments in the infrastructure. However, this result is not clear. The alternative hypothesis deals with the effect on other agents in the value chain. The higher prices charged to application providers reduce the incentive to invest in quality. The lower quality applications then reduce the incentives for consumers to use the network. This reduced consumption in turn reduces the network providers' incentive to create the infrastructure. Similar to the previous question, this is a comparison of primary versus secondary effects. The primary effect of higher prices increases the incentive to invest. The secondary effect of the higher prices is a reduction in demand, reducing the incentive to invest.

Data analysis showed that discriminatory prices did not lead to higher investments in infrastructure. Technically, the coefficient is negative although the result is not statistically significant. Instead, the primary determinants of the investment are the price charged to the consumer and, the consumer's disutility from congestion. In addition to the lack of statistical significance, the coefficient is relatively small compared to the other factors. This negative, small, and not statistically significant result shows that any increased revenue for the building of networks is offset by the reduced demand to use the more costly network.

Building on the results of the second question, the third question deals with a special case of network costs and whether discriminatory prices are justified under high cost networks. Although the previous question did not find that discriminatory prices increased network investment in general, it could be that the rationale only holds for the most expensive forms of infrastructure. For example, should network providers have greater pricing freedom when dealing with wireless networks, which have higher costs to build and operate? Under such a scenario, the ability to charge higher prices will create the incentives necessary to invest in more expensive forms of networks when traditional pricing rules would fail to fully fund the infrastructure costs.

For this argument, the simulation data analysis did support the claim that the discriminatory prices would increase the level of investment. Once again, price and congestion disutility are good determinants of the level of infrastructure built, but the interaction between price and the charging of discriminatory prices shows that the network provider did use the additional revenues for greater investment when the costs of building the infrastructure are higher.

Note however that the magnitude of the effect is still relatively small in the overall determination of the amount of infrastructure built. The demand-side factors of pricing and consumers' disutility from congestion had a greater effect. Even in cases when the costs are high and the telecommunication provider is allowed to charge discriminatory prices, the effect is still smaller than the consumers' decisions based on price and congestion.

Given that the analyses in the previous two points did not support the claim that the additional revenues resulted in greater infrastructure, except under high costs, this might imply that the network providers may be capturing and keeping a greater total of the wealth in the system. In other words, although the total investments shrink, the ability to charge discriminatory prices may enable the telecommunication provider to capture a greater portion of the wealth. Of course, this may be a greater portion of the wealth in a much smaller environment. Furthermore, as the discriminatory prices affect the overall market, it may shift how application providers charge for their services and how much the consumers are willing to pay for the basic network service. As a result, the way the network provider earns revenue may change though the fraction of the total wealth may remain approximately the same.

The data analysis indicates that the overall distribution of wealth remains approximately the same, whether price discrimination is allowed or not. This supports the view that that smaller network also harms the telecommunication provider, such that the ability to charge discriminatory prices does not enable the company to extract greater profits from the system. Furthermore, the different distribution could be explained by different behaviours by the other agents to adapt to network providers' prices. Instead, the share of wealth is positively affected by the price the network provider charges the consumer and negatively affected by the price the application provider charges. The coefficient for the network provider is 0.000014, although it is listed as 0.000 in Table 9.3 to show consistent rounding with the other fields.

CONCLUDING REMARKS

The innovation system described is complex. All the relevant stakeholders have many options to respond to the uncertainty inherent in the system. Although significant advances are made in game theoretic models of the network neutrality problem, this chapter discusses an alternative approach. Computational methods allow the more systematic modelling of incomplete knowledge and heterogeneity among players. Simulating the system also provides a method to come to grips with the high degree of interactivity among players. Even if system behaviour could be modelled analytically, it is doubtful whether equilibrium-based solutions capture the main features of the dynamic interactions, which are often adaptations to disequilibrium situations. A simulation approach turns out to be very useful in exploring the implications of alternative rule specifications (including the absence of any specific network neutrality obligations and sole reliance on ex-post competition law). An unresolved problem is that data that allow calibrating the relevant relations in the model is difficult to find. The computational model relied on 'reasonable' approximations of parameters, although the model remains largely synthetic at present.

The central theoretical claim of this chapter is that alternative specifications of the rules governing the interactions between network platform operators and content/application providers generate characteristic dynamics. The genetic programming model allowed a better understanding of the effects of the interdependencies and preliminary assessment of the effects of a simple policy rule; the prohibition of price differentiation. The model's results reemphasize the complexity of interactions derived from the conceptual analysis. A number of findings correspond with the claims and intuition of the network neutrality debate: consumer utility increases with the number of platform providers; decreases if price differentiation is allowed; telco profits decrease with the number of platform providers and application providers; and application provider profits increase with the number of platform providers. However, several findings are counter-intuitive, illustrating unexpected outcomes of the complex, dynamic interaction: consumer utility decreases with the number of application providers; telco profit decreases if price differentiation is allowed; and application provider profits also increase with telco price differentiation.

However, the analysis also revealed other aspects that shed light on contested aspects of the discussion. Although consumers' utility typically is reduced by differentiated pricing, this is not true for consumers who are very sensitive to congestion. Contrary to findings in the analytical models discussed above, in the computational approach infrastructure investment is not stimulated by the ability to price discriminate, except in situations where the cost of network upgrades is 'very high'. Lastly, the ability to price discriminate does not necessarily increase the share of network operators in total wealth generated.

Some of these findings may be due to the specific parameter constellations used in the model and further simulations will need to be conducted. At the same time, these findings provide support for the claims of opponents of stringent ex-ante network neutrality rules: that there is no clear-cut policy solution that avoids some of the undesired effects without generating additional unwanted side effects. For practical policy, this implies that cautious approaches that do not impose overly strict network neutrality regulations but establish the power to intervene swiftly if undesired abuses become visible are the most promising way forward.

ACKNOWLEDGEMENTS

Work reported in this chapter was supported with funding by the National Science Foundation under Grant No. 0941310. Any opinions, findings, and conclusions or recommendations expressed in this material are those of the authors and do not necessarily reflect the views of the National Science Foundation.

NOTES

1. Council of Europe (2010). Declaration of the Committee of Ministers on Network Neutrality. Adopted by the Committee of Ministers on 29 September 2010 at the 1094th meeting of the Ministers' Deputies.
2. The FCC Order builds the four principles of an open Internet, declared in August 2005 and subsequent policy discussions, which are condensed into three key rules: (1) transparency, (2) no blocking, and (3) no unreasonable discrimination (subject to reasonable forms of network management), FCC (2010).
3. Notice that this model only has one time period although the agents iteratively adapt their strategy to other agents' choices. It would certainly be reasonable and interesting to make this a multi-period model but this is for a future paper.
4. Finally, a coevolutionary algorithm means that the simulation consists of five separate evolutionary processes running in parallel and interacting with each other. Each evolutionary process attempts to maximize the fitness of its own agents, which contrasts to an alternative approach where a single evolutionary process maximizes the system total utility.

REFERENCES

Bauer, J. (2007), 'Dynamic Effects of Network Neutrality', *International Journal of Communication*, **1**, 531–47.

Bauer, J. (2011), 'Network Openness, Innovation, and Sector Performance', in I. Spieker and J. Krämer (eds), *Network Neutrality and Open Access*, Baden-Baden, Germany: Nomos.

Bauer, J. and DeMaagd, K. (2008), 'Network Management Practices and Sector Performance: A Genetic Programming Approach', Paper presented at the 36th Research Conference on Communications, Information, and Internet Policy.

Beltrán, F. and Sharkey, W. (2009), 'Pricing Strategies and Welfare Effects of Competition Between Two Next-Generation Platforms', Paper presented at the 37th Research Conference on Communications, Internet, and Information Policy.

Cheng, H., Bandyopadhay, S. and Guo, H. (2010), 'The Debate on Net Neutrality: A Policy Perspective', *Information Systems Research*, DOI: 10.1287/isre.1090.0257.

Choi, J. and Kim, B. (2010), 'Net Neutrality and Investment Incentives', *RAND Journal of Economics,* **41**, 446–71.

DeMaagd, K. and Bauer, J. (2010), 'Modeling the Dynamic Interactions of Agents in the Provision of Network Infrastructure', *Information Systems Frontiers*, DOI 10.1007/s10796-010-9244-2.

Dixon, K., Gifford, R., Lenard, T., May, R. and Thierer, A. (2006), *A Skeptic's Primer on Net Neutrality Regulation*, Washington. DC: The Progress and Freedom Foundation.

Economides, N. and Hermalin, B. (2010), 'The Economics of Network Neutrality', NET Institute Working Paper #10-25.

Farrell, J. and Weiser, P. (2003), 'Modularity, Vertical Integration, and Open Access Policies: Towards a Convergence of Antitrust and Regulation in the Internet Age', *Harvard Journal of Law and Technology,* **17**, 85–134.

Felten, E. (2006), *Nuts and Bolts of Network Neutrality*. Princeton, NJ: Princeton University.

Ford, G., Koutsky, T. and Spiwak, L. (2006), *The Efficiency Risk of Network Neutrality Rules*. Policy Bulletin No. 16. Washington, DC: Phoenix Centre for Advanced Legal & Economic Policy Studies.

Frieden, R. (2010). 'Assessing the Merits of Network Neutrality Obligations at Low, Medium and High Network Layers', Paper presented at the 38th Conference on Communications, Information and Internet Policy.

Friederiszick, H., Kałużny, J., Kohnz, S. and Röller, L. (2011), 'Assessment of a Sustainable Internet Model for the Near Future', ESMT White Paper No. WP-11-01. Berlin: European School of Management and Technology.

Ganley, P. and Allgrove, B. (2006), 'Net Neutrality: A User's Guide', *Computer Law & Security Report*, **22**, 454–63.

Hahn, R. and Wallsten, S. (2006), *The Economics of Net Neutrality*. Washington, DC: AEI-Brookings Joint Centre for Regulatory Studies.

Hermalin, B. and Katz, M. (2007), 'The Economics of Product-Line Restrictions with an Application to the Network Neutrality Debate', *Information Economics and Policy*, **19**, 215–48.

Herman, B. (2007), 'Opening Bottlenecks: On Behalf of Mandated Network Neutrality', *Federal Communications Law Journal*, **59**, 107–59.

Kocsis, V. and de Bijl, P. (2007), 'Network Neutrality and the Nature of Competition between Network Operators', *International Economics and Economic Policy*, **4**, 159–84.

Krämer, J. (2011), 'Net Neutrality and Congestion Sensitive Content Providers', Paper presented at the Conference of the American Economic Association.

Krämer, J. and Wiewiorra, L. (2010), Network Neutrality and Congestion Sensitive Content Providers: Implications for Service Innovation, Broadband Investment and Regulation (September 30, 2010). NET Institute Working Paper No. 10-09, available at SSRN: http://ssrn.com/abstract=1694320.

Lee, R. and Wu, T. (2009), 'Subsidizing Creativity through Network Design: Zero-Pricing and Net Neutrality', *Journal of Economic Perspectives*, **23**, 61–76.

Schuett, F. (2010), 'Network Neutrality: A Survey of the Economic Literature', *Review of Network Economics*, **9**, 1–13.

Shrimali, G. (2008), 'Surplus Extraction by Network Providers: Implications for Net Neutrality and Innovation', *Telecommunications Policy*, **32**, 545–58.

Vaishnav, C. (2010), 'From Herding Sheep to Herding Cats: Balancing Compliance and Innovation in the Modular Age of the Internet', Paper presented at the 38th Telecommunications Policy Research Council (TPRC).

Valletti, T. (2010), 'Net Neutrality: An Economist's Perspective', Paper presented at the 2nd International Symposium on Communications Regulation.

van Schewick, B. (2007), 'Towards an Economic Framework for Network Neutrality Regulation', *Journal on Telecommunications & High Technology Law,* **5**, 329–91.

Windhausen, J., Jr. (2006), *Good Fences Make Bad Broadband: Preserving an Open Internet through Net Neutrality*. Washington, DC: Public Knowledge.

Wu, T. (2003), 'Network Neutrality and Broadband Discrimination', *Journal on Telecommunications & High Technology Law*, **2**, 141–75.

Yoo, C. (2005), 'Beyond Network Neutrality', *Harvard Journal of Law and Technology*, **19**, 1–77.

10. Mobile communications: Economic and social impact

Gerald R. Faulhaber

INTRODUCTION

The rapid growth of mobile phone[1] ownership and usage is generally viewed somewhat negatively, at least in popular culture, in the United States (US) and most OECD countries. White collar workers bemoan that they are now tethered 24/7 to their jobs by their mobiles, drivers point with alarm to accidents caused by other drivers while talking on their mobiles, parents complain that their children spend much of their time (in school and at home) talking or texting on their mobiles, and many complain of loud talking by mobile users in public spaces such as streets, buses, trains and restaurants. In addition to the many TV and press stories detailing the social problems with mobile usage, there are Web sites devoted to stamping out mobiles (or at least teaching users good manners)[2], and even the Vatican has weighed in, suggesting that mobile phones may be bad for the soul.[3] With the prevalence of such negative attitudes, it is surprising that anyone actually buys and uses such devices.

Yet, mobiles are the single most ubiquitous electronic technology the US has seen, and the single most ubiquitous technology the world has seen. Currently, there are over 4.1 billion active mobile devices, representing 61 per cent of the global population. Worldwide, the annual growth rate of mobile exceeds 20 per cent and shows no sign of flagging. No other technology is even close. This extraordinary market outcome suggests the benefits of mobile telephony must be very great indeed.

This chapter presents no new data or economic models, but simply arrays the known facts of mobile telephony deployment and growth against that of other, more favoured technologies and concludes that is the dominant information technology in the world; and its dominance is set to increase over the foreseeable future.[4] Calls for a 'laptop for every child' and 'broadband to every home' are being met by mobile devices performing these functions traditionally carried out using fixed technologies. Broadband and PCs will continue to be available, of course. However, increasingly, mobile will become the portal of choice to the Internet for most of the world's population. The 'digital divide' will be conquered, for the simple reason that with mobile telephony in OECD countries, there is no digital divide, nor will there be in the future.[5]

The chapter is structured as follows. In the next section, the current US situation is examined, focusing voice subscriptions and usage growth in comparison to wireline telephony. The extensions of voice mobile into forms of data services are also discussed. World trends are then reviewed, particularly in the developing world. Specifically compared are the deployment and growth of mobile to PCs, broadband, wireline and Internet users. In the penultimate section, both empirical results and anecdotal evidence regarding the substantial impact of mobile telephony on the economies of developing countries, and the pivotal role of mobile telephony as an engine of economic development are reviewed. A final section concludes.

DEVELOPMENT OF US MOBILE MARKETS

Mobile telephones became available in the US and Europe in the 1960s, as large units, generally trunk-mounted in automobiles; high costs and limited capacity severely constrained market deployment. With the advent of cellular architecture in the 1970s (in the US, Europe and East Asia), first generation (1G) analogue mobile telephony began. Mobile handsets dropped significantly in price and weight, as did the cost per minute of mobile usage. In the mid-1990s, digital cellular phones were introduced in the US, following the first auctions of spectrum. The number of cellular operators also increased substantially, and the market for digital or second generation (2G) services entered a period of high growth. During the early-2000s, the pace of new device introductions increased, leading to higher performance, lower weight and greater battery life. Prices continued to fall, and new data services, collectively called third generation (3G) services, came on stream.

The extraordinary growth of mobile subscriptions in the US is shown in Figure 10.1, an annual growth rate of over 25 per cent. Figure 10.2 shows a strong growth in minutes of use per subscriber over the last decade, coupled with a strong decline in average revenue per minute. Total voice usage in the US is over 2 trillion minutes per year.[6]

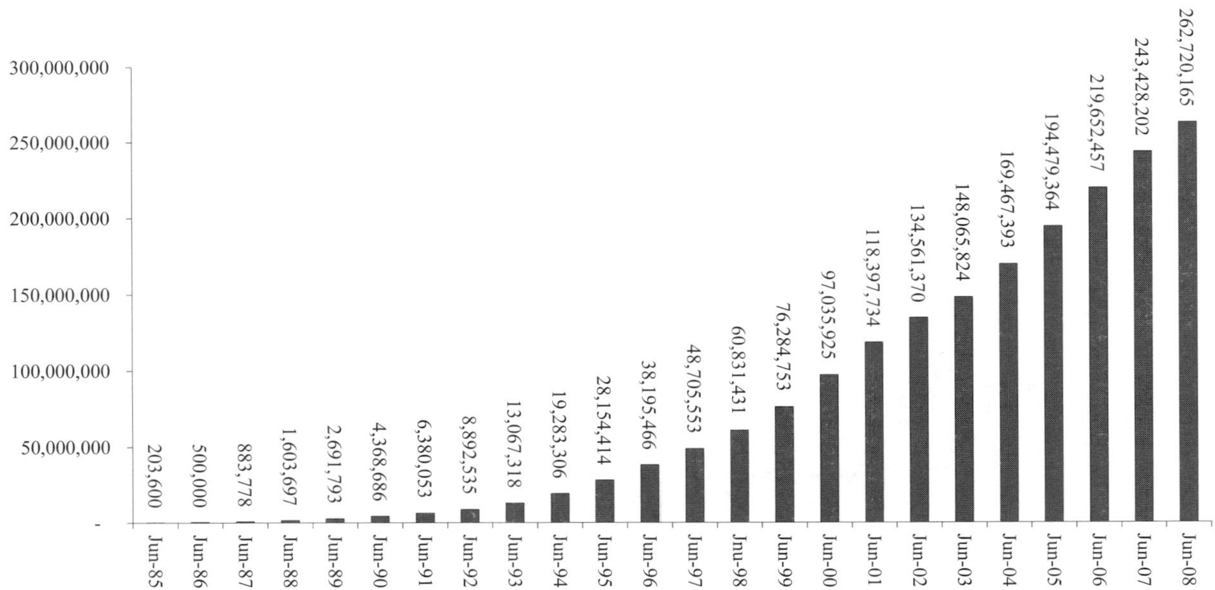

Source: CTIA Semi-Annual Survey (Roche 2009).

Figure 10.1 *US wireless subscribers, 1985-2008*

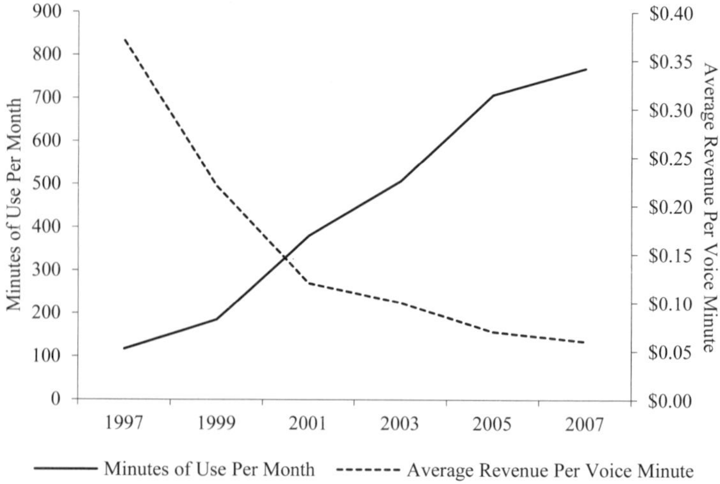

Source: FCC 13th CMRS Report.

Figure 10.2 Monthly minutes of use and revenue per minute, 1997-2007

Surveys reveal that mobile users are growing ever more attached to their devices. Table 10.1 shows that of the electronic systems (e.g., Internet, wireline phone and TV) available to customers, mobile is perceived the hardest to give up.[7]

Table 10.1 Difficulty is giving up service (%)

	2002	2006	2007
Cell phone	38	43	51
Internet	38	38	45
Television	47	44	43
Land-line telephone	63	48	40
Email	35	34	37
Wireless email device	6	22	36

Note: Survey of respondents that use a device.

Source: Pew Internet & American Life Project Surveys.

Just how impressive is this growth? Hasn't the US experienced high growth rates of other electronic innovations? Isn't this just more of the same? Why are mobile devices exceptional?

The closest US rival to the mobile phone in terms of growth and penetration is TV. The first black-and-white TV was introduced into the US market in the 1940s, and colour TV was deployed through the 1960s. Today, there are approximately 235 million TV sets in use in the US[8] compared to 263 million mobile phones. This growth of TV occurred over 30-40 years, while the growth of mobile phones occurred in less than 20 years. Further, TV is a stable product, with little recent growth, while mobile subscription continues to grow at rates of over 20 per cent per year. TV is viewed by many as the ultimate compelling application (or killer app). While there are more mobile phones than TVs, household penetration is higher for television: 99 per cent of households have at least one TV, while over 70 per cent of households have at least one mobile phone.

The obvious competitor to mobile phones is wireline telephones. The market for wireline telephones began in 1876 (with its invention) and attained market saturation in the 1970s (when household penetration reached 94 per cent), where it stabilized for decades. A recent phenomenon is the decline in fixed-line numbers. This decline includes both incumbent local exchange (ILECs) and competitive local exchange companies (CLECs). Currently, there are approximately 186 million wireline telephones in the US. Recent trends in wireless versus wireline telephony through end-2007 are shown in Figure 10.3. CLEC subscriptions peaked in 2004, but are in decline since then. Total wireline subscription peaked in 2003 and is also in decline. As these numbers suggest, mobile phones are substituting for wireline devices at an increasing rate. As of 2008, 17.5 per cent of mobile users had no wireline phone; they chose to become 'untethered', up from 13 per cent in 2007. The common thread is that mobile subscriptions continue to exhibit high growth, both absolutely and in cannibalizing wireline telephony.

However, surely mobile is outstripped by electronic technology associated with the Internet, such as PCs and broadband (local access). These data,[9] however, tell a different story. In 2007, the US had approximately 73 million Internet subscribers. Also in 2007, there were 221 million Internet users; about 70 per cent of US households were connected to the Internet, either broadband or dial-up. Perhaps even more surprising, mobile subscriptions exceed PC ownership. In 2007, there were 220 million PCs (in the US including businesses); about 75 per cent of those households had at least one PC. Growth in business PCs continues to increase, while household penetration has stabilized.

The results reviewed so far demonstrate the dominance of mobile over virtually all other recent technology save the Internet. No other service or device is close to the popularity and market acceptance of mobile telephony, and this growth is not yet over. Nevertheless, this is only the initial phase of

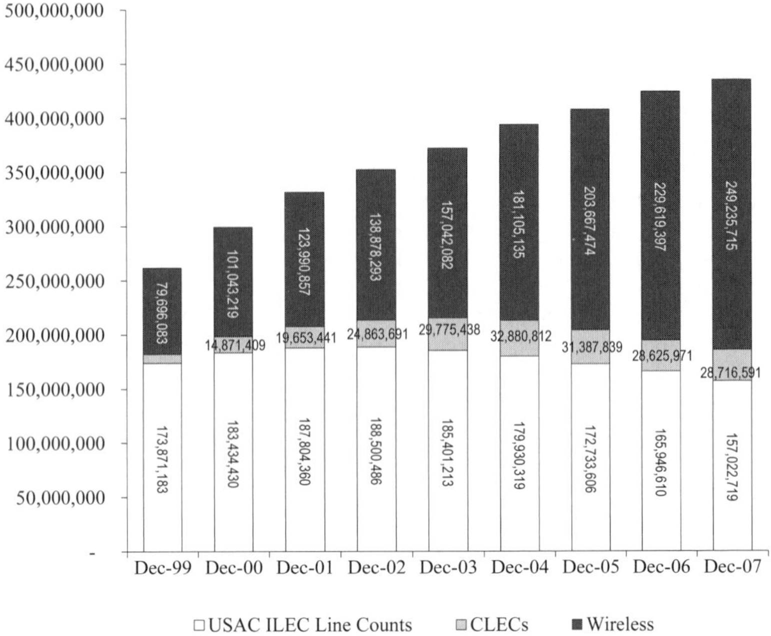

Sources: CTIA Semi-Annual Survey, FCC Local Competition Report, USAC FCC Filings (various issues).

Figure 10.3 US domestic subscription (mobile, ILEC, CLEC), 1999-2007

communications. Currently, the US use of data communications is growing faster than voice. Applications include email, Web browsing, mobile twittering, texting, remote TV and wireless hot synching. The mobile handset is becoming the device that integrates communications and computing power to provide popular social networking applications. Key to this development is 'smart phones' and high-speed Internet connections. From the Blackberry phone to the iPhone and recent successors, customers can tap into the power of the Internet to access these services. Just as experience has shown that mobiles are a substitute for wireline phones, experience is also showing that mobiles are a substitute for PCs as Internet access devices.

The growth of 3G data services in the US through 2007 is shown in Figure 10.4.[10]

Mobile wireless broadband is a very recent phenomenon; it first appears in FCC statistics[11] in June, 2004 (with merely 379,536 subscribers) relative to total broadband lines of 42.5 million. By December, 2007, mobile broadband accounted for 51 million subscribers relative to total broadband lines of 121.2

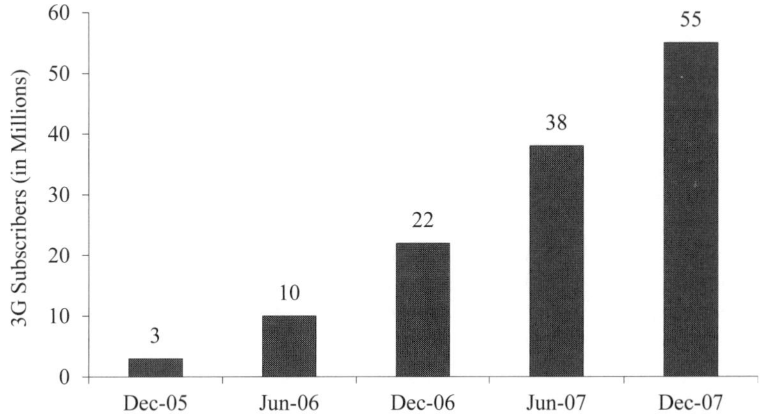

Source: US Wireless Metrics Review (Roche 2008).

Figure 10.4 Mobile broadband 3G subscription, 2005-2007

million, or 42 per cent of total broadband lines. Using the more restrictive FCC definition of broadband as 200 Kbps in both directions ('advanced service line'), mobile broadband accounted for 15.3 million lines relative to a total of 80.2 million lines, or 19 per cent of advanced service lines.[12] During 2007, mobile broadband lines increased by 28.7 million (46 per cent), or 75 per cent of total broadband net adds in that year. Mobile firms report that data revenues have increased at 40 per cent/year, from 0.6 per cent of total revenues in June, 2001 to 20.3 per cent in June, 2008.

When viewed in its entirety, the mobile telephony phenomenon is unprecedented: subscription and usage volume, voice and data, increasing applications, and exceptional growth compared to similar services. Mobile allowed Americans to talk where they want, anytime. Americans can text, email, or use a Web browser, twitter, or any number of social networking tools anywhere they want, anytime. Americans have taken to this phenomenon in record numbers at record speed. Mobile telephony substitutes for wireline phones. Mobile recently became a substitute for wired broadband, which it is significantly outpacing in the market. For many functions, it is becoming a substitute for the PC,[13] and perhaps eventually TV. Most interesting, however, is that it is a complement to the Internet. On current trends, mobile may be the most effective complement to the Internet: the ubiquitous application network connected to the ubiquitous networked device. More than the telephone, more than the PC, more than wired broadband, mobile connectivity is the likely future.

WORLDWIDE MOBILE

While the US experience with mobile telecommunications is unprecedented, global developments are even more phenomenal in social and economic impact. The worldwide experience can be broadly divided between the OECD countries and the developing world.

In broad terms, the development of mobile in the OECD is similar to that in the US. Western Europe is a world leader in the early development of mobiles, with higher penetration and faster deployment than the US, certainly through the late-1990s. Recently, the US and Western Europe have similar deployments. In East Asia, smart phones and 3G services developed more quickly than in the West, a lead which Japan and particularly South Korea maintain. South Koreans operate mobiles with broadband speeds approaching 4G, enabling lightning-fast Web browsing and high-resolution TV and a variety of high-speed services not available elsewhere. It is estimated that South Korea/Japan are 12-18 months more advanced than the US and Western Europe; for those who fear or hope for what mobile will do to or for Americans, look to South Korea to learn what the future will likely bring.

In this section, the focus is on an entirely different set of markets: developing countries. This is not to say that developments in South Korea and Japan are anything other than amazing. However, the changes wrought by mobile telephony in the developing world are even more exceptional than in the OECD.

The incremental contribution to the OECD of mobile telephony is mobility. OECD Member Countries already had established wireline connectivity by the 1980s, which also enabled data connectivity (via dial-up). Mobility is valuable, as US evidence demonstrates. However, mobile telephony brought both basic connectivity and mobility to the developing world, as wireline penetration in these countries is low. Prior to mobile telecommunications, the only means to communicate was to walk to a village. The isolation of rural communities in India, China and Africa is in stark contrast to the developed world. As such, it is hard to understand how to conduct business with minimal communication infrastructure. Information is essential to the operation of efficient markets. When information is not available, markets typically behave poorly, leading to poverty and exploitation. Mobile telephones provide, for the first time, an ability for the rural poor to utilize economic information to improve their own economic situation.

Mobile connectivity in the developing world is shown in Table 10.2.

The remainder of this section presents several case studies of the economic and social impact of mobile phones in the developing world. In doing so a series of articles in the *Washington Post* are drawn on.

Table 10.2 Developing world connectivity

	Wireline and Mobile Penetration 2007[14]		
	Main Wirelines/100	Mobiles/100	Mobile/Total
OECD countries	>40	>75	
Africa	3.21	28.44	89%
India	3.37	20	86%
China	27.52	41.19	60%

Source: International Telecommunication Union (2007).

The first article demonstrates the impact of the arrival of mobile technology on the economic conditions of traditional sardine fishermen on the Kerala coast of India.[15]

> Babu Rajan pointed off the starboard bow and shouted: 'There! There!'
>
> In choppy, gray seas four miles from shore near India's tropical southern tip, Rajan spotted the tinselly sparkle of a school of sardines. He ordered his three dozen crewmen to quickly drop their five-ton net overboard.
>
> Within five minutes, the cell phone hanging around his neck rang. [It was] a wholesale agent calling from port, who had heard by cell phone from other skippers that Rajan had just set his nets
>
> Minutes later Rajan's phone rang again -- another agent at a different port.
>
> 'When I have a big catch, the phone rings 60 or 70 times before I get to port,' he said.
>
> The cell phone is bringing new economic clout, profit and productivity to Rajan and millions of other poor labourers in India, the world's fastest-growing cell phone market.
>
> That explosive growth has meant greater access to markets, more information about prices and new customers for tens of millions of Indian farmers and fishermen. The cell phone is putting cash in the pockets of people for whom a dollar is a good day's wage. And it has made market-savvy entrepreneurs out of sheepherders, rickshaw drivers and [fishermen].

> Rajan said that before he got his first cell phone a few years ago, he used to arrive at port with a load of fish and hope for the best. The wholesaler on the dock knew that Rajan's un-iced catch wouldn't last long in the fiery Indian sun. So, Rajan said, he was forced to take whatever price was offered - without having any idea whether dealers in the next port were offering twice as much.
>
> Now he calls several ports while he's still at sea to find the best prices, playing the dealers against one another to drive up the price.
>
> Rajan's phone rang a half-dozen times in a half-hour, with calls from dealers in different ports, buyers and other boat captains. Rajan talked quickly and kept hauling. Rajan agreed to [a] deal [with a wholesale agent at his home port]. [H]e said the dealer was forced to offer a decent price, knowing that Rajan could still go elsewhere. As insurance, Rajan returned the call of the other dealer who had called him, just to keep good relations for another day.
>
> Rajan said that without his phone, his catch might have gone to waste. Because he called ahead to the port, buyers there knew that he was coming, what kind of fish he had and the size of his catch. In the past, Rajan said, he would sometimes arrive at port late in the day only to find that all the buyers had gone home, unaware that another boat was coming. His catch would go unsold, and he and his crew would go unpaid.

This particular case was studied extensively in Jensen;[16] as stated in his abstract:

> Between 1997 and 2001, mobile phone service was introduced throughout Kerala, a state in India with a large fishing industry. Using micro level survey data, we show that the adoption of mobile phones by fishermen and wholesalers was associated with a dramatic reduction in price dispersion, the complete elimination of waste, and near-perfect adherence to the Law of One Price. Both consumer and producer welfare increased.

The broader picture of mobiles in India is depicted in 'M-Powering India: Mobile Communications for Inclusive Growth.'[17] This report notes that by end-2007, India had replaced the US as the second largest mobile market (in terms of subscribers) in the world (after China) and is heading for 1/2 billion mobile subscriptions by 2010. The report also noted the importance of 'm-banking,' recommending a standard m-currency to facilitate greater 'm-commerce.'

It is no surprise to economists that information is the key to efficient markets, and that if mobiles increase the information available to market participants, the performance of markets will improve and incomes will rise. Jensen's careful empirical study of this market documents the gains from increased information due to mobile availability.

If mobiles improve the efficiency of fisheries markets, it might be expected that they can improve retail financial markets, that most information-intensive of all markets. In fact, much of the developing world is significantly under-banked at the retail level, and mobile operators are finding a profitable market niche in facilitating payments and transfers, both domestically and internationally. Referred to as M-banking, it appears to have arisen in developing countries where retail banking is unavailable or unreasonably expensive. The following case study[18] of M-banking in the Philippines (and the UK) demonstrates the power of mobile technology to facilitate cash transfers and, again, improve the efficiency of markets.

> 'It was 10:33 p.m. when Dulce Amor Bandoy's cell phone beeped with her favorite kind of message.
>
> You have received 1,321.00 of G-Cash,' read the text on her phone's glowing screen.
>
> That meant her uncle in London had just deposited 1,321 Philippine pesos - about $26 - into her Globe Telecom cell phone account, which Bandoy uses like a bank. 'My phone is now my wallet,' said Bandoy, 29, a cheerful woman with a sparkling smile.
>
> The cell phone-based system that conveys cash between Bandoy and her uncle has the potential to revolutionize the way hundreds of billions of dollars are moved around the world, according to experts who study global cash flows. But traditional methods of moving money in small, personal amounts can be slow and costly.
>
> Eugene Bandoy, 50, is a Filipino architect who lives in London and helps other expatriates buy property back home. When potential buyers want to take a look at condominiums or houses in the Philippines, his niece shows them around.
>
> Last month, Bandoy needed his niece to go to Quezon City, just outside Manila, to show a condominium to a woman who works in London but was home on vacation and interested in buying. But Dulce, like so many people struggling to get by in this country of almost 90 million people, said she didn't have the $1 for a bus or train ride to meet the client. She called her uncle and told him, 'I need money or I can't meet her'.
>
> In London, the agent typed in the amount he was sending and the day's exchange rate for the British pound and Philippine peso. Then she hit the send button to move the order to the phone company. Seconds later, a message appeared on her screen, confirming the transfer.
>
> It was 3:32 in the afternoon in London – 10:32 p.m. in Manila. At 10:33 p.m., Dulce's phone, sitting on her bedside table, pinged with the much-anticipated message.
>
> Next day, Dulce walked into the glitzy Globe phone store, where customers can browse the flashiest new phone models and pick up G-cash, as the company calls money transferred via phone . . . Less than five minutes after arriving at the store

> and after paying 26 cents – a 1 percent fee – she walked out with about $24 worth of Philippine pesos.
> By 10:30 a.m., she was walking a potential buyer through new condominiums in a middle-class area of Quezon City. 'She loved it! She signed the contract!' Bandoy recalled later.

M-banking is making an appearance to fill a need for customers, improving not only their ability to do business, but improving their lives as well. Currently,[19] India is focusing on facilitating m-commerce with plans for a standard m-currency, and m-banking spreading in sub-Saharan Africa, where the reach of traditional banks is quite limited.

However, the social impact of mobile phones is not limited to m-commerce. For example, text messaging has become a popular tool for political organizers. To quote from a recent news article:[20]

> Cell phones and text messaging are changing the way political mobilizations are conducted around the world. From Manila to Riyadh and Kathmandu protests once publicized on coffeehouse bulletin boards are now organized entirely through text-messaging networks that can reach vast numbers of people in a matter of minutes.
> The Philippines, widely called the text-messaging centre of the world, has led the way. When President Joseph Estrada was forced from office in 2001, he bitterly complained that the popular uprising against him was a 'coup de text'.

Perhaps most important is the application of mobile telecommunications to medical care. Since the dawn of the Internet, and especially since the advent of broadband, 'telemedicine' has been hailed in the US as a beneficial application of the technology. Unfortunately, there are virtually no known applications actually in place in the US. But telemedicine is alive and well in Africa, and the enabling technology is mobile, as illustrated in this case study:[21]

> Medical records and other health information can now be easily shared via mobile phones and other modern communications technologies.
>
> The small, dusty village of Mayange lies 20 kilometres from Rwanda's capital, Kigali. Its health centre has fewer than 40 beds but serves an estimated 35,000 people. The Mayange centre could well be like thousands of other health facilities across the continent struggling to meet patients' needs with very few resources and staff.
>
> But thanks to an innovative partnership involving the government, non-governmental organizations and private companies, the Mayange centre is now able to use mobile telephones to provide better treatment. With software developed by Ericsson and phones donated by the Rwandan subsidiary of Mobile Telephone Networks (MTN), a South African firm, health workers can call up the medical records of pregnant women from an online database and then, by cell phone, tell care-givers what to do during an emergency. The memory of each phone donated

> by MTN includes a maternal and child-care training manual, with images and audio directions that can be sent to mothers and families.
>
> The Mayange clinic is not alone in using mobile networks to improve health care. Across Rwanda, 143 public and private health centres that offer ARVs to people with HIV/AIDS now use Tracnet, a system that employs mobile phones to collect information on patients' infections. It helps the national drug centre keep track of which medicines are available in each health centre and when to resupply, making shortages of ARVs less common.

This is not telemedicine as envisioned by advocates in the US; but it is telemedicine in countries and markets where the need is perhaps far greater and the impact far more substantial. This case study, and the other case studies of this section, highlight: (i) how profound is the impact of mobiles in the developing world; (ii) how ingenious are the people of the developing world in devising applications that meet their needs without 'smart phones;' and (iii) how little the developed world understands the need and solutions of the developing world.

There is some empirical evidence that greater deployment of mobile leads to higher economic growth rates, and that this impact is twice as great for developing countries as for developed countries. Waverman et al. (2005)[22] estimate an endogenous growth model using World Bank data and find that for low-income countries, an additional penetration rate of 10 mobiles per 100 population raises GDP growth by 1/2 per cent per year. For high-income countries, an additional penetration rate of 10 per 1000 raises GDP growth by 1/4 per cent per year.

This, of course, is only one study, in an area notoriously difficult to obtain reliable empirical estimates (i.e., estimating the impact of infrastructure on economic growth). The estimates appear quite large; an impact of 1/2 per cent on GDP growth has a very substantial cumulative effect on national income. It is perhaps sufficient to justify the statement by development economist Jeffrey Sachs: 'The cell phone is the single most transformative technology for development.'[23]

This study included an array of numbers to demonstrate how dominant mobile telecommunications has become in daily life. However, the single number which best sums up this extraordinary growth, penetration and impacts is that there are currently 4.1 billion active mobile subscriptions worldwide, compared to a world population of 5.7 billion; a penetration rate of 61 per cent. This penetration exceeds that of PCs, wireline telephones, Internet users, and TVs.

LIMITS TO GROWTH

Perhaps the most surprising aspect of mobile markets is that both voice and data growth remains high, even though penetration is greater than any other technology. In the US, mobile subscription is growing at over 25 per cent per annum, while data services are growing at over 40 per cent. In developing countries such as India, growth in mobile subscription has been 42 per cent since 2002.

Can these high growth rates be sustained? This problem is parsed into: (i) growth in number of persons with mobiles; (ii) growth in number of subscriptions per person; and (iii) growth in data services.

Growth in Persons with Mobiles

In OECD Member Countries, the fraction of persons with mobile is high and at some point growth must level off; naturally this fraction cannot exceed 100 per cent. In the developed world, however, penetration rates are approximately 20 per cent and there is much room for future growth. While there are currently 4.1 billion mobile subscriptions globally, there may well be another billion or so to be added.[24] Eventually, everyone who wants a phone will have one, and growth will level off.

To achieve this level of penetration there are four key factors. First is price. The fastest growing developing country is India, which also has the lowest prices for both mobile devices and minutes of use. The ability of mobile operators to introduce devices to the very poor is crucial to capturing the next billion customers, and this depends upon the development of very low cost mobile technology. Market evolution thus far has shown that there is a market at the low end of the income distribution, but further effort is needed to capture more.

A second key factor is the availability of spectrum. Use of electromagnetic spectrum is the lifeblood of mobile communications. In most countries, spectrum is controlled by the government (in many cases, the military) and released to the private sector by bureaucratic processes. In some countries, spectrum is allocated via auctions, but the auctions and terms and conditions of release are still subject to bureaucratic processes. In countries that use auctions to allocate spectrum, the relatively high price received by auctioning agencies suggests that spectrum is tightly constrained relative to market demand. Using governments rather than markets to allocate scarce spectrum is a recipe to keep spectrum scarce for bureaucratic rather than technical reasons.[25] Improving the allocation of spectrum is a key factor to maintaining mobile growth rates, especially to underserved low-income areas.[26]

Another factor is 'light touch' regulation. Wireline telephony is traditionally subject to price-cost-entry regulation, while wireless telephony is subject to little regulation (other than spectrum allocation). The growth and nimbleness of mobile as compared to wireline is striking. For example, wireline telephone rate structures are determined in regulatory proceedings ('Title II' regulation in the US) and are typically distance and time sensitive. Wireless telephone rate structures are determined in a market setting, free of regulatory oversight. Mobile rates in the US are typically not distance or time sensitive, and within broad buckets, not even volume sensitive, a rate structure which customers and operators seem to prefer. As a result, wireline firms are migrating to this rate structure as the market, not regulators, revealed the structure is most suitable. Freedom from oppressive regulation has also led to technological innovation in mobile markets far more rapidly than in wireline markets, and significantly more competitive entry, and successful entry. Maintaining this light touch regulation is essential to realizing the customer benefits of mobile telephony worldwide.

A fourth key factor, which applies to poor rural areas, is the availability of reasonably reliable power. Without the ability to charge batteries, mobiles are not functional. There are, of course, alternatives to centrally distributed power. Rural customers often use solar[27] or wind power to charge mobile devices. But the lack of central power to poor rural areas is likely to hinder mobile deployment.

Growth in Subscriptions per Person

Several OECD Member Countries achieved penetrations substantially above 100 per cent, suggesting that many, perhaps most, customers carry more than one phone or at least more than one SIM card. Should countries such as the US increase penetration from 61 per cent to 120 per cent, this could lead to substantial growth. The likelihood of such growth is questionable; Kalba[28] speculates that the drivers of supra-100 per cent penetration is, among other things, the development of the prepaid market. It is unclear whether these factors apply in countries like the US. It is also unclear if increasing subscriptions per person increases usage. The US has higher usage per phone than Europe, yet penetration in the US is lower than in Europe. The value of mobile phones is from actually using it; if an individual splits usage among devices, it is not clear that this increases aggregate social value.

Growth in Data Services

The phenomenal OECD mobile data services growth demonstrates that there is much additional potential growth along this margin. There is no natural limit to such growth. Early data services such as email and texting show rapid growth, even as newer, higher bandwidth services such as TV, two-way video and high-speed access to the WWW are emerging in Korea and Japan. In these countries, mobile is evolving to a converged platform, offering voice, data communications, Internet access, and access to video content.

Such convergence has no natural limits in terms of extent and intensity of use by customers. Even in the developing world, it is clear that data services are highly valued (as demonstrated in the m-banking case study). On the supply side, this will require bringing 3G services to the developing world and 4G services to OECD Member Countries.

A key factor that determines whether the data services margin can maintain high growth is demand. That is, will customers in the OECD really want new Internet and video services, and will they be willing to pay for them? Figure 10.5 shows recent trends in wireless broadband access in the developed and developing world compared to that of wireline broadband, and demand appears to be growing rapidly worldwide. It would seem unlikely that this demand growth is likely to end in the near future.

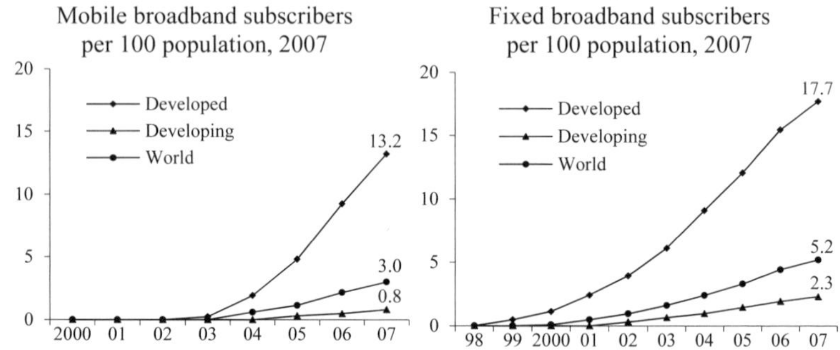

Note: The ITU defines mobile broadband to cover mobile cellular subscribers with access to data communications at broadband speeds (minimum of 256 Kbit/s).

Source: ITU World Telecommunication/ICT Indicators Database.

Figure 10.5 *Fixed and mobile broadband evolution in developed and developing countries*

Evidence from Korea and Japan suggests that the rest of the world can look forward to a mobile environment of more intense data communications, including two-way video and other bandwidth-intensive applications in the near future.

There are three key factors required to maintain high growth on the data services margin. First is the availability of spectrum. Broadband 3G and especially 4G services require substantial bandwidth, which is carried via the electromagnetic spectrum. 4G services may require 40-100 GB bandwidth which needs even more spectrum than government bureaucracy trickle out to the market. Bringing enough spectrums to market requires more than increased government largesse. It requires a new spectrum regime, moving away from command and control. Solving the spectrum allocation problem is a priority to open mobile data services to fulfil their potential.

Another factor is technical innovation in mobile devices that permits full convergence with computing and TV. Currently, mobile devices are constrained in their ability to compete effectively with computers and TV. Mobile screens and keyboards are small relative to full-sized versions associated with their fixed counterparts. In addition, for example, many customers continue to text and twitter on these keyboards. Even with the very limited input and output channels of mobile devices it is evident there is sufficient latent demand. However, there are two ways to overcome such limitations: (i) allow mobile handsets to communicate over short ranges with more capable display and input devices; using high-bandwidth Wi-Fi so that mobile handsets can stream video they receive online to a high-definition TV; (ii) use projection technologies to enable the devices to improve both display and keyboard. Technology is available which permits mobile devices to project screens onto surfaces at WVGA resolution,[29] sufficient for people to simultaneously watch movies or TV programs. Other technology permits mobile devices to project keyboard images to detect the 'keys' customer fingers are striking on the keyboard image, translating this information into a keystroke stream.[30] Such technology enable mobiles to overcome the display and keyboard limitations that hinder mobile data services growth.

The third key factor is continued light touch regulation. To encourage the rapid evolution of technology, it is essential that governments step back from this dynamic industry and let it evolve as customer demand evolves.

CONCLUDING REMARKS

Far from being one of the annoyances of modern life, mobile technology has become a defining feature in our lives. Not only has this influence affected more Americans than any other electronic technology, it has had an even greater positive influence on the lives of customers in the developing world. It is the dominant electronic technology, and growth is likely to continue.

To ensure that mobile fulfils its promise, four key items are identified: (a) release large amounts of spectrum for use by mobile service operators; this is unlikely to happen under current processes for allocating spectrum; (b) encourage more technological innovation by reducing the cost of low-end devices and systems so that the world's poor can afford connection and increase the ability of mobile devices to converge with communication, computing and TV by extending mobile's input and output capability; (c) maintain light touch regulation so that market forces for deployment and innovation have maximum play consistent with the public interest; and (d) for poor rural areas, encourage the deployment of power delivery systems so customers can charge their mobiles.

NOTES

1. Mobile refers to any mobile device capable of voice or data communication, which can be carried in a pocket, handbag or belt case. This does not include laptop computers or PDA-only devices.
2. See http://www.nophones.com.
3. See Beaumont (2008). The actual statement of the Vatican spokesman is rather more nuanced than the headline, and in fact the Vatican has used modern electronic technology (such as mobile) to communicate with the faithful.
4. Related work is reported by Kalba (2008). The Kalba paper focuses on the drivers of adoption of mobile worldwide.
5. In developing countries, penetration rates are rather lower than in OECD Member Countries, but growth rates are significantly higher. This suggests that in these countries there is a 'digital lag' rather than a digital divide.
6. Charts and data from Roche (2009).
7. See Horrigan (2008).
8. See http://www.csun.edu/science/health/docs/tv&health.html.
9. See Horrigan *op. cit.*
10. See Roche (2008).
11. Data from Federal Communications Commission (2009). The numbers quoted use the FCC's rather lax (and controversial) definition of 'high speed line' as any channel capable of 200 kbps in either direction.
12. Typically, mobile broadband data services such as EV-DO and WCDMA offer bandwidths around 500/800 Kbps, similar to that of 'starter' DSL (384 Kbps/1 Mbps), and far less than cable or premium DSL. This discrepancy in performance may account for the differing percentages of wireless broadband of total high speed lines versus advanced service lines.
13. For a discussion of the entry of PC manufacturers into the mobile device business (following Apple's iPhone lead), see Vance (2009).
14. Data are from ITU (2007).
15. See Sullivan (2006).
16. See Jensen (2007).
17. See Adler and Mahesh (2008).
18. See Jordan (2006).
19. See Adler and Mahesh, *op. cit.*
20. See Jordan (2006).
21. See Kimani (2008).
22. See Waverman et al., (2005).
23. Quoted by Ewing (2007).
24. 4.1 billion mobiles do not, of course, mean that 4.1 persons have mobiles. It is quite common in some countries for some persons to own multiple mobiles, or multiple SIM cards.
25. See, e.g., Faulhaber (2006).
26. For a discussion of problems in India with government release of spectrum, see http://www.economist. com/business/displaystory.cfm?story_id=13185 039.
27. See Ewing *op.cit.*
28. See Kalba *op cit.*
29. See Comer (2008).
30. A projection keyboard is available on Beagle Board.

REFERENCES

Adler, R. and Mahesh, U. (2008), *M-Powering India: Mobile Communications for Inclusive Growth,* Report of the Third Annual Joint Roundtable on Communications Policy, India and United States: Aspen Institute India.

Beaumont, C. (2008), 'Vatican Warns Mobile Phones are Bad for The Soul', *The Telegraph,* at http://www.telegraph.co.uk/news/newstopics/religion/3531418/Vatican-warns-mobile-phones-are-bad-for-the-soul.html.

Comer, S. (2008, March 31), 'Big Screen Projection from Your Cellphone', *ITWire.* Retrieved from: http://www.itwire.com/content/view/17386/127/.

Ewing, J. (2007), 'Upwardly Mobile in Africa', Business Week. Sept 13. Retrieved from: http://www.businessweek.com/globalbiz/content/sep2007/gb20070913_705733.htm?chan=globalbiz_europe+index+page_top+stories.

Faulhaber, G. (2006), 'The Future of Wireless Communications: Spectrum as a Critical Resource', *Information and Economic Policy,* **18**, 256–71.

Federal Communications Commission (2009), *High-Speed Services for Internet Access: Status as of December 31, 2007* (Report No. DOC-287962A1). Retrieved from: http://fjallfoss.fcc.gov/edocs_public/attachmatch/DOC-287962A1.pdf.

Federal Communications Commission (2009, January 16), *Annual Report and Analysis of Competitive Market Conditions With Respect to Commercial Mobile Services,* Thirteenth Report (WT Docket No. 08-27). Retrieved from: http://hraunfoss.fcc.gov/edocs_public/attachmatch/DA-09-54A1.pdf.

Horrigan, J. (2008), 'Mobile Access to Data and Information'. Retrieved from: http://www.pewinternet.org/~/media//Files/Reports/2008/PIP_Mobile.Data.Access.pdf.pdf.

International Telecommunication Union, *Free Statistics, By Country – 'ICT-Eye' 2007* [Data file]. Geneva, Switzerland.

ITU World Telecommunication/ICT Indicators Database. Retrieved from: http://www.itu.int/ITU-D/ict/publications/world/world.html

Jensen, R. (2007), 'The Digital Provide: Information (Technology), Market Performance, and Welfare in the South Indian Fisheries Sector', *The Quarterly Journal of Economics*, **122**, 879–924.

Jordan, M. (2006, August 25), 'Going Mobile: Text Messages Guide Filipino Protesters', *Washington Post.* Retrieved from: http://www.washingtonpost.com/wp-dyn/content/article/2006/08/24/AR2006082401379.html.

Jordan, M. (2006, October 3), 'New Conductors Speed the Global Flow of Money', *Washington Post.* Retrieved from: http://www.washingtonpost.com/wp-dyn/content/article/2006/10/02/AR2006100201462.html.

Kalba, K. (2008), *The Global Adoption and Diffusion of Mobile Phones,* Cambridge: Harvard University, Program on Information Resources Policy. Retrieved from: http://www.pirp.harvard.edu/pubs_pdf/kalba/kalba-p08-1.pdf.

Kimani, M. (2008, May), 'Rwanda: Better Health at the Click of a Button', *Africa Renewal.* Retrieved from: http://allafrica.com/stories/200805091090.html.

Roche, R. (2008, April), 'US Wireless Metrics Review', CTIA.

Roche, R. (2009, February), 'National and Rural Wireless Trends: What Does the Data Show?', CTIA.

Sullivan, K. (2006, October 15), 'For India's Traditional Fishermen, Cellphones Deliver a Sea Change', *Washington Post*. Retrieved from: http://www.washingtonpost.com/wp-dyn/content/article/2006/10/14/AR2006101400342.html.

The Hesitant Auctioneer (2009, February 26), *The Economist*.

Upwardly Mobile In Africa (2007, September 24), *Businessweek*. Retrieved from: http://www.businessweek.com/magazine/content/07_39/b4051054.htm.

Vance, A. (2009, March 15), 'Computer Makers Prepare to Stake Bigger Claim in Phones', *The New York Times*. Retrieved from: http://www.nytimes.com/2009/03/16/technology/16cell.html.

Waverman, L., Meschi, M. and Fuss M. (2005), 'The Impact of Telecoms on Economic Growth in Developing Countries' (Paper number 3), in *The Vodafone Policy Paper Series – Pushing the Debate Forward*. Retrieved from: http://www.vodafone.com/etc/medialib/attachments/cr_downloads.Par.78351.File.dat/GPP_SIM_paper_3.pdf.

11. Regulator incentives and third generation national mobile telecommunications market entry

Gary Madden, Aaron Morey and Erik Bohlin

INTRODUCTION

Mobile communications rapidly evolved since the 1980s introduction of (voice only) first generation analogue systems. Technology is characterised by relatively low network capacity and large handset size. Subsequent second generation (2G) technology developments are in response to demand for enhanced voice and data services (Gruber and Hoenicke, 1999). Digitally based 2G systems also benefit from unified European standards. Penetration of 2G mobile in advanced economies rose rapidly. More recent third generation (3G) mobile telephony, which uses packet-based broadband technology, addresses the need for global compatibility, multi-media services provision and greater speed.

Granting rights to spectrum to provide mobile service is a three-stage process. Initially, spectrum bands are allocated for particular uses cross-countries via international institutions such as the International Telecommunication Union (ITU). The process ensures interference free transmission and reception. In particular, ITU World Radio Conferences (WRCs) allocate spectrum bands to specific uses. Secondly, radio frequency channels are allotted to a particular use within a geographical area. Finally, national regulatory authorities (NRAs) assign spectrum within countries to mobile network operators (MNOs) (Gruber, 2005). While the global framework for the utilisation of radio frequency spectrum is contained in the ITU Radio Regulations, there is considerable flexibility within the framework for NRAs to assign spectrum in a manner consistent with the local environment.

In 1992 the WRC IMT-2000 project defined standards for the deployment of 3G systems. The first 3G licences were issued across most of Western Europe in 1999–2001.[1] Accordingly, European institutions initially consider 3G licensing policy positions. Directive 97/13/EC of the European Commission (EC, 1997) refers to the benefit of promoting competition in telecommunications markets. In particular, the Directive states that new operators (entrants) should be encouraged to enter markets to ensure the development of European telecommunications service markets.[2] The Directive also highlights the role NRAs should play in influencing market structure. By granting licences on the basis of transparent selection criteria which gives weight to the need to facilitate the development of competition, NRAs can assist with developing telecommunications markets (EC, 1997).

The 1997 UMTS Forum is guided by EC Directives in drafting reports on the proposed regulatory framework for 3G licensing.[3] These reports are input into the construction of a regulatory framework for spectrum licensing in Europe. The Forum notes in its initial report:

> . . . assessment of (3G licence) applications should take into account the benefits of allowing current operators into the UMTS market in terms of synergies and existing commercial experience, balanced against those of letting in new entrants whereby introducing new competition. (UMTS Forum, 1998: 11)

Thus, the UMTS Forum highlights the role of market entry to stimulate competition in European markets. In particular, the Forum notes optimum subscriber benefit is achieved when competing infrastructure provide advanced and innovative services. The briefing paper for the ITU's 2001 Workshop on Licensing of 3G Mobile considers appropriate spectrum licensing critical for 3G service developments. In particular, the successful development of 3G mobile telecommunications depends on pro-competitive licensing and market entry (Xavier, 2001).

Entrants face substantial barriers to enter mobile service markets due to high incumbent operator 3G spectrum valuations (Azacis and Burguet, 2008; Gruber, 2007; Ansari and Munir, 2008). Incumbents' spectrum valuations are higher when legacy networks can be used to provide 3G services. With entry likely to result in market share erosion, potential entry increases incumbent willingness to pay relative to that of potential entrants. Accordingly, incumbents with 'high' valuations bid more aggressively than potential entrants in auctions (Hoppe et al., 2006). In beauty contests, incumbents' market knowledge, network scale economies and existing customer base are sources of strategic advantage, especially when NRAs place greater weight in the selection criteria on meeting post-award deployment obligations (A-Focus and DotEcon, 2004). Given this, competition for 3G licences is likely to be greatest in the most 'attractive' markets. Potential entrants seemingly have a greater probability of winning licences in 'unattractive' markets, where incumbent spectrum valuations are lower.

Applicants for 3G licences in auctions and beauty contests incur substantial costs (i.e., resources used to value licences and interest foregone on deposits). Thus, when potential entrants perceive the chance of winning a licence is low bids are not made (Ansari and Munir, 2008). Given incumbents' natural advantage in bidding, NRAs can encourage participation by enhancing entrants' likelihood of success. Indeed, Gruber (2007) considers that NRAs commonly pursue more competitive national mobile market agendas.[4] Furthermore, Hoppe et al. (2006) show that NRAs influence market structure by encouraging entry to increase the number of active firms.

Facilities-based market entry in mobile telecommunications is encouraged by auction and beauty contest licensing processes.[5] In particular, NRAs attempt to influence market structure by increasing the probability of an entrant winning a licence. NRAs may use the number of licences offered (relative to incumbents), withheld licences and (price and quantity) concessions to encourage market entry. However, other factors may also influence the probability an entrant wins a licence, e.g., macroeconomic conditions, spectrum package attributes and post-award deployment obligations. This chapter examines 3G spectrum award outcomes in terms of whether an entrant wins a licence through the descriptive analysis of a unique sample of national 3G spectrum assignment data. The analysis considers the features of markets and licences where entry occurs to see whether such entry is mainly in unattractive markets. This may indicate what features of 3G markets and licences increase incumbent spectrum valuations and, ultimately, barriers to entry.

The sample consists of 141 licences from 49 national assignment processes for 1999-2008. Of these national assignments, 29 are by beauty contest and 20 by auction. Characteristics of 3G spectrum assignments are sourced from the DotEcon Spectrum Awards Database (2008). These data contain characteristics for over 100 award processes and 8500 licences in 40 countries from 1999-2008.

MNO ENVIRONMENTS

Macroeconomic and spectrum licence conditions vary across countries. Given this, some national mobile markets are deemed more attractive to potential entrants and incumbent operators. Where legacy infrastructure is able to provide 3G services incumbent valuations of the operating environment are higher.

Macroeconomic Conditions

Domestic macroeconomic conditions are likely to influence the value of national 3G spectrum licences. In particular,

(a) *National income.* Higher per capita income increases the demand for 3G services;
(b) *Population density.* Economies of density exist because shorter average length of line (per subscriber) is required in areas where subscribers are more densely located, lowering average costs; and
(c) *Mobile competition.* Local competition influences 3G revenues, especially where early-mover advantages in serving the market are realised.

Data concerning national macroeconomic conditions are listed in Table 11.1 for the periods 1999-2001 and 2002-2008. The former period coincides with the period when most Western European countries assigned 3G licences. These data show that average national income and population density values vary substantially by period.

Table 11.1 Macroeconomic conditions

	1999-2001	2002-2008	Sample
National income[a]			
Mean	21,501	13,979	18,407
Standard deviation	8,491	16,082	12,702
Population density[b]			
Mean	409	151	303
Standard deviation	1,242	184	966
Mobile competition[c]			
Mean	0.23	0.23	0.23
Standard deviation	0.05	0.05	0.05

Notes: (a) GDP per capita ($US). (b) National population per square kilometre (persons). (c) Inverse of one plus number of facilities-based mobile operators.

Licence Conditions

NRAs impose conditions that affect the value of 3G licences both to incumbents and potential entrants, viz.

(a) *Licence duration.* The number years to expiration of the licence is important, with longer licence terms offering MNOs more opportunity to realise a return on investment costs;
(b) *Geographic network coverage obligations.* NRAs commonly require MNOs to meet network coverage obligations as part of the licence conditions. For example, a percentage of the national population is often required to be served by a specified period. The higher the portion of the population to be covered, and the shorter the time to achieve coverage, the more onerous the obligations;
(c) *Annual licence fees.* Some licences require MNOs to pay an annual licence fee. Annual fees may be a predetermined amount or percentage of annual 3G revenue. NRAs can impose annual licence fees in addition to an upfront fee. Where annual fees completely substitute for large upfront fees market entry is encouraged, as payment is only made after the operator earns revenue; and
(d) *Infrastructure sharing.* Licences may enable entrants to access incumbent infrastructure to provide 3G services. Potential entrants prefer access to extant facilities while incumbents seek to prevent access.

Table 11.2 lists sample licence conditions for 1999-2001 and 2002-2008. All conditions, with the exception of duration, vary considerably across countries.

Table 11.2 Licence conditions

	1999-2001	2002-2008	Sample
Licence duration[a]			
Mean	18	15	17
Standard deviation	4	4	4
Population coverage obligation[b]			
Mean	0.55	0.33	0.46
Standard deviation	0.35	0.32	0.36
Time to achieve coverage[c]			
Mean	3.7	3.0	3.5
Standard deviation	2.4	3.0	2.7
Annual licence fee (fixed)[d]			
Mean	0.11	0.23	0.16
Standard deviation	0.32	0.58	0.45
Annual licence fee (% 3G revenue)			
Mean	0.10	0.14	0.11
Standard deviation	0.40	0.80	0.59
Infrastructure sharing[e]			
Mean	0.24	0.15	0.21
Standard deviation	0.43	0.37	0.41

Notes: (a) term (years). (b) % of population to be covered. (c) Years to achieve coverage. (d) Annual fee ($US per 100 MHz per million population). (e) = 1, if infrastructure sharing is imposed; = 0, otherwise.

Table 11.3 lists sample correlation coefficients between variables that determine the attractiveness of markets (or licence) and measures of competition for spectrum in the assignment. Competition for spectrum is greater with higher national income and population density, and lower for more intense domestic mobile competition. In terms of licence conditions, competition is greater for licences with longer duration and less onerous coverage obligations.

Table 11.3 Assignment competition

	Correlation with Assignment Competition[a]
Macroeconomic conditions	
National income	0.03
Population density	0.05
Mobile competition	0.10
Licence conditions	
Licence duration	0.21
Population coverage obligation	-0.19
Time to achieve coverage	-0.16
Annual licence fee (fixed)	-0.12
Annual licence fee (% 3G revenue)	0.07
Infrastructure sharing	-0.13

Notes: (a) Assignment competition is the number of spectrum bidders divided by number of spectrum licences available.

NRA METHODS TO ENCOURAGE ENTRY

Analysys (2007) summarises alternative NRA spectrum assignment positions with regard to new entrants. In particular, assignments can be: (a) restricted to incumbent operators; (b) open to new entrants; (c) open to entrants that receive concessions; and (d) open to entrants, and available licences exceed the number of incumbents (or at least one licence is set aside for entrants).

Spectrum and Price Concessions

Table 11.4 lists concessions provided to entice entry into spectrum markets. Concessions consist of: (a) targeted spectrum; or (b) assigning spectrum price discounts exclusively for entrants. Of the 6 assignments, only Greece did not award a licence to an entrant.[6] Importantly, Table 11.4 indicates that NRAs in only 6 of 52 assignment processes made concessions to potential entrants. The Nigerian Communications Commission (2007) is the only NRA to assign spectrum exclusively to incumbents within the period 1999-2008.[7]

Table 11.4 Entrant concessions, 1999-2008

Country	Year	Assignment Mode	Concession[a]
Italy	2000	Auction	s
UK	2000	Auction	s, p
Greece	2001	Auction	s
Israel	2001	Auction	p
Ireland	2002	Beauty Contest	s, p[b]
Slovak Republic	2002	Beauty Contest	s

Notes: (a) s indicates additional spectrum is made available only to entrants while p indicates the spectrum price is discounted to entrants; (b) The Irish entrant price advantage is via awarding additional points to entrants.

Source: DotEcon Spectrum Awards Database (2008), Analysys (2007), Börgers and Dustmann (2003).

Withheld Licences

The practice of withholding licences to encourage entry into mobile service markets is considered in Table 11.5, which lists the number and percentage of withheld licences by World Bank national income classification for 1999-2008.[8] Withholding licences for entrants is uncommon and only applied in High Income countries (8 of 116 licences). Importantly, 30 licences are awarded to entrants in High Income countries during 1999-2008. That is, entry occurs in 22 cases when no licences are withheld.

Table 11.5 Withheld licences by national income classification, 1999-2008

Income Classification[a]	Awarded Licences	Withheld Licences		Entrants	
		Number	%	Number	%
High (38)	116	8[b]	7	30	26
Upper-Middle (10)	22	0	0	4	18
Lower-Middle (4)	11	0	0	5	45
Sample	149	8	5	39	25

Notes: (a) World Bank income classification. Number of assignment processes in parentheses. (b) Belgium eventually awarded a withheld licence to an incumbent due to a lack of interest.

Excess Licences

The number of licences offered relative to incumbent operators is a metric NRAs consider in encouraging entry.[9] Table 11.6 lists the number of available licences (in excess of incumbent operators) and entrant assignment for 1999-2008. Withheld licences are excluded from the calculations. Of 49 national assignment processes (rows), in 25 cases the number of excess licences equals the number of entrants, i.e., there are 25 'matched' markets. In the remaining 24 national assignments either the: (a) number of excess licences is greater than entrant number (9 cases); or (b) number of entrants exceeds excess licences (15 cases). Where excess licences are greater than entrant numbers, the market is apparently 'unattractive' to potential entrants. Conversely, when entrant numbers are greater than excess licences, an incumbent has not valued the licence as highly as the entrant.

The relationship between entrant numbers and excess licences is explored further by considering the joint and conditional sample probabilities contained in Table 11.7 and Table 11.8, respectively. Table 11.7 shows that entrants win licences when there are no excess licences in 22 per cent of assignments. This is either due to an incumbent: (a) not bidding; or (b) being outbid by an entrant. Further, in 16 per cent of assignments no licences are awarded to entrants when at least a single excess licence is available. Thus, an excess number of licences does not assure entry. Table 11.8 shows the probability of entrant licence assignment when no excess licence is available is 0.41. Further, the probability that there are an excess number of licences when there is no entry is 0.33. These conditional probabilities indicate that entry can occur when incumbent numbers are greater than or equal to available licences, and that having an excess number of licences does not guarantee entry, respectively.

To sum, making available more licences than incumbents is common, whilst withholding licences (and awarding concessions) is rare. Further, market entry mostly occurs in the absence of such policy. Moreover, when such policies are in effect often entry does not occur. This suggests that other factors affect the entry probability, and encouraging potential entrants to participate does not necessarily overcome incumbent advantage.

Table 11.6 Excess licences and new entrants by assignment, 1999-2008

Country	Year	Excess Licences[a]	Market Entrants[b]
Finland	1999	0	0
Austria	2000	2	2
Germany	2000	2	2
Italy	2000	0	0
Japan	2000	0	0
Korea Republic	2000	0	0
Netherlands	2000	0	0
Norway	2000	1	1
Poland	2000	2	0
Portugal	2000	1	1
Spain	2000	1	1
Sweden	2000	1	2
Switzerland	2000	1	1
UK	2000	0	0
Belgium	2001	0	0
Czech Republic	2001	1	0
Denmark	2001	0	1
France	2001	1	0
Greece	2001	0	0
Israel	2001	1	0
Liechtenstein	2002	2	0
New Zealand	2001	1	2
Singapore	2001	0	0
Slovenia	2001	1	0
France	2002	1	0
Ireland	2002	0	1
Latvia	2002	0	0
Luxembourg	2002	1	1
Malaysia	2002	0	0
Slovak Republic	2002	0	0
Taiwan	2002	1	2
Estonia	2003	1	0

Luxembourg	2003	0	1
Croatia	2004	0	1
Hungary	2004	1	0
Romania	2004	0	0
Bulgaria	2005	0	0
Denmark	2005	0	1
Latvia	2005	0	1
Poland	2005	1	1
Egypt	2006	0	1
Georgia	2006	0	2
Indonesia	2006	0	1
Malaysia	2006	1	1
Philippines	2006	1	1
Slovenia	2006	0	1
Ireland	2007	0	1
Russia	2007	0	0
Slovenia	2008	0	1
Total		26	31

Notes: (a) Calculated as number of licences offered for which both entrants and incumbents can apply for in excess of incumbent operators; (b) Does not include entrants which won a withheld licence.

Table 11.7 Joint probabilities

Event	Probability
ENTRANT only	0.22
EXCESS only	0.16
ENTRANT and EXCESS	0.29
None	0.33
Total	1.00

Notes: Data are converted to binary format for the construction of this table, viz., where the number of entrants is greater than 0, ENTRANT = 1, and 0 otherwise. Further, when the number of excess licences is greater than 0, EXCESS = 1, and 0 otherwise.

Table 11.8 Conditional probabilities

	ENTRANT = 1	EXCESS = 1
$P(\cdot \mid \text{ENTRANT} = 1)$	1.00	0.56
$P(\cdot \mid \text{EXCESS} = 1)$	0.64	1.00
$P(\cdot \mid \text{ENTRANT} = 0)$	0.00	0.33
$P(\cdot \mid \text{EXCESS} = 0)$	0.41	0.00

Notes: Data is converted to binary format for the construction of this table, viz., where the number of entrants is greater than available licences, ENTRANT = 1, and 0 otherwise. Further, when the number of excess licences is greater than 0, EXCESS = 1, and 0 otherwise.

ENTRY PATTERNS

The DotEcon Spectrum Awards Database (2008) identifies the names of operators assigned 3G licences. Operator Web sites are surveyed to determine whether carriers operate a network in the particular market prior being assigned the 3G licence.[10]

Table 11.9 Licence assignments, excess licences and entry by assignment mode[a]

	Auction	Beauty Contest	Sample
National licences assigned	69	72	141
Excess licences	11	15	26
Entrants	16	15	31
Entrant-licence ratio[b]	0.23	0.21	0.22

Notes: (a) Table 11.9 is constructed using only those licences and assignments where both incumbents and entrants can bid for spectrum. Thus, withheld licences are excluded; (b) Calculated as number of entrants divided by assigned licences.

Table 11.9 presents assigned licences, excess licences and entry by assignment mode. The sample includes 141 licences approximately equally divided between auctions and beauty contests. Table 11.9 shows the percentage of licences assigned to entrants are similar for auctions (23 per cent) and beauty contests (21 per cent). Figure 11.1 plots the entrant-licence ratio against time. These data show the entrant-licence ratio is not monotonic. Figure 11.2 depicts the path of entry and excess licence availability.

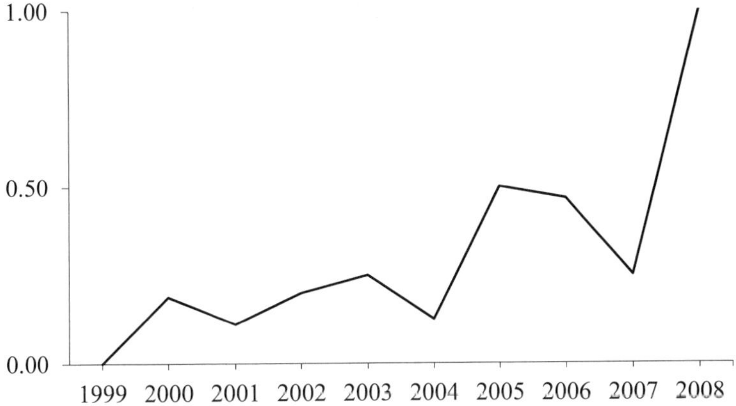

Figure 11.1 *Entrant-assigned licence ratio*

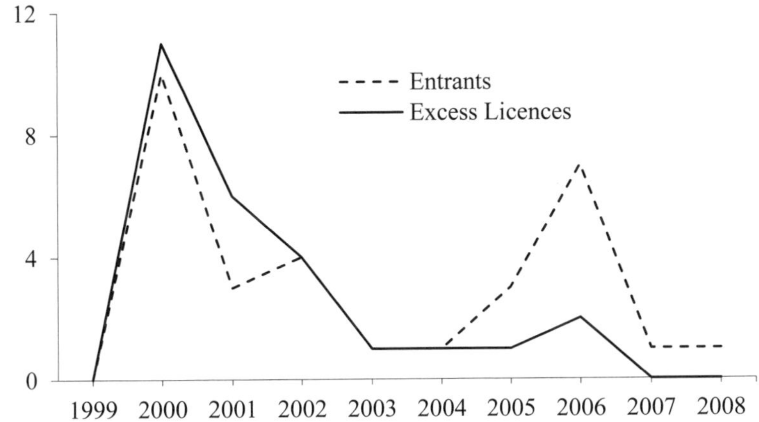

Figure 11.2 *Entry and excess licence availability*

Casual inspection of Figure 11.2 identifies three regimes. In Regime 1 (2000-2001) excess licences are always greater than entrant number. In Regime 2 (2002-2004), entry and excess licence availability match.[11] Finally, in Regime 3 (2005-2008) entrant numbers exceed available excess licences.

The payment mode may affect the probability of an entrant being assigned a licence. Spectrum pricing is either via: (a) upfront licence fees; (b) annual ex-post payments (either a percentage of 3G revenues or fixed amount); (c) combined upfront and annual fees; or (d) the spectrum is free. High upfront licence fees may act as a barrier to entry. In particular, entrants, with no subscriber base (from which to immediately draw revenue), experience longer payback periods. Further, entrants may not be able to access capital markets as readily as incumbents that have a history of mobile service provision.[12] Table 11.10 lists entrant numbers by payment mode. Table 11.10 shows that when licences require only an annual fee, entry is proportionally greater than when other pricing formats are employed. Conversely, licences paid exclusively by upfront payment have the lowest entry-licence ratio.

Table 11.10 Entry by payment mode

Mode	Assigned Licences	Entrants	Entrant-Licence Ratio
Upfront payment only	93	19	0.20
Upfront payment and annual fee	37	9	0.24
Annual fee only	7	2	0.29
Neither	4	1	0.25
Sample	141	31	0.22

Note: Withheld licences not included.

Table 11.11 lists the licences issued by regime (see Figure 11.2) and payment mode. In Regime 1 (when excess licence availability exceeds entry) most pricing plans are upfront payment only (70 per cent). Additionally, licences that require upfront and annual payments are proportionally greater in Regime 3 (31 per cent) when entry exceeds available excess licences.

An interesting question is whether post-award deployment obligations impact on the entry likelihood. More onerous obligations may favour incumbents that can rely on market experience and legacy infrastructure. Conversely, favourable deployment conditions may induce incumbents to bid more aggressively for spectrum. Table 11.12 suggests that incumbents have less onerous deployment obligations. Table 11.13 lists network deployment obligations by regime. Table 11.13 shows that entrant and incumbent coverage obligations are similar by regime. Typically, entrants have less time to meet deployment obligations in all regimes.

Table 11.11 Licence payment mode by regime[a]

Pricing Plan	Regime 1	Regime 2[b]	Regime 3	Sample
Assigned Licences	80	35	26	141
Upfront payment only	56 (70)	20 (57)	17 (65)	93 (66)
Upfront payment and annual fee	21 (26)	8 (23)	8 (31)	37 (26)
Annual fee only	0 (0)	7 (20)	0 (0)	7 (5)
Neither	3 (4)	0 (0)	1 (4)	4 (3)

Notes: (a) Percentage of total available licences in regime in parentheses. Withheld licences are excluded from this table; (b) Includes Finland (1999).

Table 11.12 Mean post-award licence obligations

	Entrant (31)[a]	Incumbent (110)	Sample
Population coverage obligation[b]	0.48	0.46	0.47
Timeframe to achieve coverage[c]	3.06	3.56	0.11

Notes: (a) Number of licences awarded in parentheses. (b) % of population to be covered by licence. (c) Years to achieve licence coverage.

Table 11.13 Mean post-award licence obligations by regime

	Regime 1	Regime 2[a]	Regime 3	Sample
Population coverage obligation[b]				
Entrant	0.60	0.30	0.44	0.48
Incumbent	0.57	0.21	0.44	0.46
Timeframe to achieve coverage[c]				
Entrant	3.77	1.83	2.92	3.06
Incumbent	3.91	2.83	3.43	3.56

Notes: (a) Finland (1999) is included in Regime 2. (b) % of population to be covered by licence. (c) Years to achieve licence coverage.

Table 11.14 lists national market conditions during assignments. Market conditions identify how attractive national markets are to potential operators. For instance, high GDP per capita and low mobile competition increase potential 3G revenue, while higher population density is associated with lower network operating costs. Table 11.14 shows entrants win licences in markets with high national income and population density.[13] Decomposing these data by regime in Table 11.15 shows that national income and population density are greater when there is entry in all regimes. Further, entry occurs in 'smaller' markets (smaller populations) in all regimes.

Table 11.14 Mean national market conditions

	National Income[a]	Population Density[b]	Mobile Competition[c]
Entry (26)[d]	22,490	384	0.24
No Entry (23)	14,507	159	0.23
Sample	18,743	279	0.23

Notes: (a) GDP per capita ($US). (b) National population per square kilometre (persons). (c) Inverse of one plus number of facilities-based mobile operators. (d) Number of assignments in parentheses.

Table 11.15 Mean national market conditions by regime

	Regime 1	Regime 2[a]	Regime 3	Sample
National Income[b]				
Entrant	23,479	33,565	16,558	22,490
No entrant	17,886	11,827	6,297	14,507
Population Density[c]				
Entrant	762.23	236.82	108.98	384
No entrant	242.44	76.35	37.90	159
Mobile Competition[d]				
Entrant	0.23	0.23	0.24	0.23
No Entrant	0.22	0.24	0.25	0.23

Notes: (a) Finland (1999) is included in Regime 2. (b) GDP per capita ($US). (c) National population per square kilometre (persons). (d) Inverse of one plus number of facilities-based mobile operators.

Entrants may win licences in markets with more attractive macroeconomic conditions because of assistance from NRAs. Thus, a distinction that should be made is between the licences won by entrants that are in direct competition with incumbents, and those that win licences with NRA assistance.

DO ENTRANTS WIN ATTRACTIVE LICENCES WITH NRA ASSISTANCE?

Table 11.16 and Table 11.17 list the macroeconomic and licence conditions, respectively, faced by entrants that: (a) win licences in direct competition with incumbents; and (b) win licences with the assistance of NRAs.

Table 11.16 Macroeconomic conditions for entrants with and without assistance[a]

	Entry with assistance	Entry without assistance	Sample
National income[b]			
Mean	21,070	21,924	18,556
Standard Deviation	11,833	22,083	12,612
Population density[c]			
Mean	183	93	301
Standard Deviation	191	42	956
Mobile competition[d]			
Mean	0.23	0.24	0.23
Standard Deviation	0.06	0.03	0.05

Notes: (a) Assistance is considered to occur when the NRA either withholds licences, makes available excess licences or offers spectrum concessions. (b) GDP per capita ($US). (c) National population per square kilometre (persons). (d) Inverse of one plus number of facilities-based mobile operators.

Table 11.16 shows that, in terms of macroeconomic conditions, NRAs have little impact in terms of markets where entry occurs. Table 11.17 similarly considers 3G licence conditions. Table 11.17 indicates some differences in licence conditions for entrants that win licences with and without assistance. In particular, fees are higher for entry without assistance, while infrastructure sharing is more likely with assistance. Entry with assistance is generally easier, viz., longer duration, more time to achieve coverage and smaller fees. However, population coverage and infrastructure sharing conditions are tougher. That is, there appears a trade-off between licence conditions. Overall, there is evidence that NRAs influence the types of markets, via licence conditions, where entry occurs. This is not surprising, given that NRAs directly determine licence conditions.

Table 11.17 Licence conditions for entrants with and without assistance[a]

	Entry with assistance	Entry without assistance	Sample
Licence duration[b]			
Mean	16.5	16.1	17.0
Standard Deviation	3.9	2.6	4.1
Population coverage obligation[c]			
Mean	0.58	0.39	0.47
Standard Deviation	0.35	0.41	0.36
Timeframe to achieve coverage[d]			
Mean	3.7	2.5	3.5
Standard Deviation	2.1	2.5	2.7
Annual licence fee (fixed)[e]			
Mean	0.14	0.27	0.15
Standard Deviation	0.44	0.61	0.45
Annual licence fee (% 3G revenue)[f]			
Mean	0.01	0.44	0.11
Standard Deviation	0.04	1.60	0.59
Infrastructure sharing[g]			
Mean	0.24	0.07	0.21
Standard Deviation	0.44	0.27	0.41

Notes: (a) Assistance is considered to occur when the NRA either withholds licences or makes available excess licences. (b) Licence term (years). (c) % of population to be covered by licence. (d) Years to achieve licence coverage. (e) Annual fee ($US per 100 MHz per million population). (f) Annual licence fee (% of 3G revenue). (g) = 1, if infrastructure sharing is imposed; = 0, otherwise.

CONCLUDING REMARKS

The potential for increased competition arising from entry into national mobile markets is recognised by the EC (1997). Recently, research on the assignment of spectrum licences concerns the design and success of auction assignments. However, the determinants of market entry have received little attention. The analysis herein suggests that ex-post payment modes encourage entry, and that incumbents win licences with less onerous deployment obligations. Further, entrants that win licences with direct assistance from NRAs appear to receive more favourable licence conditions. These findings suggest that incumbents have advantages in 3G spectrum assignments, that result in them winning licences in more attractive markets. However, the analysis also suggests NRAs can, and do, design spectrum packages that increase the likelihood of entry. Thus, it would seem that EC directives on mobile entry are consistent with NRA decision-making across the world, and that mobile markets are evolving accordingly.

ACKNOWLEDGEMENTS

The MIT Centre for Digital Business and the Columbia Institute for Tele-Information provided support during the development of the paper. Helpful comments are provided by Tom Hazlett and Eli Noam, and participants at the Australian Competition and Consumer Commission's 10th Regulatory Conference. The authors are responsible for all remaining errors. Data provided by DotEcon Spectrum Awards database is gratefully acknowledged.

NOTES

1. Japan and South Korea are the first Asian countries to assign 3G licences in 2000.
2. 3G entrants are commonly defined as an operator which does not operate a 2G network in the particular market (Jehiel and Moldovanu, 2003; Hoppe et al., 2006; Whalley and Curwen, 2006). First generation mobile markets are characterised by monopoly provision, while 2G markets are characterised by monopoly and duopoly provision.
3. The UMTS Forum is a non-profit association of operators, manufacturers and regulators with the aim of developing UMTS 3G mobile systems. The Forum participates actively in the work of the ITU.
4. Klemperer (2002) argues that NRAs aim to efficiently assign spectrum (i.e., maximise the sum of the valuations of operators awarded the licences) and, to a lesser extent, maximise revenue. When spectrum is awarded to operators that value it highly, 3G services are likely to be introduced sooner.
5. Auctions require operators to make price bids for spectrum lots. Beauty contests require that operators submit plans or bids to NRAs including spectrum use plans. After hearing proposals, NRAs award spectrum to operators that present the most 'attractive' proposals.

Potential entrants initially assess their willingness to apply (and pay) for spectrum and then, whether to submit bids. On receiving applications for spectrum the NRA's decision is whether to award a licence to an entrant or incumbent operator.

6. Greece was the only country not to have made available an excess number of licences over incumbents.
7. Nigeria is thus excluded from the sample. Analysys (2007) notes that NRAs in Moldova, Mozambique, South Africa and Sri Lanka directly granted spectrum to incumbents.
8. World Bank income classification, see www.worldbank.org.
9. Offering more licences than incumbent operators only guarantees an entrant will win a licence if there is a rule stipulating at most one licence per bidder and there is a potential entrant willing to agree to the licence terms.
10. These data augment Whalley and Curwen (2006).
11. This also occurs in Finland in 1999.
12. However, if the entrant already operates a mobile network in another country, accessing capital markets is less likely to be a problem.
13. GDP per capita is greater in markets where entry occurs than in markets where no entry occurs at the 5 per cent level of statistical significance.

REFERENCES

A-Focus and DotEcon (2004), 'The Use of Auctions in Spectrum Assignment'. Retrieved from: http://www.pts.se/upload/Documents/SE/A-focus%20auktion sstudi e%202004.pdf.

Analysys (2007), '3G Auctions: Design Options and Global Experience', FICCI Workshop on Spectrum Management, November.

Ansari, S. and Munir, K. (2008), 'How Valuable is a Piece of the Spectrum? Determination of Value in External Resource Acquisition', *Industrial and Corporate Change*, **17**, 301–33.

Azacis, H. and Burguet, R. (2008), 'Incumbency and Entry in License Auctions: The Anglo-Dutch Auction Meets Other Simple Alternatives', *International Journal of Industrial Organization*, **26**, 730–45.

Baziak, S. (2001), 'Site and Network Sharing: Cost Reducing Strategies for Rolling out 3G Networks, Coleago Consulting'. Retrieved from: http://www.coleago.co.uk/index. php/downloads.

Börgers, T. and Dustmann, C. (2003), 'European Telecom Licences', *Economic Policy*, **18**, 215–68.

Cabral, L. and Salant, D. (2009), 'Policy Standardisation in Wireless Telecommunications', in G. Madden and R. Cooper (eds), *The Economics of Digital Markets*, Cheltenham, UK: Edward Elgar.

Cartelier, L. (2003), 'Auctions versus Beauty Contests: The Allocation of UMTS Licences in Europe', *Annals of Public and Cooperative Economics*, **74**, 63–85.

Cramton, P. (2002), 'Spectrum Auctions', in M. Cave, S. Majumdar and I. Vogelsang (eds), *Handbook of Telecommunications Economics, Volume 1*, North-Holland, Amsterdam: Elsevier Science.

DotEcon, (2008), Spectrum Awards Database, DotEcon, London.

EC (1997), 'Directive 97/13/EC'. Retrieved from: http://eur-lex.europa.eu/smartapi/cg i/sga_docsmartapi!celexapi!prod!CELEXnumdoc&lg=EN&numdoc=31997L0013 &model=guichett.

EC (2002), 'Comparative Assessment of the Licensing Regimes for 3G Mobile Communications in the European Union and their Impact on the Mobile Communications Sector'. Retrieved from: http://www.euractiv.com/en/infosociety/3g-third-generation-mobile-communications/article-117436#.

Gruber, H. (2005), *The Economics of Mobile Telecommunications*, Cambridge: Cambridge University Press.

Gruber, H. (2007), '3G Mobile Telecommunications Licenses in Europe: A Critical Review', *Info*, **9**, 35–44.

Gruber, H. and Hoenicke, M. (1999), 'The Road Ahead: Towards third Generation Mobile Telecommunications', *Info*, **1**, 252–63.

Hoppe, H., Jehiel, P. and Moldovanu, B. (2006), 'License Auctions and Market Structure', *Journal of Economics and Management Strategy*, **15**, 371–96.

ITU (2004), *Trends in Telecommunication Reform: Licensing in an Era of Convergence, Sixth edition*, Geneva: ITU.

ITU (2008), 'Infrastructure Sharing, ICT Regulation Toolkit'. Retrieved from: http://www.ictregulationtoolkit.org/en/Section.3440.html.

Jehiel, P. and Moldovanu, B. (2003), 'An Economic Perspective on Auctions', *Economic Policy*, **36**, 269–308.

Klemperer, P. (2002), 'How (Not) to Run Auctions: The European 3G Telecom Auctions', *European Economic Review*, **46**, 829–45.

Noam, E. (1998), 'Spectrum Auctions: Yesterday's Heresy, Today's Orthodoxy, Tomorrow's Anachronism. Taking the Next Step to Open Spectrum Access', *Journal of Law and Economics*, **56**, 765–90.

UMTS Forum, (1998), 'Considerations of Licensing Conditions for UMTS Network Operators', Report 4. Retrieved from: http://www.umts-forum.org/component/option,com_docman/task,cat_view/Itemid,98/gid,19/.

Whalley, J. and Curwen, P. (2006), 'Third Generation New Entrants in the European Mobile Telecommunications Industry', *Telecommunications Policy*, **30**, 622–32.

Xavier, P. (2001), 'Licensing of Third Generation (3G) Mobile', Briefing paper for ITU Workshop on Licensing 3G Mobile. Retrieved from: http://www.itu.int/osg/spu/ni/3G/works hop/Briefing_paper.PDF.

12. Licensing options for digital dividend spectrum: An Australian perspective

Benoît P. Freyens

INTRODUCTION

The range of spectrum applications and management problems facing radiocommunication authorities is constantly evolving. For instance, communications technology typically requires larger spectrum space as usage density outstrips supply, while established services are concerned about the potential for interference from incoming new services. These developments have led to complex policy trade-offs. Commercial users want both service flexibility and network certainty; government and the community want guarantees over their spectrum rights; regulators wish to promote efficiency and competition without threatening commercial viability and the provision of essential public services. As in other reform-oriented International Telecommunication Union (ITU) countries, the Australian Communications and Media Authority (ACMA) uses radiocommunication licences to fine-tune these policy trade-offs.

Digital dividend allocation is such an issue. By end-2013, the switchover of analogue television for digital television (DTV) services will release a sizeable portion of 700 MHz UHF spectrum for use by non-broadcasting services. This digital dividend will be the largest release of spectrum in Australia for decades, and likely decades to come. While the size and nature of the digital dividend is yet to be determined, there are several services with a strong interest in using the dividend spectrum and licensing options that could be employed to allocate released spectrum. To ensure that the greatest public benefit is realised these licensing options must be in place to start planning for the deployment of the new services in digital dividend bands.

What are these options? The ACMA currently assigns and regulates radio frequency spectrum using alternative licensing regimes, viz., for apparatus, spectrum and class licences. Broadly speaking, these licences respectively represent command and control (C&C), property rights and unlicenced[1] approaches to spectrum management. Apparatus licensing is the traditional device centric and generally prescriptive way to allocate radio frequency. Alternatively, spectrum licensing is a space centric and service-neutral approach that confers licensees a degree of leasehold ownership over a large portion of spectrum. Class licensing is a technology-centric open access regime, which prescribes equipment standards, with minimal technical or operational requirements but otherwise abstains from regulatory intervention. Although class licensing, and particularly spectrum licensing, were seen as revolutionary at introduction under the Radiocommunications Act 1992 (RCA 1992 or the Act) none of Australia's three licensing regimes has seen substantial change during the past decade.

Should the digital dividend be allocated through a single licensing scheme or through a carefully designed mix of the three current licensing systems? Additionally, should new licensing structures be explored? Some insight into these questions can be gained by observing Australian reforms of the past 15 years. These reforms are characterized by using a wider set of spectrum management approaches than might currently be inferred from Australia's trichotomic licensing structure. Alternatively, several approaches authorised under spectrum licensing have remained largely atrophic. For this reason, the last 8 years have seen ongoing debate as to whether this wider array of approaches should be re-licenced and how.

In 2001, the Australian Communications Authority (ACA)[2] suggested a bespoke approach based on a single multi-usage adaptable licence (ACA, 2001). In 2006, the ACMA suggested the introduction of a fourth licensing regime; the private park. More recent research suggested developing a palette of specific regimes itemised and individually legislated under the Act (Freyens, 2009b). All of these licensing options incur higher management cost, with further investigation of these options repeatedly deferred. Yet, given the polyvalent nature and high value of the digital dividend, these questions are again taking much prominence. This chapter outlines Australia's current set of licences, with its own idiosyncrasies,[3] discusses the history and merits of earlier proposals for a bespoke licensing approach, and uses a conceptual model to suggest licensing opportunities for the digital dividend.

LEGAL RULES AND LICENSING IN AUSTRALIA

As an intangible resource, spectrum cannot be purchased and owned in physical units, nor legally used without regulatory consent. Spectrum users acquire spectrum by purchasing licences and adhering to licence conditions.

In Australia, licences are access rights issued by ACMA. Licences specify regulatory requirements and arrangements, mainly to govern interference management. When the demand for spectrum services is such that a highly valued band is congested, efficient band usage and interference management are of primary concern to regulators. These problems have become more acute over the last two decades, sparking waves of spectrum management reforms.

Reforms began in the late-1980s, culminating in the Radiocommunications Act 1992 and the first spectrum auctions in 1997. The legislative framework flowing from the Act and ITU radio-regulations authorises and defines the operations of apparatus, spectrum and class licences (trichotomic approach). These regimes set out the rights and obligations of spectrum users. The regimes impose minimal core specifications about frequency, bandwidth, area, power and emission types, although the means by which conditions are integrated in practice does vary. In general, apparatus and spectrum licensing have more in common than class licensing. Both provide exclusive access rights, can be auctioned, leased or traded, and are subject to regulatory approval for licence renewal - though on very different terms.

Apparatus Licensing

Apparatus licensing is a device-centric approach to radiocommunication licensing (i.e., specified through transmitter licences, receiver licences or both). Mostly, this device-centric regime is highly prescriptive, specifying the types of authorised primary services, authorised technology, the device to be used and the equipment standards along with tight technical conditions about site, band, power, and emission types. Licences are issued by ACMA after accredited persons (APs) certify the compliance of the device with specified technical conditions. Apparatus licensing is effective at controlling interferences and maximising band use. Frequency assignments require users to transmit at a particular frequency, on a particular site, with given technology to guarantee interference-controlled transmissions. This high degree of control allows apparatus licences to be issued over much narrower bandwidths than other licences. Issued for a maximum of five years, and renewable annually, apparatus licences tend to be issued in clusters to maximize the technical benefits of pooling similar services and technology over specific frequency ranges. Currently, there are 21 types of apparatus licences (mostly transmitter licences) that cover most of the radiofrequency spectrum.

Services authorised under apparatus licences are contingent to international frequency allocations specified in Australia's spectrum plan (ARSP). Conversely, the ACMA has substantial discretion in setting the regime terms of an apparatus licence. The Act does not indicate how the ARSP should be designed, nor how apparatus licences should be tailored, and

ACMA has used this discretionary power to design different categories of apparatus licence to match service designations in the ARSP. Consequently, not all apparatus licences fit the stereotype of an arch-rigid management regime ruled by government fiat. In 1992, for instance, the ACMA issued technologically flexible Personal Telecommunications Service (PTS) licences in the 900 MHz band (GSM900 licences). These licences are still in use. In 1997 the Act was amended to allow the trading of apparatus licences and third-party operations (e.g., leasing). Despite the 1997 reforms, apparatus licences generally remain a poor instrument to promote allocative efficiency among radiocommunication services.

Spectrum Licences

Introduced in 1992 under the Act, but only tested from 1997, spectrum licences confer leasehold ownership rights to licensees for fixed terms of 15 years. There is no accreditation process, although the devices need to be registered in a National Register. Spectrum licences can be issued by designation (converting existing apparatus licences into spectrum licences) or by reallocation (the band is cleared and auctioned). Overall, these spectrum licences cover a relatively small but highly valued portion of the entire spectrum. There are currently about 10 spectrum licenced bands.

Spectrum licences are service-neutral and space-centric; i.e., they theoretically permit users to operate *any* radiocommunications devices in a given spectrum space[4] subject to respecting the requirements of a technical framework. In practice, out-of-band emissions are controlled using block-edge masks (BEM) and out-of-area emissions by setting a maximum transmission power. However, spectrum licensing being a more libertarian arrangement than apparatus licences, the core conditions (bandwidth, site, area, radio emissions limits) are no longer enough to control interferences and additional conditions are imposed on the licences. Technical frameworks add coordination legal rules such as the 'unacceptable level of interference' (which determines the trade-off between spectrum space efficiency and device functionality) and the advisory guidelines on interference management (specifying guard spaces and sharing agreements with adjacent users). Once the technical framework is fully specified, device registration guarantees users against legal challenges over interferences.

Spectrum licences have added much flexibility to radiocommunications management. In February 2008, Australia's largest carrier, Telstra, was able to replace its 2G CDMA2000 network in the 850 MHz band with 3G (NextG) network without regulatory intervention by ACMA[5]. Achieving such flexibility in network self-redeployment would not have been possible prior to 1992. However, several outstanding issues which undermine this otherwise resounding success remain. For instance, there is considerable uncertainty among licensees as to whether licences will be reissued to the public or renewed, and if so under which terms. Some spectrum spaces have been left fallow.[6] Freedoms offered spectrum licensees to aid in the development of efficient spectrum markets, such as band subdivision and band management, are not often adopted, reducing technical efficiency.

Class Licences

Class licensing is another device-centric[7] approach to spectrum management with the distinct feature that it operates on an open and shared access basis. Class licences need not be applied for or issued, and in that sense are equivalent of unlicensed approaches. There is no exclusivity in usage nor fee paid. For these reasons, class licences are sometimes referred to as public parks or open access regimes. A class licence defines minimal operational conditions; band, power, types of device and emissions, standards compliance, and geographic deployment constraints (where relevant). Most class licences operate as non-interfering secondary usage easements in apparatus licenced bands.

Class licences work on the basis of free, shared, non-coordinated user access to specifically designated common bands. Since class licences are not issued to individuals, the licence conditions are not applied nor tailored to individual users (as is the case e.g. via frequency assignment certification under apparatus licensing, and through device registration under spectrum licences). Class licences do not lapse, and continue until they are revoked or amended. Conversely, class licensees cannot interfere with other licensees' transmissions and are not provided protection from interferences generated on these or other adjacent bands by other services. Consequently, this licensing regime is generally not popular with larger radiocommunications operators, such as telecommunications carriers, whose reputations depend on maintaining a minimum guaranteed level of service quality. Hence, the services and devices authorised under class licences are really only suitable for short-range, low-power applications, which considerably restricts the range of their applications.

A BESPOKE APPROACH TO RADIOCOMMUNICATIONS LICENSING?

Together, these licensing regimes authorise the ACMA to provide flexible management responses to spectrum demands. Accordingly, the *prima facie* case for expanding radiocommunication licensing options might at first appear not strong. That is, national geographical isolation and commitment to management reforms has kept Australia abreast of spectrum management liberalisation during the past two decades. Vigorous reform policy pursued by the SMA[8], ACA and later on ACMA have transformed bureaucratic rules into among the most economically efficient, flexible and transparent licensing systems in the world. Are any more radiocommunications reforms necessary, and what for purpose?

The main challenges facing spectrum management policy in Australia are: (a) limitations of the reform models used by ACMA; and (b) fast-paced technological development means that new issues appear regularly, requiring reassessment of current arrangements and anticipation of future needs. The more flexible, adaptable and responsive are licensing structures in meeting these challenges, the better placed is the nation to exploit regime potentials to efficiently deliver socio-economic benefits. In spite of its flexible spectrum management system, ACMA has signalled several times that three licence types may be insufficient and that the legal rules authorising these licences may be too restrictive. This situation has seen a revival of interest in a bespoke approach to licensing radiocommunications.

A Single Multi-Purpose Licence

In 2001, the then ACA made a submission to the Productivity Commission's Inquiry report of Radiocommunications (Productivity Commission, 2002). The ACA proposed consolidation of the 3 licensing regimes authorised under the Act into one generic licence type, from which ACA would build bespoke licences ensuring the best fit for the usage sought from a radio frequency band (ACA, 2001). This unique regime controlling standards, technical frameworks, tenure, interference management protocols, degree of usage flexibility and licence exclusivity would have been nominally equivalent to a continuous array of licences.

The idea ran counter to the mainstream 'either / or' dichotomy that guides reform arguments. In many countries, public debate over spectrum management reform is increasingly polarized between economists (advocates of an invisible hand approach) and engineers or legal scholars who support community management through shared access rights.

First, it is generally difficult to propose the bespoke approach to policy-making arenas because in polarised debates intermediate and hybrid approaches are interpreted as concessions detrimental to, rather than contributing to, reforms. Bespoke licensing appeared to imply re-entrusting the regulator with an overall command over strategic allocative and licensing choices. It is this type of power that the reform movement, led by economics, wrested from regulators.

Second, the Inquiry had by that stage developed an agenda to expand the role and scope for spectrum licences and had approached the ACA's proposal from that angle rather than from the perspective of a regime-neutral social planner. Third, negative perceptions of apparatus licensing as purely administrative management doubtless played a part in the demise of the single licence approach.

Yet this view of apparatus licensing is only partly correct. The ACMA issues both market-oriented apparatus licences and C&C-flexible spectrum licences (Freyens, 2009a). The reason the framework for apparatus licensing is more explicit, and that for spectrum licences more implicit stems from the way these licences work under enabling legislations, not from an attempt to prevent service and technology flexibility for high-value commercial services.

Apparatus licences offer short tenure compared to spectrum licences, but whether this reduced tenure confers greater certainty to spectrum licences depends on the presumption of renewal. Apparatus licences can be presumed to be renewed, whereas spectrum licences cannot.[9] Legislation only needs some fine adjustment to make apparatus licensing usage flexible. The ACA's original proposal for a bespoke approach is consistent with its current management principles emphasizing both the quest for high-value allocation and fine-tuning dilemmas; certainty vs. flexibility, allocative efficiency versus equity, interference versus technical efficiency (ACMA, 2009b).

Whichever its merits, the single licensing model was probably doomed to failure by perceptions of handing a 'blank cheque' to regulators, and by the lack of common ground between regulators and reformists. The 'either / or' approach of reformers and economic analysts raises several concerns. In particular, in many countries the reform debate has erred, focused on the need to promote property rights and markets or, to a lesser extent unlicensed regimes, together with a strange fascination for the alleged mutually exclusive nature of property rights and commons regimes (Buck, 2002; Benjamin, 2003; Brito, 2007; Freyens, 2008; Hazlett, 2008; Weiser and Hatfield, 2008). The polarisation of opinion around these regimes is an unnecessary distraction. Property rights (big space) and unlicensed approaches (short range) mostly compete for different situations and should be viewed as complementary approaches.

A Fourth Licensing Regime

In February 2006, ACMA proposed adding a fourth licensing regime by submitting a new licensing model for consultation with wireless access services (WAS) providers (ACMA, 2006a). The suggestion was to issue private park licences specifically designed to accommodate WAS. Dynamic access, technical band efficiency, black spots and competitive delivery had become major issues for these services, and there were indications the current spectrum licences may not be suitable to address all these issues. Future WAS needs required a service-neutral regime authorising any number and type of interoperable base stations in a licenced space with band coordination undertaken by users – in short a regime combining aspects of spectrum and class licensing.

The private park regime is a membership-based, fee-based licensing approach relying on device registration and self-coordination rules by users. The private park is closer to class than spectrum licensing. Conversely, the ACMA (rather than a band owner) directly issues the shared-use licences.[10] Furthermore, devices are expected to use dynamic frequency selection in similar fashion to class-licenced devices. Finally, there are no seniority privileges, and no 'hard' licence boundaries - although base stations must be sited within the geographical area of the licence. The private park approach also adopts user discrimination; prime licences are issued in short numbers to cover nation- or state-wide services, inclusive of high-density areas. Prime licences govern high-value (urban) spectrum and are auctioned. Secondary licences are sold for moderate fees, restricted to low density regional and remote areas, and issued in higher numbers (potentially unlimited). Further tiers are defined as fitting the circumstances addressed by the licence.[11]

Private park regimes resolve the crowding out of small regional operators by large carriers operating in spectrum-licenced spaces through a different mechanism than the easement. Here the regime forces users of similar size and background to coordinate and self-manage services on different geographical spectrum spaces within the band. Stakeholder feedback was mixed, with WAS providers generally resistant to change and wary of new licensing techniques (ACMA, 2006a, 2006c). As with spectrum licensing, policy-makers currently have poor visibility with respect to stakeholder interests, and further research into the behavioral economics of the issues is warranted.

The ACMA's commitment to the private park as a dynamically-efficient response to future WAS needs is firm, and has recently been reiterated in the *Five-year Spectrum Outlook 2009-2013* document (ACMA, 2009a, p. 115). It is likely that some form of privately-run WAS commons will occur, but for this alternative to succeed ACMA may develop the capacity to understand the motivations and expectations of spectrum users.

A Palette of Regimes

Shortly after submitting its proposal to develop a fourth licensing regime, the ACMA analysed the economic rationale for extending the array of licencing regimes. The resulting taxonomy of conceptual licensing regimes is based on core spectrum management regime dimensions. The first dimension is technological flexibility or discretion available in setting equipment standards. In a technology-flexible arrangement the band owner sets or adopts standards, that may complicate coordination with technology deployed on adjacent bands. By contrast, technology rigid arrangements are usually better aligned with spectrum plans and international coordination. Dimension

2 (usage flexibility) similarly indicates whether band owners (private or collective) have discretion in allocating spectrum to whichever use is deemed optimal. In the absence of this discretion, service allocation remains controlled by regulators. In Australia, several dynamic regimes are technology-neutral but service-rigid in practice.

Rights exclusivity (Dimension 3) describes the exclusivity conferred to licensees. If regulation enforces an easement for secondary users, the resulting primary rights are reduced as licensees forego the right to exclude other users. Exclusivity can be defined in a large variety of ways; easements can be of different types and the likelihood of rights expropriation for primary users introduces additional complexity. Dimension 4 (rights assignment) describes whether the regime assigns licences by price mechanism (e.g., auctions), administrative pricing or does not assign licences. Club membership (Dimension 5) captures the notion that collective use by a well-defined community does not equate to open access. This dimension plays a lesser role in less collective arrangements (e.g., purely exclusive approaches and appears as 'not applicable' for most excludable rights regimes, with the notable exception of the privately run commons regime). Dimension 6 (rules control) determines the rule setter for efficient interference management. All licensing regimes require a minimal set of rules to guarantee interference control. When formal coordination rules of control and command management (CM) are removed, other coordination arrangements must be substituted, either based on formal legal rights or informal rules. However, devices must be approved, even in unlicensed bands. So the conceptualisation of community self-rule for interference management is a matter of degree.

Figure 12.1 presents an overview of the relationship between the concepts and resulting spectrum management regimes. Dimension 1 and Dimension 2 are merged to represent service flexibility, and Dimensions 4 and Dimension 5 are implicit (i.e., not displayed). The graph is an intersection of three cubes; the left-hand cube characterises low excludability/community-managed regimes, with the right-hand cube indicating high excludability/legally-managed regimes. The facing cube represents the set of high excludability/community-managed regimes, which is largely empty due to the mutually exclusive nature of the dimensions.

At the origin is the traditional command and control regime. This regime is prescriptive in the services and technology allowed in a band, and exercises strong government control over interference management. However, the C&C is less exclusive than an ownership regime. Licences must be regularly renewed and regulators can alter conditions on renewal or require concessions from incumbents. For instance, administrative licences commonly tolerate non-interfering easements for unlicensed secondary users, as with white space users in broadcasting bands or Wi-Fi devices in ISM bands. Defence spectrum is usually available to many classes of unlicensed transmitters under the condition of vacating the band as military or emergency needs arise.

The conventional property rights regime departs from the C&C regime by providing service neutral licences and sharper exclusivity rights. For example, easements for secondary usage are subject to owner approval and may need to be purchased. Interference is managed among owners within a set of legal and technical rules. The conventional open access regime lies at the opposite end, viz., no exclusivity rights, self-management of interference under minimal government guidance, and a high degree of service and technology neutrality. Thus, command and control, open access and full property rights define the available policy space.

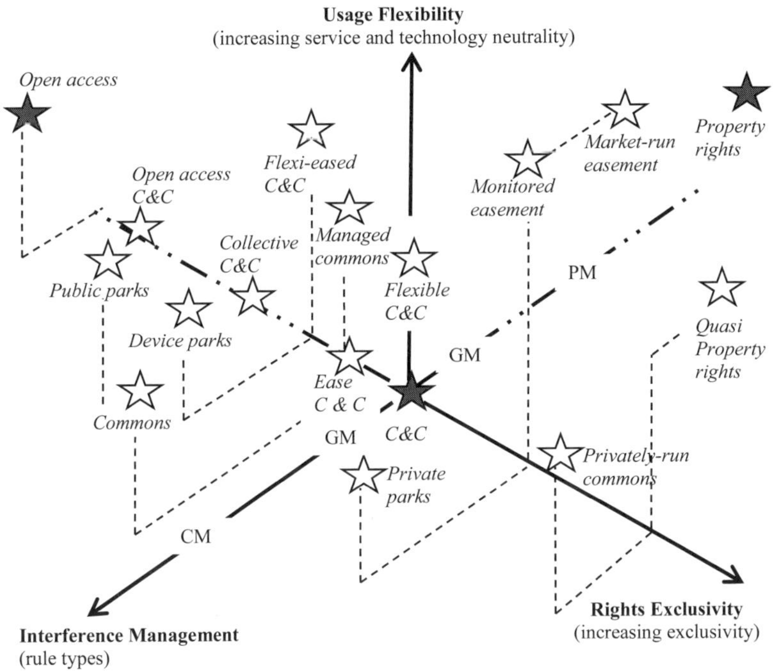

Notes: GM = government-controlled, CM = community-controlled, PM = privately managed.

Figure 12.1 Representation of bespoke regimes

The available policy space identifies intermediate regimes. An example is the main constellation that connects Open Access and C&C co-ordinates, with a possible mapping to open access with full property rights regime.

Interestingly, the regimes most discussed in the literature (C&C, property rights and open access) only populate a section of the available policy space. Depending on pre-specified levels of usage flexibility, rights exclusivity and autonomy in interference management, a complex array of potential regimes is revealed, typically near the C&C.

For instance, a commons model is more centric than an open access approach. In the commons regime, a well-defined community transmit and receive signals within a spectrum band that is flexible regarding usage and technology. Although the spectrum is shared access within the community, rights are commons owned and more exclusive than under open access. Owners of a commons (controlling authority, private or public) can exert discretion in setting and enforcing rules with regard to interference control, e.g., by government prescription (managed commons) or community management (conventional commons). Also, the owners of a commons can exclude potential users that are not part of the commons community, with the boundaries defined by accreditation or skill tests.

C&C regimes can also be repackaged, e.g., to tolerate non-interfering easements for secondary users (eased C&C) or grant service-neutral usage (flexible C&C, similar to the regime governing GSM900 licences) or both (flexi-eased C&C). The property rights approach (regimes located in the upper right of Figure 12.1) is best viewed as a federation of regimes. The full property rights regime is the most exclusive and service flexible approach. Quasi-property rights is a service-rigid but technologically-flexible version of the property rights regime. Monitored easements enforce secondary user rights in the frequency band, which weakens excludability but not flexibility. Market run easements are similar except that owners control interference management.[12]

WHICH LICENCES FOR THE DIGITAL DIVIDEND?

The switch-off of terrestrial analogue television and transition to digital services is planned to start in 2010 in remote areas of Victoria, and end in 2013 in major capital cities. The digital dividend bands are just below 820MHz (generally called the 700MHz band). The extent and allocation of the digital dividend are presently unknown. At most, the dividend will extend from 680 to 820 MHz. Wherever the start, the dividend must end at 820 MHz.

The reallocation of broadcasting channels under the current regulatory regime is a one-way planning problem. Whilst conceptually simple, the Minister must redefine the broadcasting services bands under s.31 (1) of the Act, which will then be reallocated as spectrum or apparatus licensing.[13] However, the legal process is complex, with the necessary legislation requiring consultation to build consensus among engineers and lawyers. This process could stall with the digital dividend made available but no users entitled to use it due to uncertain statutory rights.

Which services can digital dividend spectrum be used to supply? Given the highly-valued and idiosyncratic properties of the 700 MHz spectrum, and the vicinity of the 900 MHz PTS (GSM) and UMTS (3G) bands, there is little doubt among stakeholders that this spectrum will mainly be allocated to high economic value commercial services (e.g., WAS) in congested metropolitan areas and broadband wireless access (BWA) in communications poor rural areas. The nature of this spectrum is also suitable for certain land mobile and fixed-link services, but these services are unable to compete with WAS providers. As the incumbent broadcasting service on 700 MHz is also suitable for parts of the digital dividend, should broadcasters be allowed to bid?

Which licences are expected to govern digital dividend management essentially depends on government objectives (interpretation of the public interest). The Act contains many public interest objectives for assigning radiocommunications licences. In 2002, the Productivity Commission suggested that the main objective (allocative and technical efficiency) should have primacy.[14] The ACMA's management principles also tend to favour flexible and technology-neutral licensing arrangements.

It is expected that the digital dividend, when available, will be auctioned. If so, the way to licence digital dividend spectrum does not necessarily consist of spectrum licences. In practice, the apparatus licensing regime accommodating the GSM900 licences (flexi C&C) accommodates auctions, spectrum trading, and service flexibility in a way not dissimilar to spectrum licensing (at least in practice) and without the economic limitations of spectrum licences (exclusivity, unchecked band idleness).

Both regimes may contribute to the allocative efficiency objective contained in the Act, but the flexible apparatus regime may provide a better match with technical efficiency objectives. Unless legal rules governing spectrum licensing are reformed, the flexi-C&C regime may offer a better pathway to allocate the digital dividend to highest valued use (probably guaranteeing the equivalent revenues), while simultaneously ensuring a better platform to maximise band usage.

Tenure and certainty remain the major differences between flexi-C&C and spectrum licensing. Spectrum licences have a 15-year term and are not subject to sudden refarming decisions (at least not without compensation). By contrast, apparatus licences (even the most flexible) are issued for a maximum of 5 years and can be cancelled, amended or relocated by government fiat. Spectrum licences are therefore preferred for services requiring expensive investment. For this reason, spectrum licences also are favoured by operators whose market share relies on reputational capital (e.g., reliability of signal for voice communications and data transfer). Unless flexi-C&C is licenced separately under the Act to provide more certainty and tenure than apparatus licences, the costs and benefits of spectrum and flexi-C&C licences are questionable.

Are there alternative reallocation options? Class licensing or public parks are inadequate to govern high-power services that optimise the use of such high-quality, high-value spectrum. Prescriptive regimes such as traditional apparatus licences, collective-C&C, open access-C&C, and controlled easement are economically wasteful and run against the ACMA's spectrum management principles, which where feasible tend to favour user choice of service selection and technology deployment. However, semi-exclusive regimes are also an option. Easements improve the pure property rights model by enabling the operation of simultaneous, technologically compatible services subject to non-interfering conditions (Faulhaber and Farber, 2003). Users' concerns about guaranteed quality of service and network reputation, and the significant amendments required to Part 3.2., 3.3 and 3.4 of the Act[15] are the main obstacles to this approach. The success of class licences demonstrates that non-interfering secondary usage works, and is likely have improved performance when underlay and overlay radio technologies are deployed commercially.

A final set of options is by collaborative property rights, which blend shared management attributes with private rights and market incentives. For instance, privately-run commons may only require economic incentives for owners (e.g., club fees tax deductions and licence renewal guarantees) to operate under spectrum licensing (i.e., with minimal legal amendments). More importantly, the timing and design of the private park option suggests this regime as an ACMA preferred licensing option to accommodate WAS deployments on digital dividend spectrum. The dynamic, multi-tiered approach addresses both barriers to expand band usage under spectrum licensing, and reputational issues under any easement model. However, private park licences are not currently authorised under the Act and stakeholder consultations have produced a tepid response.

CONCLUDING REMARKS

The trichotomic Australian licensing model needs to expand. Apparatus licences are generally too prescriptive and provide little certainty to licensees. Spectrum licences are too exclusive, with renewal uncertain. Class licences are too restrictive for short-range low-power applications. While Australia currently benefits from an array of practical management approaches, the Act grants the ACMA much discretion in the design of apparatus licences. Ceteris paribus, the large scale expansion of spectrum licensing by conversion of apparatus licences will reduce the resilience of the licensing system.

Furthermore, such licensing resilience developed within the legal constraints of the trichotomic licensing regime, not from the free-flowing operations of a bespoke licensing approach. This has implications for digital dividend policy as many technically efficient and service neutral approaches to licensing the dividend will probably not be used. Flexi-eased C&C remains informal, rarely used and viewed as anachronic. Private parks are not unauthorised under the Act and receive mixed support. Privately-run commons are authorised but not used. A preferred mapping of potential licensing regimes to the explicit licensing structure under the Act would help clarify and promote such dynamically efficient options.

These options can assist in settling allocative conflicts. The main digital dividend allocation policy issues concern: (a) consistency with the objectives of the Act; and (ii) resolving legal conflicts over the high-value of the spectrum and incumbents' rights. A bespoke approach can contribute to clarifying both issues. First, the more tailored are licences to meet the needs of certain users in particular bands, the better the fit with market aspirations and legislated objectives. Second, resolving legal conflict concerning UHF band reallocation may require compromise. Given the deeply rooted nature of incumbent spectrum rights under the *Broadcasting Act 1997*, it is doubtful other approaches will be effective. Whereas wholesale replacement of the apparatus-licenced digital dividend by spectrum licences will polarise positions, a bespoke licensing approach may conciliate incumbent and future user views. Finally, a bespoke approach would better address the needs of providers of wireless access services that face different market structures, while addressing long-term objectives of the Act.

NOTES

1. Unlicensed usually refers to the authorised usage without the need for licences of frequencies for low-power short range devices. In Australia this usage is referred to as class licenced. The term unlicensed refers to the illegal, unauthorised use of a frequency.
2. ACA was the quasi-independent statutory agency in charge of spectrum regulation until 2005.
3. The closest analogy to Australia's licensing system is New Zealand's, which consists of management rights, radio licences and spectrum parks. However, the discussion in this chapter may be of interest to other spectrum-reforming countries, e.g., the UK recently issued Spectrum Usage Rights, a distinct variant to the property rights approach adopted in Australia, generally offering more flexibility but less certainty (Kerans et al., 2009; Webb, 2009).
4. A spectrum space is a band specified in terms of its underlying area, population density, terrain, prospective services and interference rights (receiver and transmitter). Once fully specified, the spectrum space allows a higher degree of freedom in usage and is generally favoured by large operators.
5. ACMA was heavily involved in providing a report to government about coverage issues associated with the NextG network but that was not directly related to the ability of Telstra to deploy a new network under its spectrum licences.

6. For instance, the two 4 MHz-wide spectrum licences introduced in 1997 in the 400 MHz band, or the 7 MHz- wide licences in the 2.3 GHz band in 2000, and in higher frequencies.
7. Class licensing is also referred to as technology-centric (e.g., Productivity Commission, 2002).
8. The SMA merged with the Australian Telecommunications Authority (ATA) on 1 July 1997 to become ACA, and later ACMA after the merger with the Australian Broadcasting Authority (ABA) in 2005.
9. For spectrum licences, the presumption upon expiry is that they will be reallocated through a market mechanism. As discussed earlier, licence renewal for licence holders could be granted for a specific price under various scenarios, which at the moment have more exceptional rather than routine nature. Whether increased renewal certainty should be provided to spectrum licensees and under what conditions is currently debated.
10. Note that spectrum licences in principle authorise owners to operate a similar regime, since spectrum spaces can be subdivided, and traded or leased to third parties on owners' conditions. However, the private park is initiated by government, and seeks commons-like coordination rules within the park rather than hierarchical property-based rules. Such a regime has not arisen under the management freedoms granted spectrum licences.
11. The ACMA suggests the three tier approach: business class (auctioned), economy class (over counter for a fee) and discount economy (open access). See Appendix D (ACMA, 2006a, p. 51).
12. See Pogorel (2007) and Freyens (2009a) for discussion and illustration of the approaches.
13. Note reallocation of encumbered spectrum to class licences is not authorised under s.153B of the Act.
14. Other objectives of the Act specified under s.3 comprise: (a) making adequate provision for specific government agencies and public and community users; (b) providing a responsive and flexible approach to meeting the needs of users; (c) encouraging the use of efficient technology to provide a wide range of high quality services; (d) providing efficient, equitable and transparent charging for spectrum use; (e) supporting the communications objectives of the Federal government; (f) providing a regulatory environment to maximize opportunities for the domestic communications industry; and (g) promoting Australian interests at international radiocommunications conventions.
15. The FCC made a landmark decision by authorising an open access easement (Google clause) for Block C of the auctioned 700MHz digital dividend spectrum against a reservation price guarantee from Google (Brusco et al., 2009).

REFERENCES

ACA (2001), *Submission from the Australian Communications Authority to the Productivity Commission Review of the Radiocommunications Act and the Role of the Australian Communications Authority*, Canberra and Melbourne: Australian Communications Authority.

ACMA (2006a), *Strategies for Wireless Access Services: Spectrum Planning* (Discussion Paper SPP 1/06), Canberra and Melbourne: Australian Communications and Media Authority.

ACMA (2006b), *Strategies for Wireless Access Services: Spectrum Access Options - Consultation Outcomes* (Discussion Paper SPP 08/08), Canberra and Melbourne: Australian Communications and Media Authority.

ACMA (2006c), *Strategies for Wireless Access Services: Spectrum Access Options* (Discussion paper SPP 10/06), Melbourne / Canberra : Australian Communications and Media Authority.

ACMA (2009a), *Five-year Spectrum Outlook 2009-2013*, Canberra and Melbourne: Australian Communications and Media Authority.

ACMA (2009b), *Principles for Spectrum Management*, Canberra and Melbourne: Australian Communications and Media Authority.

Benjamin, S. (2003), 'Spectrum Abundance and the Choice Between Private and Public Control', *New York University Law Review*, **78**, 2007–102.

Brito, J. (2007), 'The Spectrum Commons in Theory and Practice', *2007 Stanford Technology Law Review 1*. Retrieved from: http://stlr.stanford.edu/pdf/brito-commons.pdf.

Brusco, S., Lopomo, G.,and Marx, L. (2009), 'The "Google Effect" in the FCCs 700 MHz Auction', *Information Economics and Policy*, **21**, 101–14.

Buck, S. (2002), 'Replacing Spectrum Auctions with a Spectrum Commons', *2002 Stanford Technology Law Review 2*. Retrieved from: http://stlr.stanford.edu/STLR/Articles/02_STLR_2.

Faulhaber, G. and Farber, D. (2003), 'Spectrum Management: Property Rights, Markets, and the Commons', in L.F. Cranor and S.S. Wildman (eds), *Rethinking Rights and Regulations: Institutional Responses to New Communication Technologies*, Cambridge, MA: MIT Press.

Freyens, B. (2007), 'The Economics of Spectrum Management: A Review', Paper commissioned by the Australian Communications and Media Authority (ACMA). Retrieved from: http://www.acma.gov.au/WEB/STANDARD/pc=PC_311025.

Freyens, B. (2008), *Shared or Exclusive Radio Waves? A Dilemma Gone Astray*, Unpublished manuscript, Canberra.

Freyens, B. (2009a), 'A Policy Spectrum for Spectrum Economics', *Information Economics and Policy*, **21**, 128–44.

Freyens, B. (2009b), 'A Review of Australia's Radiocommunications Licensing', Paper commissioned by the Australian Communications and Media Authority (ACMA), 24 June 2009: Canberra.

Hazlett, T. (2008), 'Property Rights and Wireless License Values', *The Journal of Law and Economics*, **51**, 563–98.

Kerans, A., Philips, G. and Webb, W. (2009), 'Flexible Spectrum Licensing: Comparing the UK and Australia', *Policy Tracker*. Retrieved from: https://www.policytracker.com/headlines/Webb-%20Kerans-Phillips.pdf/index_html.

Pogorel, G. (2007), 'Regulation and Competition: Nine Regimes of Radio Spectrum Management: A 4-Step Decision guide', *Communications & Strategies*, **65**, 167–83.

Productivity Commission (2002), *Radiocommunications* (Report No. 22), Canberra: Productivity Commission.

Webb, W. (2009), 'An Optimal Way to Licence the Radio Spectrum', *Telecommunications Policy*, **33**, 230–37.

Weiser, P. and Hatfield, D. (2008), 'Spectrum Policy Reform and the Next Frontier of Property Rights', *George Mason Law Review*, **15**, 549–609.

13. Two-sided markets with substitution: Mobile termination revisited

Jerry A. Hausman

INTRODUCTION

In the emerging literature on two-sided markets (see Armstrong, 2006; Armstrong and Wright, 2006; Caillaud and Jullien, 2001, 2003; Rochet and Tirole, 2003, 2006), a central question of interest is how do platforms set the structure of prices across the two sides of the business, and associated with this, whether the resulting structure of prices is inefficiently distorted. This interest is motivated by the observation that in many such businesses, one side tends to pay disproportionately more than the other, and that in some cases regulators have stepped in to try to re-balance the structure of prices.

An important industry where these issues directly arise in is mobile telephony. Concerns about the high level of the charges for terminating fixed-to-mobile calls in those countries where such charges are not regulated, and the resulting high fixed-to-mobile retail prices, have led to widespread regulation of mobile termination charges. Examples of affected countries include Australia, France, Germany, Italy, Japan, and United Kingdom (UK).[1] However, above-cost mobile termination charges also imply lower charges for mobile subscribers as mobile operators have an incentive to attract mobile subscribers to earn this subsidy (so-called waterbed effect).[2] Thus, the two-sided market literature's question of equilibrium versus efficient price structure naturally arises for mobile termination.

Previous theoretical works to address this question include Armstrong (1997, 2002), Gans and King (2000), Thompson et al. (2007), Valletti and Houpis (2005) and Wright (1999, 2002). This body of work broadly argues: (1) even highly competitive mobile operators set fixed-to-mobile termination charges to maximize monopoly termination profit and thereby the subsidy they can offer to their subscribers; (2) this competitive bottleneck means equilibrium termination charges are set too high in equilibrium; and (3) yet the socially optimal termination charge can still be above cost as additional mobile subscribers provide positive externalities to fixed-line callers.

All of these works treat the two groups – fixed-line callers and mobile subscribers – as distinct consumer groups. In this chapter the literature is moved closer to reality by taking into account that fixed-line callers may also be mobile subscribers, and that such subscribers often make mobile-to-mobile calls in addition to and instead of fixed-to-mobile calls.[3] These matters given mobile-to-mobile calls are typically priced below those of fixed-to-mobile calls. The main conclusions reached are: (1) mobile operators will set fixed-to-mobile termination charges below the monopoly level; (2) equilibrium termination charges are not necessarily too high; and (3) some new network externalities arise that mean socially optimal charges can be further above cost than otherwise would be the case.

The reasons for these new results stem largely from the substitution possibilities that arise once fixed-line callers are allowed to be mobile subscribers and make mobile-to-mobile calls, the most obvious of which is that if fixed-to-mobile calls are expensive, people that subscribe to a mobile network and wish to call someone on-the-go from home may do so using their mobile phone.[4] This consideration is likely to be important since mobile penetration levels typically exceed 70 per cent in most OECD countries, so most callers can indeed substitute in this way if they wish. Moreover, in the absence of regulation, typically mobile-to-mobile prices are lower than fixed-to-mobile prices. For example, in 2004 the average price of fixed-to-mobile calls was 33 cents per minute in Australia, while the average mobile-to-mobile price was 23 cents per minute. As a result, competing mobile operators tend to limit their termination charges to avoid 'too many' subscribers substituting to cheaper mobile-to-mobile calls, which due to balanced traffic are not a source of termination profit.

The ability to use mobile phones to reach people on-the-go in turn affects the demand for mobile subscription since when fixed-to-mobile prices are high more people want a mobile phone to avoid high prices. This implies that setting termination charges above the level which maximizes the subsidy to subscribers (equilibrium level), will continue to increase mobile penetration. Since mobile subscribers generate positive externalities to other callers (both those calling from home as well as those calling from on-the-go using their mobile phones), this can create additional positive welfare effects of setting above-cost mobile termination charges. The socially optimal charge can be above that set by operators in equilibrium.

These results complement the recent findings of Baake and Mitusch (2005), who independently considered the case of substitution between fixed and mobile networks. Their focus is on mobile-to-mobile termination charge, while this chapter focuses on the setting of the fixed-to-mobile termination charge. Another important difference is that they assume differentiated mobile operators whereas here operators are assumed homogeneous competitors. This difference means they are forced to rely on a numerical example. Here general results are presented, as well as results that calibrate to real-world data.

Given the growing amount of regulatory intervention in setting mobile termination fees, the economic analysis in this paper should be useful in determining the economic factors that affect termination fees in competitive markets. In this regard, the model is calibrated to data from Australia to obtain precise implications. The equilibrium level of the termination charge predicted by the model is somewhat above the 21 cents observed in June 2004, consistent with the idea that termination charges are constrained by the threat of regulation at that time. However, it is also below the monopoly (competitive bottleneck) level predicted by existing models given the calibrated parameter values. Although the welfare-maximizing level is lower than the equilibrium level, it is still considerably higher than termination cost. Notably, regulating fixed-to-mobile termination charges to cost lowers welfare compared to the case they are left unregulated.

The rest of the chapter proceeds as follows. The next section lays out the new framework. Then, the following sections derive general results and present results based on a calibration of the model to Australian data. A final section presents concluding remarks.

THE MODEL AND PRELIMINARIES

To endogenize the choice of technology (fixed or mobile) for any given call, suppose that a fraction λ of the time people are at 'home' and a fraction $1-\lambda$ of the time people are 'on-the-go'. People at home are assumed to have access to the fixed-line network while when they are on-the-go they do not. This gives rise to several potential types of calls: λ^2 potential calls between people at home, $(1-\lambda)^2$ potential calls between people on-the-go, and $\lambda(1-\lambda)$ potential calls in each direction between people at home and on-the-go. Whether these calls can be realized or not will depend in part on whether a caller is a mobile subscriber.

In two of these situations, calls are to people at home. To reduce the number of different types of calls under consideration, it is assumed all such calls are received by people on their landlines and so do not involve mobile termination. This is consistent with the prices of calls to fixed networks being cheaper. Since the utility of such calls just shifts consumer utility in an additive way in the analysis below, they are ignored. Focusing on calls to people on-the-go, either these originate from people at home (λ of the time) or originate from people who are also on-the-go ($1-\lambda$ of the time). In either case, calls are only realized when the receiver is a mobile subscriber. When the caller is also on-the-go, the call is only realized when both parties are mobile subscribers. When instead the caller is at home, the caller may use her landline, or if she is a mobile subscriber, may choose between using her landline or her mobile phone to make the call. This decision is endogenized in the model.

Denoting the per-minute price of fixed-to-mobile (*FTM*) calls p_f and the per-minute price of mobile-to-mobile (*MTM*) calls p_m, denote the indirect utility associated with each call from home to a person on-the-go as $v(p_f, p_m)$ for mobile subscribers who have a choice of which technology to use and $v_f(p_f)$ for non-subscribers who can only make *FTM* calls. The indirect utility associated with each call from someone on-the-go to another person on-the-go is denoted $v_m(p_m)$ since such a call can only be a *MTM* call. Associated with these indirect utility functions are the demand functions $\overline{q}_f(p_f, p_m)$ and $\overline{q}_m(p_f, p_m)$ where callers choose between *FTM* and *MTM* calls, and $q_f(p_f)$ and $q_m(p_m)$ where callers cannot choose the technology. The demand functions measure the minutes people spend talking to each mobile subscriber, for each type of call. Taking into account the proportion of time a caller finds either at home or on-the-go, define the total minutes called to each mobile subscriber as $\overline{q}_f = \lambda\overline{q}_f(p_f, p_m)$, $\overline{q}_m = \lambda\overline{q}_m(p_f, p_m)$, $q_f = \lambda q_f(p_f)$ and $q_m = (1-\lambda)q_m(p_m)$, with corresponding indirect utility: $v = \lambda v(p_f, p_m)$, $v_f = \lambda v_f(p_f)$ and $v_m = (1-\lambda)v_m(p_m)$.

Some structure is imposed on these functions. It must be that $v \geq v_f$ since having the choice of which technology to use cannot make callers worse off, with $v(p_f, \infty) = v_f(p_f)$. It is assumed people sometimes make use of each technology, reflecting that in different circumstances one technology may be preferred over another. In particular, assume that over the relevant range of prices, there is positive demand for each type of call, that the own-price derivatives are negative in each case, that the cross-price derivatives are positive (i.e., $\partial\overline{q}_f / \partial p_m > 0$ and $\partial\overline{q}_m / \partial p_f > 0$), that $q_f > \overline{q}_f$ so there will be fewer *FTM* calls when a caller has the option of also using their mobile phone to make the calls, and that

$$\left|\frac{\partial\overline{q}_f}{\partial p_f}\frac{p_f}{\overline{q}_f}\right| > \left|\frac{\partial q_f}{\partial p_f}\frac{p_f}{q_f}\right|, \tag{13.1}$$

so that the price elasticity of *FTM* calls with respect to p_f is higher when people have a choice of technology use. A given percentage increase in p_f causes a greater percentage reduction in *FTM* demand by mobile subscribers given they will now partially switch to using their mobile phone for such calls, in addition to making fewer (or shorter) calls in the case they do not switch. All these properties are met, for instance, by a generalized CES specification.

People also gain some additional (exogenous) benefit from subscribing to a mobile operator. These benefits include, among other factors, being able to call people at home when on-the-go, the other services commonly available with mobile subscription, the option value of being able to be reached if necessary or to make an emergency call, and perhaps the value of receiving calls (if subscribers view this in a lump-sum manner).[5] These benefits are allowed to vary across the population, so that some people are more likely to subscribe than others.[6] The benefits are denoted b, which are drawn independently for each person from the distribution function G, with corresponding density function g and hazard function $p = g/(1-G)$. These functions are assumed to be continuously differentiable with $g > 0$ over $[\underline{b}, \overline{b}]$ and equal to 0 elsewhere. The total population is of measure one.

If the total measure of people that subscribe to one of the mobile operators is denoted N, a person's utility is summarized as follows. If a person does not have a mobile subscription, their utility arising from conversing with people on-the-go is

$$Nv_f \, . \tag{13.2}$$

In this case, people only get utility from *FTM* calls, this utility is proportional to the measure of consumers who subscribed to one of the mobile operators. If instead, a person subscribes to a mobile operator i, their utility is

$$b - r_i + N(v + v_m) \, . \tag{13.3}$$

The first term is a person's 'exogenous' benefit of subscribing. The second term is the subscription price (or rental) charged by operator i. The final term represents the utility a person gains from calling people on-the-go, both from home and when on-the-go. In both cases, the number of such calls is proportional to the measure of consumers also subscribed to the mobile network.

Assume mobile operators face a constant per-minute cost of terminating *FTM* calls on a mobile network c, and a cost per subscriber they attract f. A two-stage framework is adopted. In the first stage, each mobile operator i

sets a *FTM* termination charge a_i.[7] In the section stage, the fixed-line and mobile operators set their prices. There are $m \geq 2$ mobile operators that are homogeneous price competitors. For *MTM* calls, the standard balanced traffic assumption is adopted.

Discriminatory pricing by the fixed-line operator is allowed so that p_f can be different for calling customers on different mobile networks. Assuming the per-minute cost of originating *FTM* calls is C, the perceived cost for calling a customer on operator *i*'s network is $C + a_i$. For simplicity, it is assumed the *FTM* price to network i is $C + a_i$. The assumption is that retail prices are regulated or competitive resale is allowed over the fixed-line's network with access granted at cost. In the calibrated model, it is assumed that C includes the cost of providing this resale service.

Finally, assume *MTM* termination charges and retail prices are regulated at cost, or that competing operators agree to set their termination charges and retail prices in this way. In the absence of on-net and off-net price discrimination, Carter and Wright (2003) obtain such a result on termination charges when operators are asymmetric. Given operators set two-part tariffs, it is optimal for them to price *MTM* calls at cost in such a setting.

Even allowing for on-net and off-net price discrimination, market sharing equilibria are also possible in which operators set retail prices at cost. This is due to multiple equilibria that arise with homogeneous networks. Since calling is assumed balanced, operators still break even. Moreover, under certain expectations no individual operator can do better by raising off-net price to reflect higher termination charges, even if it lowers rentals by an offsetting amount. In particular, if each consumer expects others not to subscribe to such an operator, then each consumer does want to join the operator since if she did all her calls would have to be off-net calls at the higher off-net price. This makes such a deviation unprofitable. The level of the *MTM* termination charge is again irrelevant in this equilibrium since it does not affect prices or profits. Thus, the results of the model can be consistent with allowing higher *MTM* termination charges but having *MTM* retail prices set at cost.

ANALYSIS AND RESULTS

This section characterizes the equilibrium and welfare maximizing termination charges. First, characterize these for the general case, before doing so for a number of special cases.

Competition implies only the operator that sets the lowest possible rentals will obtain any demand. Since all operators are symmetric, this implies

$$r = f - \pi_T , \tag{13.4}$$

where π_T denotes *FTM* termination profit per subscriber. There is a subsidy to mobile customers in the sense their subscription price is set below subscription costs f. Equivalently, a subsidy on mobile phone purchases may exist, which in practice can be amortized into the subscription price.

For a particular termination charge a, the termination profit per subscriber is

$$\pi_T = (1-N)\pi_M + N\pi_C , \tag{13.5}$$

which is the weighted sum of the termination profit per subscriber $\pi_M = (a-c)q_f$ when people calling from home have no choice of technology (standard assumption) and termination profit per subscriber $\pi_C = (a-c)\overline{q}_f$ when they do have a choice. The weights are the proportion of consumers that do not subscribe to a mobile network and the proportion that do. Given $q_f > \overline{q}_f$, then $\pi_M > \pi_C$ for $a > c$ so that $\pi_M > \pi_T$. To obtain general results in Proposition 1 below assume π_M, π_C and π_T are concave in a over the relevant range of a, a property which is shown to be true in the calibrated model.

To determine the demand N for mobile subscription, define the critical value of b (denoted b^*) above which all people choose to subscribe to a mobile network and below which they do not. The number of people that subscribe is $1-G(b^*)$. At b^* the utility in (13.3) just equals that in (13.2). This implies

$$b^* = r - (v - v_f + v_m)N . \tag{13.6}$$

The demand for mobile subscription is determined by solving (13.6) together with the definition

$$N = 1 - G(b^*) . \tag{13.7}$$

For demand to be well behaved, some restriction is placed on the size of network effects. If these network effects are 'too strong' then demand is explosive (a slightly lower rental rate can lead to 100 per cent penetration.) Attracting an additional mobile subscriber increases the value of being able to make *MTM* calls so much that it leads to more than an additional subscriber. These additional subscribers then attract further subscribers, with this process snowballing until all potential subscribers have joined. Throughout, it is assumed that network effects are not 'so strong' that they make demand explosive. This assumption is correct for the calibrated model.

The number of mobile subscribers is an increasing function of the *FTM* termination charge a through two effects. First, a impacts termination profit per subscriber. Higher termination profits per subscriber result in competing mobile operators offering lower subscription prices (waterbed effect), thereby increasing mobile subscriptions. Second, a affects the price of *FTM* calls. A higher price of *FTM* calls makes it more attractive to avoid high *FTM* charges by becoming a mobile subscriber, thereby increasing mobile subscriptions. This second effect has been ignored in the literature to date.

To characterize the equilibrium termination charge, define the following benchmark termination charges. Denote the termination charge maximizing π_M as a_M, which is characterized by

$$a_M = c + \frac{q_f}{|q'_f|}, \qquad (13.8)$$

where $q'_f = \partial q_f / \partial p_f$. This is the equilibrium termination charge when there is no *FTM* to *MTM* substitution, and the one analysed in the existing literature.[8] Second, denote the termination charge maximizing π_T with N held constant as a_N, which is characterized by

$$a_N = c + \frac{G q_f + (1-G)\bar{q}_f}{G|q'_f| + (1-G)|\bar{q}'_f|}. \qquad (13.9)$$

This is the equilibrium termination charge if when setting their termination charges, mobile operators assume mobile penetration is fixed, but still allow for *FTM* to *MTM* substitution. Then:

Proposition 1: *The equilibrium termination charge* a^* *is above cost but lower than if mobile operators ignore the impact of their termination charge on mobile penetration, which is lower than the equilibrium termination charge in the absence of FTM to MTM substitution. That is* $c < a^* < a_N < a_M$.

Proof: Competition between identical mobile operators implies mobile operators set their termination charge to maximize π_T. If others do not do so, setting their termination charge to give a higher level of π_T than their rivals allows an operator to set a rental below their rivals, thereby capturing the whole market while still covering their costs. In equilibrium, at least one operator must set a_i at this level. Moreover, in equilibrium people only subscribe to operators that set their termination charge at this level. It follows that the equilibrium termination charge a^* is the one that maximizes π_T.

Termination profits π_T must be maximized for $a > c$ since by increasing a slightly above c ensures a positive level of π_T. This implies $a^* > c$.

Competition between operators implies all termination profit is competed away in the second stage. Substituting (13.4), (13.5) and (13.7) into (13.6), the marginal consumer is defined implicitly by

$$b^* = f - (a-c)\left(Gq_f + (1-G)\overline{q}_f\right) - (1-G)(v - v_f + v_m). \qquad (13.10)$$

Totally differentiating (13.10) gives

$$\frac{db^*}{da} = -\frac{\left(q_f + (a-c)\left(Gq'_f + (1-G)\overline{q}'_f\right)\right)}{1 - g\eta}, \qquad (13.11)$$

where the network effects are $g\eta$ and

$$\eta = (v - v_f + v_m) - (\pi_M - \pi_C).$$

Given the assumption that network effects are not explosive, it must be that $g\eta < 1$. Given π_M and π_C are concave in a, the function $G\pi'_M + (1-G)\pi'_C$ is decreasing in a so that $G\pi'_M + (1-G)\pi'_C > 0$ for $a < a_N$. This implies that $db^* / da < 0$ for $c \le a \le a_N$.

Differentiating π_T with respect to a gives the first-order condition

$$\pi'_T = G\pi'_M + (1-G)\pi'_C + g\frac{db^*}{da}(\pi_M - \pi_C). \qquad (13.12)$$

Since $\pi_M > \pi_C$ (given $q_f > \overline{q}_f$) for $a > c$, and $db^* / da < 0$, then $\pi'_T < G\pi'_M + (1-G)\pi'_C$. Since π_T is concave, π'_T is decreasing and equal to zero only at a^*. This implies $\pi'_T = 0$ must occur for $a < a_N$. That is, $a^* < a_N$.

Solving implicitly for a^* implies

$$a^* = c + \left(\frac{1}{1+\phi_E} \right) \frac{Gq_f + (1-G)\overline{q}_f}{G\left|q_f'\right| + (1-G)\left|\overline{q}_f'\right|} \tag{13.13}$$

where

$$\phi_E = \frac{g(1-G)(\pi_M - \pi_C)(q_f - \overline{q}_f)}{(1-g\eta)\left(Gq_f + (1-G)\overline{q}_f\right) - g(\pi_M - \pi_C)q_f}. \tag{13.14}$$

Since $c < a^* < a_N$, it must be that $\phi_E > 0$.

Finally, to show $a_N < a_M$, compare the associated first-order conditions $\pi_M' = q_f + (a-c)q_f' = 0$ and $G\pi_M' + (1-G)\pi_C' = 0$. Since π_M is concave in a, π_M' is decreasing, and so the result $a_N < a_M$ follows provided $G\pi_M' + \left(1-G\right)\pi_C' < \pi_M'$. This is true since $\pi_C' < \pi_M'$ which holds for $a > c$ given (13.1) and that $q_f > \overline{q}_f$.

Proposition 1 shows that the effect of allowing *FTM* to *MTM* substitution relative to existing models where this effect is ignored is to lower the equilibrium *FTM* termination charge and retail price. This happens for two reasons that can be best seen by examining (13.12). First, assume the number of mobile subscribers remains constant as the termination charge changes so the additional effect of $db^* / da < 0$ is ignored. The resulting equilibrium termination charge is a_N as characterized in (13.9). In this case *FTM* demand is more elastic compared to the case without substitution, which is why a_N is lower than a_M. Second, noting that the number of mobile subscribers increases as the termination charge increases, the equilibrium termination charge is even lower than a_N. This is reflected by the additional negative term in (13.12). As the termination charge is increased, more people become mobile subscribers to avoid high *FTM* charges, which further reduces the demand for *FTM* calls, thereby constraining equilibrium termination charges to be lower than a_N.

Now compare this with the termination charge that maximizes consumer surplus and that maximizes welfare. Since in equilibrium, profits of both the fixed-line and mobile operators are zero, welfare, being defined as the sum of consumer and producer surplus, just equals consumer surplus.[9] Given a symmetric second-stage equilibrium in which all mobile operators set the same rental r, welfare is written

$$W = \int_{b^*}^{\overline{b}} (b - r + N(v + v_m) + (1-N)v_f) g(b) db.$$

Total welfare is the expression in (13.3) summed up over all mobile subscribers plus the expression in (13.2) multiplied by the measure of people without a mobile subscription. Using that $r = f - \pi_T$, and $N = 1 - G$, gives

$$W = \int_{b^*}^{\bar{b}} (b - f + G\pi_M + (1-G)\pi_C + (1-G)(v + v_m) + Gv_f)g(b)db, \quad (13.15)$$

which is that sought to maximize. For the sake of obtaining general results in Proposition 2 below, assume functional forms are such that W is concave in a over the relevant range of a, a property again illustrated true in the calibrated model.

Proposition 2: *The welfare maximizing termination charge* a_W *is above cost. In general, the equilibrium termination charge* a^* *is higher or lower than* a_W.

Proof: Differentiating (13.15) with respect to a gives the first-order condition

$$W' = (1-G)\left(\pi_T' - Gq_f - (1-G)\bar{q}_f\right) - g\frac{db^*}{da}\left(Gv_f + (1-G)(v + v_M)\right). \quad (13.16)$$

Ignoring the last term by setting $db^* / da = 0$, $W' < 0$ for $a = a^*$ since at this termination charge $\pi_T' = 0$. Given W is assumed concave in a, this implies $a_W < a^*$. Incorporating the last term does not change this result when db^* / da is close to zero at a^* (it equals zero in the approach taken in the existing literature), or when the hazard rate is sufficiently low. However, given $db^* / da < 0$ from Proposition 1, the last term is positive and this means it is also possible for $W' > 0$ at $a = a^*$, so that $a_W > a^*$. This case arises when db^* / da is sufficiently negative and the hazard rate is sufficiently high (a numerical example is supplied below).

Setting (13.16) equal to zero and using (13.11), gives

$$a_W = c + \left(\frac{1+\delta}{1+\phi_S}\right)\frac{Gq_f + (1-G)\bar{q}_f}{G\left|q_f'\right| + (1-G)\left|\bar{q}_f'\right|}, \quad (13.17)$$

where

$$\delta = \frac{(1-G)\left(q_f - \bar{q}_f\right)}{Gq_f + (1-G)\bar{q}_f} > 0$$

and

$$\phi_S = \frac{1 - g\eta}{\rho v_f + g\eta}. \tag{13.18}$$

Recall $g\eta < 1$ for demand is well behaved. Also $\eta > 0$ since $v + \pi_C > v_f + \pi_M$ and $v_m > 0$. The first inequality is true given the general property that welfare is higher when a single (monopoly) firm sells to a consumer which faces the choice to buy a substitute good at cost than a consumer without such a choice. Thus $\phi_S > 0$, and so $a_W > c$.

Proposition 2 shows that the welfare-maximizing termination charge depends on an inverse elasticity rule, as does the equilibrium termination charge a^*. Moreover, the welfare maximizing termination charge exceeds cost, a result that contradicts the cost-based approach adopted by regulators in a number of countries including the UK. Setting the termination charge above cost is needed to subsidize mobile subscription, which is socially optimal given additional mobile subscribers generate a positive externality to fixed-line callers and to other mobile subscribers. This result is consistent with findings from earlier studies as discussed below.

Taking into account *FTM* to *MTM* substitution also implies a key result from the earlier literature, that the equilibrium termination charge is always too high, is no longer true. Earlier works, emphasized that starting from a_M, a small decrease in the termination charge must increase welfare since it has no first-order impact on termination profits and so on the number of mobile subscribers, but leads to a first-order benefit to *FTM* callers by reducing the deadweight loss from *FTM* prices being set above marginal cost. Allowing for *FTM* to *MTM* substitution changes this logic since a small decrease in the termination charge below a^* does lead to a first-order impact on the number of mobile subscribers. As the *FTM* price falls, fewer people obtain a mobile subscription since they have less need to avoid high *FTM* prices. Since these mobile subscribers generate positive externalities on others, welfare may be lower.

To compare the equilibrium termination charge with that which maximizes welfare, several special cases are considered. This comparison starts with the benchmark case considered previously in the literature and explains the new effects the current approach uncovers.

Comparisons with Received Literature

With the exception of Armstrong and Wright (2009), received approaches used to explore *FTM* termination, such as Armstrong (1997, 2002), Gans and

King (2000), Thompson et al. (2006), Valletti and Houpis (2005) and Wright (1999, 2002), assume there are no *MTM* calls, and therefore no scope for *FTM* to *MTM* substitution. The case without *MTM* calls is the special case of this framework, obtained by imposing $\bar{q}_f(p_f, p_m) = q_f(p_f)$ and $\bar{q}_m(p_f, p_m) = q_m(p_m) = 0$. Imposing these conditions on (13.13) implies $a^* = a_M$. In equilibrium, competing mobile operators set their termination charge at the same level chosen by a monopolist operator. Thus by ignoring *FTM* to *MTM* substitution results in equilibrium termination charges being overstated as in Proposition 1. Allowing for *FTM* to *MTM* substitution removes the 'monopoly outcome' result and demonstrates the importance of competition that exists for the majority of calls to people on-the-go.

Imposing the same conditions on (13.17) implies the welfare-maximizing termination charge is characterised by

$$a_W = c + \left(\frac{1}{1+\phi_S} \right) \frac{q_f}{|q_f'|}, \tag{13.19}$$

where

$$\phi_S = \frac{1}{\rho v_f}.$$

This implies a_W remains above cost but necessarily lower than a^*. Moreover, it also depends on the inverse elasticity rule, although only after appropriate discounting of the monopoly mark-up.[10]

The result in (13.19) is missing several important effects that arise once *MTM* calls are incorporated. Allowing for *MTM* calls, but not substitution with *FTM* calls, the discount to the monopoly mark-up becomes

$$\phi_S = \frac{1 - g v_m}{\rho v_f + g v_m}.$$

The existence of *MTM* calls leads to positive network effects, represented by the term $g v_m$, which suggests a higher termination charge than (13.19) is socially optimal.[11] In contrast, in (13.19) the only reason for setting the termination charge above cost is the positive externality on *FTM* callers. In other words, the existing approach understates the extent to which the welfare maximizing termination charge should be set above cost. More generally, the result implies that the more important are network externalities introduced by

$v_m > 0$ and $v_f > 0$, the closer is a_W to a_M. However, the welfare maximizing termination charge remains between c and a_M, as in the existing literature, a result obtained in previous models by assuming away *MTM* calls. The analysis here shows it is not necessary to do so.

If *FTM* to *MTM* substitution is allowed, three additional effects not previously considered arise. Mobile subscribers will not make as many *FTM* calls, given they can substitute to *MTM* calls, thereby reducing the 'tax base' which means a higher 'tax rate' or termination charge is socially optimal. This is captured in the positive δ term in the numerator of (13.17). Second, network effects are now different. The network effects consist of the benefits v_m arising to mobile subscribers from now being able to make calls to more people who are on-the-go (the additional mobile subscribers). If mobile subscribers do not substitute between *FTM* and *MTM* calls, this effect would be the only network effect. However, attracting additional mobile subscribers now leads to new effects reflected by the additional terms in η. The first of these effects is that additional mobile subscribers make it more attractive for non-subscribers to join the mobile network to make *MTM* calls to avoid high *FTM* prices since they increase the number of calls that can be made to people on-the-go, which is the second term in η. Alternatively, additional mobile subscribers reduce the tax base of the mobile operators, thereby reducing the subsidy available to mobile subscribers, which reduces the size of the network effect, explaining the third term in η. The second term in η is always larger than the third, as explained in the proof of Proposition 2, so that the network effects are stronger as a result of allowing mobile subscribers to substitute between *FTM* and *MTM* calls. Finally, compared to (13.19), *FTM* demand is more elastic, reflecting the ability of mobile subscribers to substitute to *MTM* calls, which means a lower level of termination charge is socially optimal (but for the same reason, the equilibrium level is also lower).

Another way of comparing the results to those of the existing literature is to examine whether the welfare maximizing termination charge is closer or further away from the equilibrium termination charge once *MTM* calls and *FTM* to *MTM* substitution is taken into account. To evaluate this focus on the ratio of mark-ups

$$\frac{a^* - c}{a_W - c}.$$

Evaluating this before taking into account *MTM* calls, this ratio equals

$$1+\frac{1}{\rho v_f},$$

which exceeds unity. After taking these features into account, the ratio is

$$\frac{1+\phi_S}{(1+\phi_E)(1+\delta)},$$

where ϕ_S, defined in (13.18), is generally lower than $1/\rho v_f$ and ϕ_E defined in (13.14) is positive (since $c < a^* < a_N$). Since $\delta > 0$, the ratio is generally lower, suggesting the extent to which the equilibrium charge exceeds the welfare-maximizing level is lower. In fact, as Proposition 2 established, the ratio may be lower than one, with the equilibrium termination charge then being too low.

New Markets

In an immature market, where in equilibrium few people subscribe. This situation reflects that the private benefits of joining are small to begin, so $\overline{b}$ is low. Mobile operators will not attract many subscribers even though it generates positive externalities. This scenario is captured by considering the limit case $G = 1$ (so $N = 0$) but with $g > 0$, so that there are no mobile subscribers in equilibrium even though some people would subscribe if their utility could be slightly increased. Then imposing $G = 1$ on (13.13) and (13.17) implies $a^* = a_W = a_M$. In equilibrium, the termination charge is set to the monopoly level, reflecting that there is no substitution to *MTM* calls given no mobile phone subscriptions in equilibrium. However, this outcome is also the welfare maximizing termination charge given it maximizes termination profits, thereby providing the greatest incentive to encourage mobile subscription, without which consumers get no surplus from *FTM* calls.

Mature Markets

At the other extreme is the case in which everyone subscribes to the mobile network. This might reflect a situation where having a mobile phone is viewed as a necessity, and so even if mobile subscribers are not subsidized, all will continue to subscribe. Provided the penetration rate is fixed so that $g = 0$ and $G = 0$, then the equilibrium charge is defined by $a^* = c + \overline{q}_f / |\overline{q}'_f|$, and the welfare maximizing termination charge equals termination cost c. Note a^* can be quite close to cost c, since $\overline{q}_f$ could be highly elastic (if *MTM* calls are quite close substitutes to *FTM* calls). The outcome in this market setting can be quite different if the marginal subscriber remains sensitive to the rentals even as the penetration rate approaches unity. Next, this case is explored in terms of the calibrated model.

CALIBRATED MODEL

Now the model is calibrated to Australian data. First, underlying parameter values are set to match observed or plausible values of variables. The mobile penetration rate N in 2003 in Australia is 0.72 from Australian Communications and Media Authority (Telecommunications Performance Report 2002-03, December 2003, p. 90). The per-minute price of *FTM* calls p_f is \$0.33, the per-minute price of *MTM* calls p_m is \$0.23, and the corresponding *FTM* termination charge a is \$0.21 (ACCC Mobile Services Review, June 2004 and data from Australian mobile company Websites). While p_f and a are directly observed, the price of *MTM* calls is the average price over all minutes. The corresponding average monthly rental for mobile subscription is set at \$22 (data from 2004 for Australian mobile operators).

A major challenge for the calibration exercise is that the underlying components of demand (q_f, $\overline{q}_f$, $\overline{q}_m$ and q_m) are not observed. Instead, the total number of calls received per mobile subscriber, broken down into *FTM* calls and *MTM* calls are observed. Denoting total *FTM* demand as Q_f and total *MTM* demand as Q_m, the relationship between individual components of demand and observed demand is

$$Q_f = (1-N)q_f + N\overline{q}_f$$

and

$$Q_m = N(q_m + \overline{q}_m).$$

These are measured as the total number of minutes called per mobile subscriber per month. Using data from an Australian carrier $Q_f = 25.687$ minutes and $Q_m = 66.713$, meaning that the typical mobile subscriber receives more than twice as many calls from people making *MTM* calls than *FTM* calls.

Interestingly, this calling pattern is reversed in the US. According to the CTIA Semi Annual Wireless Survey, June 2005, 70 per cent of calls received by a typical subscriber are *FTM* calls and only 30 per cent are *MTM* calls. This outcome is exactly what is expected if there is a lot of substitution to *MTM* calls in Australia to avoid the high price of *FTM* calls but little such substitution in the US where the price of *FTM* calls is the same as a local call.

The price elasticity of *FTM* demand per mobile subscriber is defined as $E_f = -(dQ_f / dp_f)(p_f / Q_f)$. This is estimated as low as 0.6 (ACCC op. cit., p. 103) and as high as 2 (using data from an Australian mobile carrier and econometric estimates by one of the authors). The elasticity set halfway point of 1.3. It is noted in passing that the ACCC elasticity, which is similar to elasticities that other regulatory bodies such as UK Ofcom used in their findings, is inconsistent with the claim that each mobile operator is a monopolist with respect to *FTM* calls. An operator with a monopoly over termination of calls to its subscribers always sets its termination price to the point where *FTM* demand is elastic. Unlike earlier models of competitive bottlenecks, this model, which permits substitution between *FTM* and *MTM* calls, can potentially handle inelastic demand, and therefore the implications of a range of price elasticities in the sensitivity analysis are explored.

To identify individual components of demand, additional assumptions are required. First, assume consumer utility from making calls is the same regardless of whether they are at home or on-the-go, but rather just depend on the technology used. This implies $v_f(p_f) = v(p_f, \infty)$, $v_m(p_m) = v(\infty, p_m)$, $q_f(p_f) = \overline{q}_f(p_f, \infty)$ and $q_m(p_m) = \overline{q}_m(\infty, p_m)$. Moreover, assume people do not have any particular bias towards one technology, at equal prices. The case in which the fixed-line technology is perceived superior is explored in the sensitivity analysis. The cross-price elasticity of demand ($\overline{q}_f$ with respect to p_m), denoted E_C, is set equal to one-half, although again a range of values is considered. Finally, in fitting the distribution function the estimated elasticity of penetration $E_r = -(dN / dr)(r / N)$ which equals 0.55 from Hausman (1997) is used. Similar values are estimated for Australia (Hausman, 2002).

Table 13.1 summarizes the levels of variables and parameters that allow calibration of all model parameters. All but the last variable is observed or based on estimates, while the last one is based on a plausible guess. For the estimated elasticities and the last unknown cross-price elasticity, a wide range of plausible values is allowed for as shown in the final row of the table.

The parameter c is taken to equal 12 cents, based on the ACCC's estimate of mobile termination costs. The implied cost parameter for *FTM* calls is the same $C = p_f - a = 0.12$. Based on regulatory proceedings in the US and Australia, the cost of *FTM* origination is thought to be around 3 cents per minute. The higher cost could reflect the cost of resale, which is the approach the ACCC used to try to eliminate the fixed line operator's margin from originating *FTM* calls. Alternatively, the fixed-line operator may retain a profit margin in which case the welfare analysis would still apply provided this margin remains constant in a and the policymaker's welfare criterion is consumer surplus.

Table 13.1 Values of parameters for calibration

Variable	N	p_f	p_m	a	r	Q_f	Q_m	E_r	E_f	E_c
Base value	0.72	0.33	0.23	0.21	22	25.7	66.7	0.55	1.3	0.5
Range								±0.2	±0.7	±0.25

Note: All monetary units are in Australian dollars.

A linear demand specification is adopted. For call minutes this corresponds to representative consumers having the following quadratic utility function[12]

$$U(\overline{q}_f, \overline{q}_m) = \alpha(\overline{q}_f + \omega\overline{q}_m) - \frac{\beta}{2}(\overline{q}_f^2 + 2\gamma\overline{q}_f\overline{q}_m + \overline{q}_m^2).$$

A mobile subscriber at home maximizes $U\left(\overline{q}_f, \overline{q}_m\right) + y$ subject to $p_f\overline{q}_f + p_m\overline{q}_m + y \leq M$, where y is expenditure on all other goods and M is income. This leads to the following demand functions

$$\overline{q}_f(p_f, p_m) = \frac{\alpha(1-\omega\gamma) - p_f + \gamma p_m}{\beta(1-\gamma^2)}$$
$$\overline{q}_m(p_f, p_m) = \frac{\alpha\left(\omega-\gamma\right) - p_m + \gamma p_f}{\beta(1-\gamma^2)},$$

provided p_f and p_m are sufficiently close, where using our earlier definitions $\overline{q}_f = \lambda\overline{q}_f(p_f, p_m)$ and $\overline{q}_m = \lambda\overline{q}_m(p_f, p_m)$.

Given the assumption that all calls are derived from the same demand specification, it also follows that

$$\overline{q}_f\left(p_f, p_m\right) = q_f\left(p_f\right) = \frac{\alpha - p_f}{\beta}$$

if $p_f < (p_m - \alpha(\omega - \gamma))/\gamma$. While

$$\overline{q}_m(p_f, p_m) = q_m(p_m) = \frac{\omega\alpha - p_m}{\beta}$$

if $p_f > \alpha(1-\omega\gamma) + \gamma p_m$. The corresponding indirect utility measures $v = \lambda v(p_f, p_m)$, $v_f = \lambda v_f(p_f)$ and $v_m = (1-\lambda)v_m(p_m)$ are obtained in the usual way.

Combining the relationships above we get

$$Q_f = (1-N)\lambda\left(\frac{\alpha - p_f}{\beta}\right) + N\lambda\left(\frac{\alpha(1-\omega\gamma) - p_f + \gamma p_m}{\beta(1-\gamma^2)}\right),$$

$$Q_m = N\left((1-\lambda)\left(\frac{\omega\alpha - p_m}{\beta}\right) + \lambda\left(\frac{\alpha(\omega-\gamma) - p_m + \gamma p_f}{\beta(1-\gamma^2)}\right)\right).$$

In addition $(dQ_f / dp_f)(p_f / Q_f) = -1.3$ and $(d\overline{q}_f / dp_m)(p_m / \overline{q}_f) = 0.5$, where the first elasticity is calculated assuming N is constant.[13] Using the base values of parameters from Table 13.1, imposing that $\omega = 1$ so there is no bias towards one technology over another, and solving these four equations simultaneously gives $\alpha = 0.757$, $\beta = 0.00518$, $\gamma = 0.433$ and $\lambda = 0.449$.

With these parameter values we find $q_f = 37.078$, $\overline{q}_f = 21.258$, $\overline{q}_m = 36.558$, $q_m = 56.099$, $v = 14.177$, $v_f = 7.920$, $v_m = 14.787$, $\pi_M = 3.337$ and $\pi_C = 1.913$ so that $\pi_T = N\pi_C + (1-N)\pi_M = 2.312$. The subsidy per mobile subscriber at these termination charges is \$2.31 per month. From this and the observed r

$$f = r + \pi_T = 24.312 .$$

Finally, to characterize the distribution function for b, an extreme value distribution is adopted with location parameter μ and shape parameter σ.[14] The distribution function is

$$G(b) = e^{-e^{\left(-\frac{b-\mu}{\sigma}\right)}} .$$

Using this distribution, (13.6) and (13.7) are solved to obtain values of μ and σ that match the observed penetration rate and estimated elasticity of penetration. This implies $\mu = 13.437$ and $\sigma = 27.303$.

The distribution must have mass to the left of zero to explain why 28 per cent of consumers still do not have a mobile subscription despite mobile subscription providing greater caller benefits than the charges consumers face. It implies that some people's aversion to having a mobile subscription is greater than their net benefits from using a mobile phone. Still, in the calibrated solution, the marginal subscriber who is just willing to subscribe still has a positive value of b^*, equalling 6.848, and so the fact that some non-subscribers have negative values of b does not affect the equilibrium or welfare maximizing termination charges. Finally, network effects, measured by $g\eta$, equal 0.256 which implies non-explosive but positive network effects as assumed in the theoretical analysis.

With all parameters determined, we then work out the equilibrium rental, penetration rate, termination profit and welfare for different values of the termination charge a, by solving (13.7) and (13.10) for *N* to get:

$$N = 1 - e^{-e^{\left(-\frac{f-(a-c)\left(N\bar{q}_f+(1-N)q_f\right)-N(v-v_f+v_m)-\mu}{\sigma}\right)}},$$

where q_f, $\bar{q}_f$, v and v_f are all functions of a through the *FTM* price $P = C + a$. Figure 13.1 plots termination profits in the absence of substitution (π_M), termination profits with substitution (π_T), the penetration rate N and total welfare W as a function of the *FTM* termination charge a. This illustrates the relationship between cost-based termination, the equilibrium termination charge, the monopoly termination charge, the welfare maximizing termination charge, and the termination charge which maximizes mobile penetration.

As expected from Proposition 1 the introduction of *FTM* to *MTM* substitution causes the equilibrium termination charge to fall below the monopoly one predicted by the traditional analysis. The equilibrium level of a predicted by the calibrated model (that maximizes π_T) is 29 cents, higher than the 21 cents level observed in the data in June 2004. Part of the explanation could be that there is likely some regulatory pressure on operators in Australia to lower their charges by 2004.[15] In comparison, the level of a predicted by existing competitive bottleneck theories is 38 cents, which is considerably higher than the equilibrium level.

Starting from the equilibrium level of 29 cents, an increase in termination charges increases mobile penetration even though the subsidy per mobile subscriber falls, since by raising the *FTM* price it makes mobile subscription attractive as a way to avoid high *FTM* prices. Mobile penetration is found not maximized until termination charges are set at 54 cents, which is much higher than the level which maximizes termination profit, consistent with the idea that high *FTM* prices also encourage mobile participation. Despite this finding, for this benchmark case, welfare is maximized at the lower level of 24 cents for the calibrated model. While slightly lower than the equilibrium level, this level is still twice the assumed termination cost of 12 cents, and in fact higher than the termination charges in existence in 2004. Furthermore, regulating termination charges at cost provides lower welfare than the unregulated equilibrium. Thus, cost-based regulations of FTM termination charges are undesirable in this setting. Finally, note that with the calibrated

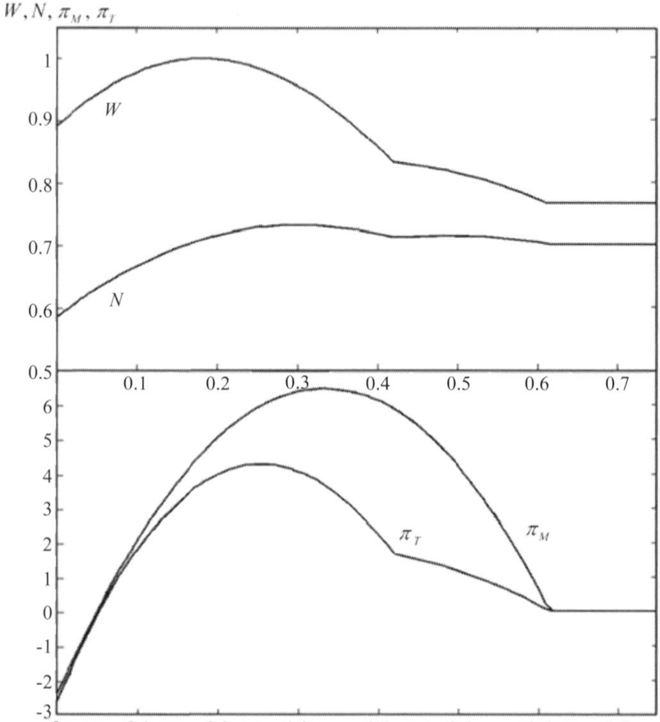

Notes: W = Welfare (normalized). N = Penetration rate. π_M = Termination profits in the absence of substitution. π_T = Termination profits with substitution.

Figure 13.1 *Welfare, penetration rate and termination profits*

parameter values, the opposite conclusion is reached if the monopoly termination charge predicted by existing theory is used as the equilibrium charge.

Sensitivity Analysis

A sensitivity analysis is conducted to see how much the calibrated results change when the underlying assumptions are changed. The range of values considered is determined by that given in Table 13.1. The results are presented in Table 13.2. The table shows the equilibrium, monopoly and welfare maximizing termination charges if the calibration had instead been conducted to match the alternative values given in the first column.

A number of interesting observations arise from Table 13.2. The first thing to note is the qualitative findings are quite robust to different assumptions about the values of the different identifying variables. The biggest variation arises from changes to the assumption about the price elasticity of *FTM* demand. If it is instead set at the regulator's estimate of 0.6, the monopoly termination charge becomes very high (one dollar). With the price elasticity of *FTM* demand being low when measured at the observed termination charge of 21 cents, a monopoly mobile operator will raise its termination charge to the point where demand becomes elastic. This requires a_M be high. However, it also implies the welfare maximizing termination charge is higher, in fact higher than the equilibrium level in this case. The possibility that the equilibrium termination charge may be too low (as suggested by Proposition 2) cannot be ruled out – in fact, it can easily arise once we allow

Table 13.2 Equilibrium, monopoly and welfare maximizing termination

	a^*	a_M	a_W
Benchmark	0.29	0.38	0.24
$E_r = 0.35$	0.29	0.38	0.21
$E_r = 0.75$	0.28	0.38	0.25
$E_f = 0.6$	0.38	1.05	1.77
$E_f = 2$	0.25	0.29	0.19
$E_c = 0.25$	0.29	0.33	0.22
$E_c = 0.75$	0.28	0.44	0.26

Note: Benchmark values of parameters are $E_r = 0.55$, $E_f = 1.3$, and $E_c = 0.50$.

two or more of the parameters to differ from their benchmark values within the stated ranges.

Comparisons with the Received Literature

To compare the results here to those obtained by using earlier models, *MTM* calls are ignored. As expected this implies $a^* = a_M = 0.38$ since the competitive bottleneck is not constrained by *FTM* to *MTM* substitution. Conversely, $a_W = 0.20$, so that the equilibrium termination charge is nearly twice the welfare-maximizing level. Compared to the equilibrium outcome, welfare is higher if termination charges are regulated at cost. This highlights the role *MTM* calls and *FTM* to *MTM* substitution can play in narrowing the gap between privately set and socially optimal termination charges.

Strong Substitution

At the opposite extreme to the case in which substitution with *MTM* calls is not possible, is the case where such substitution is assumed to be very strong. Strong substitution means that over the relevant range of termination charges, mobile subscribers always use their mobile phone to make calls to on-the-go subscribers as it is cheaper to do so. This situation is likely to be increasingly relevant with the convergence of different technologies.

From a welfare perspective, with high substitutability between types of calls, setting a very high termination charge can be desirable since raising the price of *FTM* calls drives almost everyone to subscribe. This generates positive externalities at relatively little cost since most people can substitute to *MTM* calls with little utility loss. For instance, if the degree of substitutability is increased to $\gamma = 0.75$ and the model recalibrated, such an outcome arises with a_W equal to \$1.12. In the model, an extremely high termination charge becomes socially optimal, at which point mobile subscribers never use their landline for calls from home. Corresponding to this, mobile penetration is maximized at a termination charge equal to \$1.27, with a near 95 per cent penetration rate (instead of the baseline 72 per cent level). In contrast, the equilibrium termination charge, which is limited by the ability of subscribers to easily substitute to *MTM* calls, is little changed at 31 cents.

Emerging and Mature Markets

To study different market stages, from emerging markets to mature markets, the distribution of b is exogenously shifted by Δ, to lie between $\underline{b}+\Delta$ and $\overline{b}+\Delta$. All other parameters are left the same. The parameter Δ is chosen to generate a range of penetration rates. Table 13.3 shows the corresponding equilibrium and welfare maximizing termination charges.[16] The last column shows the percentage change in welfare from regulating termination charges to cost compared to leaving them at the equilibrium level.

Table 13.3 Different degrees of market penetration

	N	a^*	a_W	$\%\Delta W$ from $a = c$
$\Delta = -40$	0.021	0.33	0.28	-100%
$\Delta = -30$	0.195	0.31	0.23	-32.86%
$\Delta = -20$	0.370	0.29	0.20	-11.44%
$\Delta = -10$	0.545	0.27	0.19	-6.25%
$\Delta = 0$	0.720	0.25	0.18	-5.01%
$\Delta = 10$	0.895	0.24	0.17	-3.04%
$\Delta = 20$	0.982	0.23	0.17	-2.78%
$\Delta = 30$	1.000	0.23	0.08	2.30%
$\Delta = 40$	1.000	0.23	0.05	2.91%

Notes: Benchmark case is $\Delta = 0$. Penetration rate N measured when $a = 0.21$.

In an immature mobile market, where few people are mobile subscribers, there is limited scope for *FTM* to *MTM* substitution. Thus, the equilibrium termination charge approximately corresponds to the monopoly one, as illustrated in the case $\Delta = -40$ in Table 13.3. However, this is also close to being welfare maximizing since with few mobile subscribers, the positive externality from subsidizing subscription are more important than any deadweight loss from *FTM* prices being above cost. For instance, when the penetration rate is just 2.1 per cent (at $a = 0.21$), lowering the termination charge to cost (in an attempt to eliminate the deadweight loss of above-cost pricing) will result in no one subscribing to the mobile network, and therefore a complete loss of surplus.

Conversely, as the penetration rate becomes high for exogenous reasons, say because all people would choose to subscribe to a mobile operator at current prices (that is, at $a = 0.21$), then there is no scope for attracting additional subscribers and so there is no reason to maintain high termination charges from a welfare perspective. However, this does not necessarily imply cost-based termination charges are socially optimal. As the $\Delta = 20$ case illustrates in Table 13.3, it could be that the socially optimal termination charge is still above cost since by lowering termination charges to cost, it is no longer the case that everyone subscribes.[17] This could provide a rationale for leaving termination charges above cost even if there is 100 per cent penetration in an unregulated equilibrium. Moreover, while the calibrated model predicts the socially optimal termination charge is close to cost in a mature market, it also implies the welfare loss (in percentage terms) of not getting it right is relatively small since everyone can substitute to *MTM* calls.

Another possibility is that marginal mobile subscribers generate fewer incoming calls and so the network benefits of subsidizing diminishes as mobile markets mature. This view arises, if people are heterogeneous in terms of how much they call out. Those that remain to join the network have not yet done so because they expect to call out little, and calling levels are highly correlated with calls received. Such a view is inconsistent with the model. In the model, everyone expects to receive the same number of calls, and people are heterogeneous only in terms of some fixed benefits of belonging to the network. Moreover, such a view is also inconsistent with empirical evidence from Australia, where new customers receive the average amount of *FTM* calls.

Fixed-line Operator Makes a Profit

Based on regulatory proceedings in the US and Australia, the cost of *FTM* origination is around 3 cents per minute. Since the observed *FTM* price is 33 cents, and the observed *FTM* termination charge is 21 cents, this still leaves 9 cents unaccounted for. The approach above is to attribute this to the cost of the fixed-line operator or of reselling the *FTM* service. Alternatively, this can be interpreted as the fixed-line operator's profit margin, as long as welfare is interpreted as consumer surplus. Adopting the latter interpretation, the results imply consumer surplus is maximized at a termination charge of 24 cents per-minute. Attributing a constant 9 cent per-minute margin to the fixed-line operator on *FTM* calls, total welfare is then maximized at 20 cents per-minute. The effect is to lower the welfare maximizing termination charge since starting from the consumer-surplus maximizing termination charge, a lower termination charge increases the total number of *FTM* calls, thereby increasing the fixed-line operator's profit which is part of total welfare.

This possibility also suggests an alternative regulatory approach to lower *FTM* prices – lower the fixed-line operator's margin on *FTM* calls (perhaps through direct price regulation). In contrast to lowering the *FTM* termination charge, lowering the margin on *FTM* calls stimulates the demand for *FTM* calls which increases rather than decreases the tax base for mobile operators. It therefore provides a more effective way to reduce the deadweight loss on *FTM* callers without limiting the subsidy to mobile subscribers that provide a positive externality to other callers (however, it does remove one reason to join the mobile network, which is high *FTM* prices). For instance, starting from the observed level of the termination charge ($a = 0.21$) and fixing c at 3 cents and *FTM* margins at 9 cents, a 9 cent drop in a results in a decrease in total welfare (including the fixed-line operator's profit) of 1.9 per cent. In contrast, by fixing c at 3 cents and a at 21 cents a reduction in the fixed-line operator's profit margin by 9 cents results in total welfare increasing by 13.2 per cent.

Receivers Care

Thus far, it is assumed that people do not get any utility from receiving calls. Suppose now people value receiving calls. This affects both the utility of a mobile subscriber who receives calls, as well as the utility of people at home who can receive calls from people on-the-go.

To model the value to people on-the-go from receiving calls, add the additional utility term $u_R = \theta(1-\lambda)(Q_f - Q_f^* + Q_m - Q_m^*)$ to the utility of a mobile subscriber described in (13.3). The parameter θ measures the marginal benefit to consumers of receiving another call. Here Q_f^* and Q_m^* refer to the observed levels of demand used in the calibration, these being 25.687 and 66.713 minutes. This specification keeps the total utility from mobile subscription the same as before at the calibrated solution, but allows utility to increase if consumers receive more calls (and decrease if they receive fewer calls). Note the utility for receiving calls is multiplied by $(1-\lambda)$ since a subscriber only obtains utility from receiving calls on their mobile phone when on-the-go, which happens a fraction $(1-\lambda)$ of the time. Writing out this expression in full, implies the extra utility is

$$\theta(1-\lambda)\left(N(q_m + \overline{q}_f + \overline{q}_m) + (1-N)q_f - Q^*\right),$$

where $Q^* = Q_f^* + Q_m^*$.

Since the number of calls received in the model is assumed independent ofoutgoing calls, this extra utility term does not affect the calibration of the demand functions. Instead it affects the calibration of the distribution function, since it changes the sensitivity of the subscription decision to the number of other subscribers. The other effect of receivers caring is on the operators' setting of a. Instead of setting a to minimize the rental they charge, they now take into account that consumers also care about the number of calls received. This causes the operators to minimize $r - u_R$ by setting a to maximize adjusted profit $\pi_R = \pi_T + u_R$.[18]

The final adjustment to the analysis is to include welfare obtained by receiving calls from people on-the-go. Previously, there was assumed no value from these 'new' calls. This additional benefit does not affect the decision about mobile subscription or demands, since people gain the same benefit whether they subscribe to a mobile operator or not. The only effect of allowing for such calls is on the final welfare analysis. For this, assume the demand for these calls is derived from the same utility function, where it is assumed the price of these calls is the same as p_m.

The parameter θ measures the (assumed constant) value of an extra minute of calls received. Since this is in the same monetary units as the prices for outgoing calls, a reasonable range of values of θ is between zero and 0.33, the price of *FTM* calls. Setting θ equal to 0.165, implying people get benefit per call received of 16.5 cents per minute of call. The result is an equilibrium termination charge of 27 cents (previously 29 cents) and a welfare-maximizing termination charge of 22 cents (previously 24 cents). Welfare is still higher at this equilibrium charge than when termination charges are set equal to cost.

The decline in the equilibrium and welfare maximizing termination charges as a result of receivers caring is consistent with the existing literature (see Armstrong, 2002 and Wright, 2002). Lower termination charges are set to encourage more *FTM* calls, thereby increasing the utility of mobile subscribers. What is more surprising about these results is how little the optimal termination charge declines despite subscribers valuing incoming calls at 16.5 cents per minute. This reflects that a high *FTM* termination charge causes more people to get mobile subscription, which has offsetting effects on the number of calls received by mobile subscribers. First, more people on-the-go that can make calls to people on-the-go (as well as those at home). Second, it means more callers that can substitute to cheaper *MTM* calls, so that the higher price of *FTM* calls does not lead to such a big decrease in calls received by mobile subscribers. To see this, note that increasing the termination charge from cost to the new equilibrium level (27 cents) results in a decline in the calls received by mobile subscribers on-the-go from non-subscribers at home of 42 per cent. This is the traditional effect emphasized in the literature. In contrast, taking into account the existence of mobile subscribers and *MTM* calls, the total minutes of calls received by a mobile subscriber decreases by 4.4 per cent.

CONCLUDING REMARKS

A view among regulators is that fixed-to-mobile prices are set too high. This inference follows typically as mobile termination is seen as a monopoly problem, where mobile carriers do not face competition to terminate calls to their customers. This view misses two important economic factors.

First, some or all of the excess of price over cost for mobile termination is used to lower prices for mobile subscription, as would be expected in a two-sided market. This results in more people obtaining mobile subscription.

Further, fixed-line caller consumer surplus increases when they are able to reach more people on-the-go via their mobile phones, as does that of existing mobile subscribers. Otherwise these people are unreachable. In other words, every new mobile subscriber attracted acts as a 'new good' to the other consumers.

The second economic factor, which this chapter considers, is that consumers who want to reach someone on-the-go can substitute mobile-to-mobile calls for fixed-to-mobile calls, and do so given relative prices. With mobile penetration at levels of 70 per cent or higher in most OECD countries, this substitution can take place for most callers. For Australia, it is found that mobile subscribers receive over two times as many mobile-to-mobile calls as fixed-to-mobile calls indicating a significant amount of substitution – exactly the reverse of the US pattern where there is little, if any, price differential between the two types of calls.

When allowed for substitution to mobile-to-mobile calls, which are assumed to be prices at cost, the monopoly termination implication no longer holds true. Indeed, fixed-to-mobile price elasticities used by regulators are inconsistent with the monopoly termination model they have based their regulatory decisions on. Empirically, when calibrated the model for Australia finds that the monopoly termination rate is much higher than the observed market determined termination rate, so it is very unlikely that the monopoly fixed-to-mobile model, ignoring mobile-to-mobile substitution, is correct. The model opens the possibility that the market may set a termination charge that is too low. More importantly, the model suggests that the market determined mobile termination rate is considerably closer to the welfare-maximizing termination rate than a regulatory-determined termination rate based on cost. Finally, it is noted that when the mobile penetration is close to 100 per cent, then although in theory welfare can be higher with cost-based termination, it can only be so by a small amount since then everyone can take advantage of mobile-to-mobile calls (assuming these are set at cost based prices).

In terms of a policy recommendation it is concluded that regulating termination charges on the basis of costs is unjustified. When prices in the mobile markets are set competitively, such market intervention seems misguided. While the calibrated results suggest welfare may be enhanced by lowering termination charges below the market determined rate, they also suggest it is well beyond usual regulatory calculations to determine the optimal prices. Rather, to a first-order approximation, regulation of mobile termination rates is redistributing income among consumers of relatively small amounts of money. Most economists agree that income redistribution is not a proper goal of telecommunications regulatory policy.

NOTES

1. In some countries like the United States (US), where mobile receivers pay for calls, termination charges are indirectly regulated to very low levels (see Littlechild, 2006 for a detailed explanation).
2. This effect is observed in the U.K. after the regulatory imposition of reduced termination rates in July of 2003. Over the period, 2003:1 to 2004:4 UK mobile subscription prices increased by approximately 6.4 per cent. This compares to a decrease in the BLS CPI for cellular telephone in the US of approximately 2 per cent. See Ofcom Website, 'The Communications Market', Appendices for August and October 2004 and US Bureau of Labor Statistics (BLS) CPI for wireless telephone services (CUUR0000SEED03).
3. Recently, Armstrong and Wright (2009) analysed the case with substitution between fixed-to-mobile and mobile-to-mobile calls. They obtain quite different results, finding the competitive bottleneck associated with mobile termination charges is only weakened indirectly by substitution. One key difference is that they analyse competition between differentiated mobile networks that set differential on-net and off-net mobile-to-mobile prices, whereas the chapter assumes mobile networks are homogeneous and that on-net and off-net mobile-to-mobile prices are both set at marginal cost.
4. They may also use text messaging, which is typically much cheaper. This model equally applies if text-messaging is considered instead of, or in addition to, mobile-to-mobile calls.
5. The calibrated version of the model is extended to allow receivers to value incoming calls.
6. The most important implication of this additive benefits assumption for the results is that the marginal subscriber receives the same number of calls as the average subscriber. This is consistent with empirical evidence from Australia, where it has been found that new customers receive close to the average amount of FTM calls.
7. This assumes mobile operators can make take-it-or-leave-it offers, motivated by the fact the fixed-line operator is typically obligated (by regulation) to interconnect with mobile operators. Binmore and Harbord (2005) provide an analysis of mobile termination as a bilateral monopoly bargaining problem, which generally results in lower termination charges set above those characterized here.
8. Assuming no FTM to MTM substitution, it is the same termination charge that a mobile operator would set if it was the only operator in the mobile sector (it has a monopoly), or in fact, regardless of the nature of competition in the mobile sector (see Wright (2002) for an analysis allowing for quite general forms of competition between mobile operators).
9. Alternatively, if C includes the margins of the fixed-line operator then the welfare analysis still applies as long as welfare is interpreted as consumer surplus.
10. This result is of the same type found in the optimal Ramsey pricing literature for regulated industries where the regulated price is compared to the unregulated monopoly price (Brown and Sibley, 1986, p. 40–1).
11. This can be confirmed by comparing first-order conditions, with the assumption that the original welfare function is concave in a.
12. In a slight abuse of notation, we temporarily use $\overline{q}_f$ and $\overline{q}_m$ in the utility function to denote the consumer's choice variables even though they are not multiplied by λ as defined earlier.
13. This involves a slight approximation given a change in price may induce a small change in N, and this in turn a small change in Q_f to the extent $q_f(p_f)$ differs from $\overline{q}_f(p_f, p_m)$. This approximation is equivalent to the actual elasticity being slightly different from the one matched, but this is immaterial given a wide range of possible elasticities is considered.
14. In an earlier version of the paper a uniform distribution is used to obtain similar results.
15. Regulatory hearings into FTM termination charges in Australia began in 1999. By 2001 carriers agreed to gradually decrease their termination prices.
16. The monopoly termination charge is 33 cents regardless of the value of Δ.

17. Valletti (2006) provides empirical evidence to suggest that the last 10-20 per cent of subscribers to join mobile networks are particularly sensitive to price.
18. Even though a higher off-net price reduces the benefit of joining a rival operator since its customers receive fewer calls, in the homogeneous Bertrand model of competition it remains an equilibrium for off-net prices to equal cost. If an operator raises its off-net price above cost and each consumer expects others will not subscribe to the operator, then consumers will join the operator and the deviation is unprofitable.

REFERENCES

Armstrong, M. (1997), 'Mobile Telephony in The UK', Regulation Initiative Discussion Paper No. 15, London Business School.

Armstrong, M. (2002), 'The Theory of Access Pricing and Interconnection', in M. Cave, S. Majumdar and I. Vogelsang (eds), *Handbook of Telecommunications Economics, Volume 1*, Amsterdam: Elsevier North-Holland.

Armstrong, M. (2006), 'Competition in Two-sided Markets', *Rand Journal of Economics*, **37**, 668–91.

Armstrong, M. and Wright, J. (2006), 'Two-sided Markets, Competitive Bottlenecks and Exclusive Contracts', *Economic Theory*, **32**, 353–80.

Armstrong, M. and Wright, J. (2009), 'Mobile Call Termination', *Economic Journal*, **119**, F270–F307.

Baake, P. and Mitusch, K. (2005), 'Mobile Phone Termination Charges with Asymmetric Regulation', DIW Berlin.

Binmore, K. and Harbord, D. (2005), 'Bargaining over Fixed-to-Mobile Termination Rates: Countervailing Buyer Power as a Constraint on Monopoly Power', *Journal of Competition Law and Economics*, **1**, 49–72.

Brown, S. and Sibley, D. (1986), *The Theory of Utility Pricing*, Cambridge: Cambridge University Press.

Caillaud, B. and Jullien, B. (2001), 'Competing Cybermediaries', *European Economic Review*, **45**, 797–808.

Caillaud, B. and Jullien, B. (2003), 'Chicken and Egg: Competition among Intermediation Service Providers', *Rand Journal of Economics*, **34**, 309–28.

Carter, M. and Wright, J. (2003), 'Asymmetric Network Interconnection', *Review of Industrial Organization*, **22**, 27–46.

Gans, J., King, S. (2000), 'Mobile Network Competition, Customer Ignorance and Fixed to Mobile Call Prices', *Information Economics and Policy*, **12**, 301–28.

Gans, J., King, S. and Wright, J. (2005), 'Wireless Communications', in S. Majumdar, I. Vogelsang and M. Cave (eds), *Handbook of Telecommunications Economics, Volume 2,* Amsterdam: Elsevier North Holland.

Hausman, J. (1997), 'Valuation and the Effect of Regulation on New Services in Telecommunications', Brookings Papers on Economic Activity: Microeconomics.

Hausman, J. (2002), 'Mobile Telephone', in M. Cave, S. Majumdar and I. Vogelsang (eds), *Handbook of Telecommunications Economics, Volume 1*, Amsterdam: Elsevier North-Holland.

Littlechild, S. (2006), 'Mobile Termination Charges: Calling Party Pays versus Receiving Party Pays', *Telecommunications Policy*, **30**, 242–77.

Rochet, J. and Tirole, J. (2003), 'Platform Competition in Two-sided Markets', *Journal of the European Economic Association*, **1**, 990–1029.

Rochet, J. and Tirole, J. (2006), 'Two-sided Markets: A Progress Report', *Rand Journal of Economics*, **37**, 645–67.

Thompson, H., Renard, O. and Wright, J. (2006), 'Mobile Termination', in R. Dewenter and J. Haucap (eds), *Access Pricing: Theory, Practice, Empirical Evidence*. Amsterdam: Elsevier.

Valletti, T. (2006), 'Mobile Call Termination – A Tale of Two-sided Markets', MPRA Paper 2344, University Library of Munich, Germany.

Valletti, T. and Houpis, G. (2005), 'Mobile Termination: What is The "Right" Charge?', *Journal of Regulatory Economics*, **28**, 235–58.

Wright, J. (1999), 'Competition and Termination in Cellular Networks', Working Paper, Centre for Research in Network Economics and Communications, University of Auckland. Retrieved from: http://ssrn.com/abstract=201988.

Wright, J. (2002), 'Access Pricing under Competition: An Application to Cellular Networks', *Journal of Industrial Economics*, **50**, 289–315.

14. Policy implications of asymmetric termination rate regulation in Europe

Edmond Baranes and Cuong Huong Vuong

INTRODUCTION

Competition policy is the best instrument through which to achieve market efficiency via the foundations of economic science. However, until the late 20th century a paucity of competition in many vertically-integrated network industries is observed, with a monopoly serving the market and controlling both inputs and outputs. Apart from political, security and technological reasons, the situation occurs, as competition is not in the public interest due to the presence of scale economies that result in natural monopoly characteristics and stranded costs.

The situation has radically changed through the past two decades due to stronger public pressure, advances in technology and especially high regulatory costs. In particular, the liberalisation and deregulation of the network industries globally provided opportunity to new market players entering potentially competitive market segments. These processes aimed at increasing market performances with more favourable consumer prices and enhanced product choices and innovation. To ensure successful transition, asymmetric regulation plays a significant role in the remaining monopolistic market, and is an effective instrument to enhance market competitiveness by promoting entry.

Conceptually, asymmetric regulation refers to the practice of imposing market constraints on a firm or group of firms whilst not subjecting competitors to similar constraints. This term, initially coined by Schmalensee (1984), depicts a stricter regulatory requirement imposed on the United States (US) telecommunications historical incumbent, AT&T, than new providers of long-distance telecommunications do. Asymmetric regulation is to correct for the position of the incumbent and entrants during the liberalisation and deregulation process. That is, from governments' perspective, there are firms or groups of firms that need favourable regulatory treatment. That is, at entry a new entrant with a zero market share is unable to compete with the incumbent. On the cost side, the telecommunications industry entry is characterised by substantial fixed costs, hence incumbent firms are likely to incur lower average costs that are a source of competitive advantage. Therefore, when services are close substitutes, no entry will occur in the absence of regulatory support. From the demand side, because of network effects (or positive network externality), which arise when the value of a network increases with subscriber numbers, and especially in the presence of the first-mover advantage[1], the first entrant has a decisive lead over competitors, and benefits from snowball effects. Hence, to enhance long-run competition in the European telecommunications industry asymmetric termination rate regulation is introduced that supports entrants against established service providers. In the next section, implementation of asymmetric termination rate regulation in the European telecommunications market is discussed. The following section analyses the efficiency of MTR regulation in Europe. A final section offers some concluding remarks.

ASYMMETRIC INTERCONNECTION POLICY IN EUROPE

The mobile phone, now part of modern life, allows personal communication with mobility that provides extra utility. Liberalisation has provided business opportunity to new market players in European mobile telephone markets including via infrastructure-based (mobile network operators; MNO) and service-based (mobile virtual network operators; MVNO) competition.

The mobile telephone industry experienced dynamic growth and in innovations service offerings. While, first-generation (1G) mobile telephony emerged in 1950s based on analogue technology (principally to deliver voice), second-generation (2G) technology, with GSM standard, is widespread in Europe since the late 1990s with European penetration exceeding a hundred per cent since 2006. Emerging third-generation (3G) technology is promising to allow higher speed access, especially to the Internet, creating a powerful platform for content and software developers[2]. Importantly, the magnitude of the mobile telephone industry contribution to European economies (average ratio revenue to GDP) of 2.9 per cent at 2008 is substantial.

Limited available spectrum resulted in relatively few firms (typically 3-5 operators) granted licences to build own networks and provide mobile service. New entrants include pan-European operators expanding market outside their national markets by leveraging their business and industry experience. Sequential entry into European mobile markets often leads to asymmetry in market positioning (Bijwaard et al., 2008).

European Asymmetric Termination Rate Regulation

Above all, interconnection between mobile networks is necessary to enhance consumer surplus by allowing subscribers to call any mobile network (any-to-any connection). Although network interoperability is required, mobile termination rates are a current debate in Europe. That is, there are two types of asymmetric access charges in place. First, between fixed and mobile networks as the fixed operators are required to provide interconnection at cost-based levels. Meanwhile, mobile network operators generally can set excessive rates for off-net calls terminated on own networks through its bottleneck[3]. These calls originate from rival mobile or fixed networks due to the discrimination rules allowed by European regulatory principles[4]. Above all, the rule is appropriate due to the high fixed-telephone penetration and the dominant position of incumbent fixed-network operator compared to mobile operators that commenced operation much later.

A second type of asymmetric termination rate regulation is associated with the different termination rates of MNOs. In particular, later entrants, with a small market share, have more freedom in setting mobile termination rates (MTRs). Similarly, asymmetric regulation arises mainly to assist late entrants with a lack of scale to create a level playing field to achieve sustainable long-run competition with infrastructure-based MNOs.

As discussed, there is current debate as to whether competition policy can replace sector-specific regulation and the temporal role of regulation in Europe. The EU regulatory framework for electronic communications, which came into force in 2002, clearly states:

> Regulation is seen as essentially a temporary phenomenon, required to make the transition from the formerly monopolistic telecommunications industry to a fully functioning market system. (Europa, 2006, p. 7)

The framework does not imply a totally unregulated environment in future but rather that a firm's actions should be monitored by competition policy, and that appropriate intervention should be made when there is abuse of market power.

Since 2002 with the European Access Directive, the national regulatory authorities (NRAs) started to set price caps to lower MTRs gradually toward the costs of providing interconnection services.[5] This 'glide path' regulation is considered an important tool to reduce regulatory asymmetry between fixed and mobile operators without incurring regulatory shock to MNOs. Also, depending on initial MTR setting and regulation, MTR levels vary different between operators and nations. In practice, there can be single (Member State) or multiple (specific mobile operator) glide paths.

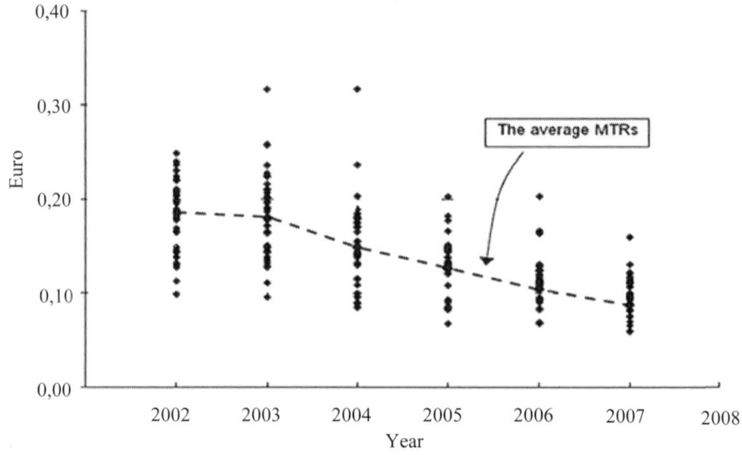

Source: European Commission (2002 – 2007).

Figure 14.1 MTR setting in Europe, 2002-2007

Figure 14.1 plots MTRs for 44 European MNOs during 2002-2007. A downward trend in MTRs values is apparent. Strikingly, a decline in the MTR dispersion between mobile operators is also observed, reflecting the harmonisation of European termination rate regulation.

Regarding asymmetric MTR regulation between MNOs, the degree of asymmetry is principally justified by exogenous factors outside firm control. This includes entry delay and cost differences due to spectrum allocations. However, in practice, control methods reflect the discrepancy/reluctance between NRAs to implement regulatory asymmetry. According to the survey made by the EC, the main control methods used by NRAs are:

(a) Incumbent fixed termination rate plus x% mark-up, ranging from 10% to 30%;
(b) Reasonable prices;
(c) Delayed reciprocity with other alternative operator's (OAO's) tariffs at time t set equal to an incumbent's tariff at $t-x$. This implies that if an incumbent's tariff is declining over time, OAO's tariffs also decline, but will not equal the incumbent's tariff (i.e. tariffs will not be symmetric); and

(d) Symmetry in some countries is reached after a glide path. This implies that OAO's tariffs at t are set higher than incumbent tariffs and must decline at a predetermined rate or ratio/mark-up, such that they equal the incumbent's tariff at $t+x$.

An interesting issue concerns the regulatory setting of MTR asymmetry in the French mobile market for operators with very different market shares, viz., 45, 35 and 20 per cent. Due to VAT implications, the bill and keep arrangements between MNOs (but the fixed-to-mobile termination rates remain high) ended in 2005. MNOs set their own MTRs, and usually set at the regulated caps designated by ARCEP, the French regulator. Almost immediately, the two largest operators strategically differentiated their service prices by offering post-paid unlimited calling toward members of the same network because of the high mobile-to-mobile termination rate setting. In response, the smallest operator (Bouygues Telecom) failed to gain new subscribers when adopting the lower on-net prices of the larger operators.[6] That is, mobile subscribers expect to incur more off-net calls on joining a small network. Furthermore, due to call externalities that arise when receivers are concerned about the price borne by the callers, mobile users are more reluctant to subscribe to small networks.

Consequently, to avoid loss of market share, Bouygues had to lower its off-net price through an unlimited 'cross net' package (NEO), which allows own network subscribers to call free to any network subscriber from 8 pm to 12 am. This offer has been available since 2006.

There are several consequences arising from operator pricing strategies. At market level, Figure 14.2 illustrates the ratio of on-net traffic to total mobile-to-mobile outgoing traffic from the 1st quarter 2000 to the 4th quarter 2008. Prior to 2005, the ratio fluctuates only slightly from 62 per cent to 64 per cent; however, the ratio rose to more than 70 per cent due to the launch of unlimited offers by the larger operators. The launch of the NEO package at end-2006 appears to rebalance these traffic ratio distortions.

With the end of bill and keep arrangements, more off-net traffic from small networks is terminated in large networks than reverse direction off-net traffic. That is, because of the lower off-net price offered by Bouygues, a higher volume of off-net calls originate from the smaller MNO network than the other networks. Furthermore, the calling party pay system ensures that subscribers benefit most from Bouygues originated and terminated calls. A natural consequence is an unbalanced traffic flow between asymmetric networks due to firm pricing strategies with an enormous volume of outgoing off-net traffic from Bouygues network with a relatively small volume of incoming off-net traffic. This traffic flow required that Bouygues pay large wholesale costs which are proportional to the margins on MNO termination rates. That is, in the absence of such margins, Bouygues could avoid such financial payments for two reasons. First, the incumbent's on-net package (or

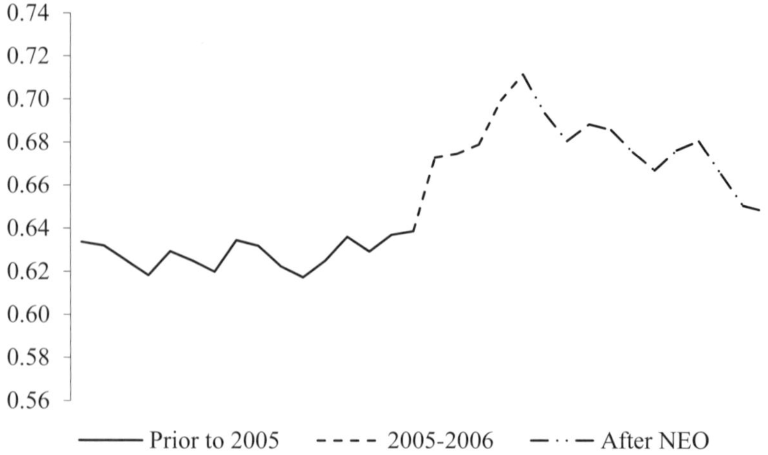

Source: ARCEP (2009).

Figure 14.2 Ratio of on-net to total mobile-to-mobile outgoing traffic

three unlimited numbers) is not justified by the competition authority. Second, Bouygues did not have to incur wholesale loss in the case of off-net traffic deficit. Consequently, ARCEP designated MTR asymmetry based not only on exogenous factors,[7] but also on a forward-looking basis that has the potential to impact on the MTR margins of Bouygues's wholesale costs due to retail market pricing strategies (See ARCEP, 2009).

EFFICACY OF EUROPEAN MTR REGULATION

This section discusses the impact of European MTR regulation. First, recent economic analyses of firm incentives over MTR settings are reviewed. Second, the principal arguments for and against implementation of glide path regulation and asymmetric MTR regulation between MNOs are discussed.

MNO Private Incentives through Termination Rates

The literature concerning the incentives for mobile operators to set own MTRs is based on models that contain different core assumptions that provide different predictions on the role of access charge setting. To simplify the following discussion firm incentives are categorised as either collusion or foreclosure.

Initially assume two symmetric MNOs that practise linear and non-discriminatory pricing of mobile service. Armstrong (1998) and Laffont *et al.* (1998a) find that MNOs choose high MTRs to weaken competition and increase joint profit. In this two asymmetric operators setting Behringer (2008) shows that high MTRs are preferable only when MNOs set the rates non-cooperatively.

MNOs often employ more sophisticated pricing structures, e.g., two-part tariff and termination-based price discrimination, and setting lower MTRs (such as bill and keep) can increase profit (Laffont *et al.*, 1998b; Gans and King, 2001). Therefore, even with a monopoly over termination, two-way access can prevent MNOs setting excessive termination rates. This result holds because mobile subscribers must bear the high MTRs for off-net calling.[8] Second, fixed fees are used to determine MNO market shares. Accordingly, high MTRs can increase revenue per subscriber and leave MNOs with an incentive to compete for market share. This intuition is clearer in the heterogeneous consumer case (Dessein, 2004; Jullien *et al.*, 2009). Authors typically assume, e.g., that post-paid subscribers call more than, e.g., prepaid subscribers. Hence, when an MTR is set low, MNOs are unlikely to compete for prepaid subscribers because of the low expected profit per subscriber. Also, recent economic analyses of two-sided markets show that it can be socially desirable to set an MTR above cost to internalise the externality on both sides, i.e., callers and receivers (see, e.g., Rochet and Tirole, 2006; Schiff, 2007).

However, this strand of the argument is not helpful in explaining the European mobile industry case in which MNOs set very high MTRs. Furthermore, setting high MTRs is considered the main cause of high off-net calling prices, and consequently tariff mediated effect that decreases the attractiveness of small MNOs (Laffont *et al.*, 1998b; Hoernig, 2007).

Accordingly, it is interesting to investigate whether large MNOs have an incentive to increase MTRs to foreclose entry when reciprocal access charge regulation is imposed.[9] At the commencement of market liberalisation, and with network effects present, there is an incentive for the incumbent to set the interconnection rate at infinity to maintain monopoly status. Following the traditional framework when two asymmetric operators set two-part prices without termination-based price discrimination the incumbent has no incentive to set MTR above-cost when reciprocity is imposed. In a slightly different model with termination-based price discrimination, Lopez and Rey (2009) argue that this possibility is likely only when the small operator is completely foreclosed. Otherwise, the incumbent makes a loss when a high reciprocal access fee is charged. However, because of the tariff mediated effects and calling club, high MTRs are a source of market power that can weaken the market share of small operators (Hoernig, 2007; Gabrielsen and Vagstad, 2008).

The Efficiency of European Asymmetric MTR Regulation

Glide-path and asymmetric fixed and mobile network regulation

Because in the Calling Party Pays (CPP) system mobile subscribers are not charged for receiving calls, regulation is required in the wholesale market because of the *bottleneck*. In particular, with the 2002 *New Regulatory Framework*, European NRAs started setting MTR caps, lowering caps gradually toward the cost of providing interconnection. Such glide path regulation can be viewed as a regulatory tool to reduce regulatory asymmetry between fixed and mobile operators.

From an economic perspective, high MTR settings in Europe can be supported for several reasons. First, in the price setting rule proposed by Ramsey the mark-up on MTR can be justified by the different consumer sensitivity to changes in call price. More precisely, as the call price elasticity for traffic initiating from a fixed network and terminated in a mobile network (fixed-to-mobile) is lower than that of reverse direction traffic (mobile-to-fixed), a mark-up on MTRs can enhance social welfare. Of course, the regulator must determine the elasticity values. However, recent economic analyses provide a wide range of values but suggest that fixed-to-mobile traffic is less elastic than outgoing traffic from mobile networks (see Elliot, 2004) because mobile and fixed networks are substitutes and more importantly, from a consumer viewpoint, the fixed telephone is less often used (rather than mobile phone) to call to other fixed subscribers because of low fixed-to-fixed call prices.

Above all, glide path regulation appears appropriate in the current context where mobile markets are becoming more saturated, which dismisses the positive role of a Pigovian tax in the presence of externalities. In particular, recent EU recommendations call for a 'sunset clause' on this form of regulatory asymmetry between fixed and mobile telephony to encourage investment by fixed operators to deploy fibre-to-the-home (FTTH) infrastructures, viz., 'The Commission decided to intervene today against these distortions of competition in the Single Market, which deter investment into upgrading fixed networks to fibre . . .'[10]

Importantly, competition authorities are aware of concerns about the impact of MTR settings on competition. In particular, with lower wholesale revenue per subscriber, lower MTRs can be employed to reduce competitiveness. Consequently, glide path regulation might lead to 'waterbed effects' whereby high retail prices result from lower MTRs. When the waterbed occurs, profitability is not substantially affected, i.e., the MNO is neutral regarding changes in MTRs (Anderson and Hansen, 2007; Schiff, 2007; Genakos and Valletti, 2008; Armstrong and Wright, 2009). In particular, Anderson and Hansen (2007) and Genakos and Valletti (2008) insist that waterbed effects probably occur in mobile networks based on empirical evidence. Genakos and Valletti (2008) select the lowest value packages of the two main MNOs in OECD Member Countries to proxy for service price and test for any link with MTRs. Genakos and Valletti show that service price increases when MTR fall, as MNOs derive less interconnection revenue implying a smaller end-subscriber transfer, and so increase retail price to rebalance profit. Anderson and Hansen (2007) with European MNO data show the impact of MTRs on operator profit is insignificant. Accordingly, glide-path regulation might not induce stronger competition, and light-hand regulation in wholesale markets should be implemented.

Finally, Baranes and Vuong (2009) provide an empirical analysis in which asymmetry between MNOs is key to explaining the differential impact of glide path regulation on MNO performance indicators, i.e., market share and EBITDA margin. In particular, they assume that European MNOs are either: incumbents or entrants. A dynamic econometric panel model shows that glide path regulation has no significant direct impact on operator profit for either group. However, since entrant market share significantly contributes to own profitability, and since glide path regulation increases entrant market share, there is an indirect increase in entrant profitability. For the incumbent group there is no corresponding indirect impact. Therefore, waterbed effect probably only applies to incumbent operators. That is, European glide path regulation induces stronger long-run competition among infrastructure-based MNOs via enhanced entrant market shares.

Asymmetric MTR between MNOs

Implementation of asymmetric regulation between MNOs varies among Member States as it depends on the relative magnitudes of operator MTRs. Especially such asymmetric regulation disappears when MTRs are regulated at provisioning costs, or when the MTRs of recent entrants are set at early entrant levels. Currently, asymmetric regulation is being implemented in most European Member Countries.[11]

By way of contrast, asymmetric MTR regulation is not based on solid economic foundations (Valletti, 2006). With an absence of empirical evidence, there are several theoretically motivated potential drawbacks to asymmetric MTR regulation. First, in the presence of a wholesale advantage, an entrant might not be required to compete with the incumbent. This is especially relevant when NRAs set MTR asymmetry based on operator market shares. Hence asymmetric MTR regulation may not provide the conditions for rent-seeking behaviour.

However, entrants do not always benefit from asymmetrically set MTRs. Large MTR asymmetries may increase the perceived cost to the incumbent of off-net calling and likely induce further on-net/off-net price discrimination. Also, when incoming off-net traffic is very elastic, raising MTRs also harm entrant wholesale profits. Second, entrants prefer low incumbent MTR asymmetry. This issue relates to the social desirability of asymmetric regulation. According to Peitz (2005a, b) asymmetric MTR regulation is not socially desirable in the short-run although it is an appropriate instrument through which to increase entrant market shares and long-run competition. In Peitz's model, due to late entry, the incumbent provides a higher reservation price. This difference is fixed[12] and acts as a parameter for the asymmetry between the networks.

Hence, implementation of asymmetric regulation whereby incumbents are obliged to provide cost-based MTRs and entrants can set MTR at above cost, increases consumer surplus via more aggressive pricing. Furthermore, under asymmetric regulation, entrant network size increases whereas the incumbent network is reduced, thus lowering social surplus. The reason is simple. Due to the fixed asymmetric reservation level, implementing asymmetric MTRs leads to distortions in market structure in which the entrant acquires too much market share. Peitz suggests that in these circumstances asymmetric regulation should be replaced by symmetric regulation where feasible.[13] Baranes and Vuong (2009), construct an asymmetric MTR regulation index[14] which is proportional to MTR differences and relative operator market shares. The index positively impacts on entrant operations, but negatively on incumbent profitability.

From the normative economic viewpoint, however, these findings do not mean that asymmetry should be set exceptionally high because of potential harm from tariff mediated effects due to stronger on-net/off-net price differentials set by the incumbent. Rather, this study provides evidence to support asymmetric MTR setting in the current European mobile industry context.

CONCLUDING REMARKS

This chapter argues that the setting of asymmetric termination rate regulation between fixed and mobile operators, and different size MNOs, should be replaced by symmetric regulation. In principle, asymmetric regulation is only appropriate when there is a demonstrated need. Furthermore, the regulator should reduce asymmetry via a glide path with MNOs well established in the market. This approach avoids the 'cash cow' problem and allows the incumbent to invest, especially in further deploying the FTTH network.

Another consideration is distortion in the MTR. In this case implementing asymmetric MTR regulation is necessary when MTRs are above cost or there are tariff-mediated effects. It may be that both types of asymmetric regulation can be replaced by symmetric regulation simultaneously. This situation is relevant in an environment in which fixed and mobile services offered by a

MNO and the incumbent become closer substitutes; and in the context when important investments are required to deploy further network infrastructure by all players.

NOTES

1. Lieberman and Montgomery (1988) discuss first-mover advantage.
2. Dunnewijk and Hultén (2007) provide a history of European mobile communications.
3. By October 2008, the average MTR in Europe is as high as 8.55 Euro centimes. While ARCEP, the French telecommunication regulator, estimate mobile termination costs around 3-4 Euro centimes, and 1-2 Euro centimes based on an efficient operator concept introduced by the European Commission. See: http://europa.eu/rapid/pressReleases Action.do?reference=IP/09/710.
4. The French telecommunications market is unique with bill and keep implemented between French MNOs until 2004 because of State tax implications. See more discussion on asymmetric regulation between mobile and fixed networks in Bomsel *et al.* (2003).
5. Retail markets are monitored by competition policy.
6. Bouygues already offered an on-net package, called Millennium, allowing its mobile users to call unlimitedly not to three or five, but to all numbers subscribed to the same network.
7. These include entry delays, different spectrum allocation cost.
8. In this case, per minute price is set at the perceived cost (see Laffont *et al.* 1998b).
9. In the context of the European mobile telecommunications industry, allowing large MNOs to increase their MTRs above that of small MNOs is inappropriate with the objective of creating long-run competition between infrastructure MNOs.
10. Stated by EU Telecommunications Commissioner Viviane Reding (Europa, 2009, p. 2).
11. For example, the Swedish regulator implemented symmetric regulation in 2005.
12. This is a crucial assumption in modeling network asymmetry. Initiated by Carter and Wright (2003) the assumption is often used with different interpretations including switching cost and brand loyalty.
13. Clearly, Peitz considers more situations than cost-based asymmetric regulation.
14. The entrant i asymmetric *MTR* index is the *MTR* difference between i and j, multiplied by corresponding relative market shares, i.e., $AR_{i,t}^{E} = \sum_{j}[MTR_{i,t} - MTR_{j,t}](\alpha_{i,t} / \alpha_{j,t})$.

REFERENCES

Albon, R. (2006), 'Fixed-to-Mobile Substitution, Complementarity and Convergence', *Agenda*, **16**, 309–22.

Albon, R. and York, R. (2005), 'Should Mobile Subscription be Subsidised in Mature Markets?', *Telecommunications Policy*, **32**, 294–306.

Anderson, K. and Hansen, B. (2007), 'Network Competition: Empirical Evidence on Mobile Termination Charges and Profitability', Working Paper. Retrieved from: http://home.bi.no/a0510011/Papers/Andersson_Hansen_MTRempirics_april_2009.pdf.

ARCEP (2009), Décision 08-1176. Retrieved from: http://circa.europa.eu/Public/irc/infso/ecctf/library?l=/france/adoptedmeasures/fr20080812/08-1176pdf/_FR_1.0_&a=d.

Armstrong, M. (1998), 'Network Interconnection in Telecommunications', *Economic Journal*, **108**, 545–64.

Armstrong, M. and Wright, J. (2009), 'Mobile Call Termination', *Economic Journal*, **199**, 270–307.

Baranes, E. and Vuong, H. (2009), 'How Does European Termination Rate Regulation Impact Mobile Operator Performance?', Working Paper, University of Montpellier, France.

Behringer, S. (2008), 'Asymmetric Equilibria and Non-Cooperative Access Pricing in Telecommunications'. Retrieved from: http://mpra.ub.uni-muenchen.de/11795/.

Benzoni, L. and Geoffron, P. (2007), *Competition and Regulation with Asymmetries: The Case of Mobile*, Paris: QUANTIFICA Publishing.

Bijwaard, G., Maarten, C. and Emiel, M. (2008), 'Early Mover Advantages: An Empirical Analysis of European Mobile Phone Markets', *Telecommunications Policy*, **32**, 246–61.

Bomsel, O., Cave, M., Le Blanc, G. and Neumann, K. (2003), 'How Mobile Termination Charges Shape the Dynamic of the Telecom Sector', Final Report, *WIK Consult*.

Carter, M. and Wright, J. (2003), 'Asymmetric Network Interconnection', *Review of Industrial Organization*, **22**, 27–46.

Dessein, W. (2004), 'Network Competition with Heterogeneous Customers and Calling Patterns', *Information Economics and Policy*, **16**, 323–45.

Dunnewijk, T. and Hultén, S. (2007), 'A Brief History of Mobile Communication in Europe', *Telematics and Informatics*, **24**, 164–79.

Elliot, D. (2004), 'Two-way Access Charges and On-net/Off-net Differentials: What are The Incentives on Operators and can Large MNOs Use High Access Charges to Foreclose the Market?'. Retrieved from: http://www.frontiereconomics.com/publications/en/88.pdf .

ERG (2008), ERG's Common Position on Symmetry of Fixed Call Termination Rates and Symmetry of Mobile Call Termination Rates (ERG (07)83 final 080312). Retrieved from: http://www.irg.eu/streaming/erg_07_83_mtr_ftr_cp_12_03_08.pdf?contentId=543020&field=ATTACHED_FILE.

EU (2008, June), Draft Commission Recommendation on The Regulatory Treatment of Fixed and Mobile Termination Rates in The EU. Brussels: EU Commission.

Europa (2006, April 6), 'Infringement Proceedings in the Field of Telecoms and Electronic Communications: What Are the Issues at Stake in This Round?'. Retrieved from: http://europa.eu/rapid/pressReleasesAction.do?reference=MEMO/06/158&format=PDF&aged=1&language=EN&guiLanguage=en.

Europa (2009, May 7), 'Telecoms: Commission Acts on Termination Rates to Boost Competition'. Retrieved from: http://europa.eu/rapid/pressReleasesAction.do?reference=MEMO/06/158&format=PDF&aged=1&language=EN&guiLanguage=en.

European Commission (2002), 'Eighth Report on the Implementation of the Telecommunications Regulatory Package', Brussels, European Commission.

European Commission (2003), 'Ninth Report on the Implementation of the Telecommunications Regulatory Package', Brussels, European Commission.

European Commission (2004), 'Tenth Report on the Implementation of the Telecommunications Regulatory Package', Brussels, European Commission.

European Commission (2005), 'Eleventh Report on the Implementation of the Telecommunications Regulatory Package', Brussels, European Commission.

European Commission (2006), 'Twelfth Report on the Implementation of the Telecommunications Regulatory Package', Brussels, European Commission.

European Commission (2007), 'Thirteenth Report on the Implementation of the Telecommunications Regulatory Package', Brussels, European Commission.

Gabrielsen, T. and Vagstad, S. (2008), 'Why is On-net Traffic Cheaper than Off-net Traffic? Access Mark-up as a Collusive Device', *European Economic Review*, **52**, 99–115.

Gans, J. and King, S. (2001), 'Using "Bill and Keep" Interconnection Arrangements to Soften Network Competition', *Economic Letters*, **71**, 413–20.

Genakos, C. and Valletti, T. (2008), 'Testing the "Waterbed" Effect in Mobile Telephony', CEIS Working Paper No. 110. Retrieved from: http://papers.ssrn. com /sol3/papers.cfm?abstract_id=1114856##.

Hoernig, S. (2007), 'On-net and Off-Net Pricing on Asymmetric Telecommunications Networks', *Information Economics and Policy*, 19, 171–88.

Jullien, B., Rey, P. and Sand-Zantman, W. (2009), 'Mobile Call Termination Revisited', IDEI Working Paper. Retrieved from: http://www.idei.fr/doc/wp/ 2009/mobile_callsept09.pdf.

Laffont, J., Rey, P. and Tirole, J. (1998a), 'Network Competition: I. Overview and Non-discriminatory Pricing', *RAND Journal of Economics*, **29**, 1–37.

Laffont, J., Rey, P. and Tirole, J. (1998b), 'Network Competition: II. Price Discrimination', *RAND Journal of Economics*, **29**, 38–56.

Lieberman, M. and Montgomery, D. (1988), 'First-mover Advantages', *Strategic Management Journal*, **9**, 41–58.

Lopez, A. and Rey, P. (2009), 'Foreclosing Competition through Access Charges and Price Discrimination', FEEM Working Paper 2009.99. Retrieved from: http://www.feem.it/userfiles/attach/20091119122514499-09.pdf.

Peitz, M. (2005a), 'Asymmetric Access Price Regulation in Telecommunications Markets', *European Economic Review*, **49**, 341–58.

Peitz, M. (2005b), 'Asymmetric Regulation of Access and Price Discrimination in Telecommunications', *Journal of Regulatory Economics*, **28**, 327–43.

Rochet, J. and Tirole, J. (2006), 'Two Sided Markets: A Progress Report', *RAND Journal of Economics*, **37**, 645–67.

Schiff, A. (2007), 'The "Waterbed" Effect and Price Regulation'. Retrieved from: http://ssrn.com/abstract=905172.

Schmalensee, R. (1984), 'Statement of Richard Schmalensee', Attachment 4 to Comments of AT&T in CC Docket No. 83-1147.

Valletti, T. (2006), 'Asymmetric Regulation of Mobile Termination Rates'. Retrieved from: http://www.npt.no/ikbViewer/Content/100464/Vedlegg_Telenor.pdf.

Vogelsang, I. (2003), 'Price Regulation of Access to Telecommunications Networks', *Journal of Economic Literature*, **41**, 830–62.

15. The absence of data for measuring the economic impact of IT in the US

Shane Greenstein

INTRODUCTION

In this chapter, I would like to assess the statistical foundations for addressing the most central economics question in Internet studies: what is the contribution of the Internet to economic growth in the United States (US) over the last decade? What will be its contribution over the next decade? My underlying motivation is that I believe statistics can inform policy debates. I make that statement as an empiricist. I have observed that economic statistics are a foundation for policy formulation in a multitude of areas.

Here is the problem: there is no shortage of Internet policy debate, but there is a shortage of facts. To be precise: there is a shortage of meaningful data. When a meaningful statistic is available it quickly becomes central to a debate. I have observed this shortage in debates about: inequality of access and use of the Internet; effect of the Internet on international trade; changing requirements for human capital accumulation in information technology markets; and the spread of electronic government.

Let me begin with a narrow motivation. The privatisation of the Internet – an event that the National Science Foundation (NSF) managed more than a decade ago – is one of the greatest gifts to the US and world economy to ever come from the US research community. Wouldn't someone love to say – with some degree of confidence – what the contribution of the Internet was to the US economy? To be sure, it is not a straightforward question to address. One must account for incremental changes from investment. Actually, it is even harder than usual (for a new technology), because one must account for all increases in productivity, as well as, the wastefulness that occurred during the boom and bust. Still, doesn't that seem like a comparatively important question to address? It turns out: we do not know the answer. More to the point, we do know pieces of it, but many pieces remain unexamined. Worse yet, there is no lively debate about the remaining open questions because scholars do not have the data to find out.

This chapter has a simple and broad point. The state of statistical information about the information economy in the US is rather mediocre. There are oases of excellence, but these are rare and not the norm. What is my benchmark for 'mediocre'? I say that primarily in comparison to other industries, e.g., cement and concrete. We have marvellous statistical data about thousands of cement and concrete plants throughout the US, as well as the users in many locales. We know a lot about the price of cement and concrete, productivity improvement in cement and concrete, the contribution of these firms to the tax base of their local economy, and, even how much they contribute to pollution in a locality. It goes on and on.

In Internet studies, by contrast, we have little comparable data about the prices, quality, taxes, employment or revenues. The frontier of research is still at a descriptive level because we do not have the data. For instance, we would like to know how economic growth changes when there is more broadband competition, but we cannot answer that because we do not know how firms respond to additional competition, or how demand responds to lower prices, higher quality and more rapid investment. In fact, we are not sure how many cities in the US have competitive broadband markets. According to industry engineers the problems run deep: we also do not know the patterns for the basic flows of traffic across the entire network. Even if we had good information about the 'branches' of the network, we are not sure whether (or how much) it would alter the quality of experience of users in a particular location on the network. We simply know a lot more about the economics of cement and concrete than about the economics of the Internet. That is because we have data about one market and do not have the data to learn more about the other.

In this chapter I will be describing the state of data. I will concentrate on the US situation, and discuss examples. My view is that we are watching an industry much like the railroad industry in 1885. By that point it was obvious to any waking observer that something dramatic was afoot, but putting together the entire picture was quite challenging. The problem was basic: the object under study changed quickly, and the problems kept getting worse because nobody documented a base year. As a result, there was not much data for documenting change over time. The community of interested users and data-collectors was largely voluntary in that era, and together they worked to improve, modify, or initiate statistical studies.

More to the point, political actors and research community did not invest in improving data collection. In that era, as now, it must have been difficult to make informed policy about the changing nature of tax collection in localities and at a national level, about the likelihood of productivity improvements across industries and locations, about changes occurring in inter-state trade, about changes in the location of economic activity, about changes in workforce requirements – in other words, about the basic parameters of economic policy.

The review proceeds as follows. First, I provide an overview of the statistical issues in the US. Next, I provide a case study to illustrate issues. This involves explaining some of the issues in the official US price index for Internet access and some basic open issues in broadband policy. Throughout I try to identify places where basic research has high value if it simply documents what is happening in a way that permits comparison over time.

GAPS IN THE STATE OF KNOWLEDGE

What type of data is required to address a basic question about the contribution of information and telecommunications technology (ICT) to the US economy? To address this fundamental question an economic researcher needs:

- An ideal data set that contains measures of variation in investment in computing and communications hardware and software, as well as provide a reasonable measurement of labour force employment. That allows researchers to identify how much information technology (IT) matters for firm performance.
- The Bureau of Economic Analysis (BEA) publishes an estimate of investment levels in ICT by industry for some recent years, and recently began publishing estimates about the wages and numbers of IT workers in some locales. The situation is better than it used to be, and many scholars have taken advantage of it.
- Brynjolfsson et al. (2002), as well as Forman et al. (2002), have made estimate for the use of ICTs or the Internet by business in 2000. Also, Arora and Forman (2007) have made estimates of local software service economies. Mark Doms has several studies that look at estimating PC use in business establishments. The CRITO research group at University of California, Irvine has also done some original survey work.
- It would be ideal to have reasonable measurement of variation in use of broadband services, between industries on average, and between firms within the same industry. This also requires some 'controls' for whether the equipment was owned by an establishment or rented from providers for monthly fees, both of which are common. As far as I know, no consistent historical data exist on this.
- Why does historical data matter? Here 'historical' usually means 'consistent time series over the last ten years'. When Forman et al.

(2002) estimated differences in use of the Internet across industries we went looking for prior census on IT use across industries. Even something from the mid-1980s would have been fine. We could not find any such list, and only much later did we learn of a project that came close – i.e., Ed Wolff's Herculean research project tracing changes in demand for information workers across post-WWII industries, using a Machlup framework. Why does this matter? Using our data we could not say, with any degree of confidence, whether the diffusion of the Internet had fundamentally altered the buying patterns for ICTs across the US economy. Hence, a fundamental question went unaddressed.

Many economic policy issues would improve with data about the geographic variation across the US economy. Many facets of electronic commerce, such as broadband or contract programming or local-area-network maintenance for hire, are inherently a local service. Their direct impact should be local. However, only some cities have robust markets for such services. It would be useful to know why this variation matters.

- For measuring the direct effect on economic growth in a metropolitan area, a researcher needs to know the availability and (especially) use by business establishments of these technologies.
- First research on this topic in Internet studies examined the registrations of domain names, including work by Zook (www.zook.info) and Kolko (www.ppic.org/main/bio.asp?i=312). Once again, the more recent work by Forman et al.[1] also tried to catalogue how areas differed. We eventually found there was plenty of good company with work by Ken Flamm[2], Tony Grubesic[3] and James Preiger[4] among others. A number of economic geographers and city planners examined related issues. Again, this is progress, but many issues are unresolved.
- When the broadband debate gained traction, policy advocates were 'shocked' to learn that they knew so little. Yet, this had been the norm for some time. Does the availability of broadband encourage entry of businesses into a local area? How does the provision of multiple suppliers affect pricing and productivity of local firms? Do these investments help some types of industries grow, and if so, which ones? In general, we did not know the answer to such questions a few years ago and we still do not.
- It remains an open question whether regional differences in using the Internet at home affects local economic conditions. Most researchers believe it does, but that is hard to measure in practice. Here is an illustration as to why: A recent Northwestern University dissertation

examined whether differences in the diffusion of the Internet altered the prices paid for airline tickets from cities. As it turned out, the answer is a long story. Yes, the Internet did make a difference, mostly at the mid and upper tail of the distribution of prices paid, but not everywhere on every route. However, to see it more clearly, one had to control for the 'Southwest' effect and the 'hub home' effect, and so on.
- Other recent work has started to see if there are price effects in other areas of the economy where we might expect to find it, such as bookstores, travel agencies, newspapers, and so on. Once again, there remains much to do.

From this brief overview it is apparent that the situation is not void of data. Rather, this is an area of study where anecdotal data typically support an imprecise impression. It is the type of environment in which a lazy investigator gives up on quickly, and a good analyst finds considerable room for speculation. More to the point, policy analysts and researchers are frustrated because these data usually cannot support inferential or predictive models with any precision, so it becomes difficult to guide policy choices.

There is variation around this trend, of course. To appreciate that variation one should be more precise about what is there. I begin with macroeconomic data then consider more micro-policy questions:

- The BEA attempted for some time to improve the situation. For example, the BEA now has estimates of differences in IT investment across industries. These data are largely contained in Jorgensen et al.'s (2006) extensive analysis of the contribution of IT to the US economy. BEA is also attempting to develop serious estimates about differences in labour markets for programmers across the US. Both of these are recent improvements.
- However, these sets of data measure IT investment at a broad level. Namely, they do not specify anything special about the Internet or technical advances in any of the sub-components of ICT. This precision about the statistics shapes the interpretation. These data are useful for learning about whether investment in ICT matters, not about whether technical change in ICT produces growth or productivity advance. For the latter concern, one needs to collect statistics that distinguish between personal computers (PC), router, software, type of software, and so on.
- It should be noted that these BEA data are a distinct improvement on earlier available information. These data come from programs initiated in cooperation with other federal agencies, such as the US Census and the Bureau of Labor Statistics (BLS). Such data collection efforts require planning, foresight, employee effort, and especially, funds for conducting surveys.

- Next, I consider challenges about whether these data are accurate. First and foremost, economic research must alter the historical focus on counting hardware as the primary source of value. Much of the value in a device resides in the underlying software. Second, much of the expense in a business resides in maintaining the hardware and software, but that frames the question: how should such expense go in the national accounts? It is just like an investment that seeks to prevent depreciation of assets due to deterioration, but it seems strange to treat human labour as capital expense rather than a variable production cost. Third, valuation questions are difficult. For instance, how does one value custom software? What is the deflator? The market value for software does not need to reflect its service value if the market price declines due to technological obsolescence. At what rate does the value of packaged software decline if its service flow does not decline?
- Just recently these initiatives led to the first survey of software at firms (not the level of the establishment). This is motivated by a desire to bring software into the estimates of capital accounts in the US. Figuring this out for just one year, 2003, was almost impossible, even using the best statistical agencies in the world, the US Census. Even the practical issues are mind-boggling. For example, who is the right person to ask in a company when there is no CIO, and how should the US Census phrase their questions?
- Many multi-establishment companies have only the vaguest estimates of how much software they own and operate across all their establishments, so how much faith should the Census put in a survey answer? Given the uncertainty for specific firms, how should the Census weight the results to make estimates for the entire economy? Of course, figuring out differences between industries, for example, is near impossible. Census is trying to improve what they do, but nobody has any ambitions for developing a precise estimate for the growth in software nationwide, one year to the next. Maybe we will get one off changes every few years.
- Overall, the state of economic knowledge about the stock of software in the US is a lot like the experts declaring that the universe is expanding, but they are unsure about the rate of expansion. Yes, the universe could be expanding a little or a lot, but there is no way to know yet.

This state has implications for some of the topics Internet researchers wish to address. For example, measurement of the productivity improvement from investment in ICTs is questioned about the extent of mismeasurement at the foundations of the exercise. And the answers go to the heart of analysis looking at the timing of economic change, whether investment yields economic benefits today or tomorrow, whether the macro economy shapes investments today, and so on. If anybody thinks this type of question is trivial, please recall that Alan Greenspan wanted to know in his own day whether investments in ICTs would yield high returns and whether the returns were measured well or not. The answer shaped whether he tried to keep interest rates low enough to encourage such investment. Greenspan decided the returns were high and under-measured, and for numerous reasons kept interest rates low – that is, during the dot-com bubble, then started to raise them after December, 1999, as it began to burst. If advances in ICTs continue to emerge (as most of us expect), then the same questions will continue to dog future chairs of the Federal Reserve.

Related, in the present era there is a call to learn about the growth in availability of broadband, as well as its use and quality. This is probably a feasible project for a US federal agency with experience conducting large surveys, like the US Census. However, to be fair, the 'dark matter' issues with software are a bigger priority because, quite frankly, it involves more money and has been mismeasured for quite a long time. Also, in a time of limited budgets to collect data, it is quite understandable why that remains the priority.

Which motivates a related question: Until such time as budgets free up, what data can researchers use?

- Outside CRITO surveys the best available data about business ICT use is the data provided by Harte-Hanks, which conducts a private survey of ICT use by business. Several groups of researchers have used this survey. To be fair, this data is reasonably good at measuring big discrete things, such as whether a business establishment uses the Internet (though, it is not particularly good at measuring 'how much'). This survey is not designed for academic economic research. Its quality for marketing is fine, but for our purposes the quality of the survey is deteriorating, especially recently, because certain data are no longer collected. Since economic researchers are rather small purchasers of these data, why should a private marketing company care about public policy uses of its data?

Finally, I must mention two initiatives at the US Census.

- First, there is a special survey conducted by the US Census on electronic commerce use at business establishments. It was a supplemental survey in 1999 of networking use by 10 per cent of US manufacturing establishments. B.K. Atrostic and colleagues at the Centre for Economic Studies have made some excellent analysis of that data. However, the survey is not economy wide nor followed with additional surveys. This situation is not ideal. For example, we do not know anything comparable about what has happened to the finance sector of the US economy, which is among the biggest users of advanced IT in the US economy. We also do not know much about IT use in the health care, services and education sectors, or warehousing, transportation services, and government agencies. Importantly, this survey will soon become rather obsolete for contemporary policy formulation.

- Second, Census has undertaken regular estimates of electronic commerce across industries. These estimates began in 2000 and have continued since. This E-Stats[5] project provides estimates of electronic shipments and revenues for many four digit industries. It is an admirable initiative, and has improved the situation. At the same time, the numbers are limited. They are large enough to suggest that the amount of dark matter must be large. They also suggest that big changes are afoot in some industries. It is less clear how to relate these data on electronic commerce to changes in productivity and concerns about economic growth. As far as I know, so far nobody has tried.

A more remarkable statistical accomplishment has been in areas concerned with the availability and use of the Internet by households. We have good statistics about household use.

- Probably the most widely used statistic is one compiled by the BLS about the adoption of the Internet by households. Collection of this statistic started in 1997, as an additional question to a supplement to a regular survey of households. This supplement had been devoted to finding out about PC use at household in 1995, so it was naturally and easily retargeted at Internet use. The basic results are widely reported in a series of reports published by the NTIA in the Department of Commerce. At some point virtually every researcher in this area has used these data.
- This series is the best continuously collected historical statistics about changes over time in the US. It uses BLS sampling procedures, which have been refined for years and, as a result, it is trusted that they are representative samples of the US – which is not a trivial feature, because it allows one to weight results for national averages without major concern about biases. The sample is also large enough, so the underlying data give large 'cells' for the two hundred largest metropolitan areas. However, these surveys do not contain good data about prices, expenditures or service quality. Many questions are discontinued. The survey also asks only basic questions about what users do on-line. Sociologists of the on-line world find the data completely uninformative about the issues they consider central. This triumph is tinged with recent absurdity. This survey continued until a few years ago, though it is my understanding that there is no plan to

continue it further. To most of us in this area this decision looks myopic to the point of tragic.

- This tragedy is partially averted by charity. Another survey is under way, by the Pew Charitable Trust, about household use of the Internet. It asks extensive questions, even more than the government survey, about what users do with their Internet, so it is quite informative about the changing nature of the on-line experience for Americans in the new millennium. John Horrigan, the principal researcher in charge, allows other researchers to examine this data, and has initiated several projects, including with Ken Flamm.
- What else can be done? A small group of researchers has also used household surveys conducted by Forester, a consulting company. Goolsbee and Klenow (2002) and Sinai and Waldfogel (2005) have made progress. A recent student at Northwestern, Jeff Prince (2004), now faculty at Cornell, also used this data for his dissertation on PC purchasing. Occasionally researchers have been able to get reasonable data of surfing behaviour from private firms such as Media Matrix.
- Related to this last set of comments, there is a small and growing literature among academics about the interplay between electronic retailing and brick-and-mortar retailing, occasionally with household behaviour included, often with a marketing question motivating the investigation. Virtually all that data come from non-government data collectors, or directly from companies. There is also a larger and still growing academic literature on Internet auctions, mostly about eBay. Virtually all that data come from 'spiders'. To my knowledge, there has not been much connection between this literature and government collected data about economy wide trends in electronic commerce. There also has not been an attempt to connect these papers back to the fundamental concerns about productivity.

When it comes to describing the availability of the Internet – in other words, who offers what service for what price and in what locations – the situation is mediocre. During the dial-up era a quirk in the telephone system helped researchers, but during the broadband era the situation has become worse.

- The best data on the availability of dial-up Internet access in the US is for the period 1996-1998. Downes and Greenstein (2002, 2007) located every commercial Internet provider in the US (the area code and prefix for a firm had an association with a unique telephone switch in a unique local calling area). The last map involved over 65,000 phone numbers. Mapping stopped after the fall of 1998. To my knowledge, nobody has tried again except in a few special places like the Appalachians and the Mississippi delta or West Texas. It is also my impression that some state development agencies know about their own situation, but there is no general sharing of this information across agencies. This is still a relevant question since broadband has failed to deploy in many low density areas, but nobody knows how good is the quality of access in such areas, especially for alternatives such as upgraded cell phones.

- The FCC publishes data on the availability of broadband across the country.[6] It ostensibly measures how many providers offer broadband in specific zip codes. It recently began to distinguish between use at households and business, and it does give state statistics. However, it does not say anything about the geographic scope of availability within a zip code, nor does it say much about the size of the firms making these offers, nor about their prices. It recently added some coarse information about bandwidth, which is a mild improvement.
- Of course, bandwidth is not the same as speed at the end point. How fast a response does a gamer get to a ping sent out to another player in another part of the country? That depends on the bandwidth of the connection to the end-point, to be sure, but it also depends on the quality of the connection, routing, and so on, and it will also vary at different times of the day. When engineers complain that they know little about the quality of the network in the US, this is in part what they mean. As it turns out, Flamm and Chaudhuri (2006) use the data about availability. This data does not particularly measure availability well without a lot of effort by a researcher, which means the published data are historically inaccurate about the details of how broadband diffused.
- The deployment of Wi-Fi is proceeding apace for some years now. There are on-line sites listing which cities have deployed city-sponsored networks. There are also a few studies of the deployment in some neighbourhoods in Los Angeles and Chicago and a few other cities (basically showing that rich neighbourhoods have more). National statistical agencies have not followed this in detail. Christian Sandvig is one of the leading researchers in that area. We know some basic things, but we do not know about the patterns of deployment across the country. The amount of dark matter has to be large because the equipment providers tell us they are doing a good business, but beyond that it is hard to tell what has happened.

PRICING INTERNET ACCESS: AN ILLUSTRATION

Let me end with an illustration of the state of things. I use the price of Internet access as the example. I want to do this because this aforementioned list of issues is long and somewhat general. I thought a very specific example might help illustrate the broader issues in play.

No statistic would seem to be as important as knowing the price of the Internet. After all, prices are the bread and butter of economics, the primary signal that markets have for indicating scarcity. You might reasonably respond: how can the Internet have a price attached to it? As it turns out, there is such a price. It is called the price index for Internet access.

The price of Internet access attracts interest for two reasons. First, the value of the Internet is unknown. The access price is one place where most users give up money in exchange for free Internet services. During the first decade of the commercial Internet the typical household spends more than three quarters of the time on-line at free or advertising supported sites.[7] Second, most of the value from the Internet is embodied in this index. Other than through access fees, there is little data from which to infer user's valuation of these sites. This component of the Web, i.e., access fees – also produced the highest fraction of total market value in the first decade of the commercial Internet. Though subscription based services are growing, the revenues spent on access fees swamp subscription services in magnitude. Fees for advertising are also growing and may exceed access revenue soon, but for the first decade they did not.[8]

The official price index for Internet access in the CPI started in late-1997, reasonably early in the market's growth (an initiative of the BLS). In 1998 the access market was a US$10.8 billion industry, with roughly half that revenue coming from access fees. At 2004 it is a US$24 billion industry.[9] In other words, it is growing. Again, that growth highlights the importance of deflating revenues properly. Is the true growth much large or much smaller than the changes in nominal growth of revenues?

Table 15.1 contains a summary of prices for Internet access in the US.[10] This is the number one would use to deflate the growth in revenue over time to figure out how much of the growth was real and nominal, with the latter being denominated in constant dollars, as any introductory economics textbook says we ought to. I want to indicate the issues with this table.

Table 15.1 US Internet access price index[11]

Year	12/97	12/98	12/99	12/00	12/01	12/02	12/03	12/04	12/05
Index	100	103.3	96.0	95.7	100.3	99.6	97.6	97.2	94.2

Table 15.1 says that the price of the Internet has declined by less than 6 per cent in 8 years. At the same time, this is not the price movement usually associated with the diffusion of a revolutionary technology. More to the point, this index seems almost unrelated to the improved experience of virtually every on-line surfer.

You might be concerned that this index has some error in it. To sharpen the focus on the right issue, consider several other closely related categories of good from the same BLS sources. During the same time period the official price indices for the US had the following patterns: computer software and accessories went down 42 per cent; personal computers and peripheral equipment (which adjusts for quality) went down 88 per cent; telephone hardware and calculators and related consumer items went down 55 per cent; and wireless telephone services went down 35 per cent. These patterns lead one to conclude that there was much price change in everything except the Internet. How can it be that Internet access did not get cheaper, but cell phones did, phone equipment did, PCs did, and software did?

First, let's be up front about the accuracy of these data: This data set is collected with exactly the same procedures as those used to collect the other indices. On one basic level, it does exactly what it is supposed to do. It is procedurally correct. Conversely, it includes some measurement error. To put it blithely, it does not adjust for quality. Some of this is straightforward to recognize though difficult to correct, such as adjusting for upgrades in bandwidth, as from 28k to 56k, (which largely occurred in 1998 and 1999), or from 56k to broadband speeds of varying qualities and availability (which is occurring since 2001). Some of it is quite subtle and difficult to correct. For example, how should the BLS measure quality when new broadband comes on-line, and half the country switches to this new source in a short period? Some issues are probably impossible to solve. For instance, the index does not adjust for the quality of the many free compliments over this time period, such as in the search engine Google or the portal Yahoo!

These errors are not the fault of the person who collects and compiles the data. They are doing exactly what they are supposed to, making a time series for the Internet that is comparable to any other price series, using the data collected by standard BLS procedures (which weight highly the prices of large and stable providers, such as AOL). The fault lies with the lack of funds to initiate anything else, and with a very conservative philosophy throughout statistical agencies in the US, who do not want to be criticized by overseers for even a slight deviation in procedures (or industry associations – yes, this does happen with alarming frequency).

While that may seem like a small thing, this little error shows up in all sorts of ways. For example, because the rate of growth in the revenues do not appear particularly high (as they are not properly deflated for improvement in quality) I have heard some macroeconomists maintain that the contribution of the Internet to the economy is small or, if large, short-lived. That conclusion is correct in a literal way, based on the data available, unless one recognizes the error in collection. And that is my point: Unless a researcher is a super expert, it is hard to recognize. Should all Internet economists ask all the macroeconomic experts in the country to be experts on the mismeasurement of broadband in the official US price index for the Internet? Of course not, we should fix it so they reach the correct conclusion when they read the numbers literally.

Think about another historical implication of that simple observation: it is one thing to say the Internet bubble was a short-lived phenomenon equal to the tulip craze in Holland centuries ago; it is quite another to say that the Internet bubble was similar to other halting ups and downs that accompanied the building of the railroads. In the first case, little economic value was created. In the latter, enormous value was created, albeit not in a calm fashion. Right now, a literal reading of the data favours the former interpretation. Most Internet insiders think that is wrong, but we do not have much data to support our case.

As another example of the difficulty with measuring prices, recently the OECD tried to issue a comparison of prices for broadband across countries, which is an ambitious and useful thing to do. Of course, the exercise is full of footnotes and qualifications, not only because the researchers are careful, but for a simple reason: there was not comparable data available across countries for even the most basic service, the price of access. Imagine how much more useful this would have been if such data were abundant?

My broad point is that something as basic as the price index for Internet access is far from perfect, but it is extremely useful. More broadly, something as basic as this has not standardized the basic definitions for price, quality and its changes over time. Is it any surprise that so much else has been neglected as well?

As one epilogue, I might add this: the recent announcements by AOL about change to its pricing – it is moving to advertising supported service in response to losing customers to broadband – will bring this index down dramatically for the first time in a long time. As of this writing, the index fell from 93.1 in September of 2007 to 77.2 in December, 2007. This is the most dramatic thing that has happened to these data over several months since the summer of 1999, when AOL attempted to give price breaks to former CompuServe users after AOL merged with CompuServe. It is a good thing if this index falls. However, the timing is all wrong. It excessively weights the behaviour of the large and established firms, such as AOL, missing the other dramatic things that have already occurred, such as half the country switching to broadband. It has delayed recording the timing of a change, putting the dramatic fall in prices many years too late.

UNANSWERED QUESTIONS

One might reasonably ask whether any of this absence of data matters. After all, maybe it is quite fine that we know more about cement and concrete than ICT in a world where we only have so much time and money to spend on collecting statistics. Maybe the basic building block for highways is more important for the economy than the basic building block for information superhighways. In response, let me give a little personal anecdote and generalize from it.

The OECD occasionally publishes a statistic comparing Internet household adoption across many countries. The last time this occurred it sent a few US Congressmen into panic because Korea, Iceland and a dozen other countries came out with larger numbers than the US. As a result, a few news reporters found the topic interesting and then searched around to call someone. Occasionally, I fielded that phone call.

The very first thing to say to a reporter is this: cross country differences in household adoption of broadband tells us about the marginal adopter and that is about it. That is useful, but not the end of the story. It is not especially informative about use by the intensive user, which are the users who generate most of the traffic. It also does not tell us about business adoption and use of broadband, which is where the productivity gains come from. Moreover, it is uninformative about the productivity impact of the Internet, because, once again, the biggest impact to productivity will come from the large adopters. I could go on, but the basic conclusion is straightforward. This index is but one piece of data. It is good to have, but it is not very informative about all of the important questions of our time.

Suffice to say, most major US newspapers have not run headlines declaring 'OECD statistic is helpful but ambiguous' with a sub-headline 'Congressmen agree to stop panicking and ask for better data'. Usually the reporter hangs up and calls someone else who is willing to be a bit more pithy about this topic.

It is just a simple statistic, but it illustrates a broad point. Simple statistics can shape policy, especially by Congressional staffers who are not going to spend much time studying the issues. If the statistics are shallow, the policies will be too.

So let's talk for just a minute about how little we know about US broadband. The best statistics on broadband come from the Federal Communication Commission (FCC) report on competition[12] in a report for high-speed services for Internet access. It is something, but it is also unsatisfying in many ways. It tells us something about the number of lines available, the number of providers available, and the type of adoption patterns found across states, and some basic distinctions between the market for business and households. It uses a comparatively low bar for 'high-speed', and recently added some gradations for that.

Here, e.g., is a short list of rather basic issues in the broadband policy for which we do not have even the most basic data:

- What industries make the greatest use of broadband? How has this improved their productivity, if at all?

- Which types of firms benefit the most when broadband becomes available? When broadband prices decline or quality improves?
- What areas of the US benefited the most from broadband in the last decade? Where have local taxes improved the most as a result?
- Which areas were hurt the most from broadband diffusion (e.g., central Nebraska lost a large part of its telemarketing industry)?
- While the data tells us a bit about different types of providers (e.g., DSL versus cable), it does not tell us much about their average quality, even though it is well known that cable firms have improved their speed over time. What is the average price per speed obtained by the typical user?
- What technologies generally go in hand with broadband? Which technologies enable or nurture a cluster of other technologies? What other investments follow?
- What happens to local wages for local programmers as broadband diffuses? Do they change at all? How about earnings at other technically-intensive industries?
- How has business use of broadband shifted in response to concerns over information security? Has this varied by industry?

CONCLUDING REMARKS

The state of data collection for the Internet economy is mediocre. I have tried to indicate that this is pervasive throughout many of the key questions in Internet economic policy. I have tried to show that some of the data used by researchers comes from the US government, but quite a lot also comes from private sources. Moreover, some of the most useful initiatives undertaken by US statistical agencies are difficult, in need of money and effort.

More to the point, US policy formulation across a range of issues is poorer as a result. This gap in knowledge pervades many issues that come up at the FCC, the US Congress, the Department of Commerce, the BEA, the Internal Revenue Service the BLS, the National Science Foundation, and elsewhere.

In closing I want to remind the reader about the purpose of this chapter. I wanted to describe the range of places that lack statistics. I wanted to identify places where we were far from any reasonable ideal. To illustrate that point I have tried to be an equal opportunity offender, citing and critiquing statistics coming from a range of government sources, in this case, BLS, the Census, the NTIA, and the FCC. I was not trying to identify these agencies for error or mistake, but to show that they are trying to address challenging issues with meagre resources. These illustrations were at hand and seemed like enough to get the point across. More to the point, these agencies need help. I hope it will motivate others to initiate projects that will fill gaps.

NOTES

1. Available at http://www.kellogg.northwestern.edu/faculty/greenstein/images/articles.html.
2. Available at http://www.utexas.edu/lbj/directory/faculty/kenneth-flamm.
3. Available at http://www.tonygrubesic.net/research.html.
4. Available at http://faculty.pepperdine.edu/jprieger/research.htm.
5. See http://www.census.gov/eos/www/ebusiness614.htm.
6. See http://www.fcc.gov/wcb/iatd/comp.html.
7. Goldfarb (2002) contains click stream data verifying this trend in detail across many categories of uses. It is also commonly verified by observers Web use, such as Media Matrix. Also see O'Donnell (2002) for an estimate of the relative magnitude of the value chain behind access and advertising on the Internet.
8. According to NAICS revenue for 514191 and 514199, access fees exceed advertising by three or four times. For example, total advertising for 1999 was 1,355 + 1,477 = 2,832, as compared with 8,979 under NAICS 514191 alone (US Census Bureau, 2001, Table 1151).
9. For 1998 see revenue for NAICS 514191 (US Census Bureau, 2001, Table 1151). This lists revenue of US$10,882 million for 1998 and US$18,025 for 1999, with access fees accounting for US$5,499 and US$8,979 respectively. These revenue estimates are based on the 1999 Service Annual Survey, Information Sector Services. In the 2004 Service Annual Survey (released by the US Census Bureau on December 29, 2005) NAICS 514191, Internet Service Providers had US$10.5 billion in access fees in 2004; NAICS 5132, Cable Network and Program Distribution, had US$8.6 billion in Internet access service; and NAICS 5133, Telecommunications Carriers, had US$4.3 billion in Internet access services. This does not count the revenue for other on-line services.
10. This is 'computer information processing services' at http://data.bls.gov, or see 'On-line information services', NAICS 514191.
11. This is the monthly price quote, as indicated, under 'Internet Services and electronic information providers'. See http://data.bls.gov/.
12. Available at http://www.fcc.gov/wcb/iatd/comp.html.

REFERENCES

Arora, A. and Forman, C. (2007) 'Proximity and Information Technology Outsourcing: How Local are IT Services Markets?', *Journal of Management Information System*, **24**, 73–102.

Brynjolfsson, E., Hitt, L. and Yang, S. (2002), 'Intangible Assets: Computers and Organizational Capital', *Brookings Papers on Economic Activity 1,* 137–82.

Downes, T. and Greenstein, S. (2002), 'Universal Access and Local Internet Market in the US', *Research Policy*, **31**, 1035–52.

Downes, T. and Greenstein, S. (2007), 'Understanding Why Universal Service Obligations May Be Unnecessary: The Private Development of Local Internet Access Markets', *Journal of Urban Economics*, **62**, 2–26.

Flamm, K. and Chaudhuri, A. (2006), 'Access and the Changing Role of Public Libraries', *Review of Policy Research*, **23**, 249–66.

Forman, C. and Goldfarb, A. (2006), 'Diffusion of Information and Communication Technologies to Business' in T. Hendershott (ed.), *Handbook of Information Systems, Economics and Information Systems, Volume 1,* Amsterdam, Elsevier.

Forman, C., Goldfarb, A. and Greenstein, S. (2002), 'Digital Dispersion: An Industrial and Geographic Census of Commercial Internet Use', *NBER Working Paper* (No. 9287).

Goldfarb, A. (2002), 'Analyzing Website Choice Using Clickstream Data', in Michael Baye (ed.), *Advances in Applied Microeconomics, Volume 11: The Economics of the Internet and E-commerce,* Oxford, Elsevier.

Goolsbee, A. and Klenow, P. (2002), 'Evidence on Learning and Network Externalities in the Diffusion of Home Computers', *Journal of Law and Economics*, **45**, 317–44.

Greenstein, S. (2005), 'The Economic Geography of Internet Infrastructure in the United States,' in M. Cave, S. Majumdar and I. Vogelsang (eds), *Handbook of Telecommunication Economics, Volume 2*, Amsterdam, Elsevier.

Greenstein, S. and Prince, J. (2007), 'The Diffusion of the Internet and the Geography of the Digital Divide' in R. Mansell, D. Quah, and R. Silverstone (eds), *Oxford Handbook on ICTs*, Oxford, Oxford University Press.

Griliches, Z. (1994), 'Productivity, R&D, and the Data Constraint', *American Economic Review,* **84**, 1–23.

Jorgensen, D., Stiroh, K. and Ho, M. (2006), 'Potential Growth of the US Economy: Will the US Productivity Resurgence Continue?', *Business Economics* , **41**, 7–16.

O'Donnell, S. (2002), 'An Economic Map of the Internet', Center for eBusiness @ MIT, Paper 162. Retrieved from: http://ebusiness.mit.edu/research/papers/162_ODonnell_Map.pdf.

Prince, J. (2004), 'The Diffusion of Durable Information Technology Products', doctoral dissertation, Northwestern University, Evanston.

Sinai, T. and Waldfogel, J. (2005), 'Do Low-income Housing Subsidies Increase the Occupied Housing Stock?', *Journal of Public Economics*, **89**, 2137–64.

US Census Bureau (2001), *2001 Statistical Abstract of US.* Retrieved from: http://www.census.gov/prod/2002pubs/01statab/stat-ab01.html.

Index